Politics and Government in the Federal Republic of Germany

Politics and Government in the Federal Republic of Germany: Basic Documents

Edited by Carl-Christoph Schweitzer,
Detlev Karsten, Robert Spencer,
R. Taylor Cole, Donald Kommers,
Anthony Nicholls

Berg Publishers

BERG PUBLISHERS LIMITED
24 Binswood Avenue
Leamington Spa
CV32 5SQ

British Library Cataloguing in Publication Data

Politics and government in the Federal Republic
   of Germany.
   1. Germany (West)—Politics and government
   I. Schweitzer, C.C.
   320.943   JN3971.A2

   ISBN 0-907582-10-9
   ISBN 0-907582-13-3 Pbk

Typesetting by MHL Typesetting Ltd, Coventry
Printed in Great Britain by Billing & Sons Ltd, Worcester

Contents

Bank (Bundesbankgesetz)—*Doc. 4:* Social Code (Sozialgesetzbuch)—*Doc. 5:* Works Constitution Act (Betriebsverfassungsgesetz): co-determination at the shop-floor level—*Doc. 6:* Act
respecting worker's co-determination (Gesetz über die
Mitbestimmung der Arbeitnehmer): co-determination at board
level—*Doc. 7:* The employers' criticisms of co-determination at
board level—*Doc. 8:* Trade Union view of co-
determination—*Doc. 9:* Federal Constitutional Court's judgment
on the Co-determination Act—*Doc. 10:* Foreign workers as a
challenge to policy

Editors' Preface

The aim of this book is to make available to those English-speaking readers interested in present day Germany access to major source materials relating to the Federal Republic's political system. The book describes the political system in Bonn as it is in 1983, although it does not neglect the appropriate historical background to the various parts of that system.

Interest in the Federal Republic has been growing throughout the Anglo-Saxon world, stimulated by the leading role that country is now playing in Western Europe, as well as by its undoubted political and economic achievements. There are many introductory accounts of the history and politics of the Federal Republic available, but the documentary basis needed to complement such explanatory books is lacking. We have tried to set out the documents in such a way that each section—be it on the Bundestag, the Federal Constitutional Court or the political parties, for example—can be read as a self-contained unit, with its own explanatory introduction and editorial comments; the book has been designed to serve both as a description of the Federal system and as a source book for students; inevitably this has meant selection, but no key point has been omitted. The editors of this volume have all had experience of teaching German politics in Anglo-Saxon universities and have themselves felt the need for a book of this kind. We hope that many teachers of political science, recent history, German studies and international relations will find it of substantial assistance in the preparation of courses and also of use as a means of stimulating interest in the subject among those students motivated to carry out further research.

The documents printed in this volume are taken from original German sources. Where a suitable English translation already existed, we have utilised and acknowledged this. These translations have not been amended, even in the few instances where this might have increased the clarity of the text or where the same German terminology has been translated by differing terms in separate instances. In the majority of cases, however, translations were commissioned by the editors. The source is normally given in German, unless translation of the title makes it more comprehensible for English-speaking readers. We ourselves have used the English translations of German terms wherever possible, but some words are in such common use—Bundestag (Federal Parliament) or Länder (Federal states) for example—that we have kept these in German. In addition a Glossary of terms and abbreviations is provided.

We would like to express our heartfelt thanks to the many institutions which have assisted us and without which this volume could not have been produced, particularly to the Presse-und-Informationsamt der Bundesregierung in Bonn, which provided *inter alia* funds for translations, the Robert-Bosch-Stiftung in Stuttgart, which generously financed editorial sessions, and the President of Duke University, North Carolina, who so kindly hosted one of those sessions. Each contributor bears the responsibility for his own chapters; the whole volume was coordinated by C.C. Schweitzer, who provided the original concept.

Summer 1983 Carl-Christoph Schweitzer, Detlev Karsten (Bonn)
Robert Spencer (Toronto)
R. Taylor Cole (Durham)
Donald Kommers (Notre Dame)
Anthony Nicholls (Oxford)

Introduction

The Federal Republic of Germany is not the first parliamentary democracy in German history, but so far it has been the most successful one. Analysts have often drawn comparisons between the Federal Republic and its antecedent, the Weimar Republic of 1919–33. Both Republics were able to invoke traditions of liberal thought and local self-government going back over several centuries; in particular, the 1848 revolutions in Germany had witnessed a widespread enthusiasm for parliamentary rule and political freedom. Both the Weimar Republic and the Federal Republic were burdened with the legacy of military defeat, which brought with it serious economic and social consequences. Here, however, similarity between the two German parliamentary democracies came to an end. In the case of the Federal Republic, there was, in addition, the hateful memory of Nazi rule and the prospect of national dismemberment. These difficulties will be referred to in the first, historical, chapter of this book. In any case, some thirty-five years after the Federal Republic was established we are able with justice to echo the words of one early observer and claim that 'Bonn is not Weimar'.

The stability and vitality exhibited thus far by the Federal Republic has been remarkable. It should not be forgotten, of course, that the Western Allied powers avoided many of the crasser errors of 1918–19. For example, they took responsibility for the administration of Germany after defeat and did not subject the new German democracy to an apparently eternal reparations burden. However, we are more concerned here with the extent to which the German founding fathers of the Federal Republic consciously learned from the mistakes of the past to establish a more secure democratic system.

This 'historical dimension' explains why a number of constitutional precautions were taken against a possible repetition of the abuses in

Weimar, not to mention the Third Reich. The rights of individuals, of associations and of political parties had to be more carefully protected. The Basic Law (Grundgesetz) of 1949 was carefully framed to meet such dangers. It is not least through such provisions in the Basic Law, as examined in chapter 5, that the resurgence of anti-democratic forces, whether of the Right or the Left has, since 1949, been effectively prevented.

Just as important as political stability has been economic growth. This particularly successful aspect of the Federal Republic's history can be attributed partly to the consistent policy of 'Social Market Economy', which is examined in chapter 10.

In economic as well as political matters, the letter of the law is of central importance. This is a very significant characteristic of the political system of the Federal Republic, and it will be reflected in almost every chapter of this volume. To an extent which may surprise Anglo-Saxon readers, the founders of the Federal Republic, successive legislators and, above all, the judges in the Federal Constitutional Court have relied upon the power of legal provisions to ensure the proper functioning of many important elements in the country's political system. This applies, for example, to the democratic administration of political parties, the observance of democratic principles in the armed forces and the safeguards which are designed to protect the parliamentary system in time of national emergency. In presenting their analysis of that system through the documents, the editors of this volume are aware how risky it is to equate constitutional theory—or the letter of the law—with what actually happens in day-to-day politics. Where it seems appropriate, therefore, they attempt to point out discrepancies between theory and practice in the working of the system.

Bearing this particular problem in mind, a political scientist or historian might then ask: what is the overall *systemic framework* within which the political actors of the Federal Republic operate? As in other Western democratic systems, he might distinguish between three different levels of activity which reinforce and complement each other. The first is the *governmental* level, comprising the three classic powers of the executive, the legislature and the judiciary. It is at this level that decision-making takes place, and here that policies are carried out and evaluated. Secondly there is an *intermediary* level of interest groups, most of which exert pressure on the governmental level—a characteristic common to all pluralist societies. Lastly there is the *primary* level, the grass roots of the system, made up of the mass of active citizens who have attained voting age. According to the democratic theory on which the

Federal Republic is based, the indivisible sovereignty of the state rests at this level. This is expressed very clearly in Article 20 of the Basic Law: 'All state authority emanates from the people'. It goes on to state that the people exercise that authority 'by means of elections and voting and by specific legislative, executive and judicial organs'.[1] This sentence leaves no doubt that the Federal Republic is based on the idea of 'representative' rather than 'direct' democracy.

So far as the political parties are concerned—as treated in chapter 8 of this volume—they can be seen as straddling all three levels through grass roots membership, representation of particular interests and participation in government or opposition. The Federal Republic is unusual in that the political parties are actually recognised in the constitution itself—i.e. in Article 21 of the Basic Law. Without political parties there could be no parliament in the Federal Republic; so far there has not been one single member of the Bundestag elected independently of a political party. Without the support of one or more political parties no chancellor can obtain power and maintain his cabinet in office. The West German system is basically one of party government.

When surveying the governmental level of the Federal Republican system, we can see that the classic division of powers between the executive and the legislative branches is more a theoretical than a practical distinction. In this the situation in Bonn is similar to that in the capitals of other Western parliamentary democracies. The reason for this is that under normal circumstances there is an identity of interest between the government and the majority which supports it in parliament (described in chapter 2). It is therefore difficult to decide 'who controls whom'.

It is certainly not possible to speak of a *de facto* supremacy of parliament in such systems. In the German context the 'chancellor in Parliament' is supreme, so long as he can muster a majority. It was in this connection that the term 'chancellor democracy' has been coined to describe the German system; it was first applied to Konrad Adenauer's remarkable period of office from 1949 to 1963. The constitution deliberately strengthened the chancellor's position by comparison with his predecessors in the Weimar Republic; in particular it was made impossible for the Bundestag to eject him from office unless it simultaneously voted for a new chancellor in the so-called 'constructive' vote of no-confidence. In the first thirty-three years of the Republic's history such a vote was only moved twice, and it only succeeded on one occasion, when Chancellor Helmut Schmidt was replaced by Helmut Kohl in October 1982.

Within the government the chancellor has a very strong position, as will be shown in chapter 3. He possesses the right to lay down the general policy guidelines and wields the ultimate executive power. That is not in the hands of the Federal President, who for the most part exercises his duties in an office concerned with what Bagehot termed the 'dignified parts', but no real authority.

However, the concept of the separation of powers in the Federal Republic has survived better the relationship between legislature and executive on the one hand and the judiciary on the other. In particular, the Federal Constitutional Court has played a very important role in controlling both legislative bodies and government activity. Chapters 4 and 6 provide striking illustrations of these functions. In a number of significant cases the Constitutional Court has effectively checked the power of both the Federal government and the Bundestag.

There is another restraint on central government. This is a phenomenon sometimes described as 'vertical' separation of powers: the federal structure of the Bonn Republic. The states—or Länder—of the Federal Republic participate in the central legislative process through the second chamber, the Bundesrat. The nature of federalism is so important in the Republic that it will be examined in two chapters—6 and 7—of this volume.

Although the answer to the question 'who governs?' might seem to be 'the chancellor', this would be an over-simplication. The chancellor and his cabinet, not to mention the political parties, can come under pressure from the intermediary level, the interest groups, and also from the mass media, which sometimes seem to act as an interest group or even independent power factor. This issue will be the subject of chapter 9, which aims to demonstrate the considerable influence of pressure groups on the decision-making process on all levels.

In the Federal Republic, as in other industrialised societies, there seems to be a danger that pressures on the legislature and the executive authorities by special interest groups must undermine a government's capacity to rule effectively. A sense of impotence can have a demoralizing effect on the political system. 'Ungovernability' (Unregierbarkeit) is perceived as a problem. This is especially true when there are conflicting priorities at stake, such as the desire to protect the environment, on the one hand, and the need for increased energy supplies on the other, or the requirements of the defence budget as against the costs of the welfare state. Governments often find it difficult to steer a straight course when buffeted by pressures from different directions and they are particularly sensitive to such influences when elections are pending. Since German governments have to content with Land elections as well as Federal ones, their position is especially difficult. These matters are touched on in this volume in the chapters relating to political parties and pressure groups (8 and 9).

One relatively new phenomenon in German politics has been the emergence of so-called 'citizens' initiative groups' (Bürgerinitiativen). Originally concerned with specific local issues, such as housing or environmental protection, they are now building an alternative type of political grouping to the conventional Bundestag parties. Styling themselves the Green movement they are currently threatening to replace the liberal party (FDP) as the third political force between the Christian Democrats and the Social Democrats. The strength of this movement should not be exaggerated. Nevertheless, it is possible to detect in it a shift of opinion amongst part of the electorate—the third level of the system mentioned above—and the emergence of a new political culture. This seems to owe a good deal to the younger and academically trained section of the population, which is consciously trying to develop a form of grass-roots democracy (Basisdemokratie) hitherto almost absent from the German political tradition.

In the last chapters of this volume we introduce documents and comments relating to specific areas of policy, including foreign affairs, Berlin, relations with the German Democratic Republic and defence. Since some of these matters have already been documented in English, we have kept the chapters fairly short, hoping to provide the reader with an up-to-date overview in more convenient form than would be available elsewhere. The literature listed at the end of the volume will be helpful for further study. Some relevant statistics and figures are provided as supporting evidence to points made in the main chapters.

Note

1. Translated passages of the Basic Law here and throughout the volume are quoted from the official translation by the Press and Information Office of the Federal Government, Bonn, 1981.

1 The Origins of the Federal Republic of Germany, 1944–1949

Robert Spencer

The Federal Republic of Germany, which came into existence in 1949, celebrates its birthday on 23 May, the date on which the Parliamentary Council (Parlamentarische Rat) meeting in Bonn formally approved its constitution (Grundgesetz).* A provisional creation, it was intended to last, as the final article of the constitution decreed, only until 'a constitution adopted by a free decision of the German people comes into force'.[1] The Federal Republic had both German and non-German origins.[2] It was a product of the Second World War, at whose end unconditional surrender and the resulting absence of any central government in Germany had led to the unprecedented assumption by the four leading Allied powers of 'supreme authority with respect to Germany, including all the powers possessed by the German Government, the High Command, and any state, municipal, or local government or authority'.[3] It was also even more directly a product of the Cold War, as East–West differences frustrated the four-power cooperation envisaged in the original post-surrender arrangements. But while Germany was a highly important object of international politics after 1945, the Federal Republic also owed to German initiatives and reflected German traditions, which merged with Allied (and especially American) policies directed towards the 'eventual reconstruction of German political life on a democratic basis'.[4] The extent to which the Federal Republic was the result of the policies of the Western Allies and the extent to which it was the consequence of the endeavours of the Germans themselves is still the subject of academic debate.[5]

Given the wartime occupation agreements between the Allied powers, this outcome was largely unforeseen. True, as late as the Crimea (Yalta)

---

* Notes for this chapter begin on p. 23.

conference in February 1945, Britain, the United States, and the USSR had indeed included among their objectives the 'dismemberment of Germany as they deem requisite for future peace and security'.[6] But they quickly abandoned this policy. At the final wartime meeting at Berlin (Potsdam) in the summer of 1945 they agreed that 'for the time being, no central German government shall be established', but also that during the period of occupation 'Germany shall be treated as a single economic unit'. In addition they envisaged the creation of 'certain essential central German administrative departments' headed by German 'under secretaries', to deal with such matters as finance, trade, transport, communications, and industry.[7] But determined French opposition to any step which appeared to threaten the revival of a centralized German power prevented their creation.[8] After 1945, the fissiparous tendencies in the occupation arrangements agreed to in the London-based European Advisory Commission in 1944–45 (Doc. 1), and the bitter East–West disagreements especially over reparations which, it was agreed at Yalta, 'Germany must pay in kind' to cover Allied losses,[9] together with the resulting dispute over economic policies in occupied Germany, led to the progressive hardening of zonal borders into frontiers dividing differing social and political systems. Within four and a half years of the German surrender, hostile governments had emerged in East and West. It was no accident that the decisive steps towards the creation of the Federal Republic in the three Western zones of occupation took place during the total blockade by Soviet forces of land and water routes connecting the Western sectors of Berlin with the Western zones which for eleven months left only the vital air links intact (Doc. 2).

But the Federal Republic also owed its origins to German efforts, and it reflected German traditions dating back to the Weimar Republic and to the ill-fated attempts to establish a national Germany on a liberal-democratic basis in 1848. The victorious powers viewed the purpose of occupation not to liberate but to control a defeated enemy nation, and at the start they discouraged 'fraternization' with German officials and the population, stressed denazification and demilitarization, and emphasized the paramountcy of Allied control. This policy was enunciated in a key directive (JCS 1067) from President Truman to General Eisenhower, the US Supreme Commander in Germany (British and French instructions were similar).[10] Two years later this post-surrender policy, with its reflection of the harshness of the Morgenthau plan (the shortlived wartime plan of the United States Secretary of the Treasury for the 'pastoralization of Germany') was replaced by a new directive which decreed that 'there should arise in Germany as rapidly as possible a form of political organization and a manner of political life which, resting on a substantial basis of economic well-being, will lead to tranquillity within Germany and will contribute to the spirit of peace among nations'.[11] And well before that date, the United States zone had been merged with the British in the interest of German economic recovery and, confronted with the failure to secure agreement on institutional and political reconstruction on a Germany-wide basis, conscious efforts had begun to recreate German administrative, political and institutional life at the local and regional level.

The occupation arrangements had paid scant attention to the old Länder boundaries. In the American zone of occupation, Land Bavaria with its capital in Munich was still intact, and by September 1945 fragments of Hesse and the old Prussian province of Hesse-Nassau had been reorganized into the new Länder of Württemberg-Baden and Greater Hesse. The northern exclave Bremen became a fourth Land a year and a half later. In the British zone, which consisted mainly of the former Prussian provinces, Lower Saxony, Hamburg, and Schleswig-Holstein became Länder in their own right, while a new Land was created, North Rhine-Westphalia, with its capital in Düsseldorf. It comprised half the population of the British zone and three-quarters of all West Germany's heavy industry. Developments in the French zone lagged in view of French designs for annexation or economic exploitation. Baden and Württemberg-Hohenzollern were left as separate Länder. The Saar and a part of the Rhine province of the Palatinate were separated, and the remainder of the French zone organized as Rhineland-Palatinate with its centre in Mainz.[12]

In the interests of effective administration, which was beyond the capacity of the occupation forces, the American and British military governors appointed as a temporary measure a hierarchy of German officials culminating in the formation of a Länder Council (Länderrat) composed of minister-presidents who, as General Lucius D. Clay, the United States Deputy Governor, reminded them, were asked to undertake a difficult transitional responsibility because of their 'known anti-Nazi past and ... liberal views'.[13] The Western allies were anxious to encourage German participation through elections on a democratic basis. From the very first months of the occupation the Germans took advantage of this policy to recreate German political life. Three major political forces soon emerged. The Social Democrats, the only party to vote against Hitler's Enabling Act in March 1933, emerged as a powerful force in the West following the tragic enforced fusion of its eastern wing with the communists in 1946. The current of traditional German liberalism revived in the Free Democratic Party. And the new political force of Christian democracy emerged in the Christian Democratic Union and its Bavarian sister party, the Christian Social Union, in the tradition of the old Centre Party, but no longer exclusively Catholic (Doc. 3). At the same time German politicians played a key role in the evolution of new institutions (and especially of the Land constitutions) authorized and encouraged by the occupation powers.[14] The pace at which the Germans regained control over their own destiny was speeded up as Western frustrations over disagreements with the Soviet Union increased. After the Foreign Ministers failed to reach agreement on an all-German solution at the Moscow conference in March–April 1947, the Germans launched their own (but abortive) attempt to stave off the looming division of their country by holding a conference in Munich, in June 1947, of minister-presidents from all the German Länder, east as well as west (Doc. 4).

As the East–West breach became manifest in 1948 Marshall Plan aid, coupled with the at first controversial but in the outcome highly successful Social Market Economy introduced into the combined United States and British zones in the summer of 1948 by Ludwig Erhard (Doc. 5), together with the currency reform of June 1948, provided the basis on which the West Germans could move along the road towards recovery and prosperity and underlined the need for the parallel political reconstruction. The decisive step in this process was the London conference of the three Western powers and the Benelux states. In a series of meetings extending from February to June 1948 it agreed on the establishment of a West German state, on measures towards Western European integration, on the creation of the International Authority under which the Ruhr industrial area would be controlled by the Occupation Powers, and on a Military Security Board to allay the fears of Germany's neighbours.[15] In accordance with the London decisions the military governors assembled the minister-presidents of the Länder in Frankfurt and authorized them to convene a constituent assembly to draft a constitution. The sixty-five members of what (to spare German sensitivities) became known as the Parliamentary Council comprised delegates chosen by the Länder legislatures. The distribution of the parties (twenty-seven each CDU/CSU and SPD, five FDP and the remaining six from three smaller parties including two from the revived Communist party) explains the narrowness of decisions on most issues, although the mood of the Council was for the most part conciliatory and pervaded by a willingness to make compromises.[16] When the Council met for the first time on 1 September it elected Konrad Adenauer as president, with vice-presidents from the SPD and the FDP. The distinguished professor of constitutional law, Carlo Schmid, was chosen chairman of the Main Committee. A draft, based on the document prepared by a meeting of the minister-presidents at Herrenchiemsee in August, was completed by 1 November.

The document which, in deference to German wishes the occupation powers eventually agreed should be termed a Basic Law, was conservative in tone. While anxious to erect barriers against any new threat of dictatorship, the members of the Parliamentary Council were also concerned to avoid the errors of 'over-democratization' which were widely believed to have contributed to the fate of the Weimar Republic.[17] Discussions, especially on 'financial federalism', continued throughout the winter, when the intervention of the military governors, who were concerned at the degree of centralization in the constitutional draft, led to further debate and compromise in Bonn and prolonged the process to the early summer.

The revised Basic Law was finally adopted by the Parliamentary Council on 8 May, four years to the day after Germany's surrender of the Third Reich. Approval by the military governors, with some significant reservations, followed on 12 May (Doc. 6), and the Occupation Statute, outlining the powers reserved to the Western Powers, came into effect on the same day. The Basic Law was approved by the Land assemblies and ratified by the Parliamentary Council in a formal ceremony on 23 May (Doc. 7).

The elections to the Federal Republic's first Bundestag which followed on 14 August foreshadowed the political pattern which was to persist for the succeeding decades. Despite a widespread belief that, as in much of the rest of Europe, the disturbed state of the old continent after the collapse of the Third Reich meant that the time was ripe for a turn to the left, the Christian Democratic Union and its Bavarian wing, the Christian Social Union, emerged as the strongest party, with a narrow majority over its principal rival, the Social Democratic Party (31.0% of the popular vote against 29.2%). On 12 September President Theodor Heuss, a respected historian and publicist who had been active in German politics before 1933, was elected federal president (Doc. 8). Three days later, Dr Konrad Adenauer, a former Centrist politician in the Weimar era and long-time mayor of Cologne, who had played a leading role in the construction of the CDU and had served as president of the Parliamentary Council, was elected federal chancellor by the narrowest of possible margins—one vote, presumably his own. Lacking an overall majority for his own party, he formed a coalition with the Free Democrats and the small, conservative German Party, the first of the successive coalitions which have conducted the government of the Federal Republic since 1949 (Doc. 9). Given his age (he was seventy-two in 1949), few could have expected that Konrad Adenauer would remain chancellor and dominate the German political scene for a further fourteen years, or that the period of CDU dominance in the chancellery would endure to 1969.[18]

Documents 1a-b

The two documents which follow constitute the basic wartime agreements for the four-power occupation of Germany within its 1937 frontiers (exclusive of the Königsberg area whose annexation to the Soviet Union was approved at Potsdam, and the remaining territories east of the Oder-Neisse line which were placed under Polish administration pending a final peace treaty).

a) PROTOCOL BETWEEN THE GOVERNMENTS OF THE UNITED KINGDOM, THE UNITED STATES OF AMERICA, AND THE UNION OF SOVIET SOCIALIST REPUBLICS, AND THE PROVISIONAL GOVERNMENT OF THE FRENCH REPUBLIC ON THE ZONES OF OCCUPATION IN GERMANY AND THE ADMINISTRATION OF 'GREATER BERLIN', 12 SEPTEMBER 1944, AS AMENDED BY THE AGREEMENTS OF 14 NOVEMBER 1944 AND 26 JULY 1945

Source: *Selected Documents on Germany and the Question of Berlin, 1944–1961*, London, HMSO, 1961, Cmnd. 1552, 27–30, 35–6, 45–8

The Governments of the United Kingdom of Great Britain and Northern Ireland, the United States of America, and the Union of Soviet Socialist Republics and the Provisional Government of the French Republic, have reached the following agreement with regard to the execution of Article 11 of the Instrument of Unconditional Surrender of Germany:

1. Germany, within her frontiers as they were on the 31st December 1937, will, for the purposes of occupation, be divided into four zones, one of which will be allotted to each of the four Powers, and a special Berlin area, which will be under joint occupation by the four Powers.

2. The boundaries of the four zones and of the Berlin area, and the allocation of the four zones as between the U.K., the U.S.A., the U.S.S.R. and the Provisional Government of the French Republic will be as follows:

Eastern Zone . . .

The territory of Germany (including the province of East Prussia) situated to the East of a line drawn from the point on Lübeck Bay where the frontiers of

Schleswig-Holstein and Mecklenburg meet, along . . . the western frontier of the Prussian province of Saxony and the western frontier of Thuringia to where the latter meets the Bavarian frontier; then eastwards along the northern frontier of Bavaria to the 1937 Czechoslovakian frontier, will be occupied by armed forces of the U.S.S.R., with the exception of the Berlin area, for which a special system of occupation is provided below.

. . .

North-Western (United Kingdom) Zone . . .
The territory of Germany situated to the west of the line defined in the description of the Eastern (Soviet) Zone, and bounded on the south by a line drawn from the point where the frontier between the Prussian provinces of Hanover and Hessen-Nassau meets the western frontier of the Prussian province of Saxony; . . . to the . . . Belgian–German frontier will be occupied by the armed forces of the United Kingdom.

. . .

South-Western (United States) Zone . . .
The territory of Germany situated to the south and east of a line commencing at the junction of the frontiers of Saxony, Bavaria and Czechoslovakia and extending westwards along the northern frontier of Bavaria to . . . where the latter meets the Austro-German frontier will be occupied by armed forces of the United States of America.

For the purpose of facilitating communications between the South-Western Zone and the sea, the Commander-in-Chief of the United States forces in the South-Western Zone will

(*a*) exercise such control of the ports of Bremen and Bremerhaven and the necessary staging areas in the vicinity thereof as may be agreed hereafter by the United Kingdom and United States military authorities to be necessary to meet his requirements;
(*b*) enjoy such transit facilities through the North-Western Zone as may be agreed hereafter by the United Kingdom and United States military authorities to be necessary to meet his requirements.

Western (French) Zone . . .
The territory of Germany, situated to the south and west of a line commencing at the junction of the frontiers of Belgium and of the Prussian Regierungsbezirke of Trier and Aachen and extending eastward along the northern frontier of the Prussian Regierungsbezirk of Trier; thence north, east, and south along the western, northern, and eastern frontier of the Prussian Regierungsbezirk of Koblenz to the point where the frontier of Koblenz meets the frontier of the district of Oberwesterwald; thence east, . . . and south-east . . . to the point where the eastern frontier of the district of Lindau meets the Austro-German frontier will be occupied by armed forces of the French Republic.

. . .

Berlin Area . . .

The Berlin area (by which expression is understood the territory of 'Greater Berlin' as defined by the Law of the 27th April 1920) will be jointly occupied by armed forces of the U.K., U.S.A., and U.S.S.R., and the French Republic assigned by the respective Commanders-in-Chief. For this purpose the territory of 'Greater Berlin' will be divided into the following four parts . . .[19]

(3) The occupying forces in each of the zones into which Germany is divided will be under a Commander-in-Chief designated by the Government of the country whose forces occupy that zone.

. . .

(5) An Inter-Allied Governing Authority (Komendatura) consisting of four Commandants, appointed by their respective Commanders-in-Chief, will be established to direct jointly the administration of the 'Greater Berlin' Area.

. . .

b) STATEMENT BY THE GOVERNMENTS OF THE UNITED KINGDOM, THE UNITED STATES OF AMERICA, THE UNION OF SOVIET SOCIALIST REPUBLICS AND THE PROVISIONAL GOVERNMENT OF THE FRENCH REPUBLIC ON CONTROL MACHINERY IN GERMANY, 5 JUNE 1945

Source: *Selected Documents on Germany and the Question of Berlin, 1944–1961*, London, HMSO, 1961, Cmnd. 1552, 43–4

(1) In the period when Germany is carrying out the basic requirements of unconditional surrender, supreme authority in Germany will be exercised, on instructions from their Governments, by the British, United States, Soviet and French Commanders-in-Chief, each in his own zone of occupation, and also jointly, in matters affecting Germany as a whole. The four Commanders-in-Chief will together constitute the Control Council. Each Commander-in-Chief will be assisted by a Political Adviser.

(2) The Control Council, whose decisions shall be unanimous, will ensure appropriate uniformity of action by the Commanders-in-Chief in their respective zones of occupation and will reach agreed decisions on the chief questions affecting Germany as a whole.

(3) Under the Control Council, there will be a permanent Co-ordinating Committee composed of one representative of each of the four Commanders-in-Chief, and a Control Staff organised in the following Divisions (which are subject to adjustment in the light of experience):

Military; Naval; Air; Transport; Political; Economic; Finance; Reparation, Deliveries and Restitution; Internal Affairs and Communications; Legal; Prisoners of War and Displaced Persons; Man-power.

There will be four heads of each Division, one designated by each Power. The staffs of the Division may include civilian as well as military personnel, and may also in special cases include nationals of other United Nations appointed in a personal capacity.

(4) The functions of the Co-ordinating Committee and of the Control Staff will be to advise the Control Council, to carry out the Council's decisions and to transmit them to the appropriate German organs, and to supervise and control the day-to-day activities of the latter.

. . .

(7) The administration of the 'Greater Berlin' area will be directed by an Inter-Allied Governing Authority, which will operate under the general direction of the Control Council, and will consist of four Commandants, each of whom will serve in rotation as Chief Commandant. They will be assisted by a technical staff which will supervise and control the activities of the local German organs.

(8) The arrangements outlined above will operate during the period of occupation following German surrender, when Germany is carrying out the basic requirements of unconditional surrender. Arrangements for the subsequent period will be the subject of a separate agreement.

Documents 2a–b

In the wartime agreements no firm arrangements were made for water and land connections between Berlin and the Western Zones. The postwar arrangements for air corridors and a four-power Berlin Air Safety Centre, however, made possible the 1948–49 air lift during which the people of West Berlin, led by Germans such as the ex-Communist, Ernst Reuter, whose election as Governing Mayor had been vetoed on Russian insistence, rallied to the Western side.

a) CONTROL COUNCIL APPROVAL OF AIR CORRIDORS, 30 NOVEMBER 1945
Source: Documents on Berlin, 1943–1963, Munich, 1963, 37ff.

. . .

(110) Proposed Air Routes for Inter-Zonal Flights
The Meeting had before them CONL/P (45) 63.

Marshal Zhukov recalled that the Coordinating Committee had approved the establishing of three air corridors, namely, Berlin–Hamburg, Berlin–Bückeburg and Berlin–Frankfurt-on-Main.

Field Marshal Montgomery expressed the hope that in due course the question of establishing the remaining air corridors would be settled satisfactorily.

General Koenig approved the paper in principle and shared the opinion of Field Marshal Montgomery.

Marshal Zhukov expressed himself confident that in due course the other air corridors would be opened ...

The Meeting

(110) (a)   approved the establishment of three air corridors from Berlin to the Western zones as defined in CONL/P (45) 63;
       (b)   agreed to refer proposal of the Soviet delegation on the placing of air-fields at the disposal of the Soviet authorities or the setting up of Soviet ground crews in the Western zones to the Air Directorate for study.

b) SPEECH OF ERNST REUTER TO AN SPD RALLY, 24 JUNE 1948

Source: Berlin. Quellen und Dokumente, 1945–51, (2. Halbband), Berlin, n.d., 1468–9

... At our large demonstration in front of our Reichstag building on 18 March I said: After the 1948 Prague incident the entire world posed the question: Whose turn will it be next? Finland maybe or even Berlin? The Berlin population gave its answer clearly and distinctly. We shall apply all the means at our disposal and repel to our utmost the claim to power which wants to turn us into slaves and helots for a political party. We lived under such slavery in Adolf Hitler's empire. We have had enough of that. We do not want a recurrence ...

We know precisely that we are an unarmed, conquered and basically defenceless nation. Our strength does not lie in the outer strength, this was taken from us. The protection from which we outwardly benefit, for instance by our police force, is more than questionable. Our strength really only lies in the fact that we defend with all means the freedom of our people, their right to self-assertion and self-government ...

There are always people who at critical moments start to talk about how one must come to terms with reality, with facts, with things and conditions. For example, people thought they were insulting me by saying I was the personification of a lack of discernment of actual conditions. Here, too, we Germans have collected enough bitter experiences. We know this way as well. Everyone who came to terms with the actual conditions in 1933 was also prepared to make peace with Hitler. There were enough excuses. People always wanted to prevent something worse. In the end Germany lay in ruins. We had not only lost our freedom but we were also retarded for a generation, condemned to a beggar's existence.

Today we are basically dealing with the same problem. Today, too, Berlin can only exist, Germany can only exist, if it learns to fight for its freedom, for its right and for its self-assertion and does not sell its birthright ...

Document 3

The revival of 'anti-fascist' political parties was authorized in the Soviet Zone by Soviet Military Administration Order No. 2 as early as 10 June, when the Red Army was still in sole occupation of Berlin. Parties were also soon authorized and emerged in the Western Zones.

THE EMERGENCE OF GERMAN POLITICAL PARTIES AFTER 1945; DIRECTIVE BY THE BRITISH MILITARY GOVERNMENT CONCERNING THE FORMATION OF POLITICAL PARTIES, 15 SEPTEMBER 1945

Source: Ossip K. Flechtheim, ed., *Dokumente zur parteipolitischen Entwicklung in Deutschland*, I, Berlin, 1962, 109–12

In order to encourage the development of a democratic spirit in Germany and prepare free elections for a date yet to be appointed, the following directives are issued herewith:

Art. 1. Formation of Political Parties

(1) Political parties can be formed in a district (Kreis) according to the directives contained herein.
(2) The military government can allow parties which have been formed according to these directives to unite with one another in larger areas, thereby dispensing with certain rules and conditions.
(3) Membership in political parties must be voluntary.

Art. 2. Method of Application

(4) Every person or group of persons who has the wish to form a political party for a Kreis can apply to the military government for permission to form such a party.

. . .

(6) Notification of permission, whether to form a party or unite already established ones, will be delivered to the applicants by the military government. This permission (in future to be called military government permission) will be issued in writing and will contain the rules and conditions according to which the political party is to be formed or according to which already established parties can be united. Neither the formation nor the union of political parties can take effect before the military government permission is granted.
(7) The grant of a military government permission according to this regulation does not include the right to hold political meetings without a permission according to Regulation No. 10 or to organize public processions without a permission according to Regulation No. 11.

. . .

Documents 4a–c

ALL-GERMAN MEETING OF MINISTER-PRESIDENTS, MUNICH, 5–7 JUNE 1947

The collapse of any hopes of four-power agreement over Germany at the Moscow conference of Foreign Ministers (March–April 1947) and the continuing serious economic situation (which inspired the Americans to launch the Marshall Plan in June) encouraged the Western powers to place greater emphasis on reconstruction, economic and political. The threat which this involved of the division of Germany along the line dividing the Soviet zone from those of the Western powers persuaded the German minister-presidents to launch an initiative of their own, ostensibly to grapple with economic issues but in fact constituting a last-ditch effort to proceed on a four-zonal basis.

a) INVITATION OF THE MINISTER-PRESIDENT OF BAVARIA, EHARD, TO A CONFERENCE OF MINISTER-PRESIDENTS OF ALL FOUR OCCUPATION ZONES, 7 MAY 1947
Source: Akten zur Vorgeschichte der Bundesrepublik Deutschland, 1945–1949, II, Munich, 1979, 424–5

In the name of the Bavarian government I hereby invite the minister-presidents of all Länder [States] of the four occupation zones to a conference in Munich. I propose as a date Friday the 6th and Saturday the 7th of June. Terms of reference of the conference should be an exploration of measures to be proposed by the responsible minister-presidents to the allied military governments with the aim of preventing the German people from sliding down further into a hopeless economic and political chaos. The Germans are no longer physically and psychologically in a position to come to grips with another winter of hunger and cold in the midst of destroyed cities on the verge of an economic collapse and in political despair. Together, therefore, we must do our best to give the German people a new hope for a gradual improvement of their overall situation. Conscious of this duty towards the Bavarian people and towards the whole German people the Bavarian government proposes to pave the way, through such a conference, for the cooperation of all Länder in Germany on the basis of an economic unity today and a political merger in the future.

The Bavarian government hopes that the minister-presidents of the Länder in all four zones will participate in these deliberations and thereby give evidence of their belief in the unifying ties comprising all parts of Germany as well as their determination to construct together a new state in whatever form . . .

b) FINAL STATEMENT OF MINISTER-PRESIDENT EHARD, 7 JUNE 1947

Source: Akten zur Vorgeschichte der Bundesrepublik Deutschland, 1945–1949, II, Munich, 1979, 586–7

. . .

Not for us alone, but for the community of all nations we want to strive to the best of our ability. We consider the exclusion of the German people from an active participation in international life especially tragic and disastrous because we are convinced that all basic problems confronting Europe and the world today can be solved if there is good will. This applies equally to the elementary question of reconstructing Germany as a state and to the problems of security, of the delimitation of frontiers, of the overall economy and even of reparations.

However, a German question cannot be solved without Germany. If others are prepared to listen to us, then we will be able to point at least to outlines of a solution to all problems. This I say with great earnestness. Fate and history have placed the German people in the midst of Europe. It cannot well be the meaning of history that we, the Germans, should constitute the line of division in Europe, its main point of dispute, an arena of terrible strife between East and West. We do not want to separate, we want to bring Europe together. We want to be in the midst of that Europe, a sanctuary of peace and security, of justice and humanity. . . .

c) REPORT OF THE GENERAL SECRETARY OF THE LÄNDERRAT, ERICH ROSSMAN, TO LT. COL. WINNING, US REGIONAL GOVERNING CO-ORDINATION OFFICE, 9 JUNE 1947

Source: Akten zur Vorgeschichte der Bundesrepublik Deutschland, 1945–1949, II, Munich, 1979, 589–92

. . .

On the basis of the impressions I got during my stay in the Eastern zone of occupation I had advised the Bavarian government most urgently to stick to their basic approach that only problems connected with the economic impasse of the German people should be dealt with at the Munich conference, that no topic should be ostensibly placed on the agenda which would, by the nature of things, be very problematic, since that could easily result in a breakdown of the whole conference . . .

The question as to whether they (the minister-presidents of the Eastern zone) would attend, remained open until June 4th. Surprisingly they then actually arrived in Munich on June 5th . . . Although I myself as well as Minister-President Ehard had . . . requested that proposals should be put forward for the agenda (in advance), no such cooperation was entered into. Whether they took up this position purposely from the beginning or only with the intention of thereby underlining more forcefully the importance attached to the one demand actually put forward at the conference itself, cannot be determined with any certainty . . .

The minister-presidents of the Western zones had hoped that joint efforts of the minister-presidents of all zones in those fields where the immediate needs are greatest would enable them to achieve more and more unanimity in their overall approach to the larger political issues and in the end bridge the differences of opinion existing in regard to those issues today. The walk-out of the minister-presidents of the Russian zone has destroyed all such hopes. This occurrence has clearly demonstrated the fact that the time does not yet seem to have come when Germany as a whole can put on record a common stance vis-à-vis the occupying powers. However, the conference of Munich has shown most impressively that the will to achieve (national) unity again is very much alive ...

Document 5

Ludwig Erhard, who had directed the Frankfurt Economic Council of the combined United States–British Zones since 1 January 1947, launched the West German 'economic miracle' by abandoning the controls which he believed were paralysing German recovery and taking full advantage of the inclusion of the Western zones in the Marshall Plan (European Recovery Plan).

LUDWIG ERHARD ON THE SOCIAL MARKET ECONOMY, 22 AUGUST 1948
Source: Prosperity through Competition, London, 1958, 14[20]

It isn't as if we had had any choice. What we had to do in this situation was to loosen the shackles. We had to be prepared to restore basic moral principles and to start with a purge of the economy of our society.

We have done more, by turning from a State-controlled economy to a market economy, than merely introduce economic measures. We have laid new foundations for our social and economic life. We had to abjure all intolerance which, from a spiritual lack of freedom, leads to tyranny and totalitarianism. We had to strive for an order which by voluntary regrouping and a sense of responsibility would lead to a sensible organic whole.

...

Document 6

Following extensive discussions in Washington, the military governors approved the Basic Law drafted by the Parliamentary Council with some significant reservations (especially over Berlin). They prepared for the new phase in the occupation by promulgating an Occupation Statute defining their more limited continuing authority, and prepared to hand over their own functions to an Allied High Commission on the entry into force of the Basic Law.

LETTER OF THE MILITARY GOVERNORS TO DR KONRAD ADENAUER, PRESIDENT OF THE PARLIAMENTARY COUNCIL, 12 MAY 1949
Source: United States Department of State, *Germany, 1947–1949: the Story in Documents,* Washington, 1950, 279–80

1. The Basic Law passed on 8 May by the Parliamentary Council has received our careful and interested attention. In our opinion it happily combines German democratic tradition with the concepts of representative government and a rule of law which the world has come to recognize as requisite to the life of a free people.
2. In approving this constitution for submission to the German people for ratification in accordance with the provisions of Article 144 (1) we believe that you will understand that there are several reservations which we must make. In the first place, the powers vested in the Federation by the Basic Law, as well as the powers exercised by Länder and local Governments, are subject to the provisions of the Occupation Statute which we have already transmitted to you and which is promulgated as of this date.
3. In the second place, it should be understood that the police powers contained in Article 91 (2) may not be exercised until specifically approved by the Occupation Authorities . . .
4. A third reservation concerns the participation of Greater Berlin in the Federation. We interpret the effect of Articles 23 and 144 (2) of the Basic Law as constituting acceptance of our previous request that while Berlin may not be accorded voting membership in the Bundestag or Bundesrat nor be governed by the Federation she may, nevertheless, designate a small number of representatives to attend the meetings of those legislative bodies.

. . .

8. In order to eliminate the possibility of future legal controversy, we would like to make it clear that when we approved constitutions for the Länder we provided that nothing contained in those constitutions could be interpreted as restricting the provisions of the Federal constitution. Conflict between Länder constitutions and the provisional Federal constitution must, therefore, be resolved in favor of the latter.
9. We should also like it to be clearly understood that upon the convening of the legislative bodies provided for in the Basic Law, and upon the election of the President and the election and appointment of the Chancellor and the Federal Ministers, respectively, in the manner provided for in the Basic Law, the Government of the Federal Republic of Germany will then be established and the Occupation Statute shall thereupon enter into force.

10. On the completion of their final task as laid down in Article 145, 1, the Parliamentary Council will be dissolved. We wish to take this occasion to compliment the members of the Parliamentary Council on their successful completion of a difficult task performed under trying circumstances, on the manifest care and thoroughness with which they have done their work and on their devotion to the democratic ideals toward the achievement of which we are all striving.

Document 7

Following approval by the Military Governors, the Basic Law was approved by the Landtage (state legislatures), not by a popular referendum. Only Bavaria withheld its consent for the time being. On 23 May 1949 the Parliamentary Council assembled for its twelfth and last sitting. The proceedings were opened by Konrad Adenauer who had presided over the Council's sessions. After his introductory remarks the members of the Council were called forward individually by the secretary, a member of the Council, to sign the completed document. Only two members refused to sign, Renner, of the Communist Party of Germany (KDP), stating 'I will not sign the division of Germany'. Dr Adenauer then announced the approval by the Landtage (noting Bavarian refusal to assent), and summoned the minister-presidents of the Länder and the presidents (or speakers) of the Landtage to sign in turn on the call of the secretary. Finally, noting the Berlin City Assembly's concurrence in the 'principles and goals' of the Basic Law, Dr Adenauer invited the president of the Berlin Assembly and the governing mayor to sign. In a closing speech Dr Adenauer noted that the Basic Law would be recorded in the Federal Gazette as Law No. 1 and would take effect as from that day.

THE SIGNING AND PROCLAMATION OF THE BASIC LAW (GRUND-GESETZ), 23 MAY 1949
Source: Parlamentarischer Rat, Stenographischer Bericht. Zwölfte Sitzung, Bonn, Monday, 23 May 1948, 270–3

President Dr Adenauer (CDU):
. . .

To-day a new chapter is being opened in the ever-changing history of the German people. To-day the Federal Republic of Germany enters the stage of history. Those who have witnessed the years since 1933 and the total breakdown in 1945 . . . are with some emotion conscious of the fact that to-day . . . a new Germany is being created. Our endeavours began with the decisions made by the Allies at the

London conference in 1948. By them we were limited in regard to the latitude of the decision permitted on some points. Forces which are stronger than the will of the German people have right up to this very day made it impossible for the whole of Germany to be reconstructed into a [new] state. However, in spite of all limitations we can state: the Basic Law which we have decided on is based on the free will, on the free decision of the German people [loud cheers are recorded at this point.] Next to the representatives of the Occupying Powers the Minister-Presidents and Presidents of the legislatures of the eleven Länder show by their presence to-day that the Länder will stand by the Federation (Bund), which also protects and guarantees their existence with affection and in good faith . . .

The Roll-call Vote

Secretary **STOCK**: President Dr. Konrad **Adenauer**. — Vice-President Adolph **Schönfelder**. — Vice-President Dr. Hermann **Schäfer**. — Hans Heinz **Bauer**. — Dr. Max **Becker**. — Dr. Ludwig **Bergstraesser**. — Dr. Paul **Binder**. — Adolf **Blomeyer**.—Dr. Heinrich **von Brentano**.—Johannes **Brockmann**.— Dr. Paul **de Chapeaurouge**. — Dr. Thomas **Dehler**. — Dr. Georg **Diederichs**. — Dr. Fritz **Eberhard**. — Adolf **Ehlers**. — Dr. Albert **Finck**. — Andreas **Gayk**. — Rudolf **Heiland**. — Wilhelm **Heile**. — Hubert **Hermans**. — Dr. Theodor **Heuss**. — Anton **Hilbert**. — Dr. Fritz **Hoch**. — Dr. Hermann **Höpker-Aschoff**. — Dr. Werner **Hofmeister**. — Dr. Rudolf **Katz**. — Dr. Ferdinand **Kleindinst**. — Dr. Gerhard **Kroll**. — Karl **Kuhn**. — Adolf **Kühn**. — Dr. Wilhelm **Laforet**. — Dr. Dr. Robert **Lehr**. — Lambert **Lensing**. — Dr. Fritz **Löwenthal**. — Friedrich **Maier**. — Dr. Hermann **von Mangoldt**. — Karl Siegmund **Mayr**. — Dr. Walter **Menzel**. — Dr. Willibald **Mücke**. — Friederike **Nadig**. — Erich **Ollenhauer**. — Dr. Anton **Pfeiffer**. — Heinz **Renner**. —

RENNER (KPD): I will not sign the division of Germany.

Secretary **STOCK**: Max **Reimann**. —

REIMANN (KPD): I will not sign.

Secretary **STOCK**: Albert **Roßhaupter**. — Hermann **Runge**. — Kaspar Gottfried **Schlör**. — Dr. Carlo **Schmid**. — Josef **Schrage**. — Carl **Schröter**. — Dr. Josef **Schwalber**. — Dr. Hans-Christoph **Seebohm**. — Dr. Kaspar **Seibold**. — Dr. Elisabeth **Selbert**. — Dr. Walter **Strauß**. — Friedrich Wilhelm **Wagner**. — Dr. Helene **Weber**. — Helene **Wessel**. — Dr. Friedrich **Wolff**. — Hans **Wunderlich**. — Gustav **Zimmermann**. — August **Zinn**. — Jean **Stock**. —

PRESIDENT Dr. ADENAUER: I now invite the delegates from Greater Berlin to sign.

Secretary **STOCK**: Jakob **Kaiser**.—Paul **Löbe**.—Ernst **Reuter** (greeted with applause).—Dr. Hans **Reif**.—Dr. Otto **Suhr**.—

PRESIDENT Dr. ADENAUER: In accordance with the resolutions of the 1948 London Conference the Basic Law was transmitted to the Military Governors who, on 12 May 1949, authorized its submission to the Landtage for ratification.

The Landtag of the State of **Baden** on 18 May approved the Basic Law.
The Landtag of the State of **Bavaria** on 20 May rejected the Basic Law.
The Citizenry of the State of **Bremen** on 20 May,
The Citizenry of the State of **Hamburg** on 18 May,
The Landtag of the State of **Hesse** on 20 May,
The Landtag of the State of **Lower Saxony** on 20 May,
The Landtag of the State of **North-Rhine-Westphalia** on 20 May,
The Landtag of the State of **Rhineland-Palatinate** on 18 May,
The Landtag of the State of **Schleswig-Holstein** on 20 May,
The Landtag of the State of **Württemberg-Baden** on 18 May,
The Landtag of the State of **Württemberg-Hohenzollern** on 20 May
approved the Basic Law.

I now invite the Minister-Presidents and the Presidents of the Landtage to sign.

Secretary **STOCK:**
The President of the State of **Baden**;
The Minister-President of the State of **Bavaria**;
The President of the Senate of **Hansestadt Bremen**;
The Senior Burgomaster of **Hansestadt Hamburg**;
The Minister-President of the State of **Hesse**;
The Minister-President of the State of **Lower Saxony**;
The Minister-President of the State of **North Rhine-Westphalia**;
The Minister-President of the State of **Rhineland-Palatinate**;
The Minister-President of the State of **Schleswig-Holstein**;
The Minister-President of the State of **Württemberg-Baden**;
The Minister-President of the State of **Württemberg-Hohenzollern**;
The President of the **Baden Landtag**;
The President of the **Bavarian Landtag**;
The President of the **Bremen Citizen Assembly**;
The President of the **Hamburg Citizen Assembly**;
The President of the **Hesse Landtag**;
The President of the **Lower Saxony Landtag**;
The President of the **North-Rhine-Westphalia Landtag**;
The President of the **Rhineland-Palatinate Landtag**;
The President of the **Schleswig-Holstein Landtag**;
The President of the **Württemberg-Baden Landtag**;
The President of the **Württemberg-Hohenzollern Landtag**;

PRESIDENT Dr. ADENAUER: The City Assembly of **Greater Berlin** in its 14th Extraordinary Sitting on 19 May 1949 unanimously approved the following **resolution**:

The City Assembly of Greater Berlin concurs in the principles and goals of the Basic Law for the Federal Republic of Germany approved by the Parliamentary Council on 8 May 1949.

I invite the President of the House of Assembly of Greater Berlin and the Governing Mayor of Greater Berlin to attest to this by their signature.

(The Governing Mayor, Professor Reuter, and the President of the House of Assembly, Dr Zuhr, added their signatures.)

PRESIDENT Dr. ADENAUER: Ladies and Gentlemen of the Parliamentary Council! I think that I may, in the name of all Council members who have been addressed by you [the SPD Altespräsident Paul Loebe, former President of the Reichstag] express the warmest thanks for the friendly and welcome words which you have found for us all. In our deliberations, it appears to me, we have all been givers and receivers. No one has merely contributed, everyone has received something. It seems to me that an essential gain from the work of the past nine months has been that we here in this Parliamentary Council have come to recognize and to respect the views of others. The sincerest wish of us all—I think I may express it—is that this achievement may not remain within these walls, but that it will be carried on in the struggle between the parties and that the election campaign, which must soon begin, will be conducted in a high-minded and businesslike fashion

(Applause)

and—let me again express it—in recognition of the honestly held views of others.

(Bravo!)

Ladies and Gentlemen! In accordance with Article 145, in the name and on behalf of the Parliamentary Council,

(The members rise from their seats)

and with the participation of the Members from Greater Berlin, I proclaim the Basic Law. It will take effect from today. It will be published today in Number 1 of the Federal Gazette.

Ladies and Gentlemen! We are firmly convinced that through our work we have achieved an essential step towards the reunification of the whole of the German people and also towards the return of our prisoners of war and displaced persons.

(Applause)

We wish and we hope that the day will soon come on which the whole German
people will be united under this flag.

(Applause and hand-clapping)

In our work we were all guided by the idea and the goal which the preamble of
the Basic Law sets forth in such a splendid manner in the following words:

conscious of its responsibility before God and men, animated by the resolve to
preserve their national and political unity and to serve the peace of the world as
an equal partner in a united Europe, the German people . . . have . . . enacted
this Basic Law . . .

May the spirit and the will expressed in these sentences be always present in
the German people.

(Lively applause—singing of the poem
Ich hab mich ergeben)

Document 8

Theodor Heuss was a representative of the Free Democratic Party in the
Parliamentary Council who had had a political career prior to 1933. A
south German liberal historian and publicist, he was a logical choice for
the presidency of a state certain to be dominated by the large forces of the
SPD and the CDU/CSU.

REPLY BY PROFESSOR THEODOR HEUSS TO THE ALLIED HIGH
COMMISSIONERS ON HIS ELECTION AS PRESIDENT OF THE FEDERAL
REPUBLIC OF GERMANY, 13 SEPTEMBER 1949
Source: Beate Ruhm von Oppen, *Documents on Germany under Occupation,
1945–1954*, London, 1955, 413–4
Transl.: Tagesspiegel, 14 September 1949

I have the honour to express to you my sincere thanks for the congratulations you
conveyed to me in the name of your heads of state and your Governments, as well
as in your own names, on my election as President of the German Federal
Republic. Simultaneously I should like to thank you for the kind words you were
good enough to address to me personally.

You mentioned the great and historic importance of the election that took place
yesterday. I know that the tasks before the German people and before me will
make almost superhuman demands on every one of us.

But our profound faith in the common high ideals, in a democracy imbued with the spirit of Christianity, and a sense of social responsibility will give us the strength to master the difficulties which today seem almost insurmountable.

I attach great value to your remarks in which you say that it is not because of your Governments if today not all German citizens form a part of the German Federal Republic. I am thinking, at this moment, of our fellow citizens in Berlin and in all those parts of our German country who have not yet had an opportunity to profess in freedom their allegiance to the motherland.

It is the sincere desire of the German people to re-enter the great European community. For this purpose we are prepared, as provided by the Constitution, to transfer sovereign rights to international institutions and we see in the consistent realization of this plan a way to the realization of a great idea in the service of peace.

We were glad to hear you say that the Governments you represent are prepared to help us find our way back into the European community.

May I ask you to rest assured that I will do everything in my power to ensure for the Constitution—which embodies the conditions for such a policy of peace—the esteem to which the Constitution of a free people must be entitled. It is in this way that I intend to carry out the mandate which the German people has given me by yesterday's election and I should be grateful if you would convey my ideas to your respective Governments.

Document 9

Dr Konrad Adenauer, a leading Centre Party politician in the Weimar Republic, had been dismissed from his post as Lord Mayor of Cologne twice, first by the Nazis, and then by the British. He emerged as the dominating figure in both the CDU and the Parliamentary Council. What is particularly striking about his Petersberg statement is its emphasis on social and economic problems.

SPEECH BY DR KONRAD ADENAUER, CHANCELLOR OF THE FEDERAL REPUBLIC, AT THE PETERSBERG CEREMONIES, 21 SEPTEMBER 1949

Source: United States Department of State, *Germany, 1947–1949: the Story in Documents*, Washington, 1950, 321–2

I have the honour to pay you a visit in company with some of the members of my Cabinet, thereby establishing the first contact between the Government of the Federal Republic of Germany and the three High Commissioners. Now that the German Federal Assembly has convened, and the Federal president been elected, and now that I have been chosen Federal Chancellor and the members of the Federal Cabinet have been appointed, a new chapter of German history of the postwar years begins.—The disaster of the second world war had left in its wake a Germany almost totally destroyed. Our cities were in ruins. Economic life was largely smashed. All vestiges of a government had ceased. The very souls of men had suffered such injuries that it seemed doubtful whether a recovery would ever be possible. During the four years following the disaster of 1945, legislative and executive power was largely vested in the occupation powers. It was only step by step that executive and legislative functions were re-delegated to German authorities on various levels, and with a limited power to make decisions. It is fitting and proper to acknowledge gratefully that the German population was saved from starvation during these trying years by Allied help in supplying food which at the time could not be purchased with the proceeds of German exports. It was this help which made possible the start of reconstruction. Now that the governmental and legislative elements of the German Federal Republic are being built up, a large part of the responsibility and the authority to make decisions will pass into German hands. We do not, of course, possess as yet complete freedom, since there are considerable restrictions contained in the Occupation Statute. We will do our part to bring about an atmosphere in which the Allied powers will see their way clear to apply the Occupation Statute in a liberal and generous manner; only in this way will the German people be able to attain full freedom. We hope that the Allied powers will, by making a corresponding use of the revision clause in the occupation statute, hasten the further political development of our country.

It is the unshakable wish of the new Federal Government first and foremost to tackle the great social problems. The Government is convinced that a sound political entity can only develop when each individual is assured a maximum of economic opportunity to earn a livelihood. Not until we succeed in converting the flotsam millions of refugees into settled inhabitants by providing them with housing and adequate opportunities for work will we be able to enjoy inner stability in Germany. Disorder and crises in this part of Europe, however, constitute a serious threat to the security of the entire continent. For this reason, the social programme of the Federal Government should at the same time act to ensure a peaceful development in Europe. We will, of course, do everything in our power to master these problems with the forces at our command. Nevertheless, I feel I am justified in believing even now that the problem of expellees is not only a national, but an international one. To solve it, the help of the rest of the world is needed....

If we want to establish peace in Europe we can, in the view of the Federal Government, achieve this only by working along entirely new lines. We see opportunities to do this in the efforts made for a European federation, which has just borne its first fruits [at] Strasbourg.[20]

Notes

1. Basic Law, Art. 146.
2. John Gimbel, *The American Occupation of Germany: Politics and the Military, 1945–1949*, Stanford, 1968, 6. Cf. Kurt Sontheimer, 'The Weimar Republic—Failure and Prospects for German Democracy,' in E.J. Feuchtwanger, ed., *Upheaval and Continuity: A Century of German History*, London, 1973, 101.
3. 'Declaration regarding the defeat of Germany and the assumption of Supreme Authority with respect to Germany . . . , 5 June 1945.' *Selected Documents on Germany and the Question of Berlin, 1944–1961*, London, HMSO, 1961, Cmnd. 1552, 38.
4. 'Directive of the United States Joint Chiefs of Staff to the Commander-in-Chief of the United States Forces of Occupation regarding the Military Government of Germany' (JCS 1067). US Department of State, *Germany, 1947–1949: The Story in Documents*, Washington, 1950, 23.
5. See, for example, Adolf M. Birke, *America and the Creation of the New Germany. Constitutional Policy in the US-occupied Zone* (forthcoming).
6. United States Department of State: *Foreign Relations of the United States: The Conferences at Malta and Yalta, 1945*, Washington, 1956, 978.
7. Ibid., *The Conference of Berlin (Potsdam), 1945*, Washington, 1960, II, 1483, 1484.
8. Gimbel, *The American Occupation of Germany*, 16–18, 23, 52. Alfred Grosser, *Germany in Our Time: A Political History of the Postwar Years*, New York, 1971, 63.
9. *The Conferences at Malta and Yalta*, 978.
10. 'Directive of the United States Chiefs of Staff . . .' (JCS 1067), in *Germany, 1947–1949: The Story in Documents*, Washington, 1950, 21 ff.
11. 'Directive of the United States Joint Chiefs of Staff to the Commander-in-Chief, United States Forces of Occupation, regarding the Military Government of Germany', (JCS 1779), 11 July 1947. Ibid., 34.
12. Peter H. Merkl, *The Origin of the West German Republic*, New York, 1963, 8–15.
13. *Akten zur Vorgeschichte der Bundesrepublik Deutschland, 1945–1949*, 1, Munich, 1979, 125.
14. For a summary of this process in the United States zone, see *Germany 1947–1949: The Story in Documents*, 169–70.
15. Merkl, *The Origin of the West German Republic*, 19; John F. Golay, *The Founding of the Federal Republic of Germany*, Chicago, 1958, 6–13; Peter Calvocoressi, *Survey of International Affairs, 1947–1948*, London, 1952, 261–3.
16. Merkl, *The Origin of the West German Republic*, 58–61.
17. Merkl, ibid., 177, cites the verdict of the distinguished (and influential) American scholar, Carl J. Friedrich, that the Basic Law was a product of a 'negative evolution'; Sontheimer, in 'The Weimar Republic,' 113, suggests that the Parliamentary Council created a 'counter-constitution' to the Weimar constitution. Ch. 3., 54f.
18. See also Ch. 3., 54f.
19. No precise definition of the French sector of Berlin is given in this document (which reflects the text of the report submitted to the four governments on 26 July 1945). It was recorded not in the EAC, but subsequently in the Allied Control Council. See also Ch. 13.
20. Cf. Ch. 10.

2 Parliamentary Democracy: the Bundestag

Carl-Christoph Schweitzer

According to democratic theory and the German Basic Law, the Bundestag, directly elected by the sovereign people, has precedence over the other two 'powers', i.e. the executive and the judiciary. The fathers of the Basic Law wanted to establish the Federal Republic of Germany very clearly as a parliamentary democracy.* Remembering their experiences with the Weimar Republic, whose head of government was responsible to both parliament and the president as Head of State, they made sure that the executive branch of government, the chancellor (Bundeskanzler) with his cabinet (Bundesregierung), is politically responsible to the Bundestag and is elected by its members by secret ballot.[1]

The president of the Bundestag (Bundestagspräsident, 'speaker'), automatically elected at the beginning of each legislative period (Wahlperiode) on the nomination of the majority party in the Bundestag, conducts the business of the House within a set of very specific Standing Orders (Geschäftsordnung des Bundestages, Doc. 1). He is assisted by Vice-presidents, representing the other parties in the Bundestag, and by the Council of Elders (Ältestenrat) made up of 'government' and 'opposition' Members of the Bundestag (MdBs, referred to below as 'members'). This body draws up, by mutual agreement, the weekly timetable of the House and in this way exercises control over its own business in a formal way not followed in Great Britain or Canada.

The members are not only governed by these Standing Orders of the Bundestag, but also by Standing Orders of their party caucuses (Fraktionsgeschäftsordnungen, Doc. 2). The party caucuses constitute themselves

---

* Notes for this chapter begin on p. 49.

formally and automatically after each general election. They are, however, recognised only when and if the elected members of a given political party make up at least 5% of the overall Bundestag membership of 518, these including twenty-two members with restricted status, delegated to the Bundestag by the parliament of West Berlin.[2] There have been so far no cases of members being elected to the Bundestag as independent representatives. Some left their party and, therefore, also their caucus in parliament during a four-year-legislative period of the Bundestag and then remained members for the rest of that period as independents. In this capacity they lost, for example, the important right to sit on Bundestag committees, because members can only be chosen for or withdrawn from those committees by party caucuses. These caucuses (Fraktionen) are highly organized bodies with working groups (Arbeitsgruppen) and coordinating committees (Arbeitskreise), comprising several working groups, which consider the various areas of policy covered by the Standing Committees of the Bundestag (Bundestagsausschüsse, Doc. 3), such as, for instance, the Budget Committee, or the Judicial Committee. These committees in turn correspond more or less to the Federal Ministries they are supposed to supervise (Docs. 3 and 4). One whole day of each weekly parliamentary timetable is devoted to meetings of the caucuses and their working-groups, another one to the meetings of the Standing Committees of the Bundestag itself.

So much for the structure of the Bundestag. Two important questions then arise: firstly, what are the functions of the Bundestag, its 'effective parts'— to use W. Bagehot's famous terminology[3]—as they are spelt out in the various Standing Orders as well as in the Basic Law itself? Secondly, what powers do the 518 supreme representatives of the people have in actual political practice—the individual members, the caucuses or the Bundestag as a whole? To begin with, the Bundestag has *elective functions*. With a so-called 'chancellor-majority' (of at least 249 members, one more than half the total membership excluding those from West Berlin) the Bundestag chooses at the beginning of each legislative period the chancellor, who then can only be voted out of office by a so-called *constructive vote of no-confidence*. This requires that the Bundestag must elect a successor to the chancellor if it wishes to remove him. The chancellor himself can also at any time ask for a *vote of confidence*. Only if he loses it can the Bundestag be dissolved within a legislative period. There is no other way than that of calling general federal elections within the constitutionally prescribed period of four years. The Basic Law says in regard to the election of a chancellor in Art. 63:

(1) The Federal Chancellor shall be elected, without debate, by the Bundestag upon the proposal of the Federal President.
(2) The person obtaining the votes of the majority of the members of the Bundestag shall be elected. The person elected must be appointed by the Federal President.
(3) If the person proposed is not elected, the Bundestag may elect within fourteen days of the ballot a Federal Chancellor by more than one-half of its members.
(4) If no candidate has been elected within this period, a new ballot shall take place without delay, in which the person obtaining the largest number of votes shall be elected. If the person elected has obtained the votes of the majority of the members of the Bundestag, the Federal President must appoint him within seven days of the election. If the person elected did not obtain such a majority, the Federal President must within seven days either appoint him or dissolve the Bundestag.

The provisions for a vote of no-confidence are stated in Art. 67:

(1) The Bundestag can express its lack of confidence in the Federal Chancellor only by electing a successor with the majority of its members and by requesting the Federal President to dismiss the Federal Chancellor. The Federal President must comply with the request and appoint the person elected . . .

and the provisions for a vote of confidence, possibly leading to new elections, are spelt out in Art 68:

(1) If a motion of the Federal Chancellor for a vote of confidence is not assented to by the majority of the members of the Bundestag, the Federal President may, upon the proposal of the Federal Chancellor, dissolve the Bundestag within 21 days. The right to dissolve shall lapse as soon as the Bundestag with the majority of its members elects another Federal Chancellor . . .

Since 1949 a vote of no-confidence has been attempted only twice. In 1972 it failed against Chancellor Willy Brandt; in 1982 it succeeded against Chancellor Helmut Schmidt (Doc. 5). Three votes of confidence were asked for: the first by Willy Brandt in 1972 in order to make new elections possible, i.e. with the members of parliament from the government bench deliberately abstaining so as to lose the vote; the second asked for and won by Helmut Schmidt in 1982; the third asked for by Helmut Kohl and again deliberately lost, in December 1982, in order again to arrive at new elections. Procedures then adopted by the majority in parliament gave rise to most heated constitutional and political debates in the Federal Republic at the turn of the year and led to a pronouncement of the Federal Constitutional Court on the subject in February

1983.[4] So far no amendments of the Basic Law have been made to enable a Parliament to dissolve itself.

The chancellor alone is responsible to the Bundestag as Head of the Cabinet. He alone can be dismissed on a vote of no-confidence, individual ministers cannot. In other words, there is collective, but no individual cabinet responsibility to parliament. In the Federal Republic of Germany there is, just as in other parliamentary democracies, no 'incompatibility' in being both a member of the Bundestag and a member of the cabinet. Consequently, with two or three exceptions, all cabinet members have been at the same time sitting members. In the first cabinet of Willy Brandt, for instance, the Minister for Science and Education, Hans Leussink, was a member of the cabinet, but not of the Bundestag, where he had no seat, no functions or privileges, but where he could speak or had to speak and answer questions for the Government.

Secondly, the Bundestag has the *function of law-making*, i.e. it is the supreme federal law-making body. However, it is important to point out that the second chamber, the Bundesrat, representing the governments of the eleven States (Länder) of the Federal Republic, has a veto on bills—a suspensive one on all, an absolute one on some, depending on the substantive matter concerned.[5] For this reason the Mediation Committee of both Houses (the Vermittlungsausschuß, Doc. 6) is a very important instrument of law-making. Here compromises are thrashed out which the two houses have then to vote on again, but which are usually carried unless the absolute veto of the Bundesrat can apply. Two points have to be taken into account: firstly, that some 80% of all federal bills later enacted are *introduced* into the Bundestag by the government (and not by the Bundestag itself, by a caucus or by the Bundesrat—all of which is constitutionally possible); such a percentage is considered fairly normal in Great Britain or Canada, where practically all business is introduced into parliament by the government.[6] However, this is not accepted as normal by German political theorists. Secondly, government bills are seldom changed in important points during their parliamentary passage. The reason for the first phenomenon is mainly that the government with its ministries has far more expertise at its disposal, even though the members have for some years now been given an assistant each, as well as access to a sophisticated Legislative Reference Service (Wissenschaftlicher Dienst) with many specialists for all fields. The reason for the second phenomenon will be referred to again below: the government can, in the law-making process as in other matters, generally rely on its majority in the Bundestag!

Thirdly, the Bundestag has (again at least on paper) a number of opportunities to exercise the function considered to be most important by theorists of parliamentary democracy, i.e. that of *controlling* the policies of the government in power. In Germany theoreticians distinguish here between control of the overall direction of policies (Richtungskontrolle) and of control of the performance of the government (Leistungskontrolle). The former means that the Bundestag can try to ascertain government policy or, having ascertained it, to criticise that policy. It can do so by means of the Question Time (Fragestunde) twice a week for ninety minutes during twenty-six weeks a year, when the Bundestag is in session. It can do so by means of an *ad hoc* debate (the so-called Aktuelle Stunde), which is a debate confined to sixty minutes with speeches limited to five minutes each. It can do so by means of a formal written question or set of questions introduced by a group of members collectively (the so-called Kleine or Große Anfrage). Finally—and most extensively in point of time—the Bundestag can control the overall direction of policies by means of a full-scale debate which any member of the cabinet or the chancellor himself can be 'compelled' to attend, in order to answer questions. That is constitutionally possible because Art. 43 of the Basic Law says in its first paragraph: 'The Bundestag and its committees may demand the presence of any member of the Federal Government'. A famous case occurred in 1974 when—on the motion of the then opposition (CDU/CSU), supported by members of the governing party —SPD Chancellor Helmut Schmidt was compelled by a vote of the House not to proceed with an intended schedule outside Bonn but instead to attend a debate on a problem of foreign policy. The Bundestag adjourned for thirty minutes in order to give the chancellor a chance to change his schedule.

Full-scale debates take place on an average of one and a half days a week when parliament is in session. Here the Bundestag exercises an important educative function, i.e. acts in the full limelight of the public as the central forum for political controversies in the nation.

The main instrument for controlling the performance of the government is provided by the Standing Committees, already mentioned. As in other Western democracies perhaps the most powerful Committee is that for the Federal Budget (Haushaltsausschuß). All committees meet, as a rule, in executive session and are closed to the public and press. Public hearings are possible, but have been extremely rare, though of late the number has increased. It is not least in such hearings that influence can be brought to bear on the political process by interest-groups, whose role in politics must also be seen in the light of historic 'affiliations' between some of these groups and certain political parties.[7]

The Bundestag provided itself in 1957 with an unique instrument for controlling the German military establishment by creating—in addition to the Defence Committee—a Defence Commissioner, or Parliamentary Ombudsman for the Armed Services (Wehrbeauftragter des Bundestages, Doc. 7). Similarly, the Bundestag has insisted on its prerogative of controlling government activities in the field of the secret services. They are supervised by a special Committee of three members (Vertrauensmännergremium, or Confidential Group), one from each caucus. So far this has not led to any security leakages.[8] It sits in secret sessions only, with no other members being able to 'listen in', as they can in most other committees. In this connection mention must also be made of the Joint Committee of twenty-two members of the Bundestag and eleven from each of the Länder (Gemeinsamer Ausschuß, in accordance with Art. 53a Basic Law), to control the government in times of national emergencies. This 'parliament in miniature' would only go into action when and if the Bundestag and Bundesrat as a whole were not in a position to assemble. Its members could be flown within minutes to the big atomic shelter-cum-command-centre near Bonn, there to 'govern' the country constitutionally from underground—a perfectionist German device to make sure that Germany remains 'safe for democracy'. Finally, there is the possibility of setting up any time, as instruments of control in addition to the Standing Committees, *ad hoc* Committees of Investigation (Untersuchungsausschüsse, Doc. 8). These Committees constitute (again on paper) a very important 'minority right', since the opposition can have them set up even if the government parties are not in favour. Art. 44 of the Basic Law states that they must be set up if one quarter of the Bundestag membership demands it. However, since *all* committees (standing or *ad hoc*) are established on the basis of proportional representation which governs the composition of the Bundestag itself, the committees 'mirror' the majority and minority in parliament at any given time. Hence, when it comes to a committee vote on resolutions, bills, treaties or reports, the opposition will, as a rule, be in a minority. The chairmanships in all committees are also distributed to the various party caucuses on a proportional basis.

At this point the overall question again poses itself as to whether in actual fact the Bundestag can *effectively* control the government in power. The answer is the same—as it would be for all parliamentary democracies of the same type: there is, firstly, no system of checks and balances between the government and the Bundestag as a whole, because the majority in parliament will generally support 'its' government through thick and thin. Since, secondly, the opposition in parliament will always be in a minority, the only effective controlling bodies of parliament are, hence, the caucuses of the government parties (or of the government party). So far it is only possible to speculate on the effectiveness of actions taken by majority caucuses of the Bundestag in controlling 'their' government, since the regular minutes of caucus-meetings are as yet 'closed' to researchers. Regular votes are taken at those meetings which cabinet ministers—including the chancellor—attending their respective party caucus would be obliged to follow politically because, after all, the government depends on the support of its basis. Votes are also taken in the opposition caucus (or caucuses as the case may be) to determine the line to be taken by the opposition in plenary sessions.[9]

The final problem is, then, basically the same in all party caucuses of the Bundestag, i.e. the question of the relationship between what is called in German terminology 'Fraktionszwang' (caucus-pressure), applied by the leadership towards rank and file members with the aim of forcing them into a certain voting behaviour (or other forms of conformity) on the one hand, and 'Fraktionsdisziplin' (a self-ordained party-discipline) on the other. To apply 'Fraktionszwang' openly would, in a very German way, be against 'the law', i.e. the Basic Law itself, whose Art. 38 clearly stipulates:

(1) The members of the German Bundestag ... shall be representatives of the whole people, not bound by orders and instructions, and shall be subject only to their conscience ...

Nevertheless, in this connection, too, one must speak of indirect deviations from the prescribed norm in so far as the party-leadership has many subtle means at its disposal to dissuade potential or actual rebels from voting against their party in the House. There have, however, been a number of recorded cases since 1949, where individual members did vote against their own party on a 'point of conscience' concerning important matters of substance.[10] What is 'conscience' and what personal-political calculation is, of course, difficult to prove (Doc. 9). But the rule in the Bundestag has been—and still is—for caucus members to observe a maximum of 'Fraktionsdisziplin'. The philosophy behind this tendency is obvious: caucuses must try to exert a maximum of influence on the political process in parliament in order to achieve their overall policy objectives. This presupposes a maximum of internal cohesion.

Political scientists and constitutional lawyers have written a good deal[11] on the *conflict* built into the Basic Law itself through its combined articles 38 and 21: Members of Parliament are supposed to be entirely free agents under Art. 38 Basic Law, but they are, in fact, elected to parliament through their affiliations to political parties, which constitute to all intents and purposes 'organs of the state' by virtue of Art. 21 Basic Law. West German parliamentary democracy is based on the principle of *party-government*[12], which is for the first time now being called into question by new movements towards 'direct democracy'—by way of citizens' action groups or by 'green' and other alternative groups of all sorts.[13]

To sum up this introduction: according to the constitutional theory of the Federal Republic of Germany the Bundestag is the supreme body in the country and constitutes the 'sovereign parliament', as in Great Britain or Canada. In Germany many aspects of parliamentary life have been laid down in very precise and detailed Standing Orders of the Bundestag as a whole and of the party caucuses. Even so, however, the political practice often does not, for the reasons mentioned above, conform to the prescribed norms—a problem for all parliamentary democracies of our time. In the Federal Republic new developments may arise in this connection due to the emergence of a fourth caucus in the Bundestag after the general elections of March 1983, that of the 'Greens' who, right from the start, have demanded a whole set of new procedural reforms to bring practice more into line with theory, at least as they see it.

Document 1

STANDING ORDERS OF THE BUNDESTAG (GESCHÄFTSORDNUNG)
Source: Text as amended by the Bundestag in June 1980 (Deutscher Bundestag, 8th legislative period, Drucksache 8/3460; cf. BGBl., I, 1237)
. . .

§ 5: The president and his deputies (vice-presidents) form the presidency.

§ 6: The *Council of Elders*
   (1) consists of the president, his deputies and twenty-three additional members to be chosen from the caucuses according to § 12 below. It is the president's duty to summon and chair its meetings. He must summon the council, if a caucus requests it.
   (2) The council of elders aids the president in conducting parliamentary business. Through it, agreements are brought about between caucuses regarding nominations to the positions of committee chairmen, as well as the weekly agenda of the Bundestag . . .
   . . .

§ 8: *The Chair*
In meetings of the Bundestag (plenary sessions) the president *pro tempore* and two
secretaries (MdBs as Schriftführer) constitute the chair . . .

. . .

§ 10: *Formation of Caucuses*
 (1) The caucuses are associations of at least five per cent of the Bundestag
membership, who belong to the same party or parties that are not in competition
with each other in any Land on the grounds that they pursue similar political
goals. . . .
 (2) The forming and naming of a caucus, the names of its chairmen, members
and guests are to be communicated to the president in writing . . .
 (4) Members of the Bundestag who wish to associate without having achieved
the minimum percentage required to form a caucus can be recognised as a
'group'. . . .

. . .

§ 12: *Positions Apportioned to the Caucuses*
 (1) The composition of the council of elders and of the Bundestag committees
as well as the apportioning of the chairmanships in those committees is determined by the proportionate strength of the different caucuses.[14] The same principle applies to the election of members to other bodies by the Bundestag . . .

§ 13: *Duties of the Members of the Bundestag*
 (1) Bundestag members are obliged to take part in the business of the
Bundestag.
 (2) On every session-day an attendance sheet will be laid out; members are to
register themselves. The consequences of non-registration and non-participation
follow from the law on remuneration for members.

. . .

Editorial comment: Non-registration is penalised by a fine for each day.

. . .

§ 19: *Plenary Sessions (Meetings)*
 (1) The meetings of the Bundestag shall be public. The public can be excluded
in accordance with Art. 42, 1, Basic Law: ' . . . on a motion of one-tenth of its
members, or upon a motion of the federal government, the public may be excluded by a two-thirds majority. The decision on the motion shall be taken at a
meeting not open to the public'.

. . .

§ 27: *Recognition of Speakers and the Way to Ask for Recognition*
 (1) . . . Members of the Bundestag who wish to speak on a point on the agenda

have, as a rule, to indicate their wish to do so to that secretary who is listing members desiring to be called . . .

. . .

§ 43: *Right to be Heard at all Times*
The members of the government (federal) and of the Bundesrat, as well as persons commissioned by them, must, upon their request, be heard any time. (Cf. Art. 43, 2, Basic Law.)

. . .

§ 54: *Standing Committees and ad hoc Committees*
(1) The Bundestag sets up standing committees which prepare the business of the day. For specific matters special committees can be set up . . .

. . .

§69: *Closed Committee Meetings*
Committee deliberations are on principle carried out in closed meetings. The committee can decide for a specific subject under debate, or parts thereof, to admit the general public. The meeting is considered to be an open one if members of the press and/or any other listeners are allowed to be present . . .

§ 70: *Public Hearings*
(1) Public hearings of experts, representatives of interest groups and other persons supplying information can be undertaken by a committee in order to become informed about a subject under deliberation . . .

Editorial comment: In the legislative period of the Bundestag 1976 to 1980 only four out of some 2000 committee meetings (see § 69 above) were open to the public. In the same period some 170 hearings with experts were conducted (see § 70 above), of those only some seventy were open to the public. Meetings of the Committee on Foreign Affairs or the Defense Committee have never been, *inter alia*, open to the public; see also Table 4.

. . .

§ 76: *Papers Submitted by Members*
(1) Any business can be brought to the attention of the Bundestag by members if a request to do so has been signed by a caucus or by five per cent of the members of the Bundestag . . .

. . .

§ 78: *Reading of Bills*
(1) Drafts of a bill are dealt with in three readings. Treaties with foreign states and similar treaties or agreements which regulate the political relations of the federation or relate to matters of federal legislation are in general deliberated

upon in two readings only, by decision of the Bundestag in three. All other business is deliberated upon only in one reading.

. . .

§ 105: *Questions by Individual Members of the Bundestag*
Any member of the Bundestag is entitled to put questions to the federal government during question-time or in writing. For details see the special rules of procedure in the annex hereof No. 4. (Cf. ibid. section II: Handing in of questions: . . . 'Questions have to be handed in to the president [his bureau for parliamentary affairs] with two copies thereof . . .'.)

Document 2

Standing orders of the SPD caucus have, basically, been in force since 1949. Their main features are the same as those of the standing orders of the other caucuses; for example, those of the CDU which, together with its Bavarian Counterpart, the CSU,[15] has since the days of Chancellor Adenauer established a joint caucus at the beginning of each new legislative period, and those of the liberal FDP. The excerpts below demonstrate once again that in practical politics there are always deviations from the prescribed norm since, for instance, § 3 stipulates that members wishing to speak in the house must channel their request through their whips, while the standing orders of the higher-ranking Bundestag stipulate in § 27 that members wishing to speak need only indicate their wish to the chair. Even more questionable is the stipulation of § 5, 3 below.

STANDING ORDERS OF THE SPD-CAUCUS (FRAKTION)
Source: Standing Orders of the SPD-Fraktion, as amended, 1970

. . .

§ 2: *Speakers for the Caucus in Plenary Sessions*
The caucus determines the speakers who are to represent its views in plenary sessions of the Bundestag.

§ 3: *Participation in Plenary Debates*
If a caucus member wishes to participate as a speaker in a plenary debate he will come to an understanding with the caucus officer in charge of the appropriate Bundestag committee (Obmann) as well as with the caucus whip (Parlamentarischer Geschäftsführer, see below § 8).

§ 4: *Nominations to Committees of the Bundestag, other Bodies and Delegations*
Nominations to such committees, other bodies and delegations are decided upon by the caucus. Candidates for offices and functions of the Bundestag who have to be put forward by the caucus are elected by the same on the proposal of the caucus's executive committee (see below § 8). If in addition nominations are put forward from the midst of the caucus, a list of all candidates proposed will be put to the vote of the caucus in alphabetical order ...

§ 5: *Introduction of Interpellations, Resolutions and Drafts for Bills*
(1) The caucus decides on the introduction of bills and other motions as well as any other interpellations (Große und Kleine Anfragen).

(2) Any initiatives taken by individual members in this respect which are not be introduced by the caucus as such, have first to be put before the caucus's executive committe via the relevant working group of the caucus ...

(3) Questions for question time have to be submitted to the parliamentary whip first.

...

§ 7: *General Duties of the Caucus Members*
The caucus members are obliged to participate in the meetings and the general work of the caucus as well as of the Bundestag and its committees. The caucus adopts more specific regulations to guarantee that participation and to grant leave of absence.

§ 8: *Caucus Executive Committee, its Composition*
(1) The caucus executive committee consists of its chairman, his deputies, the other members elected by the whole caucus and the parliamentary whips.

...

(3) ... Social Democratic members of the government and ministers of state participate in the meetings of the executive committee ...

§ 9:
The caucus elects by secret ballot, separately, the chairman of the caucus, his deputies, the parliamentary whips and the other members ...

...

§ 18: *Working Groups*
The members of a Bundestag committee form a working group of the caucus. The caucus elects for each of these a chairman (Obmann) ...

...

§ 23: *Formation of Working Committees (Arbeitskreise) and Working Groups (Arbeitsgruppen) to Deal with Specific Problems*
(1) The caucus sets up working committees for different subject matters in

order to facilitate its work in the Bundestag. In addition to the working groups in accordance with § 18 above further such groups can be set up to deal with specific problems. All working groups submit their findings to the working committees for a decision to be taken.

(2) The chairmen of the working committees and their deputies as well as the chairmen of working groups for specific problems are elected by the caucus on the proposal of the executive committee ...

§ 24: *Meetings of Working Committees and Working Groups*
All members of the caucus are entitled to take part in meetings of any such working committee or working group ...

Document 3

At the beginning of each legislative period the chairmanships of the standing committees, whose overall number has been more or less constant since 1949, are apportioned almost equally between government and opposition caucuses. The committees themselves appoint by vote, on the proposal of the senior caucus-members from all parties, 'rapporteurs' (Berichterstatter) for most matters on the agenda, such as the consideration of bills, treaties, resolutions, reports etc. There are always two, one from the government, one from the opposition parties. Ever since the days of the old German Reichstag in the last century the chairman of the important Budget Committee has been a member of the opposition.

STANDING COMMITTEES OF THE BUNDESTAG
Source: Handbuch des Deutschen Bundestages, 9th legislative period, Bonn, 1980; see also Table 4

A. Standing Committees

Number		Number of members
1	The Committee for the Scrutiny of Elections, Immunity and the Rules of Procedure	13
2	The Petitions Committee	27
3	The Committee on Foreign Affairs	33
4	The Committee on Internal Affairs	27
5	The Sports Committee	13
6	The Legal (Judicial) Committee	27
7	The Finance Committee	31
8	The Budget Committee	33
9	The Committee on Economic Affairs	31

Number		Number of members
10	The Committee on Food, Agriculture and Forestry	27
11	The Committee on Labour and Social Affairs	33
12	The Defence Committee	27
13	The Committee on Youth, Family Affairs and Health	25
14	The Committee on Transport	27
15	The Committee on Posts and Telecommunications	13
16	The Committee on Regional Planning, Building and Urban Development	27
17	The Committee on Intra-German Relations	25
18	The Committee on Research and Technology	25
19	The Committee on Education and Science	25
20	The Committee on Economic Co-operation	25

Documents 4a–d

Here we have 'typical' orders of the day for meetings of two important Bundestag committees, both restricted to committee members only: the Committee on Foreign Affairs and the Defence Committee. The case of Doc. 4a below may be taken as typical of a treaty to be ratified by parliament in accordance with Art. 59, 2, of the Basic Law:

. . .

(2) Treaties which regulate the political relations of the federation or relate to matters of federal legislation shall require the consent or participation, in the form of a federal law, of the bodies competent in any specific case for such federal legislation . . .

SOME AGENDAS OF SUCH COMMITTEES
Source: Committee publications

Document 4a

On the agenda was the treaty between the Federal Republic and Poland signed in 1975, as a further and final breakthrough in German–Polish relations after the Treaty of Warsaw of 1970.[16] The then Minister for Foreign Affairs (Genscher) was himself in attendance to answer questions and criticisms of the members. This document demonstrates the ability of the Defence Committee to transform itself (the only one which can do so) into a special 'committee of investigation' (see also below Doc. 8), the idea being that the Bundestag wished to have special emergency powers to control the new armed forces.[17]

German Federal Parliament   Bonn, 6 January 1976
7th Term [legislative period]
Third Committee
—712—2401—

Announcement

The 68th session of the Committee on Foreign Affairs takes place on Wednesday,
14 January 1976, 10.00 a.m. . . .

Agenda

1. Deliberation

   a) on a bill regarding the agreement of 9.10.1975 between the Federal
      Republic of Germany and the People's Republic of Poland on pension and
      accident insurance together with the agreements on this matter of
      9.10.1975
   b) on government information about the agreements with the People's
      Republic of Poland which were signed in Warsaw on 9.10.1975

   Rapporteurs for a) and b): Schlaga MdB
                              Dr. Wallmann MdB

2. Naming a rapporteur for the bill . . . regarding the agreement on establishing
   an association between the European Economic Community and Greece . . .
   (1975)
3. Miscellaneous

                                                              Mattick
                                                        Deputy Chairman

Document 4b

German Federal Parliament   Bonn, 20 June 1980
8th Term
Defence Committee
—715—2401—

Announcement

The 103rd session of the Defence Committee takes place on Wednesday, 2 July
1980, 9.00 a.m. . . .

Agenda

1. Decision on the FDP caucus motion of 18.6.1980 concerning infrastructure
2. Report from the Federal Ministry for Defence on a concept for an army tank in the 'nineties
3. Report from the Federal Ministry for Defence on armament planning
4. Annual report 1979 from the Defence Commissioner of the German Federal Parliament

   Rapporteurs: Ernesti MdB
   Horn MdB

5. Report of the Commission of the Federal Ministry for Defence on strengthening leadership ability and responsibility for decisions in the armed forces (de Maizière report)
   . . .

Dr. Wörner
Chairman

Document 4c

German Federal Parliament   Bonn, 26 May 1976
7th Term
Third Committee
—712—2401—

Announcement

The 78th session of the Committee on Foreign Affairs takes place on Wednesday,
2 June 1976, 3.30 p.m.
Bonn, Bundeshaus, Chamber 2704 NH

Agenda

1. Government report on the spring conference of the NATO Council of Ministers in Oslo
2. Government report on the situation in Israel
3. Government report on the Trade and Development Conference of the United Nations (UNCTAD IV) in Nairobi
4. Government report on the consular agreement between the United Kingdom and the GDR
5. Deliberation on the draft of the Ministry for Foreign Affairs concerning defence aid for Turkey (9th Tranche) . . .

6. Deliberation on the resolution of the European Parliament concerning the UN General Assembly's resolution on Zionism ...
7. Deliberation on the resolution of the European Parliament concerning the present state of the Euro-Arabian dialogue ...
8. Discussion of the CDU/CSU parliamentary caucus's motion concerning aid for the victims of the earthquake catastrophe in Northern Italy ...
9. Miscellaneous

Dr. Schröder
Chairman

Document 4d

German Federal Parliament   Bonn, 31 July 1980
8th Term
Defence Committee as the
2nd Committee of Investigation
—715—2401—

Announcement

The 110th session of the Defence Committee —8th session as the 2nd Committee of Investigation in accordance with Art. 45a, para. 2 Basic Law—takes place on Tuesday, 5 August 1980, 9.00 a.m. ...

Agenda

Questioning of the expert witness	on 1. 2, 3, 4, 5, 6
Federal Minister Gerhart Baum, MdB	in open session
Hearing	
Representatives of the 'Land Office for the Protection of the Constitution', Hamburg	in closed session
Police counsellor (Polizeirat) Elbrecht, Bremen	in open session
Under Secretary of State, Baier, Niedersachsen	in open session
Questioning of the expert witness	on 1.6
Dieter Mützelburg	in open session

. . .

Document 5

The constructive vote of no-confidence, provided for in Art. 67 of the Basic Law, prevents the Bundestag from dismissing the chancellor without at the same time electing his successor by a majority of its members. Helmut Kohl's election as the new chancellor following the no-confidence vote was the first time in the Federal Republic's history that a government had been replaced without a general election.[18] The following extract is from the parliamentary debate over the 1972 motion for a no-confidence vote against Chancellor Brandt.

CONSTRUCTIVE VOTE OF NO-CONFIDENCE
Source: Deutscher Bundestag, 183rd Parliamentary sitting, Sten. Berichte, 27 April 1972

President von Hassel: The proceedings are opened. I call for point 3 of the agenda: discussion of the motion of the CDU/CSU caucus according to Art. 67 of the Basic Law—Order Paper VI/3380—
I call on Member Dr. Kiesinger (for the motion).

Dr. h.c. Kiesinger (CDU/CSU):
. . .

We have chosen the possibility of moving a motion in accord with Art. 67 of the Basic Law for a 'Constructive Vote of No Confidence' not in order—as a speaker from the government coalition claimed yesterday—'to sneak into power', but in order to relieve a government and a policy which we are convinced has failed and has damaged the interests of our people.

(Applause from the CDU/CSU)

We have not chosen this path because we are afraid of a new election. On the contrary! But according to the Basic Law the opposition does not have the power to bring about such elections. Neither have we chosen this path out of a narrow-minded party interest with short-lived tactical considerations. Many of our friends have advised us to let this coalition, this government, this chancellor carry on even deeper into the dead-end of its failed policy in order to win better chances for ourselves in the next election. If it were only a matter of the fate of this government we would have followed this advice. But it is a matter of the interests of our people. And it was in order to avert their being further endangered that we determined on this course.

. . .

The fathers of the Basic Law, remembering the Weimar Republic, rejected with good reason a simple 'Vote of No Confidence'. For by this a heterogeneous majority could bring down a government without being in a position or wanting to form a new government itself.

The Social Democrat Member Dr. Menzel argued at the time in the Parliamentary Council that one ought to transform the 'Vote of No Confidence' as it was put to previous ill use [in the Weimar Republic, ed.] as a politically destructive mechanism into a weapon of a positively oriented parliamentary democracy.
. . .

Chancellor Brandt:

. . .

The decision of the CDU/CSU to try to bring down the government accords with the opportunities offered by the Constitution and is not difficult to understand either as power politics or psychologically. If you will allow me a judgement on the latter: This is an attempt at a 'forward escape', out of the irresponsibility of a sterile 'No' to matters of the fate of our people, but with the risk of going into a responsibility whose bitterness you would soon feel. For Dr. Barzel and his friends would only obtain this responsibility if they were to receive a 'Yes' from a few members of this respected house of whom one would be able to say that they had strained their conscience beyond the point of recognition.

(Cheers from the government side. Shouts
from the CDU/CSU: 'Rubbish, outrageous')

. . .

President von Hassel:

Ladies and Gentlemen, there are no more speakers. I hereby conclude the proceedings.

We come to the vote. The CDU/CSU proposed the motion, which is on the order paper No VI/3380 before you, that Member Dr. Barzel be elected as successor to Chancellor Willy Brandt.

According to § 98 of our rules of procedure a successor has to be elected by secret ballot. He is only elected when the votes of the majority of the members of the house—this means at least 249 votes—fall to him.

(The vote is taken. After that the
sitting is interrupted from 12.59 hrs–
13.22 hrs to count the vote)

. . .

Ladies and gentlemen, the sitting is resumed.

I will give the results of the vote. Of the members entitled to vote 260 votes were cast, from the Berlin members eleven votes. From the 260 entitled members 247 have voted yes for the motion, ten voted no, three abstained. From the Berlin members ten voted yes and one no, with no abstentions. . . .

[With few exceptions the SPD/FDP members did not take part in the vote, two from the CDU/CSU must have been 'defectors'.]

I hereby declare that the Member Dr. Barzel proposed by the CDU/CSU caucus has not obtained the votes of the majority of members of the German Bundestag.

> (Stormy applause from the government parties. The
> SPD and numerous FDP members rise to their feet.
> Dr. Barzel congratulates Chancellor Brandt and
> Minister Scheel.)

The motion of the CDU/CSU on the order paper VI/3380 is thus defeated. . . .

Document 6

As can be seen from the statistics, the Conference Committee of the two houses has a high record of achieving compromise solutions. The legislative history of the law on universities, for instance,[19] which could have been subject to a final veto by the Bundesrat, provides a good example of the way in which the original bill passed by the Bundestag finally got on the statute book in a very diluted fashion after prolonged deliberations and votes taken in the Vermittlungsausschuß. Criticism is mounting in Germany against this Conference Committee as a sort of 'second-track' law-making-body, very often finally circumventing the will of the majority of the elected Bundestag.

JOINT RULES OF PROCEDURE OF THE BUNDESTAG AND BUNDESRAT FOR THE COMMITTEE ACCORDING TO ARTICLE 77 OF THE BASIC LAW: MEDIATION (OR CONFERENCE) COMMITTEE (VERMITTLUNGS-AUSSCHUSS)
Source: BGBl.; II, 1951, 104

1 *Permanent Members*
  Bundestag and Bundesrat each delegate 12 of their members, who form the mediation committee.
2 *Chairmanship*
  The committee elects one member of both the Bundestag and Bundesrat, who act in turn as chairman every three months . . .
. . .
8 *Majority*
  The committee takes its decisions with the majority vote of its members present.
9 *Sub-committees*
  The committee can appoint sub-committees.
. . .

12 *Conclusion of the Mediation Procedures:*
   1) Should a unified motion not be decided upon in a second meeting called for consideration of the same subject matter, then any member of the committee can move that the procedures be concluded.
   2) Procedures are to be considered as concluded if a unified motion fails to get a majority at the meeting thereafter.
   3) Procedures can otherwise not be concluded without a unified motion.
   4) The chairman has to certify the conclusion of mediation procedures and give notice to this effect on the same day to the presidents of the Bundestag and of the Bundesrat . . .

Document 7

The 'Ombudsman' of the Bundestag for the members of the armed forces has, on the whole, done good work since 1957, by drawing attention to failings which are inevitable in any system. The German Basic Law of 1949 guarantees that there can be no repetition of dangerous tendencies in past Prussian–German history which were caused in part by a lack of political control over the armed forces.

DEFENCE COMMISSIONER (WEHRBEAUFTRAGTER DES DEUTSCHEN BUNDESTAGES) LAW OF 26 JUNE 1957, AS AMENDED BY THE LAW OF 2 MARCH 1974
Source: BGBl., I, 1974, 469f.

§ 1 The Defence Commissioner of the Bundestag is to observe the requirements of Article 45b of the Basic Law.

§ 2
   1. The Defence Commissioner will examine particular matters at the directive of the Bundestag or of the Standing Defence Committee. The latter can only issue the directives if it is not making the matter the subject of its own investigation. The Defence Commissioner must submit, if requested, a specific report on the result of his examination.
   2. The Commissioner will, after due consideration intervene when, in exercising his rights under § 3 (4), he learns of complaints from soldiers, passed on by members of the Bundestag, or if he learns in other ways of circumstances which lead to the conclusion that the basic rights of soldiers or the basic codes of internal conduct have been infringed.[20] He reports to the Bundestag on the result of his examination in a report about the particular case or as a part of his annual report.
   3. The Commissioner prepares a written complete report at the end of the calendar year.

§ 3

In exercising his duties the Defence Commissioner has the following powers:

1. He can demand information and access to files from the Minister of Defence and all subordinate offices and persons. This right can only be refused him where the subject in question is strictly classified. The decision about this refusal is taken by the Minister of Defence himself, or his permanent deputy in office, who is accountable for his decision to the Defence Committee . . .

. . .

3. He can pass on any complaint to the authorities responsible for initiating disciplinary actions or court procedures.

4. He can visit without previous notice any barracks, headquarters or other premises of the armed forces . . . at any time.

5. He has the right to demand from the Minister of Defence overall reports on the discharge of disciplinary powers in the armed forces and statistical reports from the Federal Minister of Justice or the ministers of justices of the Länder concerning procedures under the penal code as far as members of the armed forces and their dependants are affected thereby.

6. He can . . . sit in on proceedings of the courts, also in as far as these deliberate in closed sessions. He has the right of access to material under consideration by the courts in the same way as the public prosecutor.

. . .

§ 6

The Bundestag and its Defence Committee can demand at any time that the Commissioner be present.

§ 7

Every member of the armed forces has the right to approach the Commissioner individually or collectively without going through normally prescribed channels. He may not be . . . discriminated against by his superiors for having appealed to the Commissioner.

. . .

Document 8

The Bundestag Defence Committee constituted itself in 1980 as a special Committee of Investigation (there have been twenty such *ad hoc* committees since 1949) to probe into possible failures on the part of Bund and Länder institutions to foresee and handle violent demonstrations of the extreme left against the celebrations of the 25th anniversary of the new German armed forces within NATO in Bremen in May 1980. The Committee heard, partly in secret sessions (also above, Doc. 4d), federal ministers, chiefs of staff, heads of military intelligence and of the Offices for the Protection of the Constitution (Ämter für Verfassungsschutz). All investigating committees (Untersuchungsausschüsse) can apply the German code of court procedure, i.e. subpoena witnesses etc. In contrast to the British practice of parliamentary committees of investigation and inquiry and more analogous to the US one, there are no 'neutral' judges involved, only parliamentarians. In the case in question the result of long investigations was in the end a majority and a minority report, trying to blame or exonerate the Bonn government. The excerpts below, however, show a minimum of consensus in regard to consequences to be drawn for the future.

THE DEFENCE COMMITTEE AS A COMMITTEE OF INVESTIGATION (UNTERSUCHUNGSAUSSCHUSS): FINAL REPORT
Source: Deutscher Bundestag, 8th legislative period, Drucksache 8/4472

Section H: *Dangers and Consequences*
1. Personal injuries and damage to property
. . .
Approximately 300 Bremen police officers were injured; five police officers required hospital treatment. Nearly fifty of the assisting police officers from Lower Saxony were injured. In addition there were five injured soldiers. The number of injured demonstrators is unknown; a much lower figure is estimated.

Material damages include eight demolished and damaged army vehicles (total damages approx. DM 112 400) as well as damage to equipment in front of the Weser stadium, to streets in the area and to police clothes and equipment.

Judicial Proceedings
Seventy-four suspected persons are under investigation. The first charges have been preferred. 30% of the suspects come from the area around Bremen. Some offenders from Hamburg are thought to belong to the terrorist scene in the broadest sense. Probable offenders also come from so-called undogmatic groups. Offenders from democratic organizations or from orthodox Communist groups have not been identified . . .

Fundamental Conclusions Drawn from the Events
However much the Defence Committee supports the standpoint of the Federal Minister for Defence that the army will not allow itself to be chased from one city to another whenever organizing its official events by violent demonstrators or shut itself up in its barracks, the matter cannot be left there.

First of all, the Bremen incident throws a light on the potential of radical opponents of the Federal Republic's armed forces and its political attachment to the alliance, a potential whose size should not be exaggerated but which should be taken seriously. Various activities can be expected from this potential in the future, too . . .

[*Editorial comment:* Compare *inter alia* the violent demonstrations by a similarly violent minority during the visit of the American Vice-President to Krefeld in 1983.]

The protests and actions directed against the official event were based on a number of partly overlapping motives:

Especially widespread was the opinion that the public ceremony of the taking of the military oath, seen in a foreign policy context with the crises in Afghanistan and Iran, was considered as being adverse to détente, even conducive to promoting war. Such ideas were related to the notion of the public oath and the military tattoo being pre-democratic military rituals which were considered old-fashioned and unnecessary. Besides these voices which did not throw any basic doubt on the task of the state to provide the country with a military defence system were others which made the Bremen riots against the army, in its role as an institution upholding the state, into a symbol of the fight against this state. This opposition apparently avails itself of political–intellectual trends of a deeper dimension which can be especially observed in sections of the younger generation. This view is not only supported by the unusually large number and variety of the organizations and persons who have taken part in protests and counter-demonstrations in Bremen, but also by the number of 10,000 to 15,000 chiefly young citizens who let themselves be sent onto the streets by this topic. The main factor here is not only the defence policy opposition in the narrow sense but a basic mood which opposes the outward manifestations of the state . . .

The task of politics is to define the necessity of an efficient defence system, arising from the external and security policy conditions, but only credible and effective if it can meet the possible outside threat. State and social institutions must digest and hand on this knowledge. Left alone, the army is not capable of sufficiently promoting acceptance of the need to defend a country. Rather more, this is the task of all forces which carry responsibility in the state and in society. The committee therefore suggests examining what further and increased efforts in this basic intellectual discussion are necessary. Furthermore, the following possibilities should be considered:

Political parties, associations and Churches should stress the need for the country's defence more strongly and take part accordingly in official events. They should encourage relevant information and discussion in their field of responsibility. On the one hand, special importance is to be attached to the dialogue with critical sections of the population, above all with the younger generation. On the other, it is necessary to keep the appropriate distance from forces guided by undemocratic intentions in order to counter-balance the danger of any misleading actions by such groups; this also applies when demonstrations take place.

In the field of schooling and education, increased efforts have to be made to acquaint the younger generation more intensively with questions concerning the country's defence and compulsory military service. Here reference is made to corresponding suggestions of the Defence Committee made in June 1980. . . .

Document 9

The possible, because inherent, conflict mentioned above between Art. 38 and Art. 21 of the Basic Law explodes when 'rebels' speak and vote against their own caucus in the Bundestag. They risk being expelled from their party and caucus (the latter has never been done without the former) for their stand, as happened again in two cases in 1981/82 in regard to the then governing SPD. The excerpts to follow are part of a speech made by Dieter Lattmann, a writer who belonged to the left wing of his party and caucus and decided not to return to parliament in the following legislative period. At the time terrorism was much in evidence in West Germany and numerous laws were enacted or amended to cope with the situation, *inter alia* to prevent abuse of contacts between an accused and his lawyer (taking messages from the imprisoned on trial to outside sympathisers and followers etc.).

SPEECH BY A DISSENTING MEMBER OF THE SPD CAUCUS IN 1978

Source: Deutscher Bundestag, 72nd Parliamentary sitting, 8th legislative period, Sten. Berichte, 16 February 1978

. . .

Lattmann (SPD)
The members of the German Federal Parliament are representatives of the whole nation, not tied to orders and instructions and only bound to their conscience. With this reference to the contents of Art. 38 of the Constitution I explain why my convictions differ from those of the majority of my own caucus.
. . .

We are all faced with the question whether we submit to the terrorists' plan by letting ourselves be provoked by their murderous actions into restricting basic rights and increasingly arming the state with weapons or whether we want to defend our free basic rights even more decisively because of terrorism. Of course everybody talks about freedom. No cliché rolls off the tongue of right-wing politicians of order more often than the one about the free democratic system. People should stop making boasting noises about freedom; they should put freedom into practice!

(Applause from parts of the SPD and the FDP
—Shouts from the CDU/CSU)

This also means fearlessly describing what is happening in Parliament at a moment like this.
. . .

All of a sudden it is apparently not a matter of a bill whose meaning and usefulness are to be objectively examined but a matter of the ritual of power.

. . .

Accordingly I shall vote together with my caucus colleagues Manfred Coppik, Karl-Heinz Hansen and Erich Meinike against the bill. Our proximity to the CDU/CSU in the minutes will be only a typographical one. . . .

Notes

1. See Ch. 3 for the powers of the government and the president.
2. See Ch. 13, on Berlin, Docs. 2, 8 and Ch. 8, on Political Parties, 93 and n.9.
3. See W. Bagehot, *The English Constitution*, Oxford 1958, 118ff.
4. See Ch. 3, Doc. 9.
5. See Ch. 6, on Federalism, p. 156.
6. For the total number of laws between 1949 and 1979 which failed to get on the statutes because of an absolute veto of the Bundesrat and for the origin of bills introduced, see Table 6.
7. For instance, between the Trade Unions and the SPD or the Catholic Church and the CDU/CSU, see Chs. 8, 9.
8. On the military side there is the MAD (Militärischer Abschirmdienst, counter-espionage) and the BND (Bundesnachrichtendienst, espionage), on the civilian side the Bundesamt für Verfassungsschutz (Federal Office for the Protection of the Constitution). The latter—strictly regulated by law—gathers material on any revolutionary activities directed against the democratic order as such, not against the government in power. It has no powers to arrest etc. Parliament established by law a special supervising body of the Bundestag in 1978 for the three secret services. See also Doc. 4d and Ch. 7, 180ff.
9. It has been shown that, for instance, between 1972 to 1976 there were three or four instances of political importance, when measures already announced or announced as pending by the government, had to be cancelled because opposition within the then SPD government caucus was too strong, see: C.C. Schweitzer, *Der Abgeordnete im parlamentarischen System der Bundesrepublik*, Opladen 1979.
10. Subtle means of exerting pressure on individual MdBs could consist of offering or withdrawing nominations to certain positions in the caucus or on parliamentary committees, or to send or not to send MdBs on official trips abroad which are generally very 'popular'. Famous dissenting votes in the Bundestag were recorded in connection with the introduction of compulsory military service, the reform of the law on abortion and the law on emergency-regulations. See Schweitzer, op. cit.
11. This G. Leibholz brought out above all in his book: *Strukturprobleme der modernen Demokratie*, Karlsruhe 1967 (3rd edition).
12. See Ch. 8.
13. See Chs. 8, 9.
14. On the mathematical basis of proportional representation and formulae adopted by the Belgian mathematician d'Hondt, see also Niemeyer. See Ch. 8, also Table 7.
15. See Ch. 8.
16. See Ch. 11, 303ff.
17. See Ch. 12.
18. See Ch. 3, 63f.
19. See Ch. 1, 168ff.
20. For the concept of Internal Order (or 'Leadership') in the armed forces, see Ch. 12.

3 Chancellor, Cabinet and President

Donald P. Kommers

Executive authority in the Federal Republic is vested in the federal chancellor (Bundeskanzler) and the federal ministers who together are referred to in the Basic Law as Bundesregierung or cabinet.* The federal president (Bundespräsident) is the head of state, but, as indicated below, he has only very limited powers. Under the Basic Law the chancellor wields effective political power. He decides on the number of ministries and appoints all cabinet ministers who are directly responsible to him. For example, Chancellor Schmidt in 1974 combined the Transportation and Telecommunications Ministries into a single department. In regard to the procedures of the cabinet the chancellor is bound, as are all other members of the cabinet, by the Standing Orders of the federal cabinet (Geschäftsordnung der Bundesregierung) which, in accordance with the Basic Law, have to be approved by the federal president (Docs. 1 and 4). Constitutionally responsible for setting 'national policy guidelines', he could theoretically maintain his position in the face of an opposition which commands a majority in the Bundestag. This stems from the fact that under the constitutional provisions for the so-called 'constructive vote of no-confidence', the chancellor may not be removed unless the no-confidence vote is accompanied by the election of a successor by a majority of the members of the Bundestag. So far this has happened only once—in 1982.[1] The chancellor's powers under the constitution, combined with the fourteen-year tenure and the legacy of strong leadership provided by West Germany's first chancellor, Konrad Adenauer, have led many observers to characterize the Federal Republic of Germany as a 'chancellor democracy'.

---

* Notes for this chapter begin on p. 79.

One of the most powerful instruments of executive leadership today is the Office of the Federal Chancellor (Bundeskanzleramt), which is analogous to the White House Office of the United States President and to some extent also to the Offices of the British and Canadian Prime Ministers. Originally a small secretariat serving the chancellor's personal needs, it has developed into an agency of major political importance. It contains departments corresponding to the various federal ministries and offices which engage in long-range social and economic planning or in the coordination of policies relating to the European Community or to internal security and the secret services. Its staff of some 500 keeps the chancellor informed on domestic and foreign affairs, coordinates policy-making among the federal ministries and monitors the implementation of cabinet decisions. The office is headed by a 'chief of staff' (Undersecretary of State of the Federal Chancellery, Staatssekretär), usually a personal confidant of the chancellor. Finally the chancellor is served by a Federal Press Secretary (Bundespressechef), who in turn heads the Federal Press and Information Office (Bundespresse-und Informationsamt), with a staff of some 700. It, too, is under the chancellor's direct control.

There have been six chancellors since 1949: Konrad Adenauer (1949–63); Ludwig Erhard (1963–66); Kurt-Georg Kiesinger (1966–69); Willy Brandt (1969–74); Helmut Schmidt (1974–82); and Helmut Kohl (1982–   ) (Doc. 2). All save Brandt and Schmidt have belonged to the Christian Democratic Party. The chancellor is elected by a majority of the Bundestag in a secret ballot. Owing to the operation of the German party system, he has normally also been the leader of his party outside parliament. There is no leader of the House (Bundestag) or Leader of the Opposition in the British sense, but only a chairman of the government caucus (or caucuses) and of the opposition caucus (or caucuses).[2] Since the chancellors all came to their position via a party career, they have been politically experienced persons who have spent most of their lives in public office. The age at which they have assumed the chancellorship has been declining. Adenauer was seventy-three; Erhard and Kiesinger were in their sixties; Brandt and Schmidt were fifty-six; Kohl was fifty-two.

As Art. 65 of the Basic Law shows, the predominance of the chancellor can, theoretically, be matched by the cabinet acting as a collegial organ with the chancellor then reduced to the status of a *primus inter pares* when votes are taken. This was the case under the 'Great Coalition' of 1966–69. In other words, whether a 'chancellor democracy' prevails, or whether the focus of ultimate decision-making lies with the cabinet, depends on whether the government consists of a coalition in which the chancellor, together with his political friends inside and outside the cabinet, has to take into consideration the views expressed by the partner in the coalition. In addition, as the Adenauer years showed, it also depends on whether the office of the chancellor is held by a dominating or by a more accommodating personality.

Coalition governments have to be based on compromises. Only Adenauer—and even he only once—had the luxury of ruling with a parliamentary majority of his own party for most of the legislative period following the 1957 election. Even then, however, his majority was razor thin. The formation of a coalition government is usually preceded by negotiations between potential partners in the governing coalition. These negotiations lead to a formal coalition agreement (Doc. 3) spelling out the areas of policy consensus between the partners. Tensions between the partners may nevertheless persist. In 1966 the CDU/CSU coalition with the FDP collapsed, making way for the 'great coalition' between the CDU/CSU and the SPD. But after the 1969 election, when Social Democrats reached a new high of 42.7% of the popular vote, the SPD formed a government with the FDP as junior partner. This coalition survived three national elections. Fundamental differences over economic and social policy, however, prompted the FDP in September 1982 to drop out of the governing coalition with the SPD and join hands once again, after sixteen years, with the CDU/CSU. Schmidt fought hard to retain the chancellorship and even declared his intention to continue at the helm of a minority government, should the no-confidence vote fail to designate his successor.[3] This hope was dashed when the new CDU/CSU-FDP alliance elected Helmut Kohl as chancellor on 1 October 1982 by a vote of 256 to 235 members of the Bundestag. New general elections requested by Kohl himself on 6 March 1983 confirmed his government.[4]

As noted earlier, the chancellor is constitutionally empowered to appoint and dismiss cabinet members (Doc. 5). Yet *political* considerations limit his leverage over the formation of the cabinet. There is a practical need to distribute cabinet seats among various 'wings' of the major coalition party, and leaders of the minor party in the coalition are in a position to 'demand' the control of certain ministries. At times bitter feuding breaks out among cabinet members and occasionally between a minister and the chancellor himself. A notable example of the latter was the feuding in 1982 between Chancellor Schmidt and Economics Minister Otto Graf Lambsdorff. Schmidt actually rebuked Lambsdorff publicly, describing his proposals to limit welfare spending as 'one-sided and disappointing' and 'in flagrant contradiction to official policy'. In addition there are two principal constitutional limitations upon the chancellor in his dealing with his ministers. One concerns the special position of the minister of defence under Art. 65a of the Basic Law, the other the special veto position accorded to the minister of finance by Art. 112 of the Basic Law (Docs. 1 and 4).

The office of the parliamentary state secretary (or minister of state), to be distinguished from the permanent under secretaries of the various ministerial bureaucracies, was introduced in 1967 (Doc. 6). Parliamentary state secretaries are selected from among the more junior members of the Bundestag to help the ministers run their departments, defend their records in parliament, and to maintain contact with the public. A new element in the second Schmidt cabinet was the high number of former parliamentary state secretaries who were elevated to cabinet posts. No fewer than ten of Schmidt's 1980 cabinet appointees were former parliamentary state secretaries. The office is now widely recognized as a training ground for cabinet service.

The federal president is actually West Germany's highest ranking public official to the outside world. He is above all the formal head of state. Domestically he is without any real political power, in contrast to the Weimar Republic, where the president was directly elected and was able to wield decisive power at critical junctures. In the Federal Republic he is important as a non-partisan spokesman for the nation (Doc. 8). Although he is elected by a Federal Convention (Bundesversammlung) specially constituted for the purpose, the president is perceived as *pouvoir neutre* (Docs. 7a and b). So far, however, all office holders have reached their position on the basis of a party career and as a result either of a bargaining process within the coalition parties forming the majority in the federal convention or of a single party having a majority on its own.

The first president, Theodor Heuss, who held office for two terms from 1949 to 1959, came from the small Free Democratic Party, one of the partners in Chancellor Adenauer's first coalition government. A respected public figure, Heuss became president as a result of a bargaining process initiated by Adenauer who hoped by these means to ensure the support of the Free Democrats for his own coalition. Heuss's successor, Heinrich Lübke, who also served two terms (1959–69), was a former CDU minister. Gustav Heinemann, who became president in 1969, was a leading member of the SPD and owed his election to bargaining between the SPD and the FDP who at the time together commanded a majority in the Federal Convention. This alliance foreshadowed the socialist-liberal coalition government which took office under Willy Brandt as chancellor three months after Heinemann's election. Walter Scheel, who became president in 1974, was the FDP foreign minister and vice chancellor in Brandt's two socialist-liberal coalition governments which held office after 1969. Since 23 May 1979 Karl Carstens, a nominee of the CDU/CSU, has occupied the presidency. Despite their political background, all the occupants of the presidential office have become recognized for their fairmindedness and their ability to communicate across party lines.

In early 1983, for the first time since 1949, the president faced a court challenge over the exercise of his constitutional functions and thereby the prospect of having an important presidential decision overturned. A number of SPD and FDP members of parliament challenged President Carstens' January 1983 decision to dissolve the Bundestag on the advice of Chancellor Kohl after a contrived loss of a vote of confidence initiated by the chancellor himself. In a decision widely regarded as the most important in its history, the Constitutional Court, by a majority vote, ruled that the president's action in dissolving the Bundestag was in conformity with the Basic Law (Doc. 9).

Document 1

The following articles of the constitution relate to the powers and duties of the federal chancellor, federal president and federal ministers. Certain features of the 'executive branch' under the Bonn Constitution differ from the practice under the Constitution of the Weimar Republic. For example, prior to 1933 the president was popularly elected for a seven-year term. He had the power to appoint the chancellor and, on the latter's recommendation, the national ministers. Both chancellor and ministers were individually responsible to the national assembly. They could be removed by parliament, unshielded by the modern constructive vote of no-confidence, the net result of which was a succession of weak governments during the Weimar period.

ARTICLES OF THE BASIC LAW
Source: Press and Information Office

Art. 55. No Secondary Occupation

(1) The Federal President may not be a member of the government nor of a legislative body of the Federation or of a Land.

(2) The Federal President may not hold any other salaried office, nor engage in a trade or occupation, nor practise a profession, nor belong to the management or the board of directors of an enterprise carried on for profit.

Art. 57. Representation

If the Federal President is prevented from acting, or if his office falls prematurely vacant, his powers shall be exercised by the President of the Bundesrat.

Art. 58. Countersignature

Orders and decrees of the Federal President shall require for their validity the countersignature of the Federal Chancellor or the appropriate Federal Minister. This shall not apply to the appointment and dismissal of the Federal Chancellor, the dissolution of the Bundestag under Article 63 and the request under paragraph (3) of Article 69.

Art. 65. Distribution of Responsibility

The Federal Chancellor shall determine, and be responsible for, the general policy guidelines. Within the limits set by these guidelines, each Federal Minister shall conduct the affairs of his department autonomously and on his own responsibility. The Federal Government shall decide on differences of opinion between the Federal Ministers. The Federal Chancellor shall conduct the affairs of the Federal Government in accordance with rules of procedure adopted by it and approved by the Federal President.

Art. 65a. Power of Command over Armed Forces

Power of command in respect of the Armed Forces shall be vested in the Federal Minister of Defence.

Art. 76. Bills

(1) Bills shall be introduced in the Bundestag by the Federal Government or by members of the Bundestag or by the Bundesrat.
(2) Bills of the Federal Government shall be submitted first to the Bundesrat. The Bundesrat shall be entitled to state its position on such bills within six weeks. A bill exceptionally submitted to the Bundesrat as being particularly urgent by the Federal Government may be submitted by the latter to the Bundestag three weeks later, even though the Federal Government may not yet have received the statement of the Bundesrat's position; such statement shall be transmitted to the Bundestag by the Federal Government without delay upon its receipt.

Art. 112. Expenditures in Excess of Budgetary Estimates

Expenditures in excess of budgetary appropriations and extra-budgetary expenditures shall require the consent of the Federal Minister of Finance. Such consent may be given only in the case of an unforeseen and compelling necessity. Details may be regulated by federal legislation.

Documents 2a–f

THE CHANCELLORS FROM 1949 TO THE PRESENT WITH EXAMPLES OF
REPRESENTATIVE SPEECHES

All German governments have reflected to a greater or lesser degree the
personality of the chancellor, just as the chancellor has given expression
to the dominant views of the political party or coalition that elected him.
Presented below are brief notes on each of the six chancellors who have
held power since 1949, together with excerpts from major policy
statements which suggest aspects of their leadership.

a) KONRAD ADENAUER (1949–63)

The Federal Republic's first (and to date the longest serving) chancellor
was an unlikely candidate for the post. Aged seventy-two in 1949, he had
reached the stage when most men have sought retirement. While he had
had a long and distinguished career under the Weimar Republic as Lord
Mayor of his native Cologne, had become a member of the Prussian
State Council, and in the mid 1920s had been considered for the post of
chancellor, in 1945 he hardly ranked as a major national figure.
However, twice dismissed from his post as mayor—first in 1933 by the
Nazis and again in 1945 by the British (after having been reinstated in
office by the Americans following the capture of Cologne, six months
earlier), this elderly Catholic Rhinelander skilfully exploited his new
freedom to embark on a political role in a wider sphere. Manoeuvring his
way to the chairmanship of the newly emerged Christian Democratic
Union (which replaced the old pre-1933 Centre Party) in the British
Zone, he became chairman of the Parliamentary Council (Parlamentarischer Rat), established in 1948 to draft a constitution for the provisional government of the three Western occupation zones. Supported by
the liberal economic policies of the former Bavarian Economics Minister,
Ludwig Erhard, Adenauer emerged as the dominant political figure in
West Germany and in 1949 was elected as the Federal Republic's first
chancellor, even though by a very narrow majority (of 1). A conservative
and rather authoritarian figure, he dominated the political scene for the
next fourteen years and gave his name to an era. His chancellorship embodied a major period of post-war German history: a period of domestic
institutional reconstruction, of economic recovery, not unfairly described as the 'economic miracle', and of the re-entry of Western Germany
into the Western family of nations, its emergence as a leading advocate of
and partner in the integration of Western Europe, and especially of the

critical and hardly foreseeable reconciliation with France which culminated in the 1963 treaty.[5] While Adenauer may be criticized for his authoritarianism because he took quite literally the constitutional provisions which empower the chancellor to shape policy and may have clung too long to power (he was eighty-seven when he finally withdrew), he provided the West Germans with fourteen years of stability and prosperity during which they could become accustomed to the newly-established democratic constitutional system of government and society and win back the place in the international sphere which Hitler had gambled away.

MAJOR POLICY SPEECH BY ADENAUER IN AUGUST 1957, BEFORE THE GENERAL ELECTIONS

Source: The Bulletin, 10 September 1957
Trans.: Official

. . .

Faithful cooperation with the partners of the Atlantic Community and the peoples of the free world is and remains the cornerstone of our foreign policy. This includes friendly relations with the United States, which in our view is the nucleus of the defence alliance and the backbone of Europe's freedom. The danger of Communist infiltration and subversive attempts in many parts of the world remain unchanged. As long as we have to face this menace, the defence alliance of the free world must not be weakened.

Three Major Objectives

In the coming years we will strive for the realization of three major objectives: cementing of peace, restoration of German unity, and continuation of European integration.

It is self-evident that German re-unification is our great national concern, and all our hopes are directed towards its realization. German reunification is a true test for the sincerity of the Soviet Union and its future intentions. As long as the Soviet Union refuses to agree to Germany's reunification in peace and freedom, it is not willing to contribute toward relaxation of world tensions and to give real guarantee of world peace.

Supporting Disarmament

To promote relaxation, Germany's foreign policy will support the efforts of the London Disarmament Committee. We welcome any disarmament and control efforts that are aimed at creating security against surprise attacks and that help to prepare a world-wide relaxation for the cementing of peace.

The present border of the Soviet zone of occupation running through Germany, however, must under no circumstances become the 'central line' of an inspection area. Creation of a demilitarized zone on German or Central European soil that could be a temptation for an aggresssor must also be avoided.

The attempt to reach relaxation through controlled general disarmament is more comprehensive than the Socialist proposed European agreement with the Soviet Union ... I therefore consider such proposals not only untimely but a hopeless diversion from the more important task, already begun, of creating a feeling of security and an atmosphere which allows the tackling of hitherto un-solved problems through arms reductions and controls ...

b) LUDWIG ERHARD (1963–66)

The Federal Republic's second chancellor Ludwig Erhard, widely regarded as the 'father' of West Germany's postwar economic revival, was born in Bavaria on 4 February 1897. After service in World War I he studied economics, and from 1928 to 1942 he was special assistant and later deputy director of the Nürnberg Institute of Economic Observa-tion. After the collapse of the Third Reich he taught economics briefly at the University of Munich (1947), but more importantly he played a key role as Bavarian Minister of Economics (1945–47) and then as Director of the Economic Administration of the Western zones of occupation. A member of the CDU, he was chosen by Chancellor Adenauer in 1949 to head the Federal Ministry of Economics, a position he held until Adenauer's retirement. Adenauer had not wanted him as his successor, but in the end could not prevent it. His rather unhappy three-year chancellorship came to an end with the economic and political crisis of 1966.

The excerpts given below show one of the main characteristics of his approach to politics and government.

ERHARD'S STATEMENT OF 16 OCTOBER 1963 ON GOVERNMENT POLICY AFTER HAVING BEEN SWORN IN AS THE NEW CHANCELLOR IN THE BUNDESTAG

Source: The Bulletin, 22 October 1963

. . .

I feel sure that I am expressing the concern and, at the same time, a demand of the German people when I call upon the Government and Parliament to look beyond the wishes and interests of individual groups and to devote themselves with more determination to the essentials of our political life.

Above all, young people want to measure their actions by superordinate values and standards, and they expect the Government to adhere to these maxims as well. The youth of our country wish to be given tasks to fulfil and problems to solve. The more conscious we are of this fact and the more genuine our appeals to youth, the better we will succeed in diverting them from the wrong path of simply wanting to earn money and to enjoy being provided for.

Let us also endeavour not to hasten to stamp every demand made on the German Government with the word 'social' or 'just' when in fact they are only too often merely wishes of this or that particular group. Nor should we close our eyes to the fact that whereas distinct emphasis is placed on private and group interests the sense of civic responsibility is more and more lacking. This is all the more grave since the Federal Republic concedes to its citizens an unusual measure of freedom in their private activities and manifests its great respect for the value of individual development.

We must strive incessantly to make all our citizens aware of the values set by our Constitution, and to make clear again and again that freedom must go hand in hand with responsibility if it is not to degenerate into chaos. Thus we must repeatedly ask ourselves what in each individual case the need for a continued development of our liberal order and the need for true social justice call for. Confidence in our constitutional State will only be assured for as long as the people bearing political responsibility set a good example by their own behaviour.

If it is therefore indispensable to make clear to the pressure groups the limits to their claims, this would appear credible only if the State, too, knows how to set the right standards. The State is not an abstract entity, detached from the community of a nation, though it is certainly more than just the sum of its citizens. . . .

c) KURT-GEORG KIESINGER (1966–69)

Ludwig Erhard's successor, Kurt-Georg Kiesinger, practiced law in Tübingen after the war and in 1949 was elected as a CDU member of the first Bundestag. He was a member of the CDU/CSU national executive under Adenauer, and served as Vice-President of the Consultative Assembly of the Council of Europe from 1955 to 1958. Elected Prime Minister of the state of Baden-Württemberg in 1958, he served in Stuttgart with distinction for the next eight years. In the wake of the crisis which followed the collapse of Erhard's government (West Germans in the fall of 1966 were fearful of an economic collapse and concerned about the local successes of the neo-Nazi National Democratic Party [Nationaldemokratische Partei, or NPD])[6] it was mutually advantageous for the leaders of both parties to form a 'Great Coalition' of CDU/CSU and SPD. This was a critical step in the SPD's achievement of political dominance in the period 1969–82. Kiesinger was thus the first—and so far the last—chancellor who has had to work with a coalition government of partners equal in number and political importance—a task for which his whole 'southwest German temperament' eminently fitted him.

KIESINGER'S STATEMENT OF 16 DECEMBER 1966 ON GOVERNMENT POLICY IN THE BUNDESTAG AFTER TAKING OFFICE

Source: The Bulletin, 20 December 1966

Mr President,
Ladies and Gentlemen, ...

The formation of the present Federal Government, in whose name I have the honour to speak to you, was preceded by a long smouldering crisis, the causes of which can be traced back over a good number of years. That crisis came to a head barely a year after the elections to the fifth German Bundestag, which had proved to be an impressive vote of confidence for my predecessor, Professor Ludwig Erhard, and had enabled the ruling parties to continue their coalition. Subsequently, domestic difficulties, internal party strife, and problems of foreign policy burdened the work of the Government, until the disagreement on the balancing of the Federal budget for 1967 and on the required long-term measures of financial policy ultimately led to a split in the coalition and hence to a minority cabinet. From the following negotiations for a coalition which were an inevitable consequence of that breach the present grand coalition government emerged. In their negotiations the parties have surely carried out the most thorough stock-taking up to now of the possible courses and necessary steps open to German policy before the making of a government.

The Christian Democratic Union and the Christian Social Union and the Social Democratic Party have for the first time resolved to form a joint government at the federal level. This is without doubt a landmark in the history of the Federal Republic, an event with which many of the hopes and anxieties of our people are linked. It is hoped that the grand coalition which has such a great majority in the Bundestag exceeding by far two-thirds of its members will succeed in solving the difficult tasks ahead of it, especially of putting the public finances in order, running an economic, thrifty administration and of ensuring the growth of our economy and the stability of our currency. All these are prerequisites to the private and public weal, as much in our country as in any other country. They are the source of the strength which Government and Parliament need to enable them to act in all domains of domestic and foreign policy. Many people are worried about the possible dangers inherent in a grand coalition faced by only a comparatively small oppositon.

We are resolved to do our utmost to fulfil the hopes which have been placed in us and to ward off the dangers people are afraid of. In this coalition there will be no sharing of power and sinecures between the partners, there will be no glossing over of mismanagement, and the forces of parliamentary life will not be paralyzed by arrangements behind the scenes, as has been alleged by the slogan 'proportional democracy'. The opposition will be given all parliamentary opportunities to present and bring to bear its views.

The strongest safeguard against any possible abuse of power is the firm determination of the partners in the grand coalition to maintain the coalition only for a limited period, in other words, until the end of the present term. . . .

d) WILLY BRANDT (1969–74)

The chief beneficiaries of the Great Coalition experiment of 1966 were the SPD and Willy Brandt, who had served alongside Chancellor Kiesinger as vice-chancellor and foreign minister. Born in Lübeck in 1913, Brandt had been active in the socialist youth movement. Following the Nazi seizure of power in 1933 he managed to escape at the very last moment to Norway where as a Norwegian citizen he continued his political activities and took up journalism. When the Germans invaded that country in 1940 he was successfully hidden by Norwegian friends and eventually escaped to Sweden. After the end of the war he returned to Germany as a Norwegian press attaché and then resumed a journalistic career as editor of the *Berliner Stadtblatt*. Resuming German citizenship, he was elected to the Berlin House of Representatives in 1955 and, two years later, on the eve of the prolonged Berlin crisis of 1958–61, he was chosen Governing Mayor (Regierender Bürgermeister) of the former capital. In the meantime, as a leading exponent of the 'Berlin Course' of modernizing and reshaping the SPD to broaden its electoral appeal, Brandt had risen to prominence within it. Chosen to lead his party in the federal elections of 1961 and 1965 he substantially increased its share of the vote from 36.2% to 39.3% in 1965 (against Erhard). Political power at the national level eluded him, however, until the formation of the Great Coalition in 1966, in which his party shared power with the CDU/CSU and he became vice-chancellor and foreign minister. His success as foreign minister, and especially the initial phases of his Ostpolitik, helped to produce a further electoral gain in 1969 (42.7%) and secured enough seats in the Bundestag to enable the SPD to assume the leadership, in coalition with the smaller Free Democratic Party, which endured to 1982. Brandt, however, chose to resign in 1974 following the unmasking of a spy in his office. In the course of his chancellorship Brandt tried to usher in a series of social and economic reforms and to breathe new life into the German political system; Germany was to 'venture more democracy'. In foreign policy he was influential in pressing for further steps in European integration and through his Ostpolitik he achieved a breakthrough in West Germany's relations with the East, above all with Poland, while securing a restatement of the guarantees for West Berlin.[7]

BRANDT'S STATEMENT OF 28 OCTOBER 1969 ON GOVERNMENT POLICY IN THE BUNDESTAG

Source: The Bulletin, 28 October 1969
Transl.: Official

. . .

We are resolved to uphold the security of the Federal Republic of Germany and the coherence of the German nation, to preserve peace and to co-operate in a European peace arrangement to extend the freedoms and prosperity of our people and to develop our country in such a way that its standing will be recognized and assured in the world of tomorrow. The policy of this Government will be one of continuity and of renewal.

Our respect is due to what has been achieved in the past years—in the Federation, in the Länder and in the municipalities—by all strata of our people. I name Konrad Adenauer, Theodor Heuss and Kurt Schumacher in lieu of many others with whom the Federal Republic of Germany has lived through a period of which it can be proud. No one will deny, doubt or look down on the achievements of the past two decades. They have become history.

The stability of our democratic way of life has been reaffirmed on 28 September. I thank the voters for their unequivocal rejection of any extremism which we will have to fight also in future.

Twenty years after its constitution, our parliamentary democracy has proved its capacity for change and thus stood the test. This has been noted also outside our frontiers and has helped our State to new confidence in the world.

The strict observance of the forms of parliamentary democracy is but natural for political groups which have fought for German democracy for a good hundred years, made heavy sacrifices in its defence and taken great pains to rebuild it. Divided on material issues but united in the service of the nation, Government and Opposition have the common responsibility and duty to secure a good future for this Federal Republic.

The Federal Government knows that to cope with that task it needs loyal co-operation with the legislative bodies. For that co-operation it offers its good will to the German Bundestag and, of course, to the Bundesrat.

Our nation must have its internal order just as any other nation. In the seventies, however, we shall have order in this country only to the extent that we encourage our citizens to share responsibility. Such democratic order demands extraordinary patience in listening to others and extraordinary endeavour to understand one another.

We want to venture more democracy. We shall expose our method of working

to view and satisfy the critical mind's need for information. We shall try to ensure—through hearings in the Bundestag, through constant contact with the
representative groups of our people and through comprehensive information on
the Government's policy—that every citizen is placed in a position to participate
in the reform of state and society.

We address ourselves to the younger generation that has grown up in peaceful
times, that is not and must not be encumbered with the mortgages of the older;
those young people who want to—and should—take us at our word. These young
people must understand, however, that they, too, have obligations towards state
and society.

We shall present to this Assembly a bill to lower the franchise age from twenty-
one to eighteen and the eligibility age from twenty-five to twenty-one. We shall
also review the age of adulthood.

Joint management, joint responsibility in the various sectors of our society will
be a motive force in the years to come. We cannot create perfect democracy. But
we want a society offering more freedom and demanding greater participation in
responsibility. This Government wants discussion; it seeks the critical partnership of all those bearing responsibility, be it in the churches, in the spheres of art
and science, in economic life, or in other sectors of society.

This goes not least for the trade unions whose trustful co-operation we are seeking. There is no need to specifically certify their eminent importance to this State
and to its further development into a social state under the rule of law.

If we want to achieve what must be achieved we need to muster all the active
forces in our society. A society that wants to give room to all ideological and
religious convictions, lives on the ethical impulses which manifest themselves in
serving one's neighbour in the spirit of solidarity. We should not only have the
churches care for the families, youth, or education. We visualize our common
tasks especially where old and sick people, physically or mentally handicapped in
their distress, are in need of not only material support but of human solidarity. In
serving man—not only in our own country but also in the developing countries—the work of religious and social groups and political action converge.

We shall endeavour to bring the justified wishes of the various forces of society
and the political will of the government into harmony.

. . .

e) HELMUT SCHMIDT (1974–82)

Brandt's successor in 1974, the perennially youthful looking Helmut
Schmidt, came to the chancellery with a reputation for expertise in the
areas of economics and finance as well as in defence. Born in Hamburg
in 1918, he was of the age group involved in military service during the
Second World War. After 1945 he returned to Hamburg, joined the
SPD, and embarked on the study of economics. In 1953, after working
for the Hamburg city government, he was elected to the Bundestag and

assumed an increasingly prominent role in the leadership cadres of the SPD. In 1961 he returned to Hamburg as that state's Minister of the Interior. When flood waters devastated large parts of the city the next year, Schmidt's energetic handling of emergency measures earned him a reputation as a forceful organizer. In 1969, when the Brandt-led government was formed, he became Minister of Defence. He later headed both the Ministries of Economics and Finance. When Brandt resigned in 1974 following the discovery of an East German spy on his personal staff Schmidt, as the SPD's deputy party chairman, succeeded to the chancellor's office. In his eight years in office he dominated not only German domestic politics, but also the international arena, especially as an expert in international economic affairs.

SCHMIDT'S STATEMENT ON GOVERNMENT POLICY IN THE BUNDESTAG OF 24 NOVEMBER 1980 AFTER THE FORMATION OF HIS SECOND GOVERNMENT

Source: Statements and speeches (prepared by Press Office of the Embassy of the Federal Republic of Germany in Washington, D.C.), 28 November 1980

. . .

The basic lines of our foreign policy are:

First: Without equilibrium there is no dependable peace in the world. We can feel secure because the Atlantic Alliance maintains the equilibrium to which we have contributed by placing our whole political and military weight on the western side of the scales.

Second: Equilibrium is a necessary if insufficient condition for peace. Peace therefore has to be safeguarded by a policy of arms limitation and cooperation as well. 'Military security and a policy of détente' (Harmel Report, December 1967) have been the two main elements of the Alliance's security policy concept for over ten years. We shall continue the policy of cooperation with our eastern neighbours in the interest of peaceful development in Europe and of the future of the whole German nation.

Third: The European Community remains the indispensable basis for peace and freedom and for social and economic progress. It also helps preserve the equilibrium.

. . .

Together with our partners in the Alliance we are making efforts in the arms control negotiations with the East to achieve a stable military balance at the lowest possible level in order to halt the arms race and reduce the burden of military expenditure. Mankind could arm itself to death if the arms race were not stopped. That is why the negotiations between the superpowers on the limitation of strategic arms are of central importance. We strongly advocate the continuation of the SALT process. After my discussion with President-elect Reagan, I am pleased to be able to report to the Bundestag that he is thinking along the same lines.

...

Our long-term efforts to improve the situation of the Germans who are suffering from the division of Germany has put many things in motion: millions of people have made journeys, relatives make telephone calls to each other, families have been reunited. Roads to Berlin are being built. Trade has shown a vigorous development—to name a few examples. All in all, we have been able to keep the Germans from drifting apart from each other.

This policy is and remains an integral part of the general policy of reconciliation between West and East.

...

Our relationship with the Soviet Union is marked by the willingness for long-term cooperation. I recall the statements on the occasion of my meetings with General-Secretary Brezhnev here in Bonn two years ago and in Moscow last summer. These also express the Soviet Union's interest in cooperation between the two German states. Precisely in difficult times, the Federal Government does not want to allow the dialogue with the Soviet Union to be interrupted.

f) HELMUT KOHL (1982 to the present)

Helmut Kohl, who succeeded to the chancellorship in October 1982 following the disintegration of Helmut Schmidt's socialist-liberal coalition, was, at fifty-two, the youngest head of government in the Federal Republic's history. A tall and warm-hearted south German from Ludwigshafen, he had earned a doctorate in political science at Heidelberg University and worked in a chemical company before achieving prominence in politics. Joining the CDU as early as 1947, he became a member of the party's executive in the Rhineland-Palatinate in 1955 and four years later was elected to the state parliament in Mainz. From a strong local political base he rose steadily in the CDU national ranks to become deputy chairman in 1969 and chairman four years later. In 1976 he took on the unenviable task of leading the CDU in the electoral battle against the popular Helmut Schmidt. In the next election he was forced to step aside when the party chose to back the CSU leader, Franz-Josef Strauss, as its candidate for the chancellorship. Strauss was less successful against Schmidt than Kohl had been in 1976, however, and when Schmidt's government collapsed in 1982 Kohl was the logical choice of his party to lead a coalition of CDU/CSU and FDP. Pledged to secure ratification of the mid-term change of coalition at the polls, Kohl secured a controversial dissolution of the Bundestag and led his party to a stunning victory on 6 March 1983, turning back a strong SPD challenge and cutting deeply into traditional socialist electoral strongholds, ensuring the survival of his coalition partner, the FDP, and, by falling just short of an absolute majority, denying his rival, Strauss, a dominating position in the new government.

KOHL'S STATEMENT OF 13 OCTOBER 1982 IN THE BUNDESTAG ON TAKING OVER OFFICE.

Source: The Bulletin, 12 November 1982

. . .

The fourth priority of this Government's work in the next few months is foreign and security policy. This remains a policy for freedom, a policy for peace in Europe and worldwide, a policy for the right to self-determination of the whole German nation, a policy for the unification of Europe, a policy for human rights and against hunger and want.

This country's foreign and security policy is founded on the North Atlantic Alliance and our friendship with the United States of America. It is an Alliance that threatens no one and does not aspire to superiority, but cannot, for the sake of preserving peace, accept permanent inferiority.

. . .

The Federal Government is wholly committed to the NATO dual-track decision of 1979 which proposes negotiations on the reduction and limitation of Soviet and American intermediate-range nuclear systems. It will stand up for the two parts of the decision and put them into effect: the part relating to negotiations and, if necessary, the part on arms modernization. And it will call to mind that the credit for demanding the decision and asserting it in the Alliance goes to a Social Democratic Chancellor.

. . .

Document 3

With the exception of Adenauer's third cabinet formed in 1957—and that only for three out of four years—all German governments have been formed by party coalitions. The formation of a coalition is preceded by negotiations leading to a coalition agreement such as the following between the SPD and the FDP subsequent to the 1980 election. These agreements are not always published. The last one (1983), for instance, was not.

THE COALITION AGREEMENT BETWEEN SPD AND FDP, 1980

Source: Supplied in typescript, n.d.

On 7 October 1980 the SPD and the FDP issued a joint statement on their wish to continue the social-liberal coalition. They expressed their desire to continue their successful foreign and security policies as well as their German and Berlin policies.

In a further joint statement on co-determination, dated November 4, the SPD and FDP agreed to continue serious discussions with the aim of arriving at a mutual solution.

In addition, both coalition parties agreed to the following items:

Financial Policy
The 1981 Federal budget has to set the course for financial policy in the new legislative period: Growth rates of the 1981 Federal budget about 4 percent; net borrowing in 1981 about 27 billion DM. This will result in the following tax and subsidy policies:

a) From 1.4.1981 tax on mineral-oil will be raised by 7 pfennigs per litre for petrol, 3 pfennigs per litre for diesel oil. The possibility of giving community traffic a part sum (0.51 pfennig) out of the mineral-oil tax raise is being examined. Tax on liquors will be raised by 300 DM per 100 litres on 1.4. 1981.

The Federal Government will introduce a bill to apportion automobile tax onto mineral-oil tax; it hopes to reach an agreement with the Länder by legislative procedures.

It is not intended to increase the general tax burden during the coming legislative period. In the case of a tax reduction, the basic allowance and tax regulations for health insurance payments of the self-employed are to be improved. The Federal government is still trying to get the tax offices to disburse family allowances.

Housing and Urban Policy
Improvement of skeleton conditions for privately financed housing construction: Obligatory rent comparison, simplification of rent-raising procedure and progressive rents for first lets or lets of living-space rendered habitable after 1.1.1981. Greater consideration of market economy elements in council housing construction: continuation of yearly interest increases for construction loans. An attempt to alter present competence spheres. People living in council housing and whose income is actually too high for them to have the right to benefit from the subsidized rents should pay compensation to the community.

Better protection of the tenants against commutation, alienation, and over-modernization as well as in regard to rent deposits. Encouragement of modernizing housing by the tenant.

Policy on Women's Rights

Progress in putting women's equal rights into practice in every respect. Examine whether the non-discrimination law can confirm actual existing disadvantages for women compared to men. Further practical report on § 218 StGB, [the abortion law].

Document 4

The standing orders of the federal cabinet define the status of the ministers and their general relationship to the chancellor. They also set forth the cabinet's functions and decision-making procedures, including the method of resolving differences of opinion among cabinet members.

STANDING ORDERS OF THE FEDERAL CABINET (GESCHÄFTSORDNUNG DER BUNDESREGIERUNG)

Source: GMBl., 11 May 1951, 131ff., as amended up to and including 1 January 1970

I. The Federal Chancellor

Art. 1

(1) The Federal Chancellor shall determine general policy in domestic and foreign affairs. These policies shall be binding upon the Federal Ministers and be carried into effect by them within their sphere of competence and on their own responsibility. In cases of doubt a decision of the Federal Chancellor shall be obtained.

(2) The Federal Chancellor shall have the right and the duty to see to the adherence of the general policy [guidelines].

Art. 2

In addition to determining general policy the Federal Chancellor shall also make efforts toward the harmonizing of the operation of the Federal Cabinet.

Art. 3

The Federal Chancellor shall receive from the departments of the various Federal Ministers information on measures and plans which are of significance for the determination of general policy and for the conduct of operations of the Federal Cabinet.

Art. 4

Whenever a Federal Minister deems an extension or change of general policy necessary he shall inform the Federal Chancellor, giving his reasons and requesting the Chancellor's decision.

Art. 5

The Federal Chancellor shall keep the Federal President informed on his policies and the work of the various Federal Ministers by transmitting to him essential records or written reports on matters of particular significance, or, if necessary, by reporting in person.

Art. 6

The Federal Chancellor shall guide the operations of the Federal Cabinet in accordance with Section IV.

Art. 7

(1) The Under Secretary of the Federal Chancellery shall also act as a Secretary of State of the Federal Cabinet.
(2) He may forward directly to the appropriate Federal Minister correspondence addressed to the Federal Chancellor or transmitted to the Federal Chancellor by the Federal President. If the appropriate Federal Minister recommends a reply by the Federal Chancellor, the Under Secretary shall submit an appropriate draft reply to the Federal Chancellor.

. . .

III. The Federal Ministers

Art. 9

The spheres of competence of the various Federal Ministers shall be determined in their general outlines by the Federal Chancellor. In cases of overlapping and differences of opinion resulting therefrom among several Federal Ministers the Federal Cabinet shall decide by a resolution [vote].

Art. 10

(1) Deputations shall, as a rule, be received only by the appropriate Minister in charge, or by his deputy. Deputations shall be asked beforehand for a statement of the subject of negotiation. If a joint reception appears to be appropriate the Federal Minister appealed to shall inform the other Federal Ministers concerned.

. . .

Art. 12

Statements by a Federal Minister made in, or intended for, the public must be in accord with the general policies laid down by the Federal Chancellor.

Art. 13

(1) Each Federal Minister shall notify the Federal Chancellor whenever he shall leave the seat of the Federal Cabinet for longer than one day. Agreement shall be reached with the Federal Chancellor regarding any absence of longer than three days.

(2) The consent of the Federal Chancellor shall be necessary for the acceptance of invitations for visits abroad.

(3) Before leaving the seat of the Federal Cabinet a Federal Minister shall leave with the Federal Chancellor the address at which he can be reached during his absence.

. . .

IV. The Federal Cabinet (Federal Government)

. . .

Art. 15

(1) The Federal Cabinet shall be furnished, for its considerations and decisions, with all matters of general importance in domestic, foreign, economic, social, financial or cultural policy, particularly

(a) all legislative bills;

(b) all drafts of ordinances of the Federal Cabinet [Verordnungen];

(c) drafts of other orders, if they are of particular political importance;

(d) statements by the Bundesrat of its position on Bills submitted by the Federal Cabinet;

(e) all matters in which the Basic Law or these Standing Orders so require;

(f) differences of opinion among various Federal Ministries; . . .

. . .

Art. 17

(1) Differences of opinion among Federal Ministers shall be submitted to the Federal Cabinet only after the Federal Ministers involved, or, in the event of their disability, their deputies, have personally made an unsuccessful attempt at reaching agreement.

(2) Before discussion in Cabinet session the Federal Chancellor may first discuss the differences of opinion with the Federal Ministers involved in a ministerial conference under his chairmanship.

. . .

Art. 24

(1) The Federal Cabinet shall have a quorum when one half of the Federal Ministers, including the chairman, are present.

(2) The Federal Cabinet shall render its decisions by majority vote. In cases of tie votes the chairman shall cast the deciding vote.

. . .

Art. 25

The text of decisions of the Federal Cabinet shall be determined by the chairman at the conclusion of the oral deliberation of each subject.

Art. 26

(1) In the event that the Federal Cabinet, in cases other than those under Articles 20 and 21 of the Budget Statute (*Haushaltsordnung*), act in opposition to or without the vote of the Federal Minister of Finance in questions of financial importance, he may explicitly lodge a protest against the decision. If objections are raised the matter shall be voted upon anew at another session of the Federal Cabinet. The execution of the matter against which the Federal Minister of Finance protested must be suspended unless approved by a new vote and by a majority of all Federal Ministers, with the Minister of Finance or his deputy present and with the Federal Chancellor voting with the majority.

(2) Corresponding rules shall apply in the event that the Federal Minister of Justice or the Federal Minister of the Interior have raised objections against the draft of a law or regulation or against a measure of the Federal Cabinet on the grounds of incompatibility with existing laws.

Document 5

The Federal Ministers Act sets forth the conditions for holding office in the cabinet. The provisions of the Act deal with the tenure, discharge, financial emoluments, and retirement benefits of cabinet members. They also lay down rules designed to avoid conflicts of interest between membership in the cabinet and outside activities.

FEDERAL MINISTERS ACT (BUNDESMINISTERGESETZ)

Source: BGBl., I, 1953, 407, as amended up to and including 19 July 1968

. . .

Art. 1

The members of the Federal Cabinet have, in accordance with this Act, a public law tenure relationship with the Federation.

. . .

Art. 4

A member of the Federal Cabinet may not simultaneously be a member of a Land cabinet.

Art. 5

(1) Members of the Federal Cabinet may not in addition to their office occupy

any other salaried position, nor undertake any business or profession. Neither may they belong during their term of office to the management, board of trustees, or board of directors of a profit-making enterprise nor act as a paid arbiter nor render out-of-court expert opinions. The Bundestag may allow exceptions to the prohibition of membership on a board of trustees or a board of directors.

. . .

Art. 6

(1) The members of the Federal Cabinet shall, even after termination of their tenure, be obliged to maintain secrecy regarding matters learned by virtue of their office. This shall not apply to notifications in the course of office business nor to facts which are publicly known or which according to their significance no longer require secrecy.

. . .

Art. 18

(1) A Federal civil servant or Federal judge appointed a member of the Federal Cabinet shall vacate his office as civil servant or judge at the beginning of his tenure. For the duration of his membership the rights and duties resulting from the service condition shall be suspended, except the duty of official secrecy and the prohibition against acceptance of rewards and gifts . . .

(2) Upon termination of his tenure as member of the Federal Cabinet a civil servant or judge shall, unless assigned with his consent to another position within three months, be put at the expiration of this time on the retired list and shall receive the pension which he would have earned on the basis of his former service, with the time of his tenure as member of the Federal Cabinet added.

. . .

Document 6

The office of parliamentary state secretary, to be distinguished from the permanent under-secretaries of state of the various ministerial bureaucracies, was introduced in 1967. The parliamentary state secretaries help the ministers run their departments, defend their records in parliament, and maintain contact with the public. The document which follows describes their legal status. Cabinet and government are used synonymously.

PARLIAMENTARY UNDER SECRETARIES ACT (PARLAMENTARISCHE STAATSSEKRETÄRE)

Source: BGBl., I, 1967, 396

. . .

§1

(1) Parliamentary State Secretaries can be assigned to assist members of the Federal Government. They must be members of the Bundestag.

(2) Parliamentary State Secretaries support the members of the Federal Government to whom they are assigned in the fulfillment of government business.

(3) Under the terms of this law Parliamentary State Secretaries in their official capacity are entitled to 'public law status' within the Federation.

§2

Parliamentary State Secretaries are appointed by the Federal President. In consultation with the Federal minister for whom the Parliamentary State Secretary will work, the chancellor makes a nomination to the Federal President.

. . .

§4

Parliamentary State Secretaries can be dismissed at any time. They can also resign at any time. The chancellor will propose the dismissal to the Federal President in consultation with the Federal minister concerned. The official position of a Parliamentary State Secretary terminates with the ending of the official position . . . of the responsible member of the Federal Government. It also ends when the Parliamentary State Secretary leaves Parliament, but not with the ending of the legislative period of the Bundestag (Art. 39, 1.2, Basic Law).

. . .

§8

At the suggestion of the chancellor and with the agreement of the Federal Minister responsible, the Federal President may give a Parliamentary State Secretary the right to carry the title of 'Minister of State' for the duration of his office or for the carrying out of a particular task.

. . .

Documents 7a–b

ELECTION OF THE FEDERAL PRESIDENT

The Federal President is not elected directly by popular vote as in the Weimar Republic or the United States, but by a specially constituted *ad hoc* convention (Bundesversammlung) in accordance both with the Basic Law (Doc. 7a) and the Presidential Election Act (Doc. 7b).

a) BASIC LAW

Art. 54: Election by the Federal Convention

(1) The Federal President shall be elected, without debate, by the Federal Convention (Bundesversammlung). Every German shall be eligible who is entitled to vote for Bundestag candidates and has attained the age of forty years.

(2) The term of office of the Federal President shall be five years. Re-election for a consecutive term shall be permitted only once.

(3) The Federal Convention shall consist of the members of the Bundestag and an equal number of members elected by the diets of the Länder according to the principles of proportional resrepresentation.

(4) The Federal Convention shall meet not later than thirty days before the expiration of the term of office of the Federal President or, in the case of premature termination, not later than thirty days after that date. It shall be convened by the President of the Bundestag.

(5) After the expiration of a legislative term, the period specified in the first sentence of paragraph (4) of this Article shall begin with the first meeting of the Bundestag.

(6) The person receiving the votes of the majority of the members of the Federal Convention shall be elected. If such majority is not obtained by any candidate in two ballots, the candidate who receives the largest number of votes in the next ballot shall be elected.

(7) Details shall be regulated by a federal law.

b) PRESIDENTIAL ELECTION ACT

Source: BGBl., I, 1959, 230
Transl.: Official

I: The Federal Convention

. . .

Art. 1

The President of the Bundestag shall determine the place and date of the convening of the Federal Convention.

Art. 2

(1) The Federal Cabinet shall make a timely determination of how many members the various Länder legislatures shall have to elect. . . .

Art. 4

(1) The Land legislatures shall elect the members to which their Land is entitled on the basis of nominating lists. The provisions of the Standing Orders of the particular Land legislature shall apply accordingly.

(2) Each member of the Land legislature shall have one vote.

(3) If several nominating lists are submitted, seats shall be apportioned on the basis of the number accruing to each on the basis of the d'Hondt system of the highest average. . . .

II: Election of the Federal President

. . .

Art. 8

The President of the Bundestag shall preside over the sessions and activities of the Federal Convention. The Standing Orders of the Bundestag shall be appropriately applied to the activities of the Convention unless the Federal Convention enacts its own Standing Orders.

Art. 9

(1) Any member of the Federal Convention may make nominations for the election of a Federal President in writing to the President of the Bundestag. New nominations may be made at the second and third ballots. Nominations may contain only information necessary for the designation of the nominee; a written statement of consent by the nominee is to be attached.

(2) The Executive Committee [Sitzungsvorstand] shall scrutinize the nominations for their conformity with the legal requirements. The Federal Convention shall decide on the rejection of a nomination.

(3) Votes shall be cast with covered ballot sheets. Ballot sheets which name anyone other than a proper nominee shall be invalid.

(4) The President of the Bundestag shall inform the person who is elected of his election and shall invite him to state within two days whether he accepts the election. If the elected person does not give his statement within this time, he will be deemed to have declined his election.

(5) The President of the Bundestag shall declare the Federal Convention adjourned after the person elected has accepted his election.

Art. 10

The term of office of the Federal President shall begin with the expiration of the term of his predecessor, but not before the receipt by the President of the Bundestag of his statement of acceptance.

. . .

Document 8

The office of president is potentially an important symbol of national unity. Standing above partisan political conflict he has the opportunity to play an important educative role in the Federal Republic. He can use ceremonial occasions to his advantage by stressing the liberal constitutional values underlying German democracy. The right kind of person might even serve as the moral conscience of the nation. Gustav Heinemann came close to playing such a role during his tenure of office. He never ceased to remind Germans of their moral responsibility to redress the past by committing themselves to the creation of a living democracy infused with the values of individual freedom and social justice. The following extract is from an address celebrating the founding of the Federal Republic.

ADDRESS BY PRESIDENT GUSTAV HEINEMANN ON 24 MAY 1974
Source: Vital Speeches of the Day, n.p., n.d.
Transl.: Official

. . .

The entry into force of the Basic Law 25 years ago is one of the outstanding events in our history. It afforded us a great chance to create for the first time a liberal political system based on the rule of law and social democracy.

. . .

Considering all the improvements which still have to be made, it is an indisputable fact that the Federal Republic of Germany has, in its 25-year history, taken its place among the community of those nations who have been able to achieve a high level of civic freedom, economic prosperity, and social security. To talk away this fact by exaggerating our existing problems would be careless ingratitude and could provoke the punishment of history.

Sometimes one doubts whether we are conscious of how well off we are compared with many other nations. Who would have dared to think in 1949 that 25 years later we would have reached such a high level of prosperity and freedom and won so much respect around the world?

. . .

In conclusion I would recall that this year will be the centenary of the death of the man who composed our national anthem, Heinrich Hoffmann von Fallersleben, who was persecuted on political grounds. In 1848 he was expelled from a number of German federal states and driven from land to land as a refugee. If Article 16 of our present Basic Law had been in force then he would have had the right of asylum and would thus have been spared this fate.

Hoffmann von Fallersleben's writing shows him to be a child of his epoch. This is also manifest in his poem 'The Anthem of the Germans'. The third verse which we sing on festive occasions expresses succinctly the fundamental values cherished in the Federal Republic of Germany:

> 'Unity and right and freedom
> For our German Fatherland,
> Let us strive for this as brethren
> Strive for it with heart and hand.'

These few words state the four fundamental values around which our constitution is built: unity among ourselves and, as part of it, the unity of Germany as a national mission; the rule of law and human rights; freedom and democracy; and brotherliness or solidarity.

What the Basic Law prescribes is expressed in the 'Anthem of the Germans' as a condition of the present and as a wish for the future:

> 'Unity and right and freedom—
> On this rock our fortunes stand.
> Flourish in such fortunes splendour,
> Flourish German fatherland.'

Document 9

In October 1982 Helmut Kohl was elected chancellor on a constructive vote of no-confidence. On 6 January 1983, however, the Chancellor called for a vote of confidence, this time planning his own defeat. After losing the confidence vote as planned, the Federal President, pursuant to Chancellor Kohl's request, dissolved Parliament for the purpose of holding new elections. A number of SPD and FDP members of parliament challenged the constitutionality of the dissolution in the Federal Constitutional Court. The extracts below represent the guiding principles of the decision upholding the validity of the dissolution of the Bundestag by the President under Art. 68 of the Basic Law.

DECISION OF THE FEDERAL CONSTITUTIONAL COURT ON THE DISSOLUTION OF THE BUNDESTAG, 16 FEBRUARY 1983

Source: Xeroxed copy issued by the Court

IN THE NAME OF THE GERMAN PEOPLE

In the case of a dispute between federal organs concerning the complaint that the Federal President, through his authorization of the dissolution of the 9th German Bundestag of 6 January 1983 (BGBl. I, S.1) and his authorization of Federal elections on 6 January 1983 (BGBl. I, S. 2) contravened Article 68 Paragraph 1 of the

Basic Law and thereby directly endangered the complainants constitutional rights. . . .

Guiding Principles of the Judgement of the Second Senate of 16 February 1983:
. . .

(2) Ordering the dissolution of the Bundestag according to Article 68 of the Basic Law or refusing to do so involves a basic political decision which rests with the responsible judgement of the Federal President. A decision within the framework of Article 68 Paragraph 1, Sentence 1 of the Basic Law is thus only open to the Federal President when at the time of his decision the constitutional requirements are present.

(3) Article 68 of the Basic Law lays down a chronological sequence of events. Violations of the constitution which occurred in the previous chronological stages affect the areas of decision in which the Federal President finds himself after the Federal Chancellor has proposed the dissolution.

(4) (a) Article 68 Paragraph 1, Sentence 1 of the Basic Law is a constitutional norm, which is responsive to and requires to be given concrete expression.

(b) The authority to give concrete expression to Federal constitutional law belongs not to the Federal Constitutional Court alone, but also to other supreme constitutional organs. In this connection previously delivered judgements, basic decisions, basic principles, and constitutional norms have to be adhered to.

(c) In giving substance to the constitution as the basic legal order a particularly high degree of consensus is necessary in the analysis and assessment of the relevant facts of the case between the supreme constitutional organs concerned under considerations both of constitutional law and of political practice. It is essential that these organs act in such a given situation consistently and with due regard for durability.

(5) Confidence in the sense intended in Article 68 of the Basic Law means, pursuant to the German tradition of constitutional law, the formally manifested present endorsement, through the act of voting by the members of the Bundestag, of the person and substantive programme of the Federal Chancellor.

(6) The Federal Chancellor, who aims to secure the dissolution of the Bundestag in the manner laid down in Article 68 of the Basic Law, should only be allowed to pursue this course when it is no longer politically possible for him to ensure continued govvrning with the prevailing power constellation of the Bundestag. The power-political constellation of the Bundestag must so impair his capacity to govern that he is not in a position to pursue a meaningful policy endorsed by the continuing confidence of the majority. This is the unwritten substantive constitutional characteristic of Article 68 Paragraph 1, Sentence 1 of the Basic Law.

(7) An interpretation at this point that Article 68 of the Basic Law permits a Federal Chancellor, whose adequate majority in the Bundestag is not in question, to arrange to have the confidence question answered in the negative at a point in time convenient for him with the aim of getting a dissolution of the Bundestag is not justified by the sense of Article 68 of the Basic Law. Similarly difficulties foreseen in carrying out parliamentary business in the current legislative period

do not justify a dissolution.

(8) (a) When he proposes to initiate an application with the object of arriving at a dissolution of the Bundestag the Federal Chancellor has to examine whether a situation exists which would no longer make possible the meaningful pursuit of policy with the continuing confidence of the majority.

(b) In examining whether the application and proposal of the Federal Chancellor under Article 68 of the Basic Law is *compatible with the constitution* the Federal President does not have to rely on other yardsticks; in this respect he has to take account of the competence of the Federal Chancellor to assess and to judge, except if another evaluation which would argue against a dissolution would have to be given clear preference over the evaluative judgement of the Federal Chancellor.

(c) The unanimity of the parties represented in the Bundestag to secure new elections cannot limit the area of the Federal President's discretion; he can, however, see in this a supplementary indication that a dissolution of the Bundestag will have the result of coming closer to Article 68 of the Basic Law than a decision rejecting it.

(9) In Article 68 the Basic Law itself, through the admission of latitude for estimation and judgement, as well as the granting of discretion to the political decisions of three superior constitutional organs, has narrowed down the possibilities of constitutional review farther than in the realm of law making and of normal execution of the law; the Basic Law relies as far as this goes above all on the system of mutual political control and of political balance between the supreme constitutional organs involved as found in Article 68 itself. Only where constitutional criteria for certain political actions have been specifically spelt out in the Constitution can the Federal Constitutional Court determine their violation.

Notes

1. See Ch. 2, 25f., 41f.
2. See Ch. 2, 25, 34ff.
3. See n. 1 above
4. See Doc. 9 above, Table 17
5. See Ch. 11, Doc. 7
6. See Ch. 8, 27
7. See Ch. 2, Docs. 12–14

4 The Judiciary

Donald P. Kommers

German legal scholars often describe the Federal Republic as a *Rechtsstaat*, literally translated as a 'law state' or a state based on law.* The notion of a state based on law clearly finds its most significant manifestation in the German judiciary whose structure and jurisdiction offer the most extensive legal protection of any court system in the world.

Before discussing the judicial system as such more needs to be said about the tradition of German law associated with the idea of the *Rechtsstaat*. By the end of the nineteenth century German law had been systematically arranged and unified in several codes which still exist. Criminal law was codified in 1871; civil and criminal procedure in 1877; general private law in 1896; commercial law in 1897. These codifications followed Germany's political unification in 1871, facilitating in turn the unification of the judicial system in 1877. As Fritz Baur has pointed out, codification reflected 'the optimistic belief that all legally relevant human relations could be thus rationally comprehended and constructed'. The codification drive and the nationalistic feeling that propelled it placed a high premium upon the importance of the state in Germany's legal order. Unlike the Anglo-American or common law tradition that emphasized the importance of natural rights possessed by the individual against the state, the German tradition assumed that law and justice could be achieved only within and under the protection of the state.

The primacy of the state in German jurisprudence influenced attitudes toward the traditional role of the courts. This role is suggested by the following propositions which at one time fairly well summarized the

---

* Notes for this chapter begin on p. 112

German, and largely continental, European theory of law and judicial authority: that the state is the source of all law; that the locus of all law-making authority within the state is the sovereign legislature; that law is a closed system of logically arranged and internally coherent rules; that law, to be just, must be specific in content yet general in the sense of applying to all persons; that all legal disputes must be resolved by reference to such laws; that courts of law, independent of the legislature, are the proper agencies for interpreting the law; that laws be interpreted literally and in strict accordance with the legislator's will; the function of courts, therefore, is to administer the law as written, requiring on the part of the judge a posture of absolute neutrality, insulated from and un-moved by forces, ideas, or even notions of justice located outside the formal structure of law. This complex of attitudes was identified with the theory of legal positivism, the dominant school of legal thought in Germany.

Legal positivists in Germany have long insisted that a state based on law (*Recht*) is the only means of securing individual persons against the arbitrary exercise of power (*Macht*). Doubtless an important element of constitutional government, the *Rechtsstaat* as understood traditionally in the German context was nevertheless a long way from the Anglo-American notion of constitutionalism. It did not, for example, pre-suppose parliamentary democracy, as in English theory, or judicial review, as in American theory. The Basic Law went beyond this in im-portant aspects. Art. 20 sets up 'a democratic and social federal state' and a parliamentary system of government in which 'all state authority emanates from the people'. Additionally, Art. 20 subjects legislation to the 'constitutional order' and specifies that 'the executive and the judiciary [are] bound by law *and justice*' (italics supplied). Art. 28 stipulates that the constitutional order in the Länder must also 'conform to the principles of republican, democratic and social government based on the rule of law'; Art. 19, para. 4, guarantees to everyone in the Federal Republic recourse to ordinary courts.[1] Finally, the Basic Law's section on the administration of justice provides for the judicial review of legisla-tion and other governmental actions, vesting this power exclusively in the Federal Constitutional Court (Bundesverfassungsgericht) (Doc. 1).

German judicial organization is characterized by uniformity, specialization, and collegiality. Firstly, all courts are encompassed within a unified structure (Doc. 2). Separate Land and federal judicial systems, as in the United States, do not exist. All trial and intermediate courts of appeal are Land tribunals, while federal courts serve as courts of last resort. Secondly, the judiciary embraces separate hierarchies of administrative, labour, fiscal and social courts, while ordinary civil and criminal jurisdiction is vested in the regular courts. In addition, each Land, except for Schleswig-Holstein and Berlin, has established a constitutional court to resolve state constitutional disputes arising within its jurisdiction. Finally, the courts are marked by collegiality. Only courts of limited jurisdiction at the lowest level of the judicial hierarchy are one-judge tribunals. All other courts, trial and appellate, function in panels of three, five, or more judges.

The administration of justice in Germany is carried out by a total of 16,657 judges (as of 1981), 13,000 of whom preside over regular courts. Other legal professionals associated with the courts are some 3,500 public prosecutors. The 31,000 practicing attorneys in the Federal Republic are also regarded as 'organs' of the overall system of justice. But they are not subject to disciplinary action outside their own professional association. Their practice is by law limited to a certain level of the judiciary as well as to certain courts within a given geographical area, depending on the nature of the litigation. Finally, all judges appointed to the bench in the Federal Republic are career appointments (Doc. 3). The only exception to this rule is the Federal Constitutional Court whose judges are chosen for single nonrenewable terms of twelve years (Doc. 5). One-half of the sixteen justices must be elected by a two-thirds vote of the Bundesrat; the other half is elected by a two-thirds vote of a special Bundestag electoral committee. Judges of all other *federal* courts are elected by a judicial selection committee composed of eleven members of the Bundestag and those Länder ministers whose portfolios relate to the subject-matter jurisdiction of the particular court concerned (Doc. 4). All other judges are recruited and appointed by Land justice ministries, although here, too, electing bodies make the proposals for appointments in general.

Document 1

The following articles of the Basic Law relate to the establishment of the judicial system and the administration of justice. Especially to be noticed are provisions conferring the explicit power of judicial review on the Federal Constitutional Court. Judicial review refers to the authority of a court to invalidate statutes or other actions of government in conflict with the Constitution. It needs to be pointed out that judicial review, like the ban on extraordinary courts and capital punishment, were reactions to the abuses of governmental power tolerated, encouraged, and carried out by the Hitler regime.

EXTRACTS FROM THE BASIC LAW

Source: Press and Information Office
Transl: Official

. . .

Art. 92

Judicial power shall be vested in the judges; it shall be exercised by the Federal Constitutional Court, by the federal courts provided for in this Basic Law, and by the courts of the Länder.

Art. 93

(1) The Federal Constitutional Court shall decide:

1. On the interpretation of this Basic Law in the event of disputes concerning the extent of the rights and duties of a highest federal organ or of other parties concerned who have been vested with rights of their own by this Basic Law or by rules of procedure of a highest federal organ;
2. in case of differences of opinion or doubts on the formal and material compatibility of federal law or Land law with this Basic Law, or on the compatibility of Land law with other federal law, at the request of the Federal Government, of a Land government, or of one-third of the Bundestag members;
3. in case of differences of opinion of the rights and duties of the Federation and the Länder, particularly in the execution of federal law by the Länder and in the exercise of federal supervision;
4. on other disputes involving public law, between the Federation and the Länder, between different Länder or within a Land, unless recourse to another court exists;
4a. on complaints of unconstitutionality, which may be entered by any person who claims that one of his basic rights or one of his rights under paragraph (4) of Article 20, under Article 33, 38, 101, 103 or 104 has been violated by public authority;[2]

. . .

Art. 94

(1) The Federal Constitutional Court shall consist of federal judges and other members. Half of the members of the Federal Constitutional Court shall be elected by the Bundestag and half by the Bundesrat. They may not be members of the Bundestag, the Bundesrat, the Federal Government, nor of any of the corresponding organs of a Land.

(2) The constitution and procedure of the Federal Constitutional Court shall be regulated by a federal law which shall specify in what cases its decisions shall have the force of law. . . .

Art. 95

(1) For the purposes of ordinary, administrative, fiscal, labour, and social jurisdiction, the Federation shall establish as highest courts of justice the Federal Court of Justice, the Federal Administrative Court, the Federal Fiscal Court, the Federal Labour Court, and the Federal Social Court.

. . .

Art. 97

(1) The judges shall be independent and subject only to the law.

. . .

Art. 100

(1) If a court considers unconstitutional a law the validity of which is relevant to its decison, the proceedings shall be stayed, and a decision shall be obtained from the Land court competent for constitutional disputes if the constitution of a Land is held to be violated, or from the Federal Constitutional Court if this Basic Law is held to be violated. This shall also apply if this Basic Law is held to be violated by Land law or if a Land law is held to be incompatible with a federal law.

. . .

Art. 101

(1) Extraordinary courts shall be inadmissible. No one may be removed from the jurisdiction of his lawful judge.
(2) Courts for special fields may be established only by legislation.

Art. 102

Capital punishment shall be abolished.

Art. 103

(1) In the courts everyone shall be entitled to a hearing in accordance with the law.
(2) An act can be punished only if it was an offence against the law before the act was committed.
(3) No one may be punished for the same act more than once under general penal legislation.

Art. 104

(1) The liberty of the individual may be restricted only by virtue of a formal law and only with due regard to the forms prescribed therein. Detained persons may not be subjected to mental nor to physical ill-treatment.

. . .

Document 2

The general organization of the judiciary is specified by federal law, rendering the structure and jurisdiction of the courts rather uniform throughout the country. Other details of judicial administration are regulated by Land law. Still, a lawyer practising in the courts of Bavaria would feel perfectly comfortable in the courts of Hamburg. The following document covers the organization and decision-making procedures of courts exercising ordinary civil and criminal jurisdiction. The courts exercising this jurisdiction are called regular courts (ordentliche Gerichte). These courts are divided into civil, criminal, commercial, and juvenile chambers, not to mention special panels that deal mainly with non-contentious matters. In addition, as noted in the introduction to this chapter, there exists vertically from the Federation to the Länder a uniform system of administrative, fiscal, labour and social courts. The supreme courts of appeal for each of these areas of basic jurisdiction are federal tribunals. They include the Federal Supreme Court (Bundes-gerichtshof), Federal Administrative Court (Bundesverwaltungs-gericht), Federal Labour Court (Bundesarbeitsgericht), Federal Social Court (Bundessozialgericht), and the Federal Fiscal Court (Bundes-finanzhof).

The regular courts operate at four levels. At the lowest level are the district courts (Amstergerichte). They operate in towns or other limited geographical areas and exercise jurisdiction over minor civil suits and petty criminal offences (punishable by up to two years imprisonment). They also perform many non-judicial functions such as administering estates, drafting wills and conveyances, keeping registers, appointing guardians, and supervising executors and trustees in bankruptcy. Next come the county courts (Landgerichte). They are the trial courts of general jurisdiction; within their territorial limits they also serve as final courts of appeal for the local courts. The court of last resort in each Land is the superior court (Oberlandesgericht), although it has original jurisdiction in cases involving high treason and betrayal of the Basic

Law. The final court of appeals is the Federal Supreme Court in Karlsruhe (Bundesgerichtshof).

THE JUDICIARY ACT (GERICHTSVERFASSUNGSGESETZ)

Source: BGBl., 1950, 513, as amended up to and including 9 May 1975
Transl.: Official

I: Jurisdiction

Art. 1

Judicial power shall be exercised by independent courts that are subject only to the law.

...

Art. 12

Jurisdiction over ordinary litigation shall be exercised by District Courts (Amtsgerichte), County Courts (Landgerichte), Superior Courts (Oberlandesgerichte) and the Federal Supreme Court (Bundesgerichtshof).

Art. 13

The ordinary courts shall have jurisdiction over all civil law controversies and criminal cases over which jurisdiction either is not vested in administrative agencies or administrative courts or for which special courts have not been established or permitted on the basis of regulations of Federal law.

...

Art. 16

Extraordinary courts shall be impermissable. No one may be removed from the jurisdiction of his lawful judge.

...

III: District Courts (Amtsgerichte)

Art. 22

(1) District Courts shall be presided over by single judges.
(2) A District Court judge may simultaneously be a member or director of a superior County Court.

...

Art. 23

The jurisdiction of District Courts over civil law controversies shall include, insofar as they have not been assigned to County Courts irrespective of the value of the object in controversy:

1. Controversies over property claims whose sum or monetary value does not exceed five thousand German marks;
2. regardless of the value of the object in controversy: [disputes involving landlord and tenant, public accommodations and travel, support claims, bankruptcy proceedings, etc.]

. . .

Art. 24

(1) In criminal cases District Courts shall have jurisdiction over:

[1. misdemeanors]
[2. minor offences]
[3. major offences]

(2) A District Court may not pronounce a penalty of imprisonment in a penitentiary of more than three years. . . .

IV: Lay Judge Courts (Schöffengerichte)

Art. 28

Lay Judge Courts shall be created at the District Courts for hearing and decision on criminal cases belonging within the jurisdiction of District Courts and not decided by a District Court judge sitting singly.

Art. 29

(1) Lay Judge Courts shall be composed of a District Judge as chairman and two lay judges (Schöffen). . . .

Art. 31

The office of lay judge shall be an honorary office (Ehrenamt). It may be filled only by Germans.

. . .

Art. 36

(1) Municipalities shall compile a nominating list for lay judges every fourth year. . . .

. . .

Art. 42

The committee shall by two-thirds majority elect from the corrected nomination list for the next four business years . . . the required number of lay judges . . .

. . .

V: County Courts (Landgerichte)

Art 59

(1) County Courts shall be composed of a President and the required number of presiding judges and members. . . .

Art. 60

Civil and criminal senates shall be established at the County Courts.

. . .

Art. 75

—The civil senates shall be composed of three members including the presiding judge [unless otherwise provided by law].

Art. 76

(1) The criminal senates shall, in proceedings other than trials, decide with three members sitting, including the presiding judge.

(2) The criminal senates shall be composed as follows for trials: the presiding judge and two lay judges (minor criminal senate) if an appeal against a district court verdict is involved; and three judges, including the presiding judge, and two lay judges (major criminal senate) in all other cases.

. . .

VIII: Superior Courts (Oberlandesgerichte)

Art. 115

Superior Courts shall be composed of a president and the requisite number of senate presidents and judges.

Art. 116

(1) Civil and criminal senates shall be established at the Superior Courts. . . .
. . .

Art. 122

(1) The senates of the Superior Courts shall decide with three judges, including the presiding judge, sitting unless the procedural codes provide that a single judge shall decide instead of a senate.

(2) The criminal senates shall be composed of five judges, including the presiding judge, in trials of first instance. . . .

IX: Federal Supreme Court (Bundesgerichtshof)

Art. 123

The Federal Supreme Court shall have its seat in Karlsruhe.

Art. 124

The Federal Supreme Court shall be composed of a president and the requisite number of senate presidents.

Art. 125

(1) The judges of the Federal Supreme Court shall be chosen by the Federal Minister of Justice together with the Judicial Election Committee, and shall be appointed by the Federal President.
(2) Only persons who have reached the age of thirty-five shall be eligible for election to the Federal Supreme Court.

. . .

Art. 130

(1) Civil and criminal senates shall be established at the Federal Supreme Court. Their number shall be determined by the Federal Minister of Justice.

. . .

Art. 132

(1) A superior senate for civil cases and a superior senate for criminal cases shall be established at the Federal Supreme Court.
(2) Each superior senate shall consist of a president and eight members.
(3) The members and their deputies shall be designated by the presidium of the Federal Supreme Court for terms of two business years.
(4) The joint superior senate shall consist of the presidents and all members of the superior senates.

. . .

Art. 137

The deciding senate may solicit the decision of the superior senate in a question of fundamental importance if in its opinion the growth of the law and the assurance of uniform interpretation require it.

Art. 138

(1) The superior senates and the joint superior senate shall decide without oral proceedings and only on the question of law.

. . .

Art. 139

(1) The senates of the Federal Supreme Court shall decide with five members, including the presiding judge sitting.

(2) The criminal senate shall decide, in first instance other than the trial, with three members, including the presiding judge, sitting.

. . .

X: The Public Prosecution

Art. 141

A public prosecutor's office shall be established at each court.

Art. 142

(1) The public prosecution's functions shall be exercised:

1. By a Federal Prosecutor-General and one or several Federal Prosecutors, at the Federal Supreme Court;
2. by one or several public prosecutors, at the Superior and County Courts;
3. by one of several public prosecutors or prosecutors (Amtsanwälte), at the District Courts.

. . .

Art. 147

The power of supervision and direction shall rest with:

1. the Federal Minister of Justice in regard to the Federal Prosecutor-General and the Federal Prosecutors;
2. the Land justice administration in regard to all prosecutors in a given Land;
   . . .

Art. 150

The public prosecution shall be independent of the courts in its official business.

Art. 151

Public prosecutors may not undertake judicial business . . .

. . .

Art. 192

(1) In the rendering of decisions only the statutorily determined number of judges may participate.

. . .

Art. 194

(1) The presiding judges shall direct the deliberation, frame the questions and collect the votes.

(2) Disagreements over the subject, the framing and order of the questions or the result of the vote shall be resolved by the court.

. . .

Art. 196

(1) The court shall, unless otherwise provided by law, decide by an absolute majority of votes.

. . .

(3) If in a criminal case more than two opinions are formed on a question other than that of guilt and if none of these opinions commands a majority, then the votes most detrimental to the accused shall be added to the less detrimental votes until the requisite majority results. If two opinions are formed regarding the matter of punishment without either opinion commanding a majority, then the more lenient opinion shall prevail.

. . .

Document 3

The role and status of judges in Germany is also regulated by federal law.[3] The following document specifies their qualifications, tenure, and conditions of removal. Judgeships in Germany are life-time careers not unlike those in the civil service. A young person, upon the successful completion of his legal training, ordinarily chooses to enter one of a number of legal callings. If he chooses the judiciary he must embark upon a three-year apprenticeship in a court of law. If his stewardship meets with the approval of his superiors in the Ministry of Justice of the Land concerned, he is awarded a judgeship with lifetime tenure and security. The typical appointee begins his career at the lowest level of the judiciary. Most remain there for the duration of their careers. Promotion to higher courts usually depends on the recommendation of higher-ranking judges. Only a small percentage of all judges end their careers on the federal bench.

JUDGES ACT (DEUTSCHES RICHTERGESETZ)
Source: BGBl., I, 1961, 1665, as amended up to and including 19 April 1972
. . .

Art. 1

The judicial power shall be exercised by professional judges and by honorary judges.

Art. 2

The provisions of this Act shall apply only to professional judges unless otherwise provided.

Art. 3

The judges shall be in the service of the Federation or of a Land.

Art. 4

(1) A judge may not concurrently exercise the functions of the judiciary and the functions of the legislative or executive power.

. . .

Art. 5

(1) The qualifications for judicial office shall be attained by passing two examinations.

(2) The first examination must be preceded by legal studies of at least three and one-half years at a university. Of this, at least four semesters of the studies must be undertaken at a university within the jurisdiction of this Act.

Art. 5a

(1) Probationary service of at least two years must occur between the first and second examinations. During this time the person must serve as an apprentice to:

1. A regular civil court,
2. a criminal court or state prosecutor's office,
3. an administrative office,
4. an office of a private attorney,
5. at one of the following (by choice):
    (a) one of the offices listed in 1 to 4 above for an additional period
    (b) a Land or federal legislative body
    (c) an administrative, fiscal, labour, or social court
    (d) an office of a notary public
    (e) a trade union or other trade association
    (f) a corporation

. . .

Art. 6

(1) A candidate may not be denied admission to probationary service on the ground that he passed the first examination specified in Article 5 in another Land within the jurisdiction of this Act. Time served in probationary service in any Land within the jurisdiction of this Act must be credited in every German Land.

. . .

Art. 7

Any professor of law with tenure at a university within the jurisdiction of this Act shall possess the qualifications for judicial office.

. . .

Art. 9

Only the following may be appointed to judicial office:

1. Germans within the meaning of Article 116 of the Basic Law;
2. Those offering assurance of supporting at all times the free democratic basic order, within the meaning of the Basic Law.[4]
3. Those possessing the qualifications for judicial office (Articles 5 to 7).

Art. 10

(1) Persons who, after acquiring the qualifications for judicial office, have served in judicial office for at least three years may be appointed judges for life.

. . .

Art. 12

(1) Persons who are to serve later as judges for life or as public prosecutors may be appointed probationary judges.

(2) Probationary judges must be appointed judges for life or, as tenured civil servants, as public prosecutors for life, no later than five years after their appointment as probationary judges.

. . .

Art. 14

(1) Civil servants appointed for life or for a term may be appointed acting judges if they are later to serve as judges for life.

. . .

Art. 15

(1) Acting judges shall retain their previous office . . .

(3) Judges appointed for life or a term may, without their written consent, be dismissed only on the basis of a final judicial decision.

. . .

Art. 22

(1) Probationary judges may be dismissed at the expiration of the sixth, twelfth, eighteenth or twenty-fourth month after their appointment.

(2) Probationary judges may be dismissed at the expiration of the third or fourth year if they:

1. are unsuited for judicial office; or

2. a judicial election committee denies them entrance into judicial office for life or for a term.

. . .

Art. 23

The provisions relating to the termination of probationary judgeships shall apply to the termination of acting judgeships.

Art. 24

If a German court within the jurisdiction of this Act renders a verdict against a judge involving . . . [imprisonment or loss of civil rights] . . . the judicial office shall be terminated without further judicial decision . . .

Art. 25

The judges shall be independent and subject only to the laws.

. . .

Art. 27

(1) Judges for life and judges for a term must be assigned a judicial position at a specific court.

. . .

Art. 28

(1) Only judges for life may serve as judges at a court, except as otherwise provided by Federal law.

. . .

Art. 29

No more than one probationary judge or one acting judge . . . may participate in a court decision . . .

Art. 30

Judges for life or judges for a term may, without their written consent, be transferred into another office or be deprived of their office only:

1. pursuant to impeachment proceedings (Article 98 (2), 98 (5) of the Basic Law);
2. pursuant to a formal disciplinary proceeding;
3. in the interest of the administration of justice (Article 31);
4. for changes in court organization (Article 32).

. . .

Art. 36

(1) Judges accepting nominations as candidates for election to membership in the

Bundestag or a legislative body of a Land shall be on paid leave beginning on that day, but not earlier than two months before election day, and until two weeks after election day.

...

Art. 39

Judges must so conduct themselves in and outside their office, as well as in political activities, in such a manner that confidence in their independence is not threatened.

...

Art. 48

(1) Judges for life serving at the high Federal courts shall be retired at the end of the month in which they reach their sixty-eighth year; all other judges at the end of the month in which they reach their sixty-fifth year.

...

Art. 49

There shall be established at the Federal courts:
(1) Judges' Councils for participation in general and social matters;
(2) Presidents' Councils for participation in the appointment of judges.

...

Art. 61

(1) A special Senate of the Federal Supreme Court shall be established as the Disciplinary Court for judges in Federal service.[5]

...

Art. 62

The Disciplinary Court of the Federation is empowered to rule:
(1) on disciplinary matters . . .;
(2) on transfers [of judges] in the interest of the administration of Justice;
(3) with regard to judges chosen for life or for a term on

1. the invalidity of their appointment;
2. withdrawal of their appointment;
3. dismissal;
4. retirement on account of service disability.

...

Document 4

A federal statute also governs the appointment, qualifications, and tenure of federal judges, namely those judges sitting on the federal courts which constitute, as noted earlier, the highest courts of appeal in certain jurisdictional areas. Currently, there are 115 judges on the Federal Supreme Court, sixty-five on the Federal Administrative Court, forty-four on the Federal Fiscal Court, forty-one on the Federal Social Court, and sixteen on the Federal Constitutional Court. These high federal courts are located in cities other than the capital of the Federal Republic, in part to remove them from Bonn's highly charged political environment.

FEDERAL JUDICIAL ELECTION ACT (RICHTERWAHLGESETZ)
Source: BGBl., 1950, 368–9

For the implementation of Article 95, paragraph 3, and Article 96, paragraph 2, of the Basic Law the Bundestag has enacted the following law:

Art. 1

(1) The judges of the Federal Supreme Court and of the high Federal courts shall be chosen by the appropriate Federal Minister conjointly with the Judicial Election Committee, and shall be appointed by the Federal President.
(2) The Federal Minister of Justice shall participate in the choice of judges to the Federal Supreme Court; the Federal Minister having jurisdiction over the respective subject area shall participate in the choice of judges to other high Federal courts.

Art. 2

The Judicial Election Committee shall be composed of an equal number of ex officio and elected members.

Art. 3

(1) Ex officio members of the Committee electing judges to a high federal court shall be the Land Ministers who have jurisdiction over those lower Land courts of which the Federal court in question is the court of appeal.
(2) The Land Ministers may be represented by deputies only under the same conditions as apply to their being represented in the Land cabinet.

Art. 4

(1) The elected members must be eligible to serve in the Bundestag and must possess legal experience.
. . .

Art. 5

(1) The elected members and their deputies shall be chosen by the Bundestag according to the rules of proportional representation.
(2) Each Parliamentary Party may nominate a slate of candidates. On the basis of

the total votes cast for each slate the number of members elected from each slate shall be computed, on the basis of the d'Hondt system of the highest average. Members and their deputies shall be elected in the order in which their names appear on the slate of candidates.

. . .

Art. 8

(1) The Federal Minister of Justice shall convene the Judicial Election Committee.

. . .

Art. 9

(1) The appropriate Federal Minister or his deputy in the cabinet shall preside. He shall have no vote.
(2) Meetings shall not be public.

. . .

Art. 10

(1) The appropriate Federal Minister and the members of the Judicial Election Committee may nominate persons to be chosen as Federal judges.
(2) The appropriate Federal Minister shall present to the Judicial Election Committee the personnel records of persons nominated for judicial office.

. . .

Art. 11

The Judicial Election Committee shall examine whether a candidate for judicial office possesses the professional and personal qualifications for the office.

. . .

Art. 12

(1) The Judicial Election Committee shall decide by secret ballot by a majority of the votes cast.

. . .

Document 5

Judicial review is a relatively new departure in German constitutional history. Postwar German leaders were of the opinion that in the light of Germany's authoritarian and totalitarian past traditional parliamentary and judicial institutions were insufficient to safeguard the new liberal democratic order. So they created a national constitutional tribunal to supervise the judiciary's interpretation of constitutional norms, to enforce a consistent reading of the Constitution on the other branches of government, and to protect the basic liberties of German citizens.[5] Thus the old positivist belief separating the realm of law from the realm of politics was abandoned, together with the idea that justice could automatically be achieved through the mechanical application of general laws enacted by the legislature. The Federal Constitutional Court, unlike the United States Supreme Court, is a specialized tribunal with exclusive jurisdiction to decide constitutional questions under the Basic Law. An important structural feature of the Court is its division into two chambers, or panels, which have exclusive memberships and exclusive jurisdiction over specified constitutional disputes. The organization, jurisdiction, and internal procedures of the Federal Constitutional Court are elaborated in great detail by the following statute.

FEDERAL CONSTITUTIONAL COURT ACT (BUNDESVERFASSUNGS-GERICHTSGESETZ)

Source: BGBl., I, 1968, 949, as amended up to and including 13 September 1978

I: Constitution and Competency of the Federal Constitutional Court

Art. 1

(1) The Federal Constitutional Court shall be a federal court of justice independent of all other constitutional bodies.

(2) The seat of the Federal Constitutional Court shall be at Karlsruhe.

Art. 2

(1) The Federal Constitutional Court shall consist of two panels.

(2) Eight judges shall be elected to each panel.

(3) Three judges of each panel shall be elected from among the judges of the highest federal courts of justice. Only judges who have served at least three years with a highest federal court of justice shall be elected.

Art. 3

(1) The judges must have reached the age of forty, be eligible for election to the Bundestag, and have stated in writing that they are willing to become a member of the Federal Constitutional Court.

(2) They must be qualified to exercise the functions of a judge pursuant to the Law on German Judges.

(3) They may not be members of the Bundestag, the Bundesrat, the Federal Government, nor of any of the corresponding bodies of a Land. On their appointment they shall cease to be members of such bodies.

(4) The functions of a judge shall preclude any other professional occupation save

that of a professor of law at a German institution of higher education. The functions of a judge of the Federal Constitutional Court shall take precedence over the functions of such professor.

Art. 4

(1) The term of office of the judges shall be twelve years, not extending beyond retirement age.
(2) Immediate or subsequent re-election of judges shall not be permissible.
(3) Retirement age shall be the end of the month in which a judge reaches the age of sixty-eight.
(4) Upon expiration of his term of office a judge shall continue to perform his functions until a successor is appointed.

Art. 5

(1) Half of the judges of each panel shall be elected by the Bundestag and the other half by the Bundesrat. Of those to be selected from among the judges of the highest federal courts of justice one shall be elected by one of the electoral organs and two by the other, and of the remaining judges three shall be elected by one body and two by the other.

. . .

Art. 6

(1) The judges to be selected by the Bundestag shall be elected indirectly.
(2) The Bundestag shall elect twelve of its members as electors according to the rules of proportional representation. Each parliamentary group may submit a list of twelve candidates. The number of candidates elected on each list shall be calculated from the total number of votes cast for each list in accordance with the d'Hondt method. The members shall be elected in the sequence in which their names appear on the list. If an elector retires or is unable to perform his functions, he shall be replaced by the next candidate on the same list.
(3) The eldest elector shall immediately with one week's notice convene a meeting of the electors for the purpose of electing the judges and shall chair the meeting which shall continue until all of them have been elected.
(4) The members of the electoral committee are obliged to maintain secrecy about the personal circumstances of candidates which become known to them as a result of their activities in the committee as well as about discussions thereon in the committee and the voting.
(5) To be elected, a judge shall require at least eight votes.

Art. 7

The judges to be selected by the Bundesrat shall be elected with two-thirds of the votes of the Bundesrat.

Art. 7a

(1) If a successor is not elected in accordance with the provisions of Art. 6 above within two months of the expiration of a judge's term of office or his early retirement, the eldest elector shall immediately request the Federal Constitutional Court to propose candidates.

(2) The plenum of the Federal Constitutional Court shall decide with a simple majority on whom to propose as a candidate. If only one judge needs to be elected, the Federal Constitutional Court shall propose three candidates: if several judges are to be elected simultaneously, the Federal Constitutional Court shall propose twice as many candidates as the number of judges to be elected. Art. 16 (2) below shall apply *mutatis mutandis*.

(3) If the judge is to be elected by the Bundesrat, paragraphs 1 and 2 above shall apply save that the eldest elector shall be replaced by the President of the Bundesrat or his deputy.

(4) The right of the electoral body to elect a person not proposed by the Federal Constitutional Court shall remain unaffected.

Art. 8

(1) The Federal Minister of Justice shall draw up a list of all federal judges meeting the requirements of Art. 3 (1) and (2) above.

(2) The Federal Minister of Justice shall keep another list in which he shall enter all the candidates who are proposed for the post of judge of the Federal Constitutional Court by a parliamentary group of the Bundestag, the Federal Government or a Land government and who meet the requirements of Art. 3 (1) and (2) above.

(3) The lists shall be continually updated and be forwarded to the Presidents of the Bundestag and Bundesrat at least one week before an election.

Art. 9

(1) The Bundestag and the Bundesrat shall alternately elect the President of the Federal Constitutional Court and his deputy. The deputy shall be elected from the panel of which the President is not a member.

(2) At the first election the Bundestag shall elect the President and the Bundesrat his deputy.

(3) The provisions of Arts. 6 and 7 above shall apply *mutatis mutandis*.

Art. 10

The Federal President shall appoint the judges elected.

Art. 11

(1) On assuming office the judges of the Federal Constitutional Court shall take the following oath before the Federal President:

'I swear that as an impartial judge I shall at all times faithfully observe the Basic Law of the Federal Republic of Germany and conscientiously perform my judicial duties towards others. So help me God!'

(2) If a judge belongs to a religious denomination whose members are permitted by law to use a different form of affirmation, he may do so.
(3) The oath may be taken without the religious affirmation.

Art. 12

The judges of the Federal Constitutional Court may ask to be released from service at any time. The Federal President shall pronounce such release.

Art. 13

The Federal Constitutional Court shall decide in the cases determined by the Basic Law, to wit:

1. On the forfeiture of basic rights (Art. 18 of the Basic Law);
2. on the unconstitutionality of parties (Art. 21 (2) of the Basic Law);
3. on complaints against decisions of the Bundestag relating to the validity of an election or to the acquisition or loss of a deputy's seat in the Bundestag (Art. 41 (2) of the Basic Law);
4. on the impeachment of the Federal President by the Bundestag or the Bundesrat (Art. 61 of the Basic Law);
5. on the interpretation of the Basic Law in the event of disputes concerning the extent of the rights and duties of a highest federal organ or of other parties concerned who have been vested with rights of their own by the Basic Law or by rules of procedure of a highest federal organ (Art. 93 (1) (1) of the Basic Law);
6. in case of differences of opinion or doubts on the formal and material compatibility of federal law or Land law with the Basic Law, or on the compatibility of Land law with other federal law, at the request of the Federal Government, of a Land government, or of one third of the Bundestag members (Art. 93 (1) (2) of the Basic Law);
7. in case of differences of opinion on the rights and duties of the Federation and the Länder, particularly in the execution of federal law by the Länder and in the exercise of federal supervision (Art. 93 (1) (3) and Art. 84 (4), second sentence, of the Basic Law);
8. on other disputes involving public law, between the Federation and the Länder, between different Länder or within a Land, unless recourse to another court exists (Art. 93 (1) (4) of the Basic Law);
8a. on complaints of unconstitutionality (Art. 93 (1) (4a) and (4b) of the Basic Law);
9. on the impeachment of federal and Land judges (Art. 98 (2) and (5) of the Basic Law);

10. on constitutional disputes within a Land if such decision is assigned to the Federal Constitutional Court by Land legislation (Art. 99 of the Basic Law);
11. on the compatibility of a federal or Land law with the Basic Law or the compatibility of a Land law or other Land right with a federal law, when such decision is requested by a court (Art. 100 (1) of the Basic Law);
12. in case of doubt whether a rule of public international law is an integral part of federal law and whether such rule creates rights and duties for the individual, when such decision is requested by a court (Art. 100 (2) of the Basic Law);
13. if the constitutional court of a Land, in interpreting the Basic Law, intends to deviate from a decision of the Federal Constitutional Court or of the constitutional court of another Land, when such decision is requested by that constitutional court (Art. 100 (3) of the Basic Law);
14. in case of differences of opinion on the continuance of law as federal law (Art. 126 of the Basic Law);
15. in such other cases as are assigned to it by federal legislation (Art. 93 (2) of the Basic Law).

Art. 14

(1) The First Panel of the Federal Constitutional Court shall be competent for legal review proceedings (Art. 13 (6) and (11) above) in which mainly a legal provision is claimed to be incompatible with basic rights or with rights under Arts. 33, 101, 103 and 104 of the Basic Law, as well as for complaints of unconstitutionality with the exception of such complaints pursuant to Art. 91 below and those in the domain of electoral law.
(2) The Second Panel of the Federal Constitutional Court shall be competent for the cases stated in Art. 13 (1) to (5), (7) to (9), (12) and (14) above, as well as for legal review proceedings and complaints of unconstitutionality not assigned to the First Panel.
(3) In the cases stated in Article 13 (10) and (13) above the competency of the panels shall be governed by the provisions of paragraphs 1 and 2 above.

. . .

Art. 15

(1) The President of the Federal Constitutional Court and his deputy shall preside over their respective panels. The eldest judges present on each panel shall act as their deputies.

. . .

Art. 16

(1) If, in a point of law, a panel intends to deviate from the legal opinion contained

in a decision by the other panel, the plenum of the Federal Constitutional Court shall decide on the matter.

(2) It has a quorum if two thirds of the judges of each panel are present.

II: General Procedural Provisions

. . .

Art. 22

(1) The parties may be represented at any stage of the proceedings by an attorney registered with a German court or a professor of law at a German institution of higher education; in the oral pleadings before the Federal Constitutional Court they must be represented in this manner. Legislative bodies and parts thereof which are vested with rights of their own by virtue of their statutes or rules of procedure may, in addition, be represented by their members. The Federation, the Länder and their constitutional organs may also be represented by their officials provided that they are qualified to exercise the functions of a judge or are qualified for higher administrative service by having passed the prescribed state examinations. The Federal Constitutional Court may also permit another person to act as counsel for a party.

. . .

Art. 25

(1) In the absence of provisions to the contrary, the Federal Constitutional Court shall decide on the basis of oral pleadings, unless all parties expressly waive them.
(2) Decisions pursuant to oral pleadings shall be issued as judgments, and decisions without oral pleadings as orders.
(3) Partial and interim decisions shall be permissible.
(4) The decisions shall be issued 'in the name of the people'.

Art. 26

(1) The Federal Constitutional Court shall take evidence as needed to establish the truth. It may charge a member of the court with this outside the oral pleadings or ask another court to do so with regard to specific facts and persons.
(2) If so decided by a majority of two-thirds of the votes of the court the obtainment of individual documents may be dispensed with where their use would be detrimental to national security.

Art. 27

All courts and administrative authorities shall afford the Federal Constitutional

Court legal and administrative assistance. They shall submit files and documents to it via their highest authority.

. . .

Art. 30

(1) The Federal Constitutional Court shall decide in secret deliberations on the basis of its independent conviction resulting from the pleadings and the taking of evidence. The decision shall be drawn up in writing together with the reasons and signed by the participating judges. If oral pleadings have been held, it shall be proclaimed publicly together with the main reasons at a date announced during the pleadings and lying within three months of their termination. The date for the proclamation of the decision may be deferred by an order of the Federal Constitutional Court; in such case, the three-month time-limit may be exceeded.
(2) If, during the deliberations, a judge holds a dissenting view on the decision or the reasons, he may have it recorded in a separate opinion: the separate opinion shall be appended to the decision. In their decisions the panels may state the number of votes for and against. The details shall be laid down in rules of procedure adopted by the plenum of the Federal Constitutional Court.
(3) All decisions shall be forwarded to the parties.

. . .

Tenth Section
Procedure in cases pursuant to Art. 13 (6) above
(Review of law in general)

Art. 76

The application of the Federal Government, of a Land government or of one third of the Bundestag members pursuant to Art. 93 (1) (2) of the Basic Law shall be admissible only if one of the parties entitled to apply considers federal or Land law
1. null and void on account of its formal or material incompatibility with the Basic Law or other federal law, or
2. valid even though a court, administrative authority or a federal or Land organ did not apply the law because it deemed it incompatible with the Basic Law or other federal law.

Art. 77

The Federal Constitutional Court shall give the Bundestag, the Bundesrat, the Federal Government, and—in case of differences of opinion on the validity of federal law—the Land governments, and—in case of differences of opinion on the validity of a rule of Land law—the Parliament and Government of the Land in which the rule was announced, an opportunity to make a statement within a specified period.

Art. 78

If the Federal Constitutional Court comes to the conclusion that federal law is incompatible with the Basic Law or Land law is incompatible with the Basic Law or other federal law, it shall declare the law to be null and void. If further provisions of the same law are incompatible with the Basic Law or other federal law for the same reasons, the Federal Constitutional Court may also declare them to be null and void.

. . .

Eleventh Section
Procedure in cases pursuant to Art. 13 (11) above
(Review of specific laws)

Art. 80

(1) If the requirements of Art. 100 (1) of the Basic Law are met, the court shall directly obtain a decision by the Federal Constitutional Court.
(2) It must be stated in the reasons in what respect the decision of the court depends on the validity of the legal provision and the higher-ranking legal rule it is incompatible with. The files shall also be submitted.
(3) The application by the court shall be independent of the claim of nullity of the legal provision by a party to the proceedings.

Art. 81

The Federal Constitutional Court shall decide solely on the point of law.

Art. 82

(1) The provisions of Arts. 77 to 79 above shall apply *mutatis mutandis*.
(2) The constitutional organs named in Art. 77 above may join the proceedings at any stage.
(3) The Federal Constitutional Court shall also give the parties to the proceedings before the court making the application an opportunity to make a statement; it shall cite them to the oral proceedings and permit the agents for the case to speak.
(4) The Federal Constitutional Court may ask highest federal courts of justice or highest Land courts to state how and on the basis of what considerations they have hitherto interpreted the Basic Law with regard to the question in dispute, whether and how they have used in their exercise of justice the legal provision

whose validity is contested, and which associated points of law are awaiting decision. It may also ask them to expound their considerations on a point of law of relevance to the decision. The Federal Constitutional Court shall communicate such statement to the parties entitled to make a statement.

. . .

Art. 90

(1) Any person who claims that one of his basic rights or one of his rights under Arts. 20 (4), 33, 38, 101, 103 and 104 of the Basic Law has been violated by public authority may lodge a complaint of unconstitutionality with the Federal Constitutional Court.

(2) If legal action against the violation is admissible, the complaint of unconstitutionality may not be lodged until all remedies have been exhausted. However, the Federal Constitutional Court may decide immediately on a complaint of unconstitutionality lodged before all remedies have been exhausted if it is of general relevance or if recourse to other courts first would entail a serious and unavoidable disadvantage for the complainant.

(3) The right to lodge a complaint of unconstitutionality with the constitutional court of the Land in accordance with the provisions of the Land constitution shall remain unaffected.

. . .

Art. 93a

(1) A complaint of unconstitutionality shall require acceptance prior to a decision.

(2) A committee consisting of three judges, which shall be set up by the competent panel for one business year, shall subject the complaint of unconstitutionality to a preliminary examination. Each panel may appoint several committees.

(3) The committee may refuse acceptance of the complaint of unconstitutionality by a unanimous order if it is inadmissible or does not offer sufficient prospect of success for other reasons.

(4) If the committee does not refuse acceptance, the panel shall then decide on acceptance. It shall accept the complaint of unconstitutionality if at least two judges hold the view that a question of constitutional law is likely to be clarified by a decision or that the denial of a decision on the matter will entail a serious and unavoidable disadvantage for the complainant.

(5) The decisions of the committee or the panel shall be taken without oral pleadings and the reasons need not be stated. The order by which acceptance of a complaint of unconstitutionality is refused shall be communicated to the complainant by the committee or the presiding judge of the panel with reference to the legal aspect determining the refusal pursuant to paragraph 3 or 4 above.

. . .

Art. 95

(1) If the complaint of unconstitutionality is upheld, the decision shall state which provision of the Basic Law has been infringed and by which act or omission. The Federal Constitutional Court may at the same time declare that any repetition of the act or omission complained of will infringe the Basic Law.

(2) If a complaint of unconstitutionality against a decision is upheld, the Federal Constitutional Court shall quash the decision and in cases pursuant to the first sentence of Art. 90 (2) above it shall refer the matter back to a competent court.

(3) If a complaint of unconstitutionality against a law is upheld, the law shall be declared null and void. The same shall apply if a complaint of unconstitutionality pursuant to paragraph 2 above is upheld because the quashed decision is based on an unconstitutional law. The provisions of Art. 79 above shall apply *mutatis mutandis*.

. . .

Document 6

Official institutions in Germany are ordinarily governed by detailed standing orders or rules of procedure relating to their internal administration. The Federal Constitutional Court, however, operated for over two decades without a formal set of such rules, owing in part to the inability of the justices to agree on the partitioning of authority inside the Court. What is the relationship between the president and the plenum? (The latter consists of both panels acting together on matters of judicial administration or doctrine.) Is the former bound by the latter in matters of non-judicial administration? What authority may the president exert over other members of the Court? Who is responsible for the distribution or allocation of case loads among the justices inside the Court? Who appoints judicial research assistants and how many? These and related issues were the source of some tension over the years between the president and various justices. They were largely resolved in 1975 with the passage of the Law on the Rules of Procedure for the Federal Constitutional Court.

FEDERAL CONSTITUTIONAL COURT: RULES OF PROCEDURE [GO]
Source: BGBl., I, 1975, 2095, as amended up to and including 5 December 1978

Part A
Provisions on the Organization and Administration of the
Federal Constitutional Court

Art. 1

(1) The plenum and the President shall work together in the fulfilment of the functions of the court.

(2) The plenum shall deliberate and decide on the preparation of the budget of the court, on all questions directly concerning the judges, their status and their conditions of service, and, as required, on general principles relating to the administration of the court.

(3) The President shall exercise the powers conferred upon him by law and execute the decisions of the plenum on its behalf. He shall be in charge of the administration of the court; he shall discuss questions of fundamental importance with the plenum.

Art. 2

(1) The plenum shall be convened by the President as required, but at least once in the spring and in the autumn.

. . .

Art. 5

(1) The President shall represent the court in its external relations. If he is unable to do so, he shall deputize the Vice-President or, if this is not possible, the longest-serving judge present.

(2) The presentation of the opinions of the court and the safeguarding of its interests vis-à-vis the Federal President, the Bundestag, the Bundesrat, the Federal Government and their committees shall be the responsibility of the President in consultation with the Vice-President. They may be deputized for or supported by other judges.

. . .

Art. 13

(1) The research assistants shall assist the judge to whom they have been assigned in their official duties. They shall take instructions from such judge.

(2) Each judge is entitled to select his own research assistant. An assistant may not be assigned to him against his will.

. . .

Art. 14

(1) The President shall distribute the administrative business. He may generally assign certain business to the chief administrative officer (Director of the Federal Constitutional Court) to be conducted by the latter on his own.

(2) Administrative decisions which concern the judges and are not part of regular administrative business shall be taken by the President himself.

. . .

Part B
Supplementary Procedural Provisions

Title 1
Procedure of the Panels

Art. 20

(1) Before the start of a business year each panel shall decide, with effect from the start of that business year, on the principles according to which the applications for the institution of proceedings are to be distributed among the judges, including the presiding judge, in the capacity of rapporteurs. Deviation from these principles shall be admissible during the business year only if this becomes necessary because of an excessive workload or a judge being unable to perform his functions for an extended period.

(2) Applications which cannot be assigned in accordance with principles pursuant to paragraph 1 above shall be distributed among the judges, starting with the shortest-serving one, in the order in which they are received.

(3) Pursuant to paragraphs 1 and 2 above the presiding judge shall appoint the rapporteur. If a matter is particularly important he may, in consultation with the panel, appoint a co-rapporteur.

. . .

Art. 23

(1) For every matter to be decided by the panel the rapporteur shall produce a written report. At this point at the latest the members of the panel shall also receive the reference files containing all documents of relevance to the proceedings and the decision. In simple cases a draft decision with reasons may be produced instead of a report.

(2) There shall be a period of at least ten days between the distribution of the report and the deliberations or the oral pleadings.

Art. 24

(1) The panel shall decide whether to hold oral pleadings.

(2) As a rule, oral pleadings shall be based on an outline for the proceedings which has been approved by the panel and forwarded to the parties to the proceedings well in advance of the oral pleadings.

Art. 25

Only the judges participating in a case may attend the deliberations.

Art. 26

(1) After commencement of deliberations on a matter with less than eight judges they may not be joined by other judges. The deliberations may be recommenced only if there is not a statutory quorum for the continuation of the initial deliberations.

(2) Any judge who has participated in the decision may, until it is proclaimed or drawn up in writing for service, demand that the deliberations be continued if he intends to change his vote; he may request that the deliberations be continued if he wishes to present aspects not discussed previously or if he intends to write a separate opinion.

(3) Decisions which are not taken on the basis of oral pleadings shall be given the date on which they were finally taken.

. . .

Art. 31

(1) The decisions of the plenum pursuant to Art. 16 (1) of the Law on the Federal Constitutional Court and of the panels shall be published in a collection of the decisions of the Federal Constitutional Court, authorized by the court itself, unless the plenum or the panel rules out publication. The decision to this effect shall be recorded in the files.

. . .

Title 2
Procedure in the Committees pursuant to Art. 93a (2) of the Law on the Federal Constitutional Court

Art. 38

(1) For the purposes of the preliminary examination of complaints of unconstitutionality pursuant to Art. 93a of the Law on the Federal Constitutional Court each panel shall appoint several committees at the start of a business year and lay down their composition.

(2) The President and the Vice-president shall chair the committees which they belong to, and the longest-serving judge in each case shall chair the others.

(3) The composition of a committee shall not remain unchanged for more than three years.

Art. 39

(1) Each committee shall decide—normally on the basis of a vote—on the acceptance of all complaints of unconstitutionality which are assigned to one of its members as rapporteur. A formal decision is not necessary if the committee does not refuse acceptance.

. . .

(3) The committee may also—as long as a decision has not been taken on the acceptance of a complaint of unconstitutionality—reject by a unanimous decision an application for the issue of a temporary injunction. If the committee refuses acceptance of the complaint of unconstitutionality, the application for the issue of a temporary injunction in connection with this matter shall become invalid.

. . .

Title 4
Procedure in the Plenum pursuant to Art. 16 of the Law on the Federal Constitutional Court

Art. 47

(1) The panel which intends to deviate in a point of law from the legal opinion contained in a decision by the other panel or the plenum shall invoke the plenum by means of a decision of the panel.

(2) Invocation of the plenum shall not be necessary if the panel from whose decision deviation is intended states, upon inquiry, that it will not adhere to its legal opinion.

Art. 48

(1) The presiding judge of each panel shall appoint a rapporteur to prepare the decision of the plenum. Each rapporteur shall submit a report at least ten days before the plenary meeting.

(2) The reasons shall be stated for the decision of the plenum. It shall be treated like decisions of the panels.

. . .

Title 6
Procedure in the Event of a Separate Vote pursuant to Art. 30 (2) of the Law on the Federal Constitutional Court

Art. 55

(1) The separate vote in which a judge records the dissenting opinion on the decision or the reasons which he held during the deliberations must be submitted to the presiding judge of the panel within three weeks of completion of the decision. The panel may extend this time-limit.

(2) Anyone intending to submit a separate vote [opinion] must inform the panel of this as soon as the state of the deliberations permits.

(3) The decision shall also be signed by the dissenting judge. The separate vote shall be signed by the dissenting judge alone.

Notes

1. See also Ch. 5, 118
2. Inserted by an amendment law of 29 January 1969
3. See also Ch. 6, 165ff.
4. See also Ch. 5, Doc 6
5. For cases, see Ch. 3, Doc. 9; Ch. 5; Ch. 6, Doc. 2; Ch. 10, Doc 9

5 Basic Rights and Constitutional Review

Donald P. Kommers

The Basic Law includes an impressive charter of fundamental rights and freedoms. Such a charter of rights was also included in the Weimar Constitution. But there the relevant articles were not given the priority which they enjoy under the Basic Law of the Federal Republic. The Basic Law starts off with the charter of rights and makes certain that they cannot, as was possible in Weimar, be subjected to amendments as far as their 'substance' is concerned. The rights specifically guaranteed reflect the dominant influence both of the Social and Christian Democratic Parties in the Parliamentary Council (Parlamentarischer Rat,[1]) as well as Germany's experience with totalitarian government. One manifestation of socialist influence is the limitation on the right to property; under Art. 15, for example, natural resources, land, and the means of production may be transferred to public ownership. A manifestation of Christian influence is the basic right conferred upon parents to have their children receive religious education in public (state) schools[2] in accordance with their religious views, and the incorporation into the Basic Law of certain provisions of the Weimar Constitution concerning the public rights of religious organizations.

Apart from these and related provisions, the charter of rights also guarantees all of the fundamental freedoms against the state—so-called negative freedoms—traditionally associated with western liberal democracies. These include the freedom of speech, press, religious belief, association, and movement. Included in the Basic Rights charter are also guarantees of the right to choose a trade or occupation, the right to marry and raise a family, and the right to refuse military service for reasons of conscience. These basic liberties are defined as 'inalienable

---

* Notes for this chapter begin on p. 137

human rights', constituting 'the basis of every community, of peace and justice in the world'. Moreover, as the Federal Constitutional Court has ruled, the Basic Law establishes a value-oriented constitutional order based on human dignity. Art. 1 proclaims: 'The dignity of man shall be inviolable. To respect and protect it shall be the duty of all state authority.' Human dignity, according to the Constitutional Court, is the foundation stone of all fundamental rights and liberties. Indeed, under the terms of Art. 79 of the Basic Law, Art. 1 is beyond the amendatory power of Parliament as are in fact all the basic rights Articles. By the same token, Art. 19, para. 2, attaches a preferred status to fundamental rights by specifying that 'the essential content of a basic right [may not be] encroached upon'.

On the other hand, while obliging the state to respect human dignity and individual rights, the charter of freedoms predicates these rights upon the observance of certain principles of political obligation. Thus, every person has the right to the free development of his personality so long as 'he does not violate the rights of others or offend against the constitutional order or the moral code' (Art. 2, para. 1). Freedom of expression is 'limited by the provisions of the general laws, provisions of law for the protection of youth, and by the right to inviolability of personal honour' (Art. 5, para. 2). Freedom to teach 'does not absolve from loyalty to the Constitution' (Art. 5, para. 3). All Germans have the right to associate, but activities 'directed against the constitutional order or the concept of international understanding are prohibited' (Art. 9). Moreover, freedoms of expression, press, teaching, assembly, and association may be forfeited if used 'to combat the free democratic basic order' (Art. 18; Doc. 1).

Just as the Basic Law has absolutized Art. 1, it also renders certain concepts of the constitutional structure beyond Parliament's amendatory power. As we have seen, a number of these system values are identified in the charter of rights itself. But these values, against which the exercise of basic rights is often weighed, are also found in a number of other constitutional provisions. For example, Art. 20, which like Art. 1 cannot be changed under the terms of Art. 79, defines the Federal Republic as a 'democratic and social federal state'. Another example is Art. 21. While guaranteeing the right of political parties freely to 'form the political will of the people', it cautions that 'parties which, by reason of their aims or the behaviour of their adherents, seek to impair or abolish the free democratic basic order or to endanger the existence of the Federal Republic of Germany, shall be unconstitutional'. Such provisions spring from the abiding conviction of the founding fathers, who drafted the

Basic Law against the background of Weimar's democracy and Hitler's dictatorship, that a democracy is not an unarmed society, and that it has the right to dissolve organizations and to prohibit activities aimed at the destruction of republican and democratic (the so-called 'free democratic basic order' or 'freiheitlich-demokratische Grundordnung') government so long as the rule of law is thereby observed and protected.[3]

As the material in the previous chapter indicates, the Federal Constitutional Court serves as a principal guardian of constitutional rights in the Federal Republic. Any person who feels that one of his basic rights has been violated by the state (federal or Land) or any of its agents may lodge, after exhausting all other legal remedies, a constitutional complaint with the Federal Constitutional Court. But Länder and federal governments may also petition the Court, in appropriate cases, to vindicate the basic concepts of the constitutional system. The courts have to ask for a ruling of the Court if doubts are raised as to the conformity of any legal provision referred to in court proceedings with the constitution (Basic Law). In any case, as the constitutional cases in this chapter illustrate, the Court's job is the very difficult one of balancing competing and equally legitimate rights of the individual and of drawing the line between individual rights and system values. The Socialist Reich Party Case presented the Court with its first opportunity to interpret the meaning of the broad terms 'free democratic basic order' and to identify with greater specificity than before those principles that undergird the political system as a whole (Doc. 2). The Lüth-Harlan Case (Doc. 3) also presented the Court with one of its earliest opportunities to articulate the theory of free speech informing the Basic Law. The Religious Freedom Cases (Doc. 4) underscore not only the essential content of free exercise doctrine but also the role of religious bodies in the public life of the Federal Republic. The Abortion Case (Doc. 5) illustrates the tension between the constitutional guarantees of the right to life and to the free development of one's personality.

The remaining materials which are being presented in this chapter serve to highlight the conflict between the need for internal security and basic freedoms of speech and political association. The Civil Servant Loyalty Case (Doc. 6) is an attempt on the Court's part to reconcile conflicting rights under the Basic Law, among them the right to choose a trade or profession and the corresponding right of equality of access to the civil service. Finally, a short 'case history' of the Federal Republic's attempt to deal with a problem of internal security is presented. The three documents in this section are (1) the provision of the Basic Law guaranteeing privacy of communications, (2) the federal law limiting this

right, and (3) the Federal Constitutional Court's decision on the constitutionality of the law (Doc. 7).

Document 1

Several fundamental rights of persons quoted below trace their lineage to
the Weimar Constitution and even to the Frankfurt Constitution of
1848/9. Included also are articles from the Weimar Constitution pertaining to questions of religious freedom that have been incorporated into
the Basic Law. These articles are important for a proper understanding
of church–state relations in the Federal Republic. Absent from the list of
articles below are certain procedural rights guaranteed by the Basic Law,
particularly in criminal cases, along with the Constitution's ban on
capital punishment.[4] Finally, it should be noted that the Weimar Constitution did not empower the judiciary to enforce basic personal rights
against the state. Under the Bonn Constitution, the judiciary is clearly
empowered to enforce these rights as the documents in the previous
chapter showed.

EXCERPTS FROM THE BASIC LAW
Source: German Press and Information Office
Transl: Official

I: Basic Rights

Art. 1

(1) The dignity of man shall be inviolable. To respect and protect it shall be the
duty of all state authority.
(2) The German people therefore acknowledge inviolable and inalienable human
rights as the basis of every community, of peace and justice in the world.
(3) The following basic rights shall bind the legislature, the executive and the
judiciary as directly enforceable law.

Art. 2

(1) Everyone shall have the right to the free development of his personality in so
far as he does not violate the rights of others or offend against the constitutional
order or the moral code.
(2) Everyone shall have the right to life and to inviolability of his person. The
liberty of the individual shall be inviolable. These rights may only be encroached
upon pursuant to a law.

Art. 3

(1) All persons shall be equal before the law.
(2) Men and women shall have equal rights.
(3) No one may be prejudiced or favoured because of his sex, his parentage, his race, his language, his homeland and origin, his faith, or his religious or political opinions.

Art. 4

(1) Freedom of faith, of conscience, and freedom of creed, religious or ideological (weltanschaulich), shall be inviolable.
(2) The undisturbed practice of religion is guaranteed.
. . .

Art. 5

(1) Everyone shall have the right freely to express and disseminate his opinion by speech, writing and pictures and freely to inform himself from generally accessible sources. Freedom of the press and freedom of reporting by means of broadcasts and films are guaranteed. There shall be no censorship.

. . .

Art. 6

(1) Marriage and family shall enjoy the special protection of the state.
(2) The care and upbringing of children are a natural right of, and a duty primarily incumbent on, the parents. The national community shall watch over their endeavours in this respect.

. . .

Art. 7

(1) The entire educational system shall be under the supervision of the state.
(2) The persons entitled to bring up a child shall have the right to decide whether it shall receive religious instruction.
(3) Religious instruction shall form part of the ordinary curriculum in state and municipal schools, except in secular (bekenntnisfrei) schools. . . .

Art. 8

(1) All Germans shall have the right to assemble peaceably and unarmed without prior notification or permission.

. . .

Art. 9

(1) All Germans shall have the right to form associations and societies.

. . .

Art. 12

(1) All Germans shall have the right freely to choose their trade, occupation, or profession, their place of work and their place of training. . . .

Art. 14

(1) Property and the right of inheritance are guaranteed. Their content and limits shall be determined by the laws.

. . .

(3) Expropriation shall be permitted only in the public weal. . . .

. . .

Article 19

. . .

(4) Should any person's right be violated by public authority, recourse to the court shall be open to him. If jurisdiction is not specified, recourse shall be to the ordinary courts. . . .

Appendix to the Basic Law

Art. 135. Weimar Constitution of 11 August 1919

(1) Civil and political rights and duties shall be neither dependent on nor restricted by the exercise of the freedom of religion.
(2) The enjoyment of civil and political rights and eligibility for public office shall be independent of religious creed.
(3) No one shall be bound to disclose his religious convictions. . . .

. . .

Art. 137. Weimar Constitution

(1) There shall be no state church.
(2) Freedom of association to form religious bodies is guaranteed. . . .

. . .

(5) Religious bodies shall remain corporate bodies under public law in so far as they have been such heretofore. . . .

. . .

(7) Associations whose purpose is the cultivation of a philosophical ideology shall have the same status as religious bodies.

. . .

Art. 139. Weimar Constitution

Sunday and the public holidays recognized by the state shall remain under legal protection as days of rest from work and of spiritual edification.

. . .

Document 2

That political parties should be the principal agents of parliamentary representation is one of the tenets of modern German constitutional theory. Art. 21, paragraph 1, of the Basic Law provides: 'The political parties shall participate in forming the political will of the people. They can be freely formed. Their internal organization must conform to democratic principles. They must publicly account for the sources of their funds'.[5] Para. 2 of the same article, however, makes very clear that totalitarian parties shall not be tolerated. It provides : 'Parties which, by reason of their aims or the behaviour of their adherents, seek to impair or abolish the free democratic basic order or to endanger the existence of the Federal Republic of Germany, shall be unconstitutional. The Federal Constitutional Court shall decide on the question of unconstitutionality.' Under Art. 43 of the Federal Constitutional Court Organization Act, however, only the Bundestag, Bundesrat, or Federal Government is empowered to petition the Court for an order declaring a party unconstitutional. Up to the present time the Court has declared two parties unconstitutional: the neo-Nazi Socialist Reich Party (Sozialistische Reichspartei) in 1952 and the Communist Party of Germany (Kommunistische Partei Deutschlands) in 1956. In both instances the Federal Government, led by Chancellor Konrad Adenauer, initiated the proceeding before the Federal Constitutional Court.

THE SOCIALIST REICH PARTY CASE

Source: Entscheidungen des Bundesverfassungsgerichts, Vol. 2, 1952, 1–78
Transl: Renata Chestnut, in Walter F. Murphy and Joseph Tanenhaus, *Comparative Constitutional Law*, New York, 1977, 602–7

[Political Parties and the Free Democratic Basic Order]

German constitutions following World War I hardly mentioned political parties, although even at that time . . . the democratic constitutional life was to a large extent determined by parties. The reasons for this omission are manifold, but in the last analysis, the cause lies in a democratic ideology that refused to recognize groups mediating between the free individual and the will of the entire people composed of the sum of individual wills and represented in parliament by deputies as 'representatives of the entire people' . . .

The Basic Law abandoned this viewpoint and, more realistically, expressly recognizes parties as agents—even if not the only ones—forming the political will of the people.

. . .

In a free democratic state, as it corresponds to German constitutional development, freedom of association even for associations of a political kind are guaranteed to individual citizens as basic rights. On the other hand, it is part of the nature of every democracy that the supreme power derived from the people is exercised in elections and voting. In the reality of the large modern democratic state, however, this popular will can emerge only through parties as operating political units. Both fundamental ideas lead to the basic conclusion that establishment and activity of political parties must not be restrained.

The framer of the German Constitution was confronted with the question of whether he could fully implement this conclusion or whether he should not rather, enlightened by recent experiences, draw certain limits in this area. He had to consider whether absolute freedom to establish parties on the basis of any political idea should not be limited by principles governing a particular democracy, and whether parties seeking to abolish democracy by using formal democractic means must not be excluded from political processes. In this connection the danger had to be taken into account that the Government might also be tempted to eliminate troublesome opposition parties.

Art. 21 of the Basic Law has tried to master these problems. On the one hand, it establishes the principle that formation of political parties shall be free. On the other hand, it offers a means of preventing activity by 'unconstitutional' parties. To avert the danger of an abuse of this means, Art. 21 authorizes the Federal Constitutional Court to decide the question of unconstitutionality and attempts to determine as far as possible the factual requirements for such a declaration.

. . .

According to the constitutional-political decision made by the Basic Law, the essential constitutional order is in the last analysis founded upon the idea that man has an independent value of his own and that freedom and equality are permanent, intrinsic values of national unity. Thus, the basic order is an order heavily laden with values that oppose those of the totalitarian state which ... rejects human dignity, freedom, and equality ...

Thus, the free democratic basic order can be defined as an order which excludes any form of tyranny or arbitrariness and represents a governmental system under a rule of law, based upon self-determination of the people as expressed by the will of the existing majority and upon freedom and equality. The fundamental principles of this order include at least: respect for the human rights given concrete form in the Basic Law, in particular for the right of a person to life and free development; popular sovereignty; separation of powers; responsibility of government; lawfulness of administration; independence of the judiciary; the multi-party principle; and equality of opportunities for all political parties.

...

The behaviour of the [SRP] party and its members, as do the personnel and organizational relationships between the SRP and the NSDAP, demonstrates that the goal of the SRP is to topple the free democratic basic order.

The very same circles which made it possible for Hitler to lead Germany into the abyss are now again trying to assert their political leadership. They enjoy his means and recommend the same ways that resulted in Germany's being torn apart.

In a very unconcerned manner they declare their approval of Hitler ...

[Conclusion]

The SRP is thus unconstitutional in the sense stipulated in Art. 21, para. 2, of the Basic Law ... The party, therefore, must be dissolved.

Document 3

The Lüth–Harlan Case is a seminal decision in West German free speech jurisprudence. Harlan was a popular film director under the Nazi regime and best known for producing anti-semitic films. In 1950, several years after he had been acquitted of committing crimes against humanity, he directed a new movie, *Immortal Lover*. Erich Lüth, Hamburg's Public Press Superintendent, called upon film distributors and theatre owners not to show the movie at a German film festival because of Harlan's Nazi past. The film company obtained an injunction from a district court forbidding Lüth to call for a boycott of *Immortal Lover*. The Supreme Court of Hamburg affirmed, whereupon Lüth filed a constitutional complaint with the First Senate of the Federal Constitutional

Court, claiming that the injunction violated his rights under Art. 5 of the Basic Law.

THE LÜTH–HARLAN CASE

Source: Entscheidungen des Bundesverfassungsgerichts, Vol. 7, 1958, 198–230 *Transl.:* John C. Lane and James K. Pollock, *Source Materials on the Government and Politics of Germany*, Ann Arbor, 1964 (122–3 below); Renata Chestnut, in Murphy and Tanenhaus, ibid. (124 below)

. . . The fundamental question whether constitutional provisions have an effect in civil law and how this effect must be considered in particular instances is a matter of dispute. . . . An extreme position in this controversy is, on the one hand, the thesis that the basic rights are addressed exclusively to the state. On the other hand, there is the opinion that at least some, or at any rate the most important, of these rights are applicable in civil law relations as between anyone. The previous jurisprudence of the Federal Constitutional Court cannot be used in support of either one or the other of these extremes of opinion. . . . Nor is there occasion now for the controversy over the so-called 'third person effect' of the basic rights to be discussed in its full scope. The following will suffice for reaching an appropriate decision:

Without doubt the basic rights are above all designed to secure the sphere of individual freedom against invasions by public power (*öffentliche Gewalt*); they are the defensive rights of citizens against the state. This follows from the historical development of the idea of basic rights and from the historical events that led to the inclusion of basic rights in the constitutions of various states. The basic rights of the Basic Law have a like import. The Basic Law meant to emphasize the priority of the individual and his dignity as against the power of the state by giving the basic rights section first place. It is in accord with this that the legislature permitted the special legal relief for the protection of these rights, the constitutional complaint, only against acts of the public power.

But it is equally true that the Basic Law, which does not constitute a value-free order, erected in its basic rights section an objective order of values and it is precisely here that one finds an expression of the fundamental strengthening of the scope of the basic rights . . . This value system, whose core is the freely developing personality and its dignity within the social community must, as a basic constitutional decision, be applicable in all areas of the law; legislation, administration and adjudication receive from it direction and impetus. Thus, it naturally influences also civil law; no civil law provision may be in contradiction to it and each must be interpreted in its spirit. . . . Just as new law must be in harmony with the Basic Law's value system, so must existing old law be attuned in its content to this value system; from the latter there flows into it a specific constitutional content which henceforth determines its interpretation. A controversy between private citizens over rights and duties under civil law rules thus influenced by the basic rights remains substantively and procedurally a civil law controversy. . . .

While the Federal Constitutional Court is not competent to act as a court of appeals or as a 'super-revisional' body for civil courts, it may neither abstain from a review of their decisions and ignore any mistakings of basic law norms or standards that may possibly be evident to them. . . .

. . . The basic right of free speech, as the most direct expression of the human personality in society, is one of the highest human rights altogether. . . . The general laws must be viewed, in regard to their inhibiting effect on the basic right, in the light of the significance of this basic right, and they must be so interpreted that the particular value content of the right . . . remains in every case inviolate. . . .

Speech as such, i.e. in its purely intellectual effect, is free, but when it impairs a legally protected right of another, a right which is entitled to protection against speech, then this impairment does not become permissible just because it was committed by means of speech. A weighing of interests (*Güterabwägung*) becomes necessary: The right of speech must yield if protected interests of a higher rank would be violated by the exercise of free speech. Whether such overriding interests of others exist must be determined on the basis of all the circumstances of the case. . . .

To determine whether an invitation to a boycott . . . is contrary to public morals requires that the motives, aim and purpose of the utterances be examined first. It needs to be established, further, that in the pursuit of his aims the petitioner [in the case below] did not exceed the necessary and appropriate limits of impairment of the interests of Harlan and the film company.

. . . Clearly the motives which prompted the petitioner in his remarks are not contrary to public morals. The petitioner did not pursue his own economic interests. . . . [Furthermore] the remarks of the petitioner must be viewed in the context of his general political and cultural concerns. . . . The petitioner was legitimized to express his views publicly because of his particularly close connection with all matters of German–Jewish relations. . . .

When it is a question of forming public opinion on a question important for the public welfare, then private and particularly economic interests of individuals must generally yield (*zurücktreten*). These interests do not thereby become unprotected, for the value of the basic right becomes apparent in the very fact that everyone may avail himself of it. Whoever feels himself injured by utterances of another may reply in public himself . . . Only in the clash of opinions voiced in equal freedom can public opinion be formed and can the individuals who are addressed form their own opinions. . . .

It is beyond question that the state . . . could and can proceed against Harlan only within the limits of the laws. But this does not settle anything about what the individual citizen may undertake or say regarding Harlan. What is decisive here is that every individual is the possessor of the same basic rights. . . . The argument of the Land Supreme Court of Hamburg . . . , that 'since the state does not possess the power [to do certain things], such power can especially not be possessed by individual citizens', is erroneous. ...

The petitioner has appealed out of pure motives to the moral feelings of the affected groups and has asked them to take an irreproachably moral stand. This was not misunderstood in the public mind. ...

The complainant's statements must be seen within the context of his general political and cultural efforts. He was moved by the fear that Harlan's re-appearance might—especially in foreign countries—be interpreted to mean that nothing had changed in German cultural life since the National Socialist period. ... These apprehensions concerned a very important issue for the German people. ... Nothing has damaged the German reputation as much as the cruel Nazi persecution of Jews. There exists therefore a crucial interest in assuring the world that the German people have abandoned this attitude and condemn it, not for reasons of political opportunism, but because through an inner conversion they have come to realize its evil.

The complainant's apprehensions were not later rationalizations, but corresponded to the state of affairs as it presented itself to him at that time. This has later been confirmed by, among other things, the fact that the attempt to show the film *Immortal Lover* in Switzerland caused strong protests and even an interpellation in the National Council and an official statement by the Bundesrat ... The film was unanimously rejected not because of its content, but because of Harlan's part in it, and was not shown as a result of these numerous emphatic interventions. In several German cities, too, there were demonstrations against presentation of the film for the same reasons. ...

The District Court considers it permissible that the complainant expressed an opinion about the reappearance of Harlan, but it reprimands him for having exhorted public behaviour. This distinction overlooks the fact that the complainant, if he is permitted to express a negative opinion about Harlan's reappearance, hardly went beyond what was already contained in this value judgment. ...

Because of his especially close personal relation to all that concerned the German–Jewish relationship, the complainant was within his rights to state his view in public. Even at that time he was already known for his efforts towards reestablishing a true inner peace with the Jewish people. He held a leading position in the Society for Christian–Jewish Cooperation; a short time before, he had initiated the campaign 'Peace with Israel' on the radio and in the press. ... It is understandable that he feared all these efforts might be disturbed and thwarted by Harlan's reappearance. But he could also proceed from the assumption that the public expected him especially to make a statement on this matter. ...

The demand that under these circumstances the complainant should nevertheless, out of regard for Harlan's professional interests and the economic interests of the film companies employing him, have refrained from expressing his opinion ... is unjustified.

[Judgment reversed]

Documents (4a-b)

The religious provisions of the Basic Law have been interpreted broadly to protect both religious and non-religious belief systems (Weltanschauungen). In addition, the protection of all faiths and beliefs is reinforced by the anti-discrimination clauses of Art. 3 and 33, together with Art. 140, provisions that bar any prejudicial or favoured treatment based on a person's 'faith or his religion or political opinion'. The state's neutrality with respect to religious matters is the central concept behind the Basic Law's church–state provisions. The neutrality, however, is one that emphasizes a cooperative rather than a separationist mode of church–state relations. The Weimar articles carried over into the Basic Law confer public corporate status on the major denominations and guarantee self-governing autonomy to 'religious bodies', including their right to own and maintain property for religious, educational, and charitable purposes, an acknowledgement of the importance ascribed by the Constitution to the social role that religion plays in the life of society.

The extracts below are taken from two cases challenging certain applications of the church tax.[6] All wage earners are subject to a church tax ranging between 8 and 10 percent of their net taxable income. An employee must formally resign his or her church membership—as did 238,000 persons in 1975—to be exempted from the tax. Collected by state revenue officers, these taxes are distributed to the major denominations in amounts proportionate to their total membership. The Federal Constitutional Court has sustained the general validity of the church tax, although it has occasionally invalidated its application to particular persons in situations where the tax has been deemed to infringe religious freedom. The following passages summarize the general theory of religious freedom and church-state relations in West Germany.

a) CHURCH TAX, I, 1965

Source: Entscheidungen des Bundesverfassungsgerichts, Vol. 18, 1965, 386f.; Vol. 19, 1966, 217ff.

. . .

There can be no state church under the system of church-state relations prescribed by the Basic Law. Every religious community has the right to order and administer its affairs independently within the limits of law applicable to all. Neither the state nor the civic community is permitted to involve itself in the selection of church officials. Churches are institutions endowed with the right of self-determination. Their nature is such as to render them independent of state influence. Thus the state may not interfere in their internal affairs.

Churches are defined by the constitution as corporate bodies under public law (Art. 140 of the Basic Law and Art. 137 of the Weimar Constitution). But their independence is not thereby compromised. This legal characterization does not signify an equality in status to other public law corporations within the organic structure of the state. It is only a recognition of their public status. That status, while higher than that of religious societies organized under private law, does not subordinate the churches to the supreme authority of the state or to close administrative supervision. To the extent that they exercise power conferred by the state, adopt measures beyond their authority as church bodies, or intrude into the domain of the state, they indirectly exercise governmental authority; but in such cases their self-determination is limited. . . .

b) CHURCH TAX, II, 1966

Source: Ibid.

. . .

Art. 137, para. 6, of the Weimar Constitution authorizes religious societies organized as corporate bodies under public law to levy taxes 'on the basis of the state's civil tax lists'. The state is obligated to establish the conditions for the levying of such taxes, thus providing for the possibility of their compulsory collection. This sovereign right of tax collection granted by the state is quite different from the process of collecting contributions, which is an internal affair of the church. Pursuant to Art. 137, para. 3 (of the Weimar Constitution), religious societies are able to impose fees and contribution requirements without state interference. The levy of the church tax, on the other hand, is a common affair of both church and state. Here the state makes its own administrative apparatus available to the church for the collection of the tax. State regulation is necessary to administer the tax. For that reason, the levying of the church tax is also subject to judicial review.

. . .

According to Art. 4, para. 1, Art. 3, para. 3, and Art. 33, para. 3 of the Basic Law, together with Art. 136, paras. 1 and 4 and Art. 137, para. 1 of the Weimar Constitution in conjunction with Art. 140 of the Basic Law the state as the home of all citizens is bound by ideological and religious neutrality. The Basic Law prohibits the introduction of official religious forms as well as the granting of any privilege to a religious denomination. This requirement of religious and denominational neutrality means that the state is not permitted to confer on a religious society any sovereign authority over individuals who are not among its members.

Religious societies exercise sovereign authority, however, when pursuant to state law they tax persons who are not among their members. . . . In the exercise of this authority the state by means of its taxing power is effectively providing financial support for religious societies. This the state may not do when the taxing power reaches persons who do not belong to those religious societies. The churches in their corporate character may only obligate their own members through the power of taxation.

No significance is to be derived from the historical fact that religious societies once held a privileged position under the law. State churches in the sense that they were formally known no longer exist in the light of the prohibition against an official church. Churches no longer have the legal capacity unilaterally to enrol persons, without regard to their wishes, who settle within their territorial jurisdiction. Indeed, the Weimar Constitution had already deprived them of any such territorial control; rather their authority was to extend only to persons within their membership.

Documents 5a-b

In 1974 the Bundestag passed the Abortion Reform Act. Prior to that time an abortion carried out at any stage of pregnancy and for any reason other than to preserve the life and health of the woman was a criminal offence under German law. Backed by a majority of SPD and FDP members of the liberalized act provided as follows: firstly, termination of pregnancy would no longer be punishable during the first twelve weeks after conception if performed by a licensed physician with the consent of the pregnant woman; secondly, destruction of the foetus would be permissible after the first twelve weeks if warranted by medical or eugenic indications and procured prior to the twenty-second week of pregnancy; finally, the person or physician terminating the pregnancy—not the pregnant woman—would be punishable under the act. Criminal penalties would continue to operate with respect to abortions performed after the third month of pregnancy, except in those instances where medical, eugenic, or ethical indications would justify the foetus' destruction. Christian Democratic members of the Bundestag and five of the ten Länder under CDU or CSU control challenged the validity of the statute in the Federal Constitutional Court. The law was declared invalid, the consequence being that Parliament was required to amend the law in conformity with the Court's decision. Abortion is now permited, but only under four specified conditions.

a) THE ABORTION REFORM ACT

Source: Entscheidungen des Bundesverfassungsgerichts, Vol. 39, 1975, 1–95

1. The embryonic life which grows up in the womb possesses, as far as the law is concerned, a value in itself which enjoys the protection of the Constitution (Art. 2, Section 2, Clause 1; Art. 1, Section 1 of the Basic Law).

2. The duty of the state to provide protection not only prohibits direct state interference with the embryomic life; it also requires the state to offer its protection and support to this embryo.

3. The protection of the life of the embryo takes, as a matter of principle, precedence over the right of self-determination of the pregnant woman. It does so for the entire period of the pregnancy and must not be called into question for a specific time-span.

4. The law-maker may also use other means than that of a threat of punishment in order to express legal rejection of abortion which is prescribed as a matter of principle. What is decisive is whether the sum-total of the measures which are taken to protect the unborn child guarantees actual protection to a level which is commensurate with the value of this protected subject. In an extreme case, when the protection of the Basic Law can in no way be provided by other means, the law-maker is under an obligation to use the means of criminal prosecution in order to safeguard the embryonic life.

5. A continuation of a pregnancy is intolerable, if an abortion is necessary in order to remove a threat to the pregnant woman's life or the danger of serious damage to her health. Beyond this, the law-maker is at liberty to define as intolerable other extraordinary burdens upon the pregnant woman, which have a similarly heavy weight, and not to impose criminal sanctions in these cases.

6. The Fifth Law on the Reform of the Criminal Code of 18 June 1974 (BGBl. I, p. 1297) has failed to live up to the required extent to the constitutional duty of protecting the embryonic life.

b) THE ABORTION REFORM ACT (COMMENTARIES)

Source: Entscheidungen des Bundesverfassungsgerichts, Vol. 39, 1975, 1–95
Transl: Robert E. Jones and John D. Garby, 'West German Abortion Decision: A Contrast to Roe V. Wade—With Commentaries', *The John Marshall Journal of Practice and Procedure,* Spring 1976, 605–84

. . .

1) Article 2, Paragraph 2, Sentence 1, of the Basic Law also protects the life developing itself in the womb of the mother as an intrinsic legal value.

a) The express incorporation into the Basic Law of the self-evident right to life—in contrast to the Weimar Constitution—may be explained principally as a reaction to the 'destruction of life unworthy of life', to the 'final solution' and 'liquidations', which were carried out by the National Socialistic Regime as measures of state. Article 2, Paragraph 2, Sentence 1, of the Basic Law, just as it contains the abolition of the death penalty in Article 102, includes 'a declaration of the fundamental worth of human life and of a concept of the state which stands, in emphatic contrast to the philosophies of a political regime to which the individual life meant little and which therefore practiced limitless abuse with its presumed right over life and death of the citizen' (Decisions of the Federal Constitutional Court, 18, 112, 117).

b) In construing Article 2, Paragraph 2, Sentence 1, of the Basic Law, one should begin with its language: 'Everyone has a right to life . . .'. Life, in the sense of historical existence of a human individual, exists according to definite biological-physiological knowledge, in any case, from the 14th day after conception (nidation, individuation) (*cf.* on this point the statements of Hinrichsen before the Special Committee for the Reform of the Penal Law, Sixth Election Period, 74th Session, Stenographic Reports, p. 2142 ff.). The process of development which has begun at that point is a continuing process which exhibits no sharp demarcation and does not allow a precise division of the various steps of development of the human life. The process does not end even with birth; the phenomena of consciousness which are specific to the human personality, for example, appear for the first time a rather long time after birth. Therefore, the protection of Article 2, Paragraph 2, Sentence 1, of the Basic Law cannot be limited either to the 'completed' human being after birth or to the child about to be born which is independently capable of living. The right to life is guaranteed to everyone who 'lives'; no distinction can be made here between various stages of the life developing itself before birth, or between unborn and born life. 'Everyone' in the sense of Article 2, Paragraph 2, Sentence 1, of the Basic Law is 'everyone living'; expressed in another way: every life possessing human individuality; 'everyone' also includes the yet unborn human being. . . .

. . .

II

1. The duty of the state to protect is comprehensive. It forbids not only—self-evidently—direct state attacks on the life developing itself but also requires the state to take a position protecting and promoting this life, that is to say, it must, above all, preserve it even against illegal attacks by others. It is for the individual areas of the legal order, each according to its special function, to effectuate this requirement. The degree of seriousness with which the state must take its obligation to protect increases as the rank of the legal value in question increases in importance within the order of values of the Basic Law, an ultimate value, the particulars of which need not be established; it is the living foundation of human dignity and the prerequisite for all other fundamental rights.

2. The obligation of the state to take the life developing itself under protection exists, as a matter of principle, even against the mother. Without doubt, the natural connection of unborn life with that of the mother establishes an especially unique relationship, for which there is no parallel in other circumstances of life. Pregnancy belongs to the sphere of intimacy of the woman, the protection of which is constitutionally guaranteed through Article 2, Paragraph 1, in connection with Article 1, Paragraph 1, of the Basic Law. Were the embryo to be considered only as a part of the maternal organism the interruption of pregnancy would remain in the area of the private structuring of one's life, where the legislature is forbidden to encroach (Decisions of the Federal Constitutional Court, 6, 32 41; 6, 389 433; 27, 344 350; 32 373 379). Since, however, the one about to be born is an independent human being who stands under the protection

of the constitution, there is a social dimension to the interruption of pregnancy which makes it amenable to and in need of regulation by the state. The right of the woman to the free development of her personality, which has as its content the freedom of behaviour in a comprehensive sense and accordingly embraces the personal responsibility of the woman to decide against parenthood and the responsibilities flowing from it, can also, it is true, likewise demand recognition and protection. This right, however, is not guaranteed without limits—the rights of others, the constitutional order, and the moral law limit. *A priori*, this right can never include the authorization to intrude upon the protected sphere of right of another without justifying reason or much less to destroy that sphere along with the life itself; this is even less so, if, according to the nature of the case, a special responsibility exists precisely for this life.

A compromise which guarantees the protection of the life of the one about to be born and permits the pregnant woman the freedom of abortion is not possible since the interruption of pregnancy always means the destruction of the unborn life. In the required balancing, 'both constitutional values are to be viewed in their relationship to human dignity, the center of the value system of the constitution' (Decisions of the Federal Constitutional Court, 35, 202 225). A decision oriented to Article 1, Paragraph 1, of the Basic Law must come down in favor of the precedence of the protection of life for the child *en ventre sa mere* over the right of the pregnant woman to self-determination. Regarding many opportunities for development of personality, she can be adversely affected through pregnancy, birth and the education of her children. On the other hand, the unborn life is destroyed through the interruption of pregnancy. According to the principle of the balance which preserves most of competing constitutionally protected positions in view of the fundamental idea of Article 19, Paragraph 2, of the Basic Law; precedence must be given to the protection of the life of the child about to be born. This precedence exists as a matter of principle for the entire duration of pregnancy and may not be placed in question for any particular time.

. . .

Document 6

Since the end of the eighteenth century professional civil servants have enjoyed an esteemed and privileged position in Germany, especially in the former state of Prussia. Art. 33 of the Basic Law carries on this historical tradition. It provides that the 'exercise of state authority as a permanent function shall as a rule be entrusted to members of the public service whose status, service, and loyalty are guaranteed by public law'. Loyalty to the state—not to be confused with an existing government—is of course among the highest principles governing the professional civil service anywhere. Federal and state laws seek to ensure the loyalty of civil servants by requiring, as a condition of entry into the bureaucracy, that they 'defend at all times the free democratic basic order within the spirit of the Basic Law'.[7] Against the background of violent demonstrations by university students together with the renewed determination of radical groups to 'march through the institutions' of the Federal Republic, the federal chancellor and all ten state prime ministers issued, on 28 January 1972, a new loyalty decree setting forth guidelines for the recruitment of civil servants. The first such guidelines went into effect in both Federation and Länder after the outbreak of the Korean War in 1950. They included provisions barring from the public service applicants who have engaged in 'anticonstitutional' activities and permitting the exclusion of persons who were or are members of 'an organization pursuing anticonstitutional goals'. Pursuant to these provisions the Land of Schleswig-Holstein refused to admit a law graduate who had once attended meetings of a radical student group at Kiel University from entering the practical phase of his training in various governmental agencies. He appealed to the courts to vindicate his right to continue his legal training. The Supreme Administrative Court of Schleswig-Holstein referred constitutional questions involved in the case to the Federal Constitutional Court for decision.

THE CIVIL SERVANT LOYALTY CASE
Source: Entscheidungen des Bundesverfassungsgerichts, Vol. 39, 1975, 334

... Constitutionally, civil servants have the duty of loyalty towards the free democratic state to which they are particularly closely related. ... The democratic state requires a body of civil servants supportive of the existing constitutional order. Civil servants are duty-bound to defend the state in times of crisis by fulfilling the tasks entrusted to them in faithful harmony with the spirit of the constitution along with its system of values and prescriptions. Such loyalty is required of civil servants in the interest of the state's preservation. The realization of this constitutional value in Art. 33, para. 5, of the Basic Law is not opposed to Art. 21, para. 2; Art. 33, para. 5, requires civil servants to support the constitutional order. Art. 21, para. 2, on the other hand, grants to the citizen the freedom to reject the constitutional order and politically to oppose it, so long as he employs permissible means of opposition and operates within a political party that is not prohibited.

The special duties of civil servants have not been imposed to hinder their political activities, but rather to maintain the security of the constitutional state against threats from its civil servants. Without the requirement of political loyalty, civil servants could use their special status and competence for the purpose of altering or subverting the existing constitutional order by means not authorized in the Constitution. It is not a question of discriminating against a civil servant on the grounds of his membership of a political party. Rather, it is one of requiring his loyalty as a state official and insuring that applicants will at all times, with their whole being, stand up for the free democratic basic order. Whether such loyalty can be expected of applicants for the civil service can be determined by their previous activities. Affiliation with or membership in an anti-constitutional party, whether or not it has been declared unconstitutional by the Federal Constitutional court, is an admissible factor in evaluating the credentials of an applicant. . . .

. . .

The legal position thus far expounded does not conflict with the fundamental right to freedom of expression . . . Owing to his official status [the civil servant] is charged with special duties *vis-à-vis* the state; at the same time, he is a citizen who may assert his fundamental rights against the state. Thus, two basic values of the Basic Law clash within the person of the civil servant: the assurance that the state will be served by an indispensable and reliable body of civil servants who will support the state and affirm the free democratic basic order . . . and the fundamental right freely to express one's opinion . . . All conduct involving the expression of political opinion is constitutionally protected by Art. 5 of the Basic Law only to the extent that it is compatible with the duty of political loyalty required by the civil servant under Art. 33, para. 5.

. . .

(3) According to Art. 3, para. 3, no person may be 'discriminated against or favoured because of . . . his political opinions.' . . . [Yet] the formal prescription of Art. 3, para. 3, is not absolute. It should be obvious that it is not impermissible to require acknowledgement of a particular creed on the part of a teacher about to be employed at a denominational school, or to give preference to a female for the position of principal at a girl's school, . . . Art. 3 prohibits only 'purposeful' discrimination; it does not prohibit favourable or prejudicial treatment based on a different order of intentionality (e.g., rules for the protection of the pregnant mother or for the protection of the constitutional order.) . . .

Finally, a constitutional provision should not be interpreted in isolation; on the contrary, it must be interpreted within the context of the Constitution itself. With this understanding, it is simply inconceivable that the constitution which, in the wake of the bitter experience of Weimar's democracy, intended the Federal Republic of Germany to be a strong and valiant democracy also permits the surrender of this state to its enemies under the protection of Art. 3, para. 3, of the Basic Law.

. . .

Documents 7 a – c

The following three extracts constitute a short case history in documents of Germany's attempt to provide for its internal security against enemies both domestic and foreign, while simultaneously seeking to preserve the liberties of its citizens. When the Constitution was originally adopted Art. 10 contained a simple declaration: 'Privacy of the mail and privacy of posts and telecommunications shall be inviolable. Restrictions may be imposed only pursuant to a law.' In 1968, however, the year the Constitution was amended to include a new and substantial section providing for the defence of the Federal Republic in the event of a serious military threat, Art. 10 was also amended (at the special request of the former occupying powers) to allow the state to interfere with private communications in the interests of protecting the 'free democratic basic order'. Subsequently, the Bundestag passed a law implementing this provision. The law, like the amendment, permitted telephone taps and other interferences with private communications but did not require those under surveillance to be informed of that fact. In addition, the legislature provided for administrative and parliamentary rather than judicial review of this process. The states of Bremen and Hesse challenged the validity of the statute and the amendment before the Second Panel of the Federal Constitutional Court in an abstract judicial review proceeding. It may seem anomalous that the validity of an amendment to the Basic Law could be challenged as unconstitutional. But in a very early case the Constitutional Court hinted *in dicta* that an amendment to the Constitution might itself be unconstitutional if it were to offend a basic principle on which the Constitution as a whole is based. The petitioners seized upon this theory in their argument before the Court.

a) ARTICLE 10 OF THE BASIC LAW
Source: Press and Information Office
Transl: Official

(1) Privacy of posts and telecommunications shall be inviolable.
(2) This right may be restricted only pursuant to a law. Such law may lay down that the person affected shall not be informed of any such restriction if it serves to protect the free democratic basic order or the existence or security of the Federation or a Land, and that recourse to the courts shall be replaced by a review of the case by bodies and auxiliary bodies appointed by Parliament.

b) LAW ON THE CURTAILMENT OF PRIVACY IN THE MAILS AND TELECOMMUNICATIONS (SUPPLEMENTARY LAW TO ARTICLE 10 OF THE BASIC LAW)
Source: BGBl., 1968, I, 949, as amended up to and including 13 September 1978

The Bundestag has approved the following law:

Art. 1

§ 1. (Purpose of surveillance and responsibility for it)

    1) Both the Federal and Länder Offices responsible for the protection of the Constitution (Bundesamt für Verfassungsschutz, Landesämter), the Security Office of the Federal Armed Forces (Militärischer Abschirmdienst) and of the Intelligence Service (Bundesnachrichtendienst) are entitled to open and read any communications which enjoy privacy as letters, post or telecommunications. They are also entitled to read telexes, listen in to telephone conversations and record them on tape recorders. The above is in order to avert dangers which threaten the free democratic basic order, the stability or the security of the Federal Republic or of the Länder, including the safety of troops stationed in the Federal Republic from non-German treaty states of the North American Treaty Organization and troops of the Three Powers stationed in Berlin.

    2) The German Federal Post Office (Deutsche Bundespost) must, when authorized, give information to the office which is entitled to it about postal and telephone communications, release messages which have been entrusted to it for delivery or transmission by the postal or telephone systems and also make it possible for telephone conversations and telexes to be intercepted.

§ 2. (Pre-conditions for surveillance)

    1) Curtailment of the right to privacy according to § 1 may be authorized under the conditions set down therein when definite reasons for suspicion exist that someone is committing or has committed:

        1. Offences which endanger peace or offences of high treason.

        2. Offences endangering the democratic constitutional state . . .

        3. Offences of treason and those which endanger external security . . .

        4. Offences against national defence . . .

§ 4. (Requirements for application and those entitled to apply)

    1) Curtailment according to § 1 of rights to privacy may only be authorized when application has been made.

    2) Those entitled to apply within the sphere of their work are the following:

        1. In the cases of § 2

        a) The Federal Office for the Protection of the Constitution through its president or his deputy.

        b) The official Länder bodies for the protection of the constitution through their directors or their deputies.

        c) In the case of activities against the Federal Armed forces, its Army Security Office through its director or his deputy.

        d) In the case of activities against the Intelligence Service, the latter through its President or his deputy.

. . .

§ 5. (Responsibility for authorization according to § 1. Contents of an Authorization)

 1) The office responsible for authorization according to § 1 is the highest responsible Länder official body in the case of application from the Länder bodies for the protection of the constitution. A Federal minister appointed by the Federal Chancellor is responsible for this over and above this.

. . .

§ 9. (Monitoring of surveillance methods by a body of members of parliament or by a commission—elimination of legal proceedings).

 1) The Federal Minister responsible for the authorization of curtailment (of rights of privacy) according to § 5 No. 1 will report every six months at the most to a committee consisting of five members of parliament selected by the Bundestag concerning the carrying out of this law.

 2) . . . the minister reports monthly to a commission.

 3) The commission consists of a chairman with legal qualifications and other members . . . [all] appointed by . . . the body mentioned in § 9.1.

. . .

c) PRIVACY OF COMMUNICATIONS CASE

Source: Entscheidungen des Bundesverfassungsgerichts, Vol. 30, 1970, 1
Transl: Renata Chestnut, in Murphy and Tanenhaus, ibid., 659–66

JUDGMENT of the Court . . .

 C.-I. . . .

1. . . . a) From the outset, the Basic Law did not unreservedly protect privacy of mails and telecommunications; rather, restrictions were always admissible, but in all cases had to be based on a law. . . . In this respect, the newly added sent. 2 of Art. 10, para. 2, does not introduce anything novel. . . .

Wherever the Basic Law restricts basic rights, it is always to protect effectively another individual or supra-individual legal interest which has priority. . . . The existence of the Federal Republic and its liberal constitutional order are a predominant legal interest for whose effective protection basic rights may, if absolutely necessary, be restricted.

What is really new in the constitutional amendment is . . . authorization not to inform the person affected of those restrictions, and to replace recourse to the courts by a review of the case by bodies . . . appointed by Parliament. The connection between these special measures and the restrictions . . . is clear. Efforts, plans, and measures directed against the constitutional order and against the security and existence of the state are mostly initiated by groups who disguise their work and manoeuver in secret, who are well-organized and rely to a great extent on undisturbed functioning of their communications system. An Office to protect the Constitution can effectively counter such an 'apparatus' only if its measures of surveillance remain secret. . . . Even subsequent disclosure . . . can furnish forces hostile to the Constitution with clues as to methods of operation and specific areas of observation by the Office for the Protection of the Constitution. . . .

b) Constitutional provisions must not be interpreted in isolation, but rather so that they are consistent with the Basic Law's fundamental principles and its system of values [citing a case]. . . . In the context of this case, it is especially significant that the Constitution . . . has decided in favour of a 'militant democracy' that does not submit to abuse of basic rights for an attack on the liberal order of the state [citing a case]. Enemies of the Constitution must not be allowed to endanger, impair, or destroy the existence of the state while claiming protection of rights granted by the Basic Law (cf. Art. 9, para. 2, Arts. 18 and 21). To protect the Constitution, the Basic Law explicitly provides for an institution, the Office for the Protection of the Constitution (cf. Art. 73, 10, and Art. 87, para. 1). The Basic Law cannot mean to set the constitutionally highest bodies of the state a task and to provide for a special agency for this purpose, while at the same time denying this agency means necessary to fulfill its assigned mission.

. . .

Interpretation of the amendment's substitution of review of administrative action by an agency or agencies appointed by Parliament for protection normally provided by the courts is very important. The principle of the rule of law demands that any statute implementing the amendment must establish agencies and procedures that produce a system of control which, even though the suspect does not participate in the process, functions as an effective equivalent to judicial control.

Accordingly, Art. 10, para. 2, sent. 2, requires that the law which is issued to implement it provides for *one* agency among those appointed by parliament which decides in judicial independence, and can bind all persons who are involved in the preparation, administrative decision making, and execution of the surveillance . . . and which can prohibit illegal measures of surveillance. This agency may be established within or outside parliament. It must, however, have sufficient expert and legal knowledge; it must be truly independent; and its members must be irrevocably appointed for a specific period of time. It must be competent to supervise all measures taken by all agencies involved in choosing, preparing, implementing, and supervising encroachment upon the privacy of mails and telecommunications. . . . For this purpose, all files relevant to deciding a case must be made available to the agency of control. This control must be a legal control. Art. 10, para. 2, sent. 2, also authorizes creation of a controlling agency that can, for appropriate reasons, order a surveillance discontinued or not exercised, even where legal prerequisites for surveillance are present. . . .

. . .

1. The second sentence of Art. 10, para. 2, authorizes the Government to keep secret from a suspect the fact that he is under surveillance. This provision does not violate the dignity of man.

. . .

A regulation or instruction that restricts a citizen's freedom or imposes duties on him does not violate human dignity. Neither does a measure which subjects a citizen, even without his knowledge or consent, to governmental surveillance. Under the circumstances at hand, absence of notification is not an expression of disrespect for a human being and his dignity, but a burden imposed upon a citizen . . . to protect the existence of his state and of the free democratic order. . . . Possibility of illegal and unconstitutional abuse does not make the rule unconstitutional; in interpreting and assessing a regulation one must rather proceed from the assumption that in a free democracy based on the rule of law it will be applied in a correct and just manner.

. . .

The guarantee of recourse to the courts laid down in Art. 19, para. 4, serves the purpose of legal protection for the individual. . . . The essential aspect of this constitutional provision is that legal protection is furnished by a materially and personally independent body, separate from the executive and legislative and therefore neutral. . . . If the Constitution is amended so that 'recourse to the courts' is 'replaced by a review of the case by bodies and auxiliary bodies appointed by parliament', then the entire system of legal protection is replaced.

. . .

Furthermore, one cannot infer from the constitutional amendment any tangible limitation on the number of people who may be kept under surveillance. Restrictions on privacy may be ordered in a very general manner, whenever they serve to protect the free democratic basic order or the existence or security of the Federation or a Land. . . .

Notes

1. See Ch. 1
2. See also Ch. 6, 146f.
3. See also Ch. 4
4. These articles appear in Ch. 4, Doc. 1
5. See also Ch. 8
6. See also Ch. 9, 234
7. See also Doc. 2 above, 161, 197

6 Federalism:
Bund and Länder

R. Taylor Cole

The legalistic criteria of classical federalism* are certainly present in the West German political system: powers under a rigid constitution are divided between three different levels of government, each of which possesses autonomous powers of decision-making in specific areas.† Though this legalistic classification has been the subject of much controversy in the Federal Republic, and doubts persist as to its appropriateness, the formal federal features of the political system have a continuing importance for policy making, adjudication, and other purposes.

As defined in the Basic Law, the division of functions between the three levels of government, the Federation (Bund)¹, the constituent states (Länder), and local authorities pertains to three fields:

(1) *Legislation.* The division of legislative powers between Bund and Länder is spelled out in the Basic Law (Doc. 1). In this field the Bund plays a dominant role and, with some exceptions deriving from Länder autonomy such as cultural policy, the interests of the Länder are taken care of by the second chamber in the Bonn parliament, the Bundesrat (Doc. 3), which has an important role in the federal legislative process.

(2) *Administration.* Here the main responsibility rests with the Länder. While the Bund has an administrative structure of its own for a limited number of areas such as the execution of foreign and defence policy, most federal laws are executed by Länder administrations. This not only gives the Länder administration discretionary powers, but it also explains why roughly half of the federal laws require the consent of the

---

* The term 'federalism' is used here throughout in the European rather than the North American sense to denote decentralizing rather than centralizing tendencies.

† Notes for this chapter begin on p. 162

Bundesrat (p. 152 below). Local administrations in the municipalities depend directly on the Länder governments, but they enjoy considerable discretionary powers of their own.

(3) *Finance.* Some taxes or shares of taxes go directly to the municipalities, while other taxes go to the Länder or to the Bund. Some taxes are shared between the three levels. For example, income and corporation taxes are shared in a fixed proportion between the three levels of government, and the value added tax (VAT) is divided between the Bund and the Länder on a ratio which is subject to often highly controversial negotiations. A fixed proportion of the revenue from the VAT goes to the European Community, thus adding a supra-national element to the financial picture. The municipalities are notoriously weak financially, because they have to provide most public services but have relatively low tax revenues of their own. In order to secure *uniform living standards* in the Federal Republic (an important objective which is laid down in Art. 72 (2), Art. 106 (3) of the Basic Law), there are arrangements for financial equalization between the 'rich' and the 'poor' Länder (by the so-called horizontal equalization) and between Bund, Länder and the municipalities (the so-called vertical equalization) (Ch. 7, Doc. 2). On the whole, the West German federal system is based on the principle of 'subsidiarity', that is, problems should be solved where they emerge. (This principle finds its expression e.g. in Arts. 30, 70 and 83 of the Basic Law). Only if problems cannot be solved locally, should a higher level take over.

Beyond the formal division of functions between the Bund, the Länder and the local authorities, federalism can also be viewed as a process marked by shifting and flexible relationships between the Bund and its constituent states. In this connection three basic points can be raised:

Firstly, the West German federal system can be understood only when viewed in its historical context. For example, the present territorial boundaries of the West German Länder owe as much to the political fiat of the occupying powers after World War II as to their evolution in previous centuries. Once the boundaries of the Länder had crystallized the possibility of making changes in them largely disappeared (Doc. 4).

Secondly, many factors have accelerated the movement in postwar Germany towards centralization of political life and an increasing dominance of the Bund in relation to the Länder. However, two very important institutions in the system operate to monitor the extent to which the balance shifts and indeed on occasion to limit its progress: the Bundesrat and the Federal Constitutional Court (Doc. 2). These 'federalizers' are far more than trivial features of a constitutional structure, as will be seen in the documents to follow.

Thirdly, the traditional concept of dual federalism, which denotes the classical division of power between the two levels of the central state on the one hand and the constituent states on the other, has been superseded in the Federal Republic by the development towards *cooperative federalism*. Cooperative federalism emphasizes joint programmes and institutionalized forms of cooperation, many of which have their bases not in constitutional provisions, but in various types of fiscal arrangements. These include above all Bund financial assistance, contributions, and grants-in-aid for specific projects. Some of these institutional connections involve new intergovernmental relations between Bund, Länder and local communities and regions.

The future of German federalism has been the focus of several official, as well as non-official, reviews in the past years. Among the first was the Troeger Commission, a creation of the Bund and the Länder governments, which submitted a final report on financial reform in 1966. Mention must also be made in this connection of the Commission of Inquiry on Constitutional Reform (the so-called 'Enquête-Kommission für Verfassungsreform').[2] In both official and non-official discussions of the future contours of German federalism there have been at least three separate, though interconnected, paradigms. The first assumes that rapidly increasing centralization is inevitable in German post-industrialized society and that the Länder will eventually be recognized as anomalies, useful only as administrative units. In this view, federalism does not reflect, except perhaps formally, the social realities and 'real forces' of the day. A second, while recognizing that the pulls toward the centre will continue, assumes that these will be accompanied by structural changes that would maintain and might even increase the autonomy of the Länder. Crucial here is the proposed reorganization—the 'Neugliederung'—of the German Länder to reduce their number and to provide greater equality of population, resources and capabilities. However, there is little possibility of creating a limited number of more viable Länder as a counterbalance to the Bund in the light of the amendments of the Basic Law in 1976.

The third paradigm assumes that the existing trend towards centralization is exaggerated. According to this 'theory' there is likely to be a heavier emphasis on coordinating machinery, both vertical (between the Bund and the Länder) and horizontal (between the Länder themselves). The integrity of the Land structure, reflecting the rigidity of boundaries once established, would be safeguarded within limits by the existence of 'federalizers' in the political system. There would thus not be any sudden or fundamental changes in the existing arrangements, but rather a gradual evolution to new types of federal relationships in which the Länder would continue to play an indispensable part.[3]

The last conclusion is buttressed by data dealing with the 'attitudes of the people towards federalism' provided by the Institut für Demoskopie in Allensbach. In reply to the regularly administered key-question: 'What would you say if all Länder legislatures and all Länder governments were abolished and all political decisions came from Bonn?', in 1960 25 per cent of the respondents were in favour and 41 per cent were opposed; in 1970 27 per cent were in favour and 44 per cent opposed; in 1980 *only* 9 per cent gave a favourable reply, reflecting reactions during the 'dual majority period' when the Bundestag and the Bundesrat had differing party majorities. Elisabeth Noelle-Neumann of the Institute concluded that the 'pro-federal' trend in public opinion since the 1950s has been consistently on the rise and today represents the viewpoints of a 'great majority' of the people. These pro-federal attitudes are present in somewhat varying degrees irrespective of age, sex, occupation or affiliation to a political party as well as to regions, though it is somewhat stronger in the Rhine district, the southwest and Bavarian areas than in other regions of the Federal Republic.

Document 1

Although many other provisions of the Basic Law have some bearing on federal relationships, the most pertinent provisions are:

a) Arts. 30–31 dealing with the 'functions of the Länder' and the 'priority of federal law';

b) Arts. 70–75 dealing with the 'legislative powers of the Bund', and especially those provisions outlining and enumerating the exclusive, concurrent and 'framework' or skeleton powers of the Bund; by now, however, the wide field of concurrent legislation has to all intents and purposes been absorbed by the Bund.

The exclusive and concurrent powers catalogued in the Basic Law have been almost completely monopolized by the Bund with the consequence of limiting the legal competence of the Länder in such fields as culture and education, police, communal affairs, and to some extent planning for land use and problems of the environment.

c) For Arts. 91a and 91b, as amended in 1969 to deal with so-called 'joint tasks', see Chap. 7, Doc. 3a.

d) for Arts. 104a and 109, which deal with the division of revenues and fiscal administration, see Chap. 7, Doc. 2a; for Arts. 83 to 86 dealing with the execution of federal laws by the Länder, see Chap. 7, Doc. 1a.

CONSTITUTIONAL PROVISIONS GOVERNING THE RELATIONSHIP BETWEEN BUND AND LÄNDER (BASIC LAW, GRUNDGESETZ)
Source: Press and Information Office of the Federal Republic
Transl.: Official

The Bund and Länder

Art. 30. Functions of the Länder

The exercise of governmental powers and the discharge of governmental functions shall be incumbent on the Länder insofar as this Basic Law does not otherwise prescribe or permit.

Art. 31. Priority of Federal Law

Federal law shall override Land law.

. . .

Art. 70. Legislation of the Bund and the Länder

(1) The Länder shall have the right to legislate insofar as this Basic Law does not confer legislative power on the Bund.
(2) The division of competence between the Bund and the Länder shall be determined by the provisions of this Basic Law concerning exclusive and concurrent legislative powers.

Art. 71. Exclusive Legislation of the Bund, Definition

In matters within the exclusive legislative power of the Bund the Länder shall have power to legislate only if, and to the extent that, a federal law explicitly so authorizes them.

Art. 72. Concurrent Legislation of the Bund, Definition

(1) In matters within concurrent legislative powers the Länder shall have power to legislate as long as, and to the extent that, the Bund does not exercise its right to legislate.
(2) The Bund shall have the right to legislate in these matters to the extent that a need for regulation by federal legislation exists because:

   1. a matter cannot be effectively regulated by the legislation of individual Länder, or

2. the regulation of a matter by a Land law might prejudice the interests of other Länder or of the people as a whole, or
3. the maintenance of legal or economic unity, especially the maintenance of uniformity of living conditions beyond the territory of any one Land, necessitates such regulation.

Art. 73. Exclusive Legislation, Catalogue

The Bund shall have exclusive power to legislate in the following matters:

1. foreign affairs as well as defence including the protection of the civilian population;
2. citizenship in the Bund;
3. freedom of movement, passport matters, immigration, emigration, and extradition;
4. currency, money and coinage, weights and measures, as well as the determination of standards of time;
5. the unity of the customs and commercial territory, treaties on commerce and on navigation, the freedom of movement of goods, and the exchanges of goods and payments with foreign countries, including customs and other frontier protection;
6. federal railroads and air transport;
7. postal and telecommunication services;
8. the legal status of persons employed by the Bund and by federal corporate bodies under public law;
9. industrial property rights, copyrights and publishers' rights;
10. co-operation of the Bund and the Länder in matters of
    a) criminal police,
    b) protection of the free democratic basic order, of the existence and the security of the Bund or of a Land (protection of the constitution), and
    c) protection against efforts in the federal territory which, by the use of force or actions in preparation for the use of force, endanger the foreign interests of the Federal Republic of Germany,
    as well as the establishment of a Federal Criminal Police Office and the international control of crime.
11. statistics for federal purposes.

Art. 74. Concurrent Legislation, Catalogue

Concurrent legislative powers shall extend to the following matters:

1. civil law, criminal law and execution of sentences, the organization and procedure of courts, the legal profession, notaries, and legal advice (Rechtsberatung);
2. registration of births, deaths, and marriages;
3. the law of association and assembly;

4. the law relating to residence and establishment of aliens;

4a. the law relating to weapons and explosives;

5. the protection of German cultural treasures against removal abroad;

6. refugee and expellee matters;

7. public welfare;

8. citizenship in the Länder;

9. war damage and reparations;

10. benefits to war-disabled persons and to dependents of those killed in the war as well as assistance to former prisoners of war;

10a. war graves of soldiers, graves of other victims of war and of victims of despotism;

11. the law relating to economic matters (mining, industry, supply of power, crafts, trades, commerce, banking, stock exchanges, and private insurance);

11a. the production and utilization of nuclear energy for peaceful purposes, the construction and operation of installations serving such purposes, protection against hazards arising from the release of nuclear energy or from ionizing radiation, and the disposal of radioactive substances;

12. labour law, including the legal organization of enterprises, protection of workers, employment exchanges and agencies, as well as social insurance, including unemployment insurance;

13. the regulation of educational and training grants and the promotion of scientific research;

14. the law regarding expropriation, to the extent that matters enumerated in Arts. 73 and 74 are concerned;

15. transfer of land, natural resources and means of production to public ownership or other forms of publicly controlled economy;

16. prevention of abuse of economic power;

17. promotion of agricultural and forest production, safeguarding of the supply of food, the importation and exportation of agricultural and forest products, deep sea and coastal fishing, and preservation of the coasts;

18. real estate transactions, land law and matters concerning agricultural leases, as well as housing, settlement and homestead matters;

19. measures against human and animal diseases that are communicable or otherwise endanger public health, admission to the medical profession and to other health occupations or practices, as well as trade in medicines, curatives, narcotics, and poisons;

19a. the economic viability of hospitals and the regulation of hospitalization fees;

20. protection regarding the marketing of food, drink and tobacco, of necessities of life, fodder, agricultural and forest seeds and seedlings, and protection of plants against diseases and pests, as well as the protection of animals;

21. ocean and coastal shipping as well as aids to navigation, inland navigation, meteorological services, sea routes, and inland waterways used for general traffic;

22. road traffic, motor transport, construction and maintenance of long-distance highways as well as the collection of charges for the use of public highways by vehicles and the allocation of revenue therefrom;
23. non-federal railroads, except mountain railroads;
24. waste disposal, air purification, and noise abatement.

Art. 74a. Wider Competence of Bund for Pay Scales

(1) Concurrent legislation shall further extend to the pay scales and pensions of members of the public service whose service and loyalty are governed by public law, insofar as the Bund does not have exclusive power to legislate pursuant to item 8 of Art. 73.

(2) Federal laws enacted pursuant to para. (1) of this Article shall require the consent of the Bundesrat.

(3) Federal laws enacted pursuant to item 8 of Art. 73 shall likewise require the consent of the Bundesrat, insofar as they prescribe for the structure and computation of pay scales and pensions, including the appraisal of posts, criteria or minimum or maximum rates other than those provided for in federal laws enacted pursuant to para. (1) of this Article.

(4) Paras. (1) and (2) of this Article shall apply *mutatis mutandis* to the pay scales and pensions for judges in the Länder. Para. (3) of this Article shall apply *mutatis mutandis* to laws enacted pursuant to para. (1) of Art. 98.

Art. 75. General Provisions of the Bund, Catalogue

Subject to the conditions laid down in Art. 72 the Bund shall have the right to enact skeleton provisions concerning:

1. the legal status of persons in the public service of the Länder, communes, or other corporate bodies under public law, insofar as Art. 74a does not provide otherwise;
1a. the general principles governing higher education;
2. the general legal status of the press and the film industry;
3. hunting, nature conservation, and landscape management;
4. land distribution, regional planning, and water regime;
5. matters relating to the registration of changes of residence or domicile (Meldewesen) and to identity cards.

Documents 2a – c

Two institutions maintain a balance between the Bund and the Länder. One of these is the Federal Constitutional Court.[4]

The manner in which federalism is protected by the Federal Constitutional Court is illustrated by its 1957 decision on the continuing validity of the Concordat concluded in 1933 between the Hitler government and the Vatican. The Court had to decide whether the treaty-making power of the Reich government exercised in 1933 could, if the treaty were still valid, nullify school legislation of a Land passed in accordance with the provisions of the 1949 Basic Law, which accorded exclusive powers to the states over public instruction. The case, brought on petition of the federal government as plaintiff, was dismissed on the grounds that certain provisions of the constitution, and especially those dealing with the Land powers in educational matters, absolved the Land from abiding by the conflicting Concordat provisions regarding the establishment of public (or state) schools.

a) CONCORDAT DECISION OF THE FEDERAL CONSTITUTIONAL COURT
Source: Entscheidungen des Bundesverfassungsgerichts, Vol. 6, 1957, 309ff.

A difference of opinion exists between the Land Government of Lower Saxony and the Federal Goverment over the rights and obligations of the Federal government and the Länder under the Basic Law. The Federal Constitutional Court decides where such differences exist (Art. 93, para. 1, item 3, Basic Law; Art. 13, item 17, Federal Constitutional Court Law).

According to Art. 68 of the Federal Constitutional Court Law, the petitioner for the Federal Republic in such cases may only be the Federal Government. . . . The resolution of the Federal Government was adopted on 9 March 1955 and requested the Federal Constitutional Court to determine whether the Reich Concordat is valid, and whether the Lower Saxony Education Act was compatible with the Reich Concordat.

The Reich Concordat remained in effect under international and domestic law throughout the duration of the National Socialist regime. The repeated and serious violations of the Reich Concordat . . . by the National Socialist Government and party agencies did not detract from its legal validity. Rather it gave the injured party the right to withdraw from the contract or to demand its fulfillment. However, the Holy See adhered to the Reich Concordat and in numerous instances, which were climaxed by the Encyclical 'With Deep Anxiety' of 24 March 1937, never ceased protesting against the 'evasion of contract, erosion of contract and finally more or less public breach of contract' by the National Socialist state. In spite of violations of the Concordat and their attacks on the Church and Christianity, the National Socialists never renounced the Concordat or declared it void. . . .

During the period of the increasing attack on the Church in the years from 1937–1939, efforts were made by National Socialist party agencies and by government circles to declare certain articles of the Concordat invalid. Later they conspired to nullify the entire agreement. The Reich Government in fact considered issuing a Reich Education Act which would have been incompatible with the education provisions of the Reich Concordat. Nevertheless, this proposal did not progress beyond internal discussion and no notice of cancellation was ever issued. . . .

Although the National Socialist regime disregarded the Reich Concordat to an ever increasing degree and the Church regarded it from the beginning as more of a *concordatum defensionis* than a *concordatum amicitiae*, neither party ever questioned its continuing validity.

The Reich Concordat . . . did not lose its validity through the collapse of National Socialist tyranny. . . .

The Occupation Powers did not abrogate the Reich Concordat. Such action would have had no effect under international law. The Concordat, like other treaties with neutral states, lay outside the unilateral jurisdiction of the Occupation Powers. Decrees of the Occupation Powers could at most have had only domestic application. . . .

The continuing validity of the Reich Concordat under international law has resulted in a situation in which the mutual obligations arising from the treaty must be honoured by the treaty partners. Within the purview of the Basic Law, the Federal Republic, that is, constitutionally the Federal Government and the Länder as a whole, is considered to be a party to the Concordat. According to the constitutional law of the Federal Republic, the obligations arising from the education provisions of the Concordat can only be fulfilled by the Länder, since the Federal Government does not possess legislative authority in education matters. The outcome of the present litigation hinges on the question of whether the Federal Government can demand that the Länder comply with the educational provisions [of the Concordat]. This must be answered affirmatively if it is established that the Länder have a constitutional obligation to the Federal Republic to observe those provisions in formulating their education laws.

. . .

As has already been stated, the Basic Law denied the Federal Government legislative and administrative jurisdiction over education matters, assigning this field to the exclusive responsibility of the Länder. It did not thereby ignore the education provisions of the Reich Concordat, but instead left it to the Länder to decide on their own responsibility and with complete freedom how to fashion their education laws in view of the obligations of the Federal Republic to the Reich Concordat under international law. In addition, it did not give the Federal Government the authority constitutionally to interfere in the formulation of objectives in the fulfilment of this task. . . .

This treaty was concluded under international law within the competence of the German Reich. The Federal Republic of Germany inherited the obligations arising from this treaty itself since, as a result of her identification with the German Reich, she assumes responsibility for its state treaties under international law. But the Basic Law made available to the Federal government no vehicle by which it could either satisfy the education provisions of the Reich Concordat itself or ensure their observance. . . .

[It could be] conjectured that the Basic Law intended to provide the greatest possible insurance that the treaty would be honoured. This conjecture cannot however be sustained where, as here, it is clear that the framers of the Basic Law were not prepared to equip the Federal Government with the necessary means to ensure the fulfilment of the education provisions of the Reich Concordat. The legal consequences flowing from the treaty under international law which binds the Federation rests for its member states exclusively on the provisions of constitutional law. . . . This relationship cannot be based on international law.

It is not necessary to determine whether the Federal Republic of Germany is liable for violating the Concordat. Even the liability of the Federal Government under international law cannot change its relation to the Land under constitutional law.

The petition of the Federal Government is unfounded. If the Education Act of Lower Saxony conflicts with the education provision of the Reich Concordat, the rights of the Federal Government vis-à-vis the Land are not violated as a result. Thus it will not be necessary to examine the technical compatibility of the Lower Saxony Education Act with the provisions of the Reich Concordat. The petition of the Federal Government is therefore rejected.

A second case had considerable political undertones and must be read in the light of the intentions and actions of Chancellor Adenauer who was at the time strongly opposed by the SPD-governed Länder. Adenauer had established by administrative fiat a second television channel (German Television Limited). This action was challenged by all of the Länder with SPD governments as a violation of both their rights over cultural affairs and the principle of federal comity (Bundestreue) in the procedures which the Bonn government had followed. In the court hearings the aggrieved Länder placed reliance on Art. 30 of the Basic Law ('The exercise of governmental powers and the discharge of governmental functions shall be incumbent on the Länder insofar as the Basic Law does not otherwise prescribe or permit') and on Art. 70, para. 1 ('The Länder shall have the right to legislate insofar as the Basic Law does not confer legislative power on the Federation'). The federal government relied chiefly on Art. 73, para. 7, and Art. 87, para. 1, which granted exclusive authority to the federal government to legislate regarding 'postal and telecommunication services' and, as a matter of direct federal administration, to administer 'the federal postal service'.

The case represented the high water mark in the Court's sharp rejection of certain of the federal government's expansionist claims and, while its impact has been modified over time, it still provides a legal bulwark for Länder powers over broadcasting and television. This famous decision led in fact to the setting up of a 'Second German Television' (Zweites Deutsches Fernsehen—ZDF) in 1961 by means of an interstate treaty (Staatsvertrag zwischen den Ländern). On the governing board of the ZDF, however, are represented not only all the Länder and the Bund, but also all political parties with caucuses in parliament and the most important interest groups.[5]

b) 'TELEVISION DECISION' OF THE FEDERAL CONSTITUTIONAL COURT
Source: Entscheidunges des Bundesverfassungzgerichts, Vol. 12, 1961, 205ff.

As a method of mass communication, the broadcasting system belongs to the same family as the press and film. Art. 5, para. 1 of the Basic Law mentions all three in one line. The legislative competence of the Federal Government is expressly limited to the general legal status of the press and films in Art. 75, item 2 of the Basic Law. The broadcasting system is not mentioned in this Article. Any interpretation which takes into account the context of the provisions of the Basic Law cannot presume that exclusive legislative competence over broadcasting as a whole is vested in the Federal Government, while for the press and films this competence is limited to the enactment of framework legislation governing legal status.

In defining the legislative competence of the Federal Government and the Länder the Basic Law begins with the concept of Land jurisdiction. The Federal Government has legislative jurisdiction only when expressly granted in the Basic Law (Art. 70, para. 1). Thus, as a rule the legislative competence of the Federal Government can be based only on the express grant of such jurisdiction in the Basic Law. Doubt as to the jurisdiction of the Federal Government must therefore be resolved against its competency, as the Basic Law calls for a strict interpretation of Arts. 73ff.

Added to the above is the fact that the broadcasting system belongs to the cultural sphere. According to fundamental decisions of the Basic Law, insofar as cultural matters can be administered and regulated by the state, ... they fall under the jurisdiction of the Länder, so long as no specific provisions of the Basic Law introduce limits, restrictions or exceptions in favour of the Federal Government. This basic principle of the Basic Law, which is one favouring the federal structure in the interests of an effective division of power, precisely excludes any federal jurisdiction in cultural matters in the absence of any clauses containing exceptions in the Basic Law. No such clause exists. ... The Bund lacks any authority to regulate broadcasting beyond the technical aspects of transmission.

In the German federal state, all constitutional relationships between the state as a whole and its members, as well as the constitutional relationship between Länder, are governed by the unwritten constitutional principle of reciprocal obligation of the Bund and Länder to behave in a pro-federal manner. ... From this the Federal Constitutional Court has developed a number of concrete legal obligations. In connection with the consideration of the constitutionality of the so-called horizontal financial equalization, the Federal Constitutional Court stated: 'By its nature the federal principle establishes not only rights, but also obligations. One such obligation is the duty of the financially stronger Länder to assist the weaker Länder, within certain limits. . . .' This constitutional principle can further impose an increased obligation on all participants to cooperate in instances in which the law calls for agreement between the Federal Government and the Länder. . . . In the decision to grant Christmas bonuses to public employees the Länder must comply with the principle of federal comity (Bundestreue) and thus take into account the overall financial structure of the Federal Government and the Länder. This restriction resulting from the concept of federal comity is even more applicable in the exercise of legislative authority. If the effects of a law extend beyond the boundaries of a Land, then the Land legislators must take into account the interests of the Federal Government and the other Länder. . . . The constitutional principle of the obligation to act in a pro-federal manner can further include the obligation of the Länder to respect treaties of the Federal Republic under international law. . . . On the basis of its obligation of federal comity, a Land may be potentially obliged to use its supervisory authority over local government to intervene against communities whose actions are encroaching on matters under expressly federal jurisdiction. As has been indicated, the principle of pro-federal behaviour is also of fundamental importance . . . in the area of broadcasting.

The case in question presents an opportunity to develop another aspect of the constitutional obligation to act in a pro-federal manner. Even the procedure and the style of the negotiations necessary in constitutional life between the Federal Republic and its member states and between Länder are subject to the rule of pro-federal behaviour. In the Federal Republic all Länder have the same constitutional status and have the right to the same treatment in dealing with the Federal Government. In seeking a relevant agreement to a constitutional question which involves all of the Länder, the obligation to behave in a pro-federal manner prohibits the Federal Republic from working from the premise of 'divide and conquer'. In other words, the Federal Republic may not take advantage of rifts between Länder by seeking an agreement with some and then pressuring the others to join as well. In negotiations which affect all of the Länder, that principle also prevents the Federal Republic from treating the Länder governments differently according to their political leanings and especially from including in politically decisive discussions only those representatives who are closely connected with politically friendly Länder governments. . . . [The procedures followed by the Federal Government in this and other respects] violated the obligation to act in a pro-federal manner. . . .

In an unpublished paper on 'The West German Federal System and the Constitutional Court' (1981), Professor Wolfgang Zeidler, the Vice-President of the Court, commented on the role of the Court:

c) EVALUATION OF DECISIONS BY THE FEDERAL CONSTITUTIONAL COURT RESPECTING FEDERALISM GENERALLY

Source: Federal Constitutional Court

Decisions of the Federal Constitutional Court have ranged, in the realm of taxation, from the validation of Länder taxes on juke-boxes, pinball machines and other entertainments ... to that of special federal duties on the wine trade or road freight traffic or that on incomes in accordance with the requirements of the economy ...; from the disallowance of a special local import tax for Heligoland to that of a Land tax on the sale of ice cream. ... Decisions concerning social matters have upheld federal provisions for family allowances, for employers' contributions to employees' pension insurance and for accident insurance. ... In the field of criminal law and public order decisions have covered a variety of subjects, from the assignment to federal or Länder jurisdiction of provisions of Reich laws on explosives and weapons to the denial that existing law on casinos belonged to the federal sphere of competence ...; from the constitutionality of Land legislation for the expropriation of Hamburg's dikes to confirmation of federal road traffic provisions ...; from the federal law on the dissemination of literature harmful to young people, to the power to prohibit the importation of films for reasons of public order and security. ...

The importance for the federal system of some of these cases taken individually may appear to be slight. Yet the cumulative effect is substantial. In an examination of these decisions affecting the balance of power between Bund and Länder, ... some differentiation is necessary. As those judgments which went in favour of the Bund were in conformity with the general trend towards the expansion of federal power, they have remained in effect and unchallenged. If this is also true of many decisions in favour of the Länder, the explanation is that many of these decisions concerned relatively minor questions or activities. ... However, other federalist decisions favouring the Länder are more far-reaching in their effects, and it might be expected that some of these would in time be reversed, ignored or eroded. Yet, so far, this has occurred only to a limited extent. ...

Documents 3a–d

The 'Council of the Constituent States' (Bundesrat) is the other important institution which helps to preserve a flexible balance between Bund and Länder. Excluding the members from Berlin who have a special status, it has forty-one members, with Land representation varying from three to five. Members of the Bundesrat represent the governments of the Länder and vote as blocs, with twenty-one votes providing an absolute majority and twenty-eight votes a two-thirds majority. The Bundesrat represents the Länder interest in the full range of federal legislation. In this respect the Bundesrat has assumed an increasingly important role hardly envisaged in 1949.[6]

The result has been an increasingly important use of the Bundesrat's two-fold veto power: a *suspensive* veto, which the Bundesrat can use against any law passed by the Bundestag and which the latter can in the end override by a simple majority[7] and an *absolute* veto against certain bills passed by the Bundestag, which the latter cannot then override. An absolute veto can be directed against measures which would seriously affect financial or administrative interests of the Länder, as well as amendments to the constitution which have to be passed by the Bundesrat (as well as the Bundestag) by a two-thirds majority. In case of either a suspensive or an absolute veto against a bill passed by the Bundestag, a special committee of both houses of the German parliament, the so-called joint Mediation Committee (Vermittlungsausschuß, Ch. 2) is called together at the request of either house. In accordance with Art. 77 of the Basic Law the Bundesrat can request a meeting within fourteen days after the receipt of the bill from the Bundestag. Composed of an equal number of members of the Bundestag and Bundesrat, the joint committee seeks to resolve differences between the two bodies. When opposition parties to the party or parties forming the government have a majority in the Bundesrat, as they have had for some years prior to the defeat of Chancellor Schmidt in October 1982, they can thus influence the political scene and parliamentary process in many—and perhaps even decisive—ways.

The constitutional provisions regarding the Bundesrat concern:

(1) organisation structure, Arts. 50–53;

(2) the procedures by which the Bundesrat is involved in meeting national emergencies, Art. 53a.[8]

(3) Arts. 83–86 regarding the execution of federal laws and the federal administration (Chap. 7, Doc. 1a).

a) CONSTITUTIONAL PROVISIONS CONCERNING THE BUNDESRAT (BASIC LAW)
Source: Press and Information Office
Transl.: Official

Section IV: The Council of Constituent States (Bundesrat)

. . .

Art. 50. Function

The Länder shall participate through the Bundesrat in the legislation and administration of the Bund.

Art. 51. Composition

(1) The Bundesrat shall consist of members of the Land governments which appoint and recall them. Other members of such governments may act as substitutes.
(2) Each Land shall have at least three votes; Länder with more than two million inhabitants shall have four, Länder with more than six million inhabitants five votes.
(3) Each Land may delegate as many members as it has votes. The votes of each Land may be cast only as a block vote and only by members present or their substitutes.

Art. 52. President, Rules of Procedure

(1) The Bundesrat shall elect its President for one year.
(2) The President shall convene the Bundesrat. He must convene it if the members for at least two Länder or the Federal Government so demand.
(3) The Bundesrat shall take its decisions with at least the majority of its votes. It shall draw up its rules of procedure. Its meetings shall be public. The public may be excluded.
(4) Other members of, or persons commissioned by, Land governments may serve on the committees of the Bundesrat.

Art. 53. Participation of the Federal Government

The members of the Federal Government shall have the right, and on demand the duty, to attend the meetings of the Bundesrat and of its committees. They must be heard at any time. The Bundesrat must be currently kept informed by the Federal Government of the conduct of affairs.

Section IVa: The Joint Committee

Art. 53a

(1) Two-thirds of the members of the Joint Committee shall be deputies of the Bundestag and one-third shall be members of the Bundesrat. The Bundestag shall delegate its deputies in proportion to the sizes of its parliamentary groups; such deputies must not be members of the Federal Government. Each Land shall be represented by a Bundesrat member of its choice; these members shall not be bound by instructions. The establishment of the Joint Committee and its procedures shall be regulated by rules of procedure to be adopted by the Bundestag and requiring the consent of the Bundesrat.

(2) The Federal Government must inform the Joint Committee about its plans in respect of a state of defence. The rights of the Bundestag and its committees under paragraph (1) of Art. 43 shall not be affected by the provision of this paragraph.

. . .

Art. 79. Amendment of the Basic Law

(1) This Basic Law can be amended only by laws which expressly amend or supplement the text thereof. In respect of international treaties the subject of which is a peace settlement, the preparation of a peace settlement, or the abolition of an occupation regime, or which are designed to serve the defence of the Federal Republic, it shall be sufficient, for the purpose of clarifying that the provisions of this Basic Law do not preclude the conclusion and entry into force of such treaties, to effect a supplementation of the text of this Basic Law confined to such clarification.

(2) Any such law shall require the affirmative veto of two-thirds of the members of the Bundestag and two-thirds of the votes of the Bundesrat.

(3) Amendments of this Basic Law affecting the division of the Federation into Länder, the participation on principle of the Länder in legislation, or the basic principles laid down in Arts. 1 and 20, shall be inadmissible.

As the Rules of Procedure clearly imply, most of the work of the Bundesrat is done in standing committees of which there were fourteen in 1980. In the so-called 'political' committees (Foreign Relations, Defence and Inner-German Affairs) the Länder are usually represented by their heads of government or plenipotentiaries, while in the 'technical' committees, the responsible Länder ministers or their representatives serve (i.e. Länder Ministries of Finance on the Bundesrat Finance Committee). The initial stages in the legislative process often involve the relations between Federal ministries and the concerned ministries of the Länder. As Gerhard Ziller, the Bundesrat Director, has commented there also exist informal means of coordination which work as follows:

'.... As a rule, the ministries concerned of the Länder are the first to be informed of the legislative plans of the Federal Government. In accordance with the Rules of Procedure of the Federal ministries, these plans are formulated as rough drafts of bills to be examined by the responsible Länder ministries. These contacts take place as a rule at an informal 'working level' ... The 'political level' in the Länder ... is informed after the bill has been considered by the Federal Cabinet. After this action by the Federal Cabinet, formal proceedings begin in the Bundesrat. ... The material [the proposed legislation] is printed and is distributed to the Länder. Then the technical departments of the Länder have three weeks to ... study the bill, prepare amendments and supplementary proposals ... Four weeks after the distribution of the government bill, the committees of the Bundesrat meet. The ministers concerned of the Länder ... now have the opportunity to discuss the proposed law, to ask questions, and to defend their own suggestions. ....'[9]

b) RULES OF PROCEDURE OF THE BUNDESRAT (GESCHÄFTSORDNUNG)
Source: Bundesrat Sekretariat

Art. 1. Members

The governments of the Länder furnish the President of the Bundesrat with names of the members of the Bundesrat, the date of their appointment as members of the Bundesrat and of the Land government and the date on which their membership expires.

Art. 2. Incompatibility of Office

Members of the Bundesrat may not simultaneously be members of the Bundestag.

. . .

Art. 5

1) The Bundesrat elects without debate one President and three Vice-Presidents from among its members for one year.

. . .

Art. 8. The Presidency

1) The Presidency consists of the President and the three Vice-Presidents.
2) On the advice of a Permanent Advisory Council, it prepares the draft budget of the Bundesrat. It makes decisions on the internal affairs of the Bundesrat so long as the power of decision is neither reserved for the Bundesrat as a whole nor incumbent on the President.

. . .

Art. 11. Committees

(1) The Bundesrat establishes standing committees. It may set up additional committees to deal with particular business.
(2) Each of the Länder is represented on every committee by a member of the Bundesrat, another member or a delegate from its government.

. . .

Art. 18. Participation in Debate

(1) The rapporteur of the Mediation Committee and the Under Secretary of State of the Federal Republic may also take part in the discussions of the Bundesrat. Other persons may do so with the permission of the President.
(2) Representatives of the Länder and the Federal government may be called in to assist the members of the Bundesrat and the Federal Government as well as other participants in the discussions.

. . .

Art. 25. Reports

(1) The committees are to make oral reports in the sessions of the Bundesrat on matters of importance currently under discussion. With the permission of the President an oral report on technical or legal questions may be replaced by a written report. . . .

. . . .

Art. 30. Voting Rules

(1) According to Arts. 76 to 78 of the Basic Law questions to be put to a vote in legislative proceedings are to be put in such a way that the voting shows conclusively whether the Bundesrat has decided by a majority. . . .

. . .

Art. 34. Participation in the Debates of the Bundestag

The Bundesrat may authorize its members to defend its resolutions in the Bundestag and its committees. The committees may make suggestions in this regard.

. . .

Art. 40. Participation and Right to Question

(1) Members of the Bundesrat and delegates of the Land governments who are not members of the committees, as well as representatives of the Federal government may participate in the discussions of the committees and subcommittees, but do not enjoy voting rights.

(2) In session, members of the committees as well as delegates of the Land governments may question the members of the Federal government and its representatives.

. . .

In accordance with the Basic Law the Bundesrat has an absolute veto, above all in matters connected with taxation. In most cases a compromise acceptable to the Bundestag is reached, but not always. The document below gives the official reasons advanced by the Bundesrat in 1976 for rejecting, in accordance with Art. 106, para. 3 of the Basic Law, the proposed increase in the value added tax which would have raised the Bund's percentage of the revenues realized from it. This document illustrates the possibilities the Bundesrat has to protect the financial integrity of the Länder.

c) DECISION OF THE BUNDESRAT REGARDING THE ACT TO AMEND THE VALUE ADDED TAX AND OTHER ACTS, 6 JUNE 1976

Source: Deutscher Bundesrat, Drucksache 329/76

The Bundesrat had previously in its examination of the bill on its first submission indicated its intention not to approve the proposed increase in the value added tax. The objections raised during this examination are justified.

The developments of the subsequent period have increased the doubts about the necessity for the tax increase. The most recent economic predictions indicate that there will be an increase in tax income; the budget of the Bund for 1975 has provided a more favourable estimate of projected expenditures. In the opinion of the Bundesrat, there is also the possibility of more careful budget oversight and of economies so as to reduce in course of time the budget deficit without the necessity of increasing the value added tax.

. . .

This speech on the occasion of the 400th meeting of the Plenum of the Bundesrat suggests the continuing influence of the Bundesrat in the legislative process of the Federal Republic and the importance of the joint Mediation Committee.

d) 'THE FEDERAL PRINCIPLE HAS JUSTIFIED ITSELF IN THE BASIC LAW', SPEECH BY THE PRESIDENT OF THE REPUBLIC, KARL CARSTENS, 4 JUNE 1981

Source: Bundesrat Sekretariat

This occasion provides the opportunity to assess the importance of the Bundesrat for our constitutional system and for the well-being and future welfare of our Republic. The founding fathers of the Basic Law decided on a federal framework for our state. This reflected centuries of German constitutional tradition, the approval of the overwhelming majority of the Parliamentary Council, and, above all, the internal orientation of the Germans, who since the beginning of their history have been divided into more or less closely-bound family groups and territories.

Today, thirty-two years after the founding of the Federal Republic, we can be pleased that the federal principle has justified itself. It has been a stabilizing factor, and it has particularly facilitated cultural development.

. . .

The Bundesrat has a central role in the federal structure. In it, the Länder jointly participate in the legislative and administrative work of the Bund. They do this not only separately as Länder of the Bund, that is in their autonomous capacities, but they also work together as an organ of the Bund with unified responsibility for the good of the whole.

In the Bundesrat, above all in its committees, the expertise of the Land governments is made available for advice on Bund legislation. . . . Their experience in this advisory role on proposed federal legislation is of great value. . . .

It is occasionally alleged that important decisions are negated by the Bundesrat—that is, that it pursues a policy of obstruction of policies of the Bund Government and Bundestag. A careful examination of the allegation disproves it. In the last legislative period, from 1976 to 1980, there were 354 bills presented to the Bundesrat. Of these 277, around 78 per cent, were accepted by the Bundesrat without any major reservations. In seventy-seven instances, around 21 per cent of the cases, a joint Mediation Committee for consideration of bills was activated. Final action on six of the proposed bills had not been completed by the end of the legislative period. Including these six, there were fifteen proposed bills, less than 5 per cent, which were not finally enacted into law. By and large, this experience was typical of earlier legislative periods.[10]

One can, of course, contend that in one-fifth of the instances where the joint committees had to be activated, compromises became necessary. But, in my opinion, the process of discussion, of negotiation and of compromise is an indispensable ingredient of the democratic process.

Likewise, as it is unacceptable to view the Bundesrat as an organ of obstruction, so it is inappropriate to consider the differences between the Bundesrat and other Bund organs as primarily the reflection of political partisanship. . . . The viewpoints of the Länder as such also have a very significant influence. . . . But, in the final decisions . . . when there are basic political questions at issue, it is entirely proper that each political party should seek to realize its objectives.

. . .

Documents 4a – b:

The question of redrafting the boundaries of the German Länder has roots which go back beyond the collapse of the Third Reich. Throughout the Weimar Republic, whose twenty-five constituent states were inherited from the Bismarckian empire, the question of the division of the large state of Prussia was a live one. After the collapse in 1945 the map of their part of Germany was radically altered by the three Western occupying powers. The irrationality of the original territorial arrangements was especially complicated by the new zonal lines when the French zone was carved out of those originally assigned to Great Britain and the United States. In the American zone, after some makeshift adjustments, three states, Bavaria, Hesse and Württemberg-Baden, emerged. Bremen was later added to the Länder under American control.

The consequences of the zonal division were exhibited at their worst in the partition of historic Württemberg and Baden between the French and American zones (Ch. 1). The famous 'Southwest Case' brought before the Federal Constitutional Court grew out of these territorial divisions. Three states resulting from the fiat of the occupying powers, Baden, Württemberg-Baden, and Württemberg-Hohenzollern, provided an unsatisfactory solution for the German southwest. A special provision in the Basic Law (Art. 118) provided for reorganization on the basis of agreement among the three states and, if agreement could not be reached, by federal legislation which had to incorporate provisions for a plebiscite. Two federal laws, the First and Second Reorganization Acts, were enacted. Both of these were challenged before the Federal Constitutional Court. The Court, in its first major decision in 1951, issued a temporary injunction postponing the required referendum until several major issues could be examined fully. In this decision, the Court in effect held the First Reorganization Act to be unconstitutional though the essential features of the Second Reorganization Act were sustained.[11]

In fact, there has been only one other major change in the territorial boundaries of the Federal Republic since the early 1950s. This was the addition in 1957, as the Republic's tenth Land, of the Saar area, which had been occupied by and given a special status by France after 1945.

From the start, however, the Basic Law had contained provisions in Art. 29 to make a territorial reorganization possible. In 1976, as a result of several internal political pressures, an amendment of that Article made it permissive rather than compulsory to reorganize the Länder by law. The crucial change was in the wording of para. 1, which was altered to read: 'The Federal Territory *may be* reorganized . . .' from the original 'The Federal territory *must be* reorganized . . .'. In the light of the realities of the German political system, territorial reorganization of German states appears at present to be a dead issue.

Alternative proposals for the territorial reorganization of the German Länder were outlined by a special Commission appointed by the Federal Minister of Interior in 1970 to consider the avenues for executing Art. 29, para. 1. In its 1973 report the Commission presented possible alternative territorial rearrangements for consolidating and reducing the number of the existing Länder from ten to five or six units. These alternatives were depicted in four maps, along with the 'pros' and 'cons' of each proposal. In general, the Commission argued that the smaller number of units would provide Länder more equality in population and make them more economically viable. The Länder would presumably be better able thereby to withstand centralizing pressures from the Bund. One of the four maps is included below (Doc. 4b).

a) BASIC LAW

Source: Press and Information Office

Art. 29. Reorganization of the Federal Territory

(1) The federal territory may be reorganized to ensure that the Länder by their size and capacity are able effectively to fulfill the functions incumbent upon them. Due regard shall be given to regional, historical and cultural ties, economic

b) MODEL 1 FOR THE REORGANIZATION OF THE FEDERAL TERRITORY
(SPECIAL COMMISSION)

Schleswig-Holstein

Hamburg

Bremen

BUNDESLAND NORD

Niedersachsen

Berlin

NORDRHEIN
WESTFALEN

Nordrhein-Westfalen

Hessen

BUNDESLAND
MITTELWEST C

Rheinland-Pfalz

Saarland

BAYERN

Bayern

BUNDESLAND
SÜDWEST C

Baden-Württemberg

▬▬ Boundaries of the Federal Republic
— Present Boundaries of the Länder
▬▬ Projected Boundaries after Reorganization

expediency, regional policy, and the requirements of town and country planning. (2) Measures for the reorganization of the federal territory shall be introduced by federal laws which shall be subject to confirmation by referendum. The Länder thus affected shall be consulted.

. . .

(7) Other modifications of the territory of the Länder may be effected by state agreements between the Länder concerned or by a federal law with the approval of the Bundesrat if the territory which is to be the subject or reorganization does not have more than 10,000 inhabitants. The details shall be regulated by a federal law requiring the approval of the Bundesrat and the majority of the members of the Bundestag. It must make provision for the affected communes and districts to be heard.

Notes

1. For the purpose of Chs. 6 and 7 we are using the term Bund rather than Federation, even deviating from the official translations to do so, since Bund is always used in connection with Länder
2. The Enquête Kommission published its report in 1976; see Drucksache 7, Deutscher Bundestag, Bonn
3. See also R. Taylor Cole, 'West German Federalism Revisited', *American Journal of Comparative Law*, Spring 1975, 234–36
4. See also Ch. 4, Docs. 5, 6
5. See also Ch. 9, Doc. 11
6. See Philip M. Blair, *Federalism and Judicial Review in West Germany*, Oxford, 1981
7. A two-thirds majority in the Bundestag would, in fact, be necessary if the Bundesrat were to pass its suspensive judgement with a two-thirds majority, never so far achieved. Between 1949 and 1983, out of a total of 3,671 laws promulgated 1,863 required the consent of the Bundesrat (Zustimmings Gesetze)
8. See also Ch. 2, 29
9. See 'Gewichtiges Mitspracherecht . . .', *Das Parlament*, 24 August–1 September 1979, 6
10. See Table 6
11. See Gerhard Leibholz, 'The Federal Constitutional Court and the "Southwest Case"', *American Political Science Review* 46, 1952, 723 ff.

7 Federalism: Intergovernmental Relations and Finance

R. Taylor Cole

Documents 1a–c

Considerable attention is given in the Basic Law to administrative matters, especially in Part VIII, 'The Execution of Federal Laws and the Federal Administration'.* In accordance with German traditions, the responsibility for the administration of most federal laws belongs to the Länder. While the Länder, of course, execute their own laws, for example, those dealing with education, cultural affairs, police and local goverment—there is a division of responsibility between the Bund and the Länder for the execution of the federal laws by the civil services of the Bund and Länder. Directly administered by federal civil service are such matters as the foreign service, armed forces, and postal services. Administered by the Länder acting as agents of the Bund are, in particular, laws relating to federal taxes and federal highways (Auftragsverwaltung); administered by the Länder civil services as 'matters of their own concern' are all those laws which do not fall in the other categories (Doc. 1a). Where the Länder have autonomy in the administration of federal laws, any exercise of supervision by the Federal Government requires Bundesrat approval. Though the degree of flexibility allowed to the Länder in administration of federal laws varies, it is clear that most federal laws are administered by Land officials. The resulting system is often and properly referred to as one of administrative decentralization.

---

* Notes for this chapter begin on p. 191

a) THE EXECUTION OF FEDERAL LAWS AND THE FEDERAL ADMINISTRA-
TION UNDER THE BASIC LAW
Source: Press and Information Office
Transl.: Official

Art. 83. Execution of Federal Laws by the Länder

The Länder shall execute federal laws as matters of their own concern insofar as
this Basic Law does not otherwise provide or permit.

Art. 84. Land Administration and Federal Government Supervision

(1) Where the Länder execute federal laws as matters of their own concern, they
shall provide for the establishment of the requisite authorities and the regulation
of administrative procedures insofar as federal laws consented to by the
Bundesrat do not otherwise provide.
(2) The Federal Government may, with the consent of the Bundesrat, issue pertinent general administrative rules.
(3) The Federal Government shall exercise supervision to ensure that the Länder
execute the federal laws in accordance with applicable law. For this purpose the
Federal Government may send commissioners to the highest Land authorities
and with their consent or, if such consent is refused, with the consent of the
Bundesrat, also to subordinate authorities.
(4) Should any shortcomings which the Federal Government has found to exist in
the execution of federal laws in the Länder not be corrected, the Bundesrat shall
decide, on the application of the Federal Government or the Land concerned,
whether such Land has violated applicable law. The decision of the Bundesrat
may be challenged in the Federal Constitutional Court.
(5) With a view to the execution of federal laws, the Federal Government may be
authorized by a federal law requiring the consent of the Bundesrat to issue individual instructions for particular cases. They shall be addressed to the highest
Land authorities unless the Federal Government considers the matter urgent.

Art. 85. Execution by Länder as Agents of the Bund

(1) Where the Länder execute federal laws as agents of the Bund, the establishment of the requisite authorities shall remain the concern of the Länder except insofar as federal laws consented to by the Bundesrat otherwise provide.
(2) The Federal Government may, with the consent of the Bundesrat, issue pertinent general administrative rules. It may regulate the uniform training of civil
servants (Beamte) and other salaried public employees (Angestellte). The heads
of authorities at the intermediate level shall be appointed with its agreement.
(3) The Land authorities shall be subject to the instructions of the appropriate
highest federal authorities. Such instructions shall be addressed to the highest
Land authorities unless the Federal Government considers the matter urgent.
Execution of the instructions shall be ensured by the highest Land authorities.

Art. 86. Direct Federal Administration

Where the Bund executes laws by means of direct federal administration or by federal corporate bodies or institutions under public law, the Federal Government shall, insofar as the law concerned contains no special provision, issue pertinent general administrative rules. The Federal Government shall provide for the establishment of the requisite authorities insofar as the law concerned does not otherwise provide.

The relations between the Bund and Länder in the execution of the law are also reflected in the legislation regulating the status of the career of professional civil servants (Beamte). The civil servants include not only those in the limited areas of administration under exclusive federal control, but also the much larger numbers which are employed by the Länder and local governments and which are frequently engaged also in the execution of federal laws. These include professors, teachers, policemen, tax collectors and many others. These officials are distinguished from the more numerous public employees who occupy respected positions of governmental authority but who are legally classified as salaried employees or wage earners. Such a three-class system in the German Civil Service has long roots in German history. Differences, once considerable in regard to salaries, social security and pensions, have by now been largely abolished. However, even today, only 'Beamte' can perform acts expressing state authority—such as the signature of reports in state schools or signing of birth certificates. Civil servants in the narrower sense traditionally owe a special loyalty to the constitutional order, not to the particular government in power.

b) FEDERAL CIVIL SERVICE FRAMEWORK ACT 1977 (BEAMTENRECHT-SRAHMENGESETZ)
Source: BGBl., 6 January 1977, 23ff.

General

Art. 2. Status of the Civil Service

(1) The civil servant is bound to his employer by the terms of his employment and by loyalty.
(2) Only those can be appointed to the civil service who will exercise official functions or such functions which for reasons of state or public security generally cannot be entrusted exclusively to persons whose professional status is subject to private law.

(3) The exercise of official authority is ordinarily to be entrusted to the civil service if permanent functions are involved.

Art. 3. Nature of the Status of the Civil Service

(1) The civil service status can be based on:

1. lifetime appointment if the civil servant is to be permanently employed . . .;
2. term appointment if the civil servant is to be employed in such functions for a specific period;
3. trial appointment if the civil servant must complete a probationary period before future employment on a lifetime basis;
4. temporary appointment if the civil servant (a) must complete a preparatory service, (b) will only be employed incidentally or temporarily for assignments.

. . .

Art. 4. General Personal Requirements

(1) To be appointed to the civil service one must:

1. be a German citizen as defined by Art. 116 of the Basic Law;
2. swear to defend the free and democratic constitutional order as defined by the Basic Law;
3. have the educational background prescribed for this career or, in the absence of such prescription, the standard educational background.

. . .

Termination of the Civil Service Status

Art. 21. Reasons for Termination

(1) The civil service status ends, other than because of death, through:

1. dismissal . . .;
2. loss of the rights of the civil service;
3. removal from service in accordance with disciplinary laws;

. . .

Retirement

Art. 25. Retirement Age

The retirement age for the civil service is to be determined by law. Career civil servants retire after reaching retirement age. The point in time for the beginning of retirement is to be determined by law.

. . .

Art. 34. Members of the Governments of the Länder

It may be determined by law that the civil servant leaves office when he becomes a member of the government of his Land. In this case, it may be further specified that the civil servant who has left office enters into retirement after the end of his term in government. The same holds for any official status which corresponds to the Undersecretary of State as defined by the law governing the legal status of Undersecretaries of State [Staatssekretäre].

. . .

Functions of the Civil Servant

Art. 35. Impartial, Democratic and Political Behaviour

(1) The civil servant serves the whole people, not one party. He must fulfill his duties in an impartial and equitable manner. He must take into consideration the welfare of the general public in the administration of his office. He must defend the free and democratic constitutional order as defined in the Basic Law in every aspect of his behaviour and help preserve it.

(2) In his political activity the civil servant must observe the moderation and discretion which befits his position relative to the general public and out of consideration for the duties of his office.

Art. 36. General Professional Obligations and Behaviour

The civil servant must practice his profession with complete dedication. He must administer his position unselfishly and conscientiously. His behaviour on duty and off must evidence the respect and trust demanded of his profession.[1]

The Framework Act for Higher Education is a further example of the 'framework legislative powers' of the federation, that is, the federation's competence to enact skeleton legislation within whose terms Land legislation and administrative practice must fit. The basic objective of framework legislation is to ensure a minimum of uniformity of living conditions. In the course of the history of the Federal Republic additional fields for this legislative power were added to the Basic Law:

Art. 75. General Provisions of the Bund, Catalogue

Subject to the conditions laid down in Art. 72[2], the Federation shall have the right to enact skeleton provisions concerning:

1. the legal status of persons in the public service of the Länder, communes, or

other corporate bodies under public law, in so far as Art. 74a does not provide otherwise;

1a. the general principles governing higher education;
2. the general legal status of the press and the film industry;
3. hunting, nature conservation and landscape management;
4. land distribution, regional planning, and water regime;
5. matters relating to the registration of changes of residence or domicile
   (Meldewesen) and to identity cards.

Education, traditionally a recognized reserved field for the Länder, was
also the subject of attention during the 'reform period' beginning in
1969. In addition to the amended Art. 75, empowering the Bund to
enact framework legislation incorporating the 'general principles
governing higher education', the amendments passed in 1969/70 (Arts.
91a and 91b) contain important provisions dealing with the facilities for
higher education, educational planning in general and the promotion of
supra-regional institutions and projects of scientific research.

Impelled by a variety of pressures (the demands for more student
capacity, adequate staffing, democratization, rising costs, relevance of
programmes to social need, rationalization of administrative and budget
arrangements amongst others) as presented in a number of reports, the
SPD–FDP coalition government sought after 1970 to implement provision 1a of Art. 75 through the enactment of a framework law on higher
education.

The original drafts of this proposed legislation—passed by the
Bundestag in 1975—faced considerable opposition from CDU and CSU
ranks, especially in the Bundesrat, which had an absolute veto in the
matter due to certain administrative aspects of the framework law. The
passage of the resulting compromise was, therefore, delayed until 1976.
The new law provided the skeleton confines for the legal guidance of the
Land legislators, who were obliged to change their Land university laws
in order to implement the legislation. The law established uniform
guidelines for internal university organization, student admissions, participation of staff and all other groups in the university community
(teaching and research) programmes of study, the planning of integrated
universities, inter-university relationships, and other matters. All these
reforms changed the traditional structures of German universities as
basically established in the nineteenth century. Especially controversial,
both within and without the academic community, were the provisions
for new modes of participation in the decision-making machinery, doing
away, *inter alia*, with the absolute monopoly of Germany's so-called
'chairholders' (Ordinarien). Though the reform ethos has been ebbing

since the early 1980s, the Hochschulrahmengesetz represents an important milestone in German university development. It also provides a significant illustration of the use of the newly acquired powers of the Bund to restrict the jurisdiction of the Länder over education.

c) FRAMEWORK ACT FOR HIGHER EDUCATION (HOCHSCHULRAHMEN-GESETZ)

Source: BGBl., I, 1976, 185ff.
Transl.: Official

Section 1

(1) Reform of higher education shall be a task to be carried out jointly by the institutions of higher education themselves and the competent government authorities.

(2) The higher education system shall be reformed with a view to combining the functions in research, teaching and studies at present performed by different types of institutions of higher education.

(3) The aim of such reform shall in particular be the following:

1. a range of interrelated study courses, phased in coordinated stages with regard to contents, schedule and final qualification in appropriate fields; to the extent that this is compatible with the contents of courses, common study segments or successive courses shall be organized;

2. a structure of courses which will permit the greatest possible transfer of credit for studies performed and examinations passed when a student transfers to another course in the same or a related field of study;

3. a combination of theoretical and practical studies appropriate for each subject;

4. the formulation and implementation of research and teaching programmes of an interdepartmental and interinstitutionnal nature as well as the concentration of research and teaching subjects, i.e. in coordination with other institutions of research and education and with organizations concerned with the advancement of research;

5. subject-related and interdisciplinary promotion of higher education didactics;

6. effective academic counselling;

7. the optimum use of each institution's facilities;

8. provision of research opportunities for professors at those institutions of higher education where such research opportunities do not exist or are inadequate for the fulfilment of such professors' official duties;

9. coherent planning for the higher education sector as a whole and a balanced provision of institutions of higher education both in regional and supraregional terms.

. . .

Section 9: Study Reform Commissions

(1) In order to promote the reform of studies and examinations and to coordinate and support the reform work already carried out at the individual institutions, study reform commissions shall be set up. Joint study reform commissions shall be established by the Länder for the area of application of the present Act.

(2) The study reform commissions shall be set up by the competent Länder authorities in cooperation with the institutions of higher education concerned.

. . .

Section 31: Central Allocation of Study Places

(1) Study places in courses for which admission quotas have been laid down for several institutions may be allocated by the Central Office set up jointly by the Länder. The decision to allocate places in a particular course of study by means of the procedure of the Central Office must be taken—at the earliest possible point in time—if the Central Office finds that admission quotas have been laid down for the course in question for all State institutions within the purview of this Act, and if it is to be expected that the number of applicants will exceed the total number of available places, unless the decision is left to the institutions themselves on account of the special nature of the admission requirements or the selection criteria for specific courses. Places in a particular course of study shall be allocated by means of the procedure of the Central Office if, according to the facts as registered by the latter, admission quotas have been laid down for the majority of the State institutions within the purview of this Act.

. . .

Section 38: Composition and Voting Rights

(1) The type and the extent of participation as well as the number of members in the composite bodies, committees and other bodies shall depend on the latters' tasks as well as on the qualifications, function, responsibility and involvement of the members of the institution concerned. The proportion of the votes assigned to the different groups (see subsection 2) represented on the composite central bodies and on the departmental councils (Fachbereichsräte) shall be governed by law.

(2) Each of the following shall be represented as a group on the various bodies:

1. professors,
2. students,
3. scientific assistants, artistic assistants and university assistants,
4. other staff members.

. . .

(4) In the case of decisions already affecting research, creative arts projects, teaching or the appointment of professors, the following members of the body concerned shall have the right to vote: the professors, the principal of the institution or a member of the institution's governing board (Leitungsgremium), the university, scientific and artistic assistants, the students and those persons assimilated in status under subsections (2) and (3) of section 36. . . .

(5) Any decisions directly affecting research, creative arts projects and the appointment of professors shall be based not only on the overall majority vote of the whole body but also on that of the professors in that body. If no decision is reached even in the second round of voting, the majority vote of the professors in that body shall suffice for taking the decision concerned. In the case of decisions to be taken on proposals for professional appointments, the majority within the body shall be entitled to submit an alternative proposal of its own.

. . .

Section 62: Governance of Institutions of Higher Education

(1) Each institution shall have a full-time principal[3] elected for a term of office of at least four years; he shall be solely reponsible for running the institution concerned, maintaining order and exercising authority within the institution, except where provision for the exercise of these duties by other person or persons obtain. He shall give an annual account of the fulfilment of the institution's tasks.

(2) The place of the principal of an institution may be taken by an elected governing board with at least one full-time member; the senior administrative officer shall be an ex officio member of this body. The provisions of this Act relating to the composite and other bodies shall not apply to the governing board.

(3) The principal or the members of the governing board to be determined by vote shall be elected for a limited term by a composite central body on the basis of a proposal made by the institution concerned and appointed by the organ responsible under Land law. Removal from office by vote shall not be possible.

. . .

Section 64: The Department (Fachbereich)

(1) The department shall be the basic organizational unit of institutions of higher education; nothwithstanding the overall responsibility of the institution and the sphere of competence of the institution's central bodies, the department shall fulfil the functions of the institution within its own area. Within the framework of the facility-provision plans, it shall ensure that its members, its scientific establishments and its operational units can fulfil the functions incumbent on them.

(2) The organs of the department are the departmental council and the departmental spokesman (Fachbereichssprecher).

(3) The departmental council shall be responsible for all matters within the department concerning research and teaching, except for those for which Land law places responsibility with the departmental spokesman.

. . .

(5) The departmental spokesman shall be elected by the departmental council from among the council's professorial members.

. . .

Documents 2 a–c

The allocation of tasks to the various levels—Bund, Länder, municipalities—requires appropriate economic and financial structures. In 1969 the need to improve fiscal administration and budgetary procedures and to secure a higher degree of uniformity of living standards within the federal territory led to a series of financial reforms effected by means of amendments to the Basic Law. The following Arts. 104a–109 embody the most significant of the provisions in this field.

But even after this reform, one of the major problems remained unsolved; the municipalities have to provide most public services and are responsible for a large proportion of public investment but do not receive adequate funds from the share of public revenue directly accruing to them. This partly explains their growing financial indebtedness.

a) PROVISIONS OF THE BASIC LAW ON FINANCIAL EQUALIZATION, FISCAL ADMINISTRATION AND BUDGETARY PROCEDURE

Source: Press and Information Office
Transl.: Official

Art. 104a. Apportionment of Expenditure, Financial Assistance

(1) The Bund and the Länder shall meet separately the expenditure resulting from the discharge of their respective tasks insofar as this Basic Law does not provide otherwise.

(2) Where the Länder act as agents of the Bund, the Bund shall meet the resulting expenditure.

(3) Federal laws to be executed by the Länder and involving the disbursement of

funds may provide that such funds shall be contributed wholly or in part by the Bund. Where any such law provides that the Bund shall meet one-half of the expenditure or more, the Länder shall execute it as agents of the Bund. Where any such law provides that the Länder shall meet one-quarter of the expenditure or more, it shall require the consent of the Bundesrat.

(4) The Bund may grant the Länder financial assistance for particularly important investments by the Länder or communes or associations of communes, provided that such investments are necessary to avert a disturbance of the overall economic equilibrium or to equalize differences of economic capacities within the federal territory or to promote economic growth. Details, especially concerning the kinds of investments to be promoted, shall be regulated by federal legislation requiring the consent of the Bundesrat, or by administrative arrangements based on the federal budget.

(5) The Bund and the Länder shall meet the administrative expenditure incurred by their respective authorities and shall be responsible to each other for ensuring proper administration. Details shall be regulated by a federal law requiring the consent of the Bundesrat.

Art. 105. Customs Duties, Monopolies, Taxes—Legislation

(1) The Bund shall have exclusive power to legislate on customs matters and fiscal monopolies.

(2) The Bund shall have concurrent power to legislate on all other taxes the revenue from which accrues to it wholly or in part or where the conditions provided for in para. (2) of Art. 72 apply.

(2a) The Länder shall have power to legislate on local excise taxes as long and insofar as they are not identical with taxes imposed by federal legislation.

(3) Federal laws relating to taxes the receipts from which accrue wholly or in part to the Länder or communes or associations of communes shall require the consent of the Bundesrat.

Art. 106. Apportionment of Tax Revenue

(1) The yield of fiscal monopolies and the revenue from the following taxes shall accrue to the Bund:

1. customs duties,
2. excise taxes insofar as they do not accrue to the Länder pursuant to para. (2) of this Article or jointly to the Bund and the Länder in accordance with paragraph (3) of this Article or to the communes in accordance with paragraph (6) of this Article.
3. the road freight tax,
4. the capital transfer taxes, the insurance tax and the tax on drafts and bills of exchange,
5. non-recurrent levies on property, and contributions imposed for the purpose of implementing the equalization of burdens legislation,

6. income and corporation surtaxes,
7. charges imposed within the framework of the European Communities.

(2) Revenue from the following taxes shall accrue to the Länder:

1. property (net worth) tax,
2. inheritance tax,
3. motor-vehicle tax,
4. such taxes on transactions as do not accrue to the Federation pursuant to para. (1) of this Article or jointly to the Federation and the Länder pursuant to para. (3) of this Article.
5. beer tax,
6. taxes on gambling establishments.

(3) Revenue from income taxes, corporation taxes and turnover taxes shall accrue jointly to the Bund and the Länder (joint taxes) to the extent that the revenue from income tax is not allocated to the communes pursuant to para. (5) of this Article. The Bund and the Länder shall share equally the revenues from income taxes and corporation taxes. The respective shares of the Bund and the Länder in the revenue from turnover tax shall be determined by federal legislation requiring the consent of the Bundesrat. Such determination shall be based on the following principles:

1. The Bund and the Länder shall have an equal claim to coverage from current revenues of their respective necessary expenditures. The extent of such expenditures shall be determined within a system of pluri-annual financial planning;
2. the coverage requirements of the Bund and of the Länder shall be coordinated in such a way that a fair balance is struck, any overburdening of taxpayers precluded, and uniformity of living standards in the federal territory ensured.

(4) The respective shares of the Bund and the Länder in the revenue from the turnover tax shall be apportioned anew whenever the relation of revenues to expenditures in the Bund develops substantially differently from that of the Länder. Where federal legislation imposes additional expenditures on, or withdraws revenue from, the Länder, the additional burden may be compensated by federal grants under federal laws requiring the consent of the Bundesrat, provided such additional burden is limited to a short period. Such laws shall lay down the principles for calculating such grants and distributing them among the Länder.

(5) A share of the revenue from income tax shall accrue to the communes, to be passed on by the Länder to their communes on the basis of income taxes paid by the inhabitants of the latter. Details shall be regulated by a federal law requiring the consent of the Bundesrat. Such law may provide that communes shall assess communal percentages of the communal share.

(6) Revenue from taxes on real property and businesses shall accrue to the communes; revenue from local excise taxes shall accrue to the communes or, as may

be provided for by Land legislation, to associations of communes. Communes shall be authorized to assess the communal percentages of taxes on real property and businesses within the framework of existing laws. Where there are no communes in a Land, revenue from taxes on real property and businesses as well as from local excise taxes shall accrue to the Land. The Bund and the Länder may participate, by assessing an impost, in the revenue from the trade tax. Details regarding such impost shall be regulated by a federal law requiring the consent of the Bundesrat. Within the framework of Land legislation, taxes on real property and businesses as well as the communes' share of revenue from income tax may be taken as a basis for calculating the amount of such impost.

(7) An overall percentage, to be determined by Land legislation, of the Land share of total revenue from joint taxes shall accrue to the communes and associations of communes. In all other respects Land legislation shall determine whether and to what extent revenue from Land taxes shall accrue to communes and associations of communes.

(8) If in individual Länder or communes or associations of communes the Bund causes special facilities to be established which directly result in an increase of expenditure of a loss of revenue (special burden) to these Länder or communes or associations of communes, the Bund shall grant the necessary compensation, if and insofar as such Länder or communes or associations of communes cannot reasonably be expected to bear such special burden. In granting such compensation, due account shall be taken of third-party indemnities and financial benefits accuring to the Länder or communes or associations of communes concerned as a result of the institution of such facilities.

(9) For the purpose of this Article revenues and expenditures of communes and associations of communes shall be deemed to be Land revenues and expenditures.

Art. 107. Financial Equalization

(1) Revenue from Land taxes and the Land share of revenue from income and corporation taxes shall accrue to the individual Länder to the extent that such taxes are collected by revenue authorities within their respective territories (local revenue). Federal legislation requiring the consent of the Bundesrat may provide in detail for the delimitation as well as the manner and scope of allotment of local revenue from corporation and wage taxes. Legislation may also provide for the delimitation and allotment of local revenue from other taxes. The Land share of revenue from the turnover tax shall accrue to the individual Länder on a per capita basis; federal legislation requiring the consent of the Bundesrat may provide for supplemental shares not exceeding one-quarter of a Land share to be granted to Länder whose per capita revenue from Land taxes and from the income and corporation taxes is below the average of all the Länder combined.

(2) Federal legislation shall ensure a reasonable equalization between financially strong and financially weak Länder, due account being taken of the financial capacity and financial requirements of communes and associations of communes.

Such legislation shall specify the conditions governing equalization claims of Länder entitled to equalization payments and equalization liabilities of Länder owing equalization payments as well as the criteria for determining the amounts of equalization payments. Such legislation may also provide for grants to be made by the Bund from federal funds to financially weak Länder in order to complement the coverage of their general financial requirements (complemental grants).

Art. 108. Fiscal Administration

(1) Customs duties, fiscal monopolies, excise taxes subject to federal legislation, including the excise tax on imports, and charges imposed within the framework of the European Communities, shall be administered by federal revenue authorities. The organization of these authorities shall be regulated by federal legislation. The heads of authorities at the intermediate level shall be appointed in consultation with the respective Land governments.

(2) All other taxes shall be administered by Land revenue authorities. The organization of these authorities and the uniform training of their civil servants may be regulated by federal legislation requiring the consent of the Bundesrat. The heads of authorities at the intermediate level shall be appointed in agreement with the Federal Government.

(3) To the extent that taxes accruing wholly or in part to the Bund are administered by Land revenue authorities, those authorities shall act as agents of the Bund. Paras. (3) and (4) of Art. 85 shall apply, the Federal Minister of Finance being, however, substituted for the Federal Government.

. . .

Art. 109. Separate Budgets for Bund and Länder

(1) The Bund and the Länder shall be autonomous and independent of each other in their fiscal administration.

. . .

The percentages of the total tax income from all sources for the period from 1971 to 1982 (estimates for 1981 and 1982) are included in the following table. As Doc. 2b indicates, the percentages received by the Länder and the municipalities have increased slightly since 1971, while, when account is taken of the tax revenues allocated to the European Community, that of the Bund has declined. The big increase in the tax revenues for the local communities occurred between 1970 and 1971, when the new provisions regarding allocations to them came into effect. In the constitutional distribution of tax revenues to the Bund, the Länder and the municipalities separate allocations are made from a number of less important taxes. Of the three most productive taxes, the revenues from the corporation and income taxes are divided evenly between the Bund and the Länder, with a legally fixed proportion going to the municipalities. The third, the value added tax, is reexamined regularly. The percentage received by the Bund in 1980 was some 67.5 per cent of the total.

The primary apportionment of the financial revenue is that between the Bund and the Länder. It is the result of what is known as 'vertical' financial equalization and is reflected in Doc. 2b below. But although in 1969 the apportionment of revenues was reformed, there remained a need for a redistribution among the 'rich' and the 'poor' Länder themselves, termed 'horizontal' financial equalization. The comparatively disadvantaged Länder, with the amounts received between 1970–1981 (1980 and 1981 estimated), are listed in Doc. 2c.

b) PERCENTAGE OF TAX REVENUE ANNUALLY ALLOCATED TO THE BUND, LAF*, LÄNDER, MUNICIPALITIES AND EUROPEAN COMMUNITY (1971–1982)

(Adapted from Bundesministerium des Finanzen, *Finanzbericht*, 1982, 25)

Year	Bund	LAF	Länder	Municipalities	European Community
1971	54.0	0.8	32.8	12.3	0.6
1972	51.6	0.7	34.0	12.9	0.8
1973	51.1	0.6	34.0	13.3	1.0
1974	49.5	0.5	35.1	13.7	1.2
1975	49.2	0.5	34.0	13.8	2.5
1976	48.8	0.5	34.1	14.1	2.4
1977	48.1	0.4	34.8	14.1	2.6
1978	48.3	0.3	35.0	13.7	2.8
1979	48.5	0.1	35.4	13.1	3.0
1980	48.3	0.0	34.8	14.0	2.9
1981	45.5	0.0	34.6	13.4	3.5
1982*	48.7	0.0	34.7	13.2	3.4

* Decisions of the Bund Government as of Sept. 2–3, 1981 regarding 1982 Bund Budget are included. LAF are burden sharing funds (Lastenausgleichsfonds). Other explanatory footnotes for table above are omitted.

c) EQUALIZATION-ENTITLED LÄNDER*

(Adapted from Bundesministerium des Finanzen, *Finanzbericht*, 1982, 108)

Year	Bavaria	Lower Saxony	Palatinate	Schleswig-Holstein	Saarland	Bremen	Total
1970	148.2	407.3	228.4	199.1	142.8	89.5	1 215.3
1971	198.9	450.5	238.7	207.9	143.0	50.3	1 289.3
1972	178.3	610.7	291.5	246.9	155.6	72.7	1 555.7
1973	167.0	679.3	247.7	276.7	184.6	70.5	1 625.8
1974	346.4	742.8	298.6	272.6	194.8	54.8	1 910.0
1975	368.6	717.6	294.3	239.4	178.9	45.5	1 844.3
1976	332.1	768.3	340.7	369.3	195.5	51.5	1 957.4
1977	399.3	929.1	286.6	321.8	210.8	144.7	2 292.3
1978	299.0	885.7	355.5	354.4	216.0	154.8	2 265.4
1979	327.9	1 002.2	291.1	401.6	228.0	235.0	2 485.8
1980	400.6	747.7	246.6	320.3	284.1	178.8	2 178.1
1981	347.0	969.0	345.0	379.0	279.0	158.0	2 477.0

In millions of German Marks

Documents 3a–h

Apart from the constitutional amendments in this connection, already cited (thirty-four in all since 1949), there are a myriad of emerging and shifting intergovernmental relationships involving cooperation between Länder, the federal financing of Länder activities and 'joint tasks' (Art. 91 of the Basic Law). These provide a multifaceted legal web of increasingly complex design governing relationships between Bund and Land, between the Länder, between the Bund and the municipalities, as well as between the Länder and the municipalities and between the municipalities themselves. The last two fields will not be covered by the documents to follow.

———————————

Parliamentary bills enacted after 1969 under Art. 91 have been and continue to be important. By this constitutional amendment the Bund acquired additional powers, for instance, in the field of higher education.

———————————

* Sharing ratio in value added tax:
  1970: Bund 60.0%   Länder 30.0%
  1974: Bund 63.0%   Länder 37.0%
  1980: Bund 67.5%   Länder 32.5%

Under these augmented powers, the Framework Act for Higher Education, cited above, was enacted. In the era of so-called 'domestic reforms', initiated by the socialist-liberal government of Willy Brandt in the early 1970s, the Bund also consented to contributions for constructing new universities. Of even greater importance have been the measures referred to in Art. 91a, 2 and 3.

a) THE DEFINITION OF 'JOINT TASKS' ADDED TO THE BASIC LAW IN MAY 1969
Source: Press and Information Office
Transl.: Official

Art. 91a

(1) The Bund shall participate in the discharge of the following responsibilities of the Länder, provided that such responsibilities are important to society as a whole and that federal participation is necessary for the improvement of living conditions (joint tasks):

1. expansion and construction of institutions of higher education including university clinics;
2. improvement of regional economic structures;
3. improvement of the agrarian structure and of coast preservation.

(2) Joint tasks shall be defined in detail by federal legislation requiring the consent of the Bundesrat. Such legislation should include general principles governing the discharge of joint tasks.

(3) Such legislation shall provide for the procedure and the institutions required for joint overall planning. The inclusion of a project in the overall planning shall require the consent of the Land in which it is to be carried out.

(4) In cases to which items 1 and 2 of para. (1) of this Article apply, the Bund shall meet one-half of the expenditure in each Land. In cases to which item 3 of para. (1) of this Article applies, the Federation shall meet at least one-half of the expenditure, and such proportion shall be the same for all the Länder. Details shall be regulated by legislation. Provision of funds shall be subject to appropriation in the budgets of the Bund and the Länder.

(5) The Federal Government and the Bundesrat shall be informed about the execution of joint tasks, should they so demand.

Art. 91b. Co-operation of Federation and Länder in Education Planning and in Research

The Bund and the Länder may both, pursuant to agreements, co-operate in educational planning and in promotion of institutions and projects of scientific research of supraregional importance. The apportionment of costs shall be regulated in the pertinent agreements.

After 1945 the Western occupying powers and the Germans alike sought to develop a decentralized police administration. Under the occupation regime the police were organized along zonal lines, with the United States zone achieving the greatest degree of decentralization and local control. When the Basic Law was being developed, the Germans responded to the abuses of the Nazi period by recognizing the police as falling under the reserved power of the Länder. Consequently, in a return to the pre–1933 pattern, there is today no federal police force. Each Land has its own separate force under the direction of its Ministry of the Interior. None the less, the indirect influence and participation of the Bund in police affairs are substantial. The Länder are parties to administrative agreements with the Bund to provide collective action—especially in cases of national emergencies and crises.[4] Land police officers are classified as civil servants and are covered by the Federal Civil Servants Framework Law (Doc. 1b). Above all, in the early 1950s, under the impact of the Korean war with its demonstration of the 'clear and present' communist danger, special federal services were created, including the Federal Border Police (Bundesgrenzschutz), the Federal Office for the Protection of the Constitution (Bundesamt für Verfassungsschutz) and the Federal Crime Office (Bundeskriminalamt).[5] As well as the complex Bund–Land relationships, there are agreements covering various relationships between the police forces of the Länder themselves. Police matters thus not only involve Bund–Land but also inter-Land levels of contact under the overall federal umbrella.

In addition to its main responsibilities as a central repository of crime statistics and crime research centre, the Federal Crime Office serves as a coordinating agency for the Länder in nationwide pursuit of criminals.

b) ACT REGULATING THE ESTABLISHMENT OF THE FEDERAL CRIME OFFICE (BUNDESKRIMINALAMT)

Source: BGBl., I, 29 June 1973, 704ff.

Art. 1. Establishment and Function

(1) The Bund establishes a Federal Crime Office for the purpose of procuring cooperation in criminal investigations between the Bund and the Länder. Its function is to pursue any criminal element insofar as it operates, or will potentially operate, internationally or beyond the jurisdiction of a single Land.

(2) The Federal Crime Office is also the national headquarters of the International Police Organization (Interpol) for the Federal Republic of Germany.

Art. 2. Functions in Detail

(1) It is the function of the Federal Crime Office as a central agency to:

1. compile and evaluate all information and data relating to the combating of crime. In this respect it is also the headquarters for the data centre shared by the Federal Government and the Länder;
2. advise the prosecuting authorities of the Federal Government and the Länder immediately of any relevant information and of any connection which it might discover between crimes;
3. maintain the facilities for police records;
4. maintain the facilities necessary for all aspects of criminal investigation and for research on criminal practices, as well as coordinate the cooperation of police in these areas;
5. study crime patterns and compile criminal investigation analyses and statistics based on its findings;
6. conduct research on the development of police practices and on methods of combatting crime;
7. give support to the police of the Länder in the prevention of crime;
8. hold continuing education sessions on special areas of criminal investigation.

At the request of police headquarters, the public prosecutor and the courts, the Federal Crime Office gives expert advice based on police records and criminal practices.

Art. 3. Criminal Investigation Departments of the Länder

(1) To ensure cooperation between the Federal Government and the Länder, the Länder are obliged to maintain Crime Offices for their areas. These centres are to relay to the Federal Crime Office any information or data necessary for it to perform its functions.

Art. 4. Obligation of Notification of the Crime Offices of the Länder

(1) The Land Crime Offices notify the Federal Crime Office of the beginning, the interruption and the termination of a term of imprisonment imposed by the courts.
(2) The same obligation of notification is incumbent on the judicial and administrative authorities vis à vis the Land Crime Offices.

. . .

Art. 6. The Dispatch of Officials to the Police Authorities of the Länder

(1) To assist in criminal prosecutions the Federal Crime Office may dispatch of-

ficials to the Länder if so required by the responsible police authorities of the Länder.

(2) The highest Land authority is to be informed immediately.

Art. 7. Central Exercise of Police Functions in Different Länder

(1) If a crime affects more than one Land or if a connection exists with another crime in another Land, and if it is desirable that the functions of the police in regard to criminal prosecutions be carried out from a central location, the Federal Crime Office will inform the Attorney General (Generalstaatsanwalt) and the highest Land authorities in whose areas jurisdiction lies. The Federal Crime Office assigns responsibility in criminal prosecutions to a Land in agreement with the Attorney General and the highest authority of the Land on the understanding that the responsibility wil be fully assumed.

(2) The Land Crime Office is responsible for the fulfilment of the responsibility assigned to the Land. . . . The highest Land authority may designate another police authority other than the Land Crime Office as the appropriate agency.

Art. 8. Official Acts of the Executive Officers of the Federal Republic and the Länder

(1) Executive officers . . . must notify the local police authorities immediately of any investigation within their jurisdiction unless there is good reason why this should not be done. Whenever possible local responsible police authorities should be included in the investigation proceedings.

(2) The police authorities of the Land provide information and permit inspection of its records in cases under its jurisdiction to the Federal Crime Office and to the officials dispatched by it. . . . The same holds true for police officials of the Länder. . . .

(3) The locally responsible police authorities furnish personal and practical assistance to the officials of the Federal Crime Office, or in the case of an assignment under Art. 7, para. 1, to officials of another Land who are carrying out an investigation.

. . .

The Federal Office for the Protection of the Constitution, established by federal law in 1950, collects and passes on information to other authorities but has itself no police powers such as the power of arrest. The need to provide for special safeguards for the constitutional order must be viewed against the background of the Nazi seizure of power in 1933 and especially in the light of the present division of Germany, with the 'other German state', the German Democratic Republic (DDR), forming the western outpost of Moscow's empire. While the frontier separating the DDR from the Federal Republic is heavily fortified and sealed off to prevent movement from East to West[6], it is possible for East Germans (and East German agents) to cross the frontier to the West without any visa or other formalities. There is ample evidence of extensive East German subversive activities in the Federal Republic, including considerable financial assistance to the Moscow-dominated Deutsche Kommunistische Partei (DKP) annually.[7]

Since the Länder governments also established similar offices, the cooperation between the Bund and the constituent states had to be laid down in special agreements, published in excerpts below.

c) ACT REGULATING THE COOPERATION OF THE FEDERAL GOVERN-MENT AND THE LÄNDER IN MATTERS RELATING TO THE PROTECTION OF THE CONSTITUTION (BUNDESAMT FÜR VERFASSUNGSSCHUTZ, LANDESÄMTER FÜR VERFASSUNGSSCHUTZ)

Source: Federal Gazette, I, 7 September 1950, 282

Art. 1. Duty of the Bund and the Länder to Cooperate

(1) The Bund and the Länder are obliged to cooperate in matters relating to the protection of the Constitution.
(2) Cooperation involves mutual support and assistance.

Art. 2. Federal Office for the Protection of the Constitution

(1) The Federal Government establishes a Federal Office for the Protection of the Constitution as the highest federal authority to realize cooperation between the Federal Government and the Länder. It is placed under the jurisdiction of the Federal Minister of the Interior.
(2) Each Land appoints an authority to deal with matters relating to the protection of the Constitution to implement the cooperation of the Länder with the Federal Government.

Art. 3. Functions of the Federal Office for the Protection of the Constitution

(1) The function of the Federal Office for the Protection of the Constitution and the authorities established under Art. 2, para. 2 is the compilation and interpretation of information, intelligence and other data dealing with:

1. efforts which are directed against the stability and security of the Federal Republic or of a Land, or which have as an objective unlawful infringement on the administrative activities of members of constitutional bodies of the Federal Republic;
2. threats to security or espionage activities within the scope of this law on behalf of a foreign power;

3. activities falling within the scope of this law which endanger the foreign interests of the Federal Republic and which involve the use of force or a conspiracy to use force.

(2) Further, the Federal Office for the Protection of the Constitution and the authorities appointed under Art. 2, para. 2, will co-operate in:

1. the investigation of persons who will be entrusted with data, subject matter or information which must be kept secret in the public interest, and of persons who are believed to have access to or who are capable of gaining access to such materials;
2. the investigation of persons who are employed or who will be so employed in sensitive security areas which are essential to life and defense;
3. technical security measures for the protection of data, subject matter or information which must be kept secret from unauthorized persons.

(3) The Federal Office for the Protection of the Constitution has no police or supervisory powers. To carry out its duties in accordance with paras. 1 and 2, it may make use of intelligence service resources. The Office may not become affiliated with a police authority.

(4) The courts and authorities and the Federal Office for the Protection of the Constitution cooperate with each other in providing legal and administrative assistance (Art. 35, Basic Law).

Art. 4. Reciprocal Information

(1) The Federal Office for the Protection of the Constitution gives the authorities established in each Land under Art. 2, para. 2, all data required by the Land to protect the constitution.

(2) The authorities established in the Länder keep the Federal Office informed of all those matters relating to the protection of the constitution which come to their attention and which are important either to the Federal Republic, to the Länder, or to both.

(3) If an authority other than the supreme Land authority is appointed under Art. 2, Sec. 2, the supreme Land authority is to be so advised.

Art. 5. Authority to Issue Directives

(1) When an attack on the constitutional order of the Federal Republic is initiated, the Federal Government may issue to the highest Land authorities directives requiring the cooperation of the Länder with the Federal Republic in the protection of the Constitution.

. . .

The Federal Border Police (Bundesgrenzschutz), established in 1951 has the statutory responsibility to do duty on the frontier crossings of the Federal Republic and to observe, more especially, the tragic division line between the two Germanies, sealed off with barbed wire with electronic and explosive devices by the East German government.[8] As a result of terrorist activities in the 1970s, the Bundesgrenzschutz established a special anti-terrorist unit (the so-called GSG 9 force). Only the Land Bavaria has its own, separate border police force, the Bayrische Grenz-schutzpolizei. The working relationships between it and the Federal Border Police were outlined in a special agreement of 1976.

d) LAW CONCERNING THE ORGANIZATION OF THE BAVARIAN LAND POLICE, 10 AUGUST 1976 (POLIZEIORGANISATIONSGESETZ)

Source: GVB., 1976, 303ff.

. . .

Art. 4. The Land Police

(1) The Bavarian Land Police has the responsibility within the entire state [*sic*] territory for all tasks incumbent on a police force except when particular local and specialized units . . . are responsible.

. . .

Art. 5. The Border Police

(1) the Bavarian Border Police are charged with the protection of the state territory . . . . The [border protection] consists of:

1. the surveillance of the borders of the Land,
2. the supervision of the border-crossing traffic including
    (a) the checking of the legal documents required for border crossing,
    (b) criminal investigation emanating outside federal territory,
    (c) the prevention of disturbances and protection against threats and dangers which jeopardize the security of the border territory, within an area of up to 30 km from the frontier.

(2) The State Ministry of the Interior can within the border territory authorize the Border Police to substitute for the Land Police.

. . .

Art. 7. Land Crime Office

(1) The Land Crime Office is the central office in charge of criminal investigations. It is directly subordinate to the State Ministry of the Interior. Furthermore, the Land Crime Office is also the central headquarters for the criminal

police within the meaning of the Act for the Creation of the Federal Crime Office, for data processing and data transmission for the police . . . .

The Königstein Administrative Agreement of 31 March 1949 provided for the financing of scientific research institutions, including the world famous Max Planck Institutes (especially for the natural sciences). This agreement was subsequently extended several times. It is a good example of early cooperative agreements between the Länder which were arranged outside of the provisions of the Basic Law.

e) THE KÖNIGSTEIN AGREEMENT OF THE LÄNDER OF THE FEDERAL REPUBLIC OF GERMANY ON THE FINANCING OF SCIENTIFIC RESEARCH FACILITIES, 31 MARCH 1949
Source: Xerox copy, Archives Kultusmiknisterkonferenz, Bonn

The Länder of Baden, Bavaria, Lower Saxony, North-Rhine-Westfalia, Rhineland-Palatinate, Schleswig-Holstein, Württemberg-Baden, Württemberg-Hohenzollern, represented by their Minister Presidents, the Hanseatic city of Hamburg, represented by the Senate, the Free Hanseatic city of Bremen, represented by the President of the Senate, have concluded the following agreement:

Art. 1

Under the terms of this agreement, the signatories undertake to raise jointly the necessary funds for German scientific research facilities whose functions and significance exceed the general sphere of activity of a single Land and whose need for support exceeds the financial capability of a single Land. . . .

Art. 2

In order to spend the public funds available for research purposes efficiently and to keep the budgetary accounts straight, the signatories assume that the research facilities to be financed jointly by the Länder are not simultaneously receiving subsidies from the Bund. . . .

. . .

Art. 4

The signatories agree that the Länder should be afforded due representation in the Senate of the Max Planck Institute.

Art. 5

The signatories will determine annually the total demands on the funds to be made available by the Länder. They may make the availability of these funds conditional on an appropriate portion of the subsidy requirements of a research facility being covered by the Land in which that research facility has its headquarters.

Art. 6

The sum of the funds to be raised jointly will be assessed for each Land at two-thirds based on tax income and one-third based on population. Tax income is increased or reduced relative to the amounts which a Land receives from other Länder or which they pay other Länder within the framework of the general financial settlement.

Art. 7

The agreement will run initially for five years. It enters into force on 1 April 1949.

An early example of another type of intergovernmental cooperation is the agreement made between the Federation and the Länder in 1967.

f) ADMINISTRATIVE AGREEMENT BETWEEN THE BUND AND THE LÄNDER CONCERNING THE ESTABLISHMENT OF A SCIENCE COUNCIL, 5 NOVEMBER 1957
Source: GMBl., No. 20, 558

Art. 1

The parties agree to establish a Science Council

Art. 2

The Science Council is charged:

1. to work out an overall programme for the furtherance of the sciences, based on the plans devised by the Bund and the Länder within their respective competences and, thereby, to harmonize the programs of the Bund and the Länder; . . .
2. to arrange annually for an emergency programme;
3. to make recommendations for the use of those funds which are provided by the Bund and the Länder for the furtherance of the sciences.

Art. 4

(1) The Science Council is composed of 39 members. The members shall be scientists, or qualified persons in public life, or individuals closely associated professionally with the sciences and their furtherance.

(2) 22 members are to be appointed by the President of the Federal Republic; 16 of these are to be jointly nominated by the German Research Society, the Max Planck Society and the West German Rectors Conference, and the other six to be jointly nominated by the Federal Government and the governments of the Länder. . . .

(3) 17 members shall be selected by the Federal Government and the governments of the Länder; of these, the Federal Government designates six members, the governments of the Länder one member each.

. . .

Art. 9

The expenditures for personnel and material will be equally borne by the Bund and the Länder. Two-thirds of the total amount of the funds, which are to be appropriated by the Länder, will be apportioned among the Länder in proportion to their tax income, and one-third in proportion to the size of their respective populations. . . .

———————————

An important example of intergovernmental cooperation is the Standing Conference of the Länder Ministers of Education which also provides an example of inter-Land cooperation. This agreement was designed to secure a minimum of uniformity in the educational systems throughout the Bund.

g) STANDING CONFERENCE OF THE MINISTERS OF EDUCATION, SCIENCE AND CULTURAL AFFAIRS OF THE LÄNDER (STÄNDIGE KONFERENZ DER KULTURSMINISTER)
Source: Secretariat of Standing Conference, 1982
Transl.: Secretariat

The Standing Conference is a voluntary body of the ministers (in some cases called senators) in the Länder, including Berlin (West), responsible for education, science and research, and cultural affairs. This institution which, since 1948, has evolved under the shortened name *Kultursministerkonferenz* is not provided for in the constitution. It operates along pragmatic lines, by consultation, mutual information-gathering and discussion. Its function is to deal with 'matters of cultural policy of supraregional importance with the objective to reach common opinions and aims, and representing common interests' (preamble of the standing orders). One of the main tasks of the Standing Conferences is that of coordination. According to the Basic Law, the legislative body and the government in each Land are responsible for all educational and cultural affairs within the area of the respective territory. However, as each Land in the Federal Republic of Germany is a member of the Bund, the activity of one Land is never without influence upon its neighbour; in addition, each Land must be aware of its joint responsibility.

The *plenary* of the Conference consists of the ministers of education, science and cultural affairs of the Länder of the Federal Republic of Germany, including Berlin. It meets at intervals of about eight weeks. Each minister, i.e., each Land, has only one vote. Problems must be discussed as long as it takes to reach a conclusion which is acceptable to all parties concerned. The resolutions of the Conference can only be adopted unanimously. The *ministers' deputies* (senior officials) also meet regularly.

Four major *standing committees* are concerned with the preparation of the decisions to be taken by the plenary:

1. the schools committee
2. the committee on higher education
3. the committee on art and adult education
4. the committee on German, European and International schools abroad

The Conference has also set up various *commissions*: for international affairs, statistics, forecasting and educational economics (i.e., the data commission), and sport. The Länder are represented on the committees and commissions by the officials concerned with these fields of activity. The standing commission for study reform, likewise appointed by the Standing Conference, consists half of representatives of institutions of higher education.

. . .

Secretariat

The Standing Conference is served by a Secretariat located at Bonn. . . . The Secretariat prepares the plenary, committee and commission meetings and undertakes the evaluation and implementation of the results. It also maintains the flow of information among the education ministries and is a point of contact between them and the federal authorities and other supra-regional institutions, especially as concerns external cultural relations and international and supranational co-operation in the field of educational and cultural policy. . . .

―――――――――――

The amendments to the Housing Modernization Act of 1978 illustrate several of the salient points made in this chapter; the federal financing of

Länder activities in the field of joint tasks, the execution of federal law in Länder and municipalities, and the possibilities of the municipalities to get federal aid.

h) AMENDMENTS TO THE HOUSING MODERNIZATION ACT

Source: Federal Gazette, I, 1978, 878

Art. 1

The Housing Modernization Act of 23 August 1976 ... will be amended as follows: ...

Art. 2

(1) Aims of government support:

1. The Bund and the Länder support the modernization of housing as a means of improving the availability of good, low-priced housing to a wider sector of the population, thus contributing to the aid of cities and communities and
2. measures to conserve heating energy in homes.

. . .

Art. 7 (6) Financial Contribution of the Federal Republic

1. The Bund will contribute to the financing of modernization as called for by the Länder in accordance with this law. Federal funds as provided in the federal budget will be made available to the Länder as financial assistance under the terms of Art. 104a, Sec. 4 of the Basic Law. They will constitute up to half of the expenditures in subsidies.

. . .

3. The financial assistance of the Bund will be made available on the basis of administrative agreements between the Federal Republic and the Länder, unless otherwise decided. To encourage energy conservation measures the Bund will grant the Länder financial assistance to the amount of 1,170 million DM in the years 1978 to 1982.

Notes

1. See also Ch. 5, Doc 6
2. See also Ch. 6, Doc. 1
3. Traditionally a German university was headed by a *rector magnificus*, elected for two years as a *primus inter pares* by the faculties
4. See also Ch. 12, 316
5. See also Ch. 2, n. 8
6. See also Ch. 14
7. Cf. Annual Reports of the Federal Ministry of the Interior, Bonn
8. See Ch. 14

8 Political Parties

Anthony Nicholls

Political parties in Germany are not only recognized in law and regulated by it, they are even referred to in the Federal German Constitution (Basic Law).* Art. 21 of the Basic Law is clearly designed to ensure that political parties respect the principles of democracy. It reads as follows:

(1) Political parties shall participate in the forming of the political will of the people. They may be freely established. Their internal organisation must conform to democratic principles. They must publicly account for the sources of their funds.

(2) Parties which, by reason of their aims or the behaviour of their adherents, seek to impair or abolish the free democratic basic order or to endanger the existence of the Federal Republic of Germany shall be unconstitutional. The Federal Constitutional Court shall decide on the question of unconstitutionality.

(3) Details shall be regulated by federal laws.[1]

This provision in the Basic Law was designed to prevent a recurrence of the situation which had developed in the Weimar Republic, when parties like the Nazis and Communists had abused the freedom given to them under the constitution to attack democracy itself. In the early years of the Republic the restrictions in the Basic Law were indeed implemented against threats from the right and left. The neo-Nazi Socialist Reich Party (SRP) was banned in 1952, and in 1956 the German Communist Party (KPD) suffered the same fate.[2]

Nevertheless, it took some time before the Federal legislation referred to in the last paragraph of Art. 21 passed through parliament. It was not

---

* Notes for this chapter begin on p. 229

until July 1967 that the Law on Political Parties was finally approved by the Bundesrat (Doc. 1).

The law defines political parties and lays down rules about their statutes and organization. The rights of members, election of officers, and the regulation of finances are established in this law.

The question of party finances has been the subject of both legislation and judicial proceedings. In general, strict rules are established about the public declaration of financial contributions. On the other hand parties are generously treated by comparison with Anglo-Saxon counterparts, in that they receive direct financial assistance from the state in direct proportion to their performance at the polls. Contributions to party funds are also, if only to a limited extent, exempt from personal taxation. The way in which these matters are regulated in the Party Law is set out in Doc. 2.

The electoral process in the Federal Republic is also carefully circumscribed by statute. Art. 38 of the Basic Law stipulates that the members of the Bundestag shall be elected in 'general, free, equal and secret elections'.

The Bundestag and Land parliaments are elected according to a system which combines direct election with proportional representation (Doc. 3). The aim is to combine fairness of representation with political stability; it is assumed that 'pure' proportional representation would lead to a multiplicity of small parties and weak coalition governments.

Normally the Bundestag has a total of 518 members, of whom twenty-two are elected from West Berlin. Half the remaining 496 are directly elected in constituencies—the other half from party lists drawn up in each Land. This illustrates the importance of legally defining parties in Germany, since the electoral process would not work if the fiction were maintained that such parties did not exist.

Electors have two votes, the first of which is given to a candidate and the second to a party list. In each of the 248 constituencies one candidate is directly elected by simple majority. Then electors' second votes are put together with those from other constituencies and a total figure for each party in the Federal Republic is obtained (Electoral Law, section 6, paras. 1 and 2). The 248 'list' seats are then divided among the parties using the d'Hondt system of calculation.[3] Once each party's total entitlement has been defined, its seats are divided among the Land lists according to the second votes cast in the various Länder, although the number of directly elected members is subtracted from the total entitlement in each case. If a party has more directly elected members than its total of second votes in any one Land would warrant, it is allowed to keep the extra members and the number of seats in the Bundestag from that Land is increased accordingly. This occurred, for instance, in Schleswig-Holstein in 1980.[4] Voters may, of course, choose different parties with their first and second votes and such 'tactical' voting is not uncommon. The decisive vote for determining the strength of the parties is the second vote. In order to gain seats from the Land lists at all, parties must obtain at least 5 per cent of the valid votes cast or be successful in direct elections in three constitutencies (section 6, para. 11). This so-called '5 per cent hurdle' has been a serious obstacle to the emergence of small parties in the Bundestag and is a constant threat to the FDP. The law also sets out rules for the presentation and selection of party candidates. All such candidates must be elected by constituency parties according to defined procedures (sections 20 and 21).

In comparison with some Anglo-Saxon countries, membership of political parties is high in the Federal Republic. In 1981 the Social Democratic Party claimed 956,490 members. In the same period the two Christian Parties mustered well over three-quarters of a million members between them.[5]

Electoral participation is also very impressive. Since 1957 the turnout for Bundestag elections has never dropped below 85 per cent and in 1972 it was as high as 91 per cent.[6] At the last election, in March 1983, it was 89.1 per cent. One reason for this may be the attention paid to political education in German schools. More important is possibly the fact that elections in Germany are held on a Sunday, so that working people are given a fair chance to go to the polling booths. It is also relatively easy to obtain a postal vote. However, it should be remembered that proportional representation itself encourages a high turnout because no elector needs to feel that he is wasting his vote.

In accordance with the laws established for political parties, their statutes set out in detail their aims, membership, organization and financing arrangements. The laws require that the parties should be organized on strictly democratic lines.

Examples from contrasting political groups illustrate the extent to which party life is based on firm legal foundations.

The first example is the statute of the Christian Democratic Union, Germany's most important conservative party and a ruling party in Bonn coalitions, 1949–1969 and 1982 to the present (Doc. 4).

The second example is that of the Social Democratic Party, the main opposition group, 1949–1965, and the foundation of coalition governments, 1969–82 (Doc. 5).

The third example is taken from the statute of the Greens' Party, an ecological movement (Doc. 6). This is a relatively new party. It openly rejects many of the values which have informed previous political discussions in Bonn, although it fully accepts the democratic constitution. The nature of its statute and organization is not markedly different from that of the other parties, although it does stress the desire to decentralize party politics and create democracy from the 'grass roots' (Section 10, Arts. 1 and 2), and it does specifically commit itself to try and obtain proportionally just representation for women at all levels in the party structure (Section 7, Art. 3). The Greens also make a point of restricting their leaders' terms of office to ensure rotation of personnel and the maximum influence from the 'grass roots'.

So far as the Christian Democrats and Social Democrats are concerned, their statutes do not reveal striking differences, except that the SPD is rather more centralized in its organization than the CDU. This reflects different attitudes to the issue of Federalism; the Christian Democrats have always stressed the importance of the Land divisions within the Federal Republic.

In all parties policy is defined by the party conference. Party leaders, even when they are in government, cannot dispense with the confidence of the party conference. An example of this was Chancellor Schmidt's difficulty in carrying his party with him on defence and economic matters in 1982.

Party Finances
The financial affairs of political parties are carefully regulated in their statutes. Both the CDU and the SPD assess contributions in relation to income, so that wealthier members pay more than poorer ones (Docs. 7 and 8).

Party Programmes
In the early years of the Federal Republic there were clear programmatic differences between the parties. The Christian Democrats stood for a decentralized Germany, integrated into Western Europe and NATO. They were in favour of Church influence on German cultural life, believed in private property and, by 1949, they were committed to free enterprise in the economy. However, this was tempered by a commitment to social welfare—the so-called 'Social Market Economy'.[7] The Social Democrats wanted a centralized Germany with a strong emphasis on social equality. They favoured an economic policy involving state planning and the socialization of major industries. The Free Democrats also wanted a strong central government and were specially concerned to

see Germany reunified. They, like the Social Democrats, were opposed to clerical influence in education. However, they were completely against state interference in the economy or state control of industry. If anything, the Free Democrats, despite their liberal-sounding name, were socially more conservative, more nationalist and more committed to laissez-faire economics than the CDU.

After the first decade of Federal German politics, differences between the parties began to blur. The SPD, for example, discouraged by poor Federal election results and headed by a new generation of leaders, changed its programme so that it accepted the free market, at least in modified form, and committed itself to national defence. This was enshrined in the Godesberg Programme of November 1959 (Doc. 9).

Towards the end of Chancellor Schmidt's administration differences of opinion surfaced within the SPD, above all over defence policy. These divisions have become more marked since the 1983 Bundestag elections. However, so far no serious split is discernible. In the 1960s the Free Democrats also faced divisions of loyalty and began to move towards a form of liberalism which stressed individual freedom rather than national-ism or business interests. In October 1971 at their Congress in Freiburg, they enshrined this humane liberalism into the 'Freiburg theses' which formed the basis of their programme and the theoretical justification for political collaboration with the Social Democrats (Doc. 10).

The Christian Democrats have found it possible to retain most of their basic principles, though they have felt the need to put a new gloss on some aspects of their policies, such as those dealing with the protection of the environment or women's rights. They have clashed with Free Democrats and Social Democrats over the attitude to be adopted towards the Soviet Union and other Eastern European countries, not to mention, of course, the German Democratic Republic. The CDU/CSU stress the need to resist Soviet pressure and strengthen the West. They also tend to favour stronger measures to uphold law and order, and vigilance against subversion in the public services. The general principles of Christian Democracy are well set out in the fundamental programme of the CDU's Bavarian sister party, the Christian Social Union, passed by the Party Congress at Munich in March 1976 (Doc. 11).

It will be seen that at least by the early 1970s the area of common ground between the parties represented in the Bundestag had become very large. Today differences in electoral programmes rarely concern fundamental matters of principle, but are about the priority to be given to different objectives. In many ways this is a source of stability in the system. From time to time, however, there have been signs that the consensus is under strain. In the early 1980s, for example, a new party, the Greens, has emerged to challenge the traditional ones. The Greens were founded on 17 March 1979 in Frankfurt/Sindligen, also calling themselves the 'Other Political Association' (Die Sonstige Politische Vereinigung). They were formed out of an amalgam of ecological and citizens' action groups from various parts of Germany. On 13 January 1980 they established themselves as a Federal Party. Although they only obtained 1.5 per cent of the vote* in the Bundestag elections of 1980, they went on to achieve increasing success in Land elections, and gained representation in several Land parliaments. In March 1983 they polled 5.6 per cent, or over two million, of the second votes cast in the Bundestag elections and gained twenty-seven seats. The Greens owe their rising popularity to disillusionment with the established parties at a time of economic stagnation, and to their ability to exploit local environmental problems. They are opposed to nuclear power and nuclear armaments. Their programme involves a fundamental rejection of the premises upon which West Germany's post-war prosperity has been based—especially the concept of economic growth (Doc. 12).

There have also been threats from the extreme Right and Left. In the middle years of the 1960s, when a minor economic set-back occurred, the political system in the Federal Republic was challenged by a radical nationalist party, the National Democrats or NPD. It obtained some impressive results in Land elections, but was never able to overcome the 5 per cent hurdle in a Bundestag election. Since 1969 it has dwindled in importance. In the 1980 Bundestag elections it only achieved 0.2 per cent of the vote. Although its founders were careful to pay lip-service to the Basic Law of the Federal Republic, their extreme nationalism and dislike of Bonn's parliamentary democracy was thinly disguised (Doc. 13). On the Left, Radical Marxist parties also exist, despite the banning of the Communist Party (KPD) in 1956. The party which claims to be the successor to the KPD, although carefully defining itself as compatible with the Basic Law, is the German Communist Party (DKP), which was set up in 1968. Unlike some other Communist parties, it is completely loyal to Soviet policies, and expresses itself in the language of the class war (see Doc. 14). Electorally it is very weak, gaining only 0.2 per cent of the votes at the last Bundestag election. However, it does have some influence over radical students and young people, and encourages demonstrations against NATO or other aspects of Western policy.

---

* The figures for the Greens, the NPD and the DKP (below) refer to second votes—cast for party lists

More extreme in methods and aims are the 'New Left' groups supporting fundamentalist Marxist-Leninism and hard-line Maoism.[8] Such
groups are volatile and fissiparous. They are committed to international
revolution and reject both Western capitalism and 'Russian Social Imperialism'. One example of such a group is the Communist League of
West Germany (KBW) (Doc. 15). From the electoral viewpoint these
groups have no significance, but they do try to exert some influence on
student politics, citizens' initiatives and the ecological movement.

It is not likely, however, that the German people will lightly leave the
path of parliamentary democracy or the policies which have accompanied it. These may be summarized as a mixed economy with free competition softened by enlightened social policies; commitment to NATO
and the European Community and a willingness to seek trade and
diplomatic dialogue with Eastern Europe. In this sense the electoral laws
and party system have proved highly successful.

Document 1

THE LAW ON POLITICAL PARTIES (PARTEIENGESETZ): INTERNAL
ORGANIZATION, 24 JULY 1967
Source: Documents on Politics and Society in the Federal Republic of Germany (Inter
Nationes, Bonn, 1978) citing BGBl. I, 1967, 773
Transl.: Official

I: General Provisions

Art. 1. Constitutional Status and Functions of the Parties

(1) Political parties form a constitutionally integral part of a free democratic
system of government. Their free and continuous participation in the formation
of political opinions amongst the population enables them to discharge the public
tasks which are incumbent upon them pursuant to the Basic Constitutional Law
(Grundgesetz) and which they undertake to fulfil to the best of their ability.
(2) The parties participate in the formation of the political will of the people in all
fields of national life, in particular by:

bringing their influence to bear on the shaping of public opinion;
inspiring and furthering political education;
promoting an active participation by individual citizens in political life;
training talented people to assume public responsibilities;
participating in Federal, Land and Local Government elections by nominating
candidates;
exercising an influence on political trends in parliament and the government;
initiating their defined political aims in the national decision-making processes;

and
ensuring continuous, vital links between the people and the public authorities.
(3) The parties define their aims in the form of political programs.

Art. 2. Definition of the Term 'Political Party'

(1) Parties are associations of citizens who set out to influence either permanently or for a long period of time the formation of political opinions at Federal or Land level and to participate in the representation of the people in the . . . Bundestag or regional parliaments.

. . .

Art. 4. Designation

(1) The name of a party must be clearly distinguishable from that of any existing party . . . .

. . .

Art. 5. Parity of Treatment

(1) Where a public authority provides facilities or other public services for use by a party, it must accord equal treatment to all other parties . . . .

II: Internal Organisation

Art. 6. Statutes and Program

(1) A party must have written statutes (articles of association) and a written program.

. . .

(2) The statutes must contain provisions on:

1. the name and abbreviation (if used), the registered seat and the activities of the party;
2. the admission and designation of members;
3. the rights and duties of members;
4. admissible disciplinary measures against members and their exclusion from the party (Art. 10, paras. 3 to 5);
5. admissible disciplinary measures against regional associations;
6. the general organisation of the party;
7. composition and powers of the executive committee (Vorstand) and other bodies (Organe);
8. matters which may only be decided upon by a meeting of members and representatives pursuant to Art. 9;

9. the preconditions, form and time limit for convening meetings of members and representatives and the official recording of the resolutions;
10. regional associations and bodies which are authorised to submit or sign election proposals for elections to parliaments inasmuch as there are no legal provisions on this matter;
11. an overall vote by members and the procedure to be adopted when the party-congress (convention) has passed a resolution to dissolve the party or a regional association or to merge with another party;

. . .

Art. 7. Organisation

(1) Parties are subdivided into regional associations. The size and scope of these units are determined in the statutes. The regional structure of the party must be developed to a sufficient degree to enable individual members to participate on an appropriate scale in the formation of political opinions within the party . . .

. . .

Art. 8. Party Bodies (Organe)

(1) The members' meeting and executive committee constitute the essential organs of the party and the regional associations . . .

. . .

Art. 9. Meetings of Members and Representatives (Party Congress, General Meeting)

(1) The members' or representatives' meeting constitutes the supreme body in the given regional association. It is designated as a party congress (Parteitag) in higher level regional associations and general meeting (Hauptversammlung) at the lower levels. . . . Party congresses are convened in at least every second calendar year.

(2) Pursuant to the statutes, members of the executive committee and members of other bodies in a regional association . . . may participate in a representatives' meeting. However, in this case they may only be given voting rights on a scale corresponding to one-fifth of the total number of members at the meeting who are entitled to vote.

(3) . . . the party-congress decides on programmes, statutes, contribution subscriptions, arbitral procedure, dissolution of the party and merging with other parties.

(4) The party-congress elects the chairman (Vorsitzender) of the regional association, his representatives and the other members of the executive committee. . . .

Art. 10. The Rights of Members

(1) . . . . No justification need be given for refusing an application for member-

ship. Neither general nor temporary embargoes on new members are permissible. . . .

(2) Members of the party and representatives in the party bodies have equal voting rights. . . .

(3) The statutes contain provisions governing:

1. admissible disciplinary measures against members;
2. reasons for such measures;
3. those bodies within the party which may order the implementation of disciplinary measures.

If a member is deprived of his party offices or his qualification to hold them, the justification for such a decision must be stated.

(4) A member may only be expelled from the party if he deliberately infringes the statutes or acts in a manner quite contrary to the principles or discipline of the party and thus seriously impairs its standing.

(5) The arbitral court competent in accordance with the arbitration procedure code decides upon expulsion from the party. The right to appeal to a higher court is guaranteed. . . .

Art. 11. Executive Committee (Vorstand)

(1) The executive committee must be elected at least every second calendar year. It must comprise at least three members.

(2) . . . the executive committee may include members of parliament and other high-ranking persons in the party if they hold office by virtue of an election. The proportion of members not elected under the provisions of Art. 9, para. 4, may not exceed one-fifth of the total number of executive committee members.

. . .

Art. 13. Composition of Representatives' Meetings

The composition of a representatives' meeting or that of any other body wholly or partly comprising representatives from regional associations is laid down in the statutes. The number of representatives from a regional association is primarily calculated on the basis of the number of represented members. The statutes may provide that the composition of the rest of the representatives from the regional associations, at most one-half of the total, shall be determined in accordance with the proportion of votes polled at regional association level in previous parliamentry elections. . . .

Art. 14. Party Courts of Arbitration

(1) The party and the highest-level regional associations set up courts of arbitration to settle and decide disputes between the party or a regional association and individual members as well as differences of opinion about the interpretation and implementation of the statutes. . . .

Art. 15. Decision-Making in the Party Bodies

(1) The party bodies adopt their resolutions on the basis of a simple majority vote inasmuch as an increased majority vote is not stipulated by law or by the statutes.
(2) The ballots for members of the executive committee and representatives for representatives' meetings as well as for the bodies of higher-level regional associations are secret. . . .
(3) The statutory provisions governing the submission of motions must be such as to ensure a democratic formation of opinions and in particular adequate discussion of the proposals put forward by minorities. . . .

Art. 16. Measures against Regional Associations

(1) The dissolution and exclusion of subordinate regional associations . . . are only permissible in cases of serious infringement of party principles or discipline. The statutes stipulate:

1. the reasons in justification of the measures;
2. which higher-level regional association and which regional association body may adopt such measures. . . .

III: Nomination of Candidates for Election

Art. 17. Nomination of Candidates

The proposing of candidates for election to parliament must be carried out by secret ballot. The nomination procedure is governed by the election laws and the party statutes. . . .

Document 2

The Law regulates the manner in which political parties may be assisted from public funds when meeting election expenses. The accounting procedures of the parties are also strictly defined.

THE LAW ON POLITICAL PARTIES: FINANCES
Source: Documents on Politics and Society in the Federal Republic of Germany

IV: Reimbursement of Election Expenses

Art. 18. Principles and Scale of Reimbursement

(1) Parties which have taken part in the Bundestag Elections with their own candidates and programmess are reimbursed for the requisite expense of a suitable election campaign. In the current Bundestag election, campaign expenses are re-

imbursed by the payment of a flat-rate sum of DM 3.50 per person entitled to vote (Wahlkampfkostenpauschale).

(2) The payment of this flat-rate sum is allocated amongst parties which, in accordance with the final result of the election, obtain at least:

1. 0.5% of the valid second votes cast in a given district
   or
2. 10% of the valid first votes cast in a given district if a Land list was not permissible for the party in question in this Land.

(3) The share of the flat-rate reimbursement sum granted to the parties is computed on the following basis:

1. parties covered by para. (2) fig. 1 are compensated in accordance with their share of the second votes polled in the given district (Wahlgebiet);
2. a party covered by para. (2) fig. 2 is compensated by payment of a sum of DM 3.50 for every first vote cast in an electoral district (constituency) where the minimum vote of 10% was achieved . . .

. . .

Art. 22. Reimbursement of Election Campaign Expenses in the Länder

The Länder are empowered to adopt legislation containing provisions governing the reimbursement of election campaign expenses in Landtag (Land Diet) elections . . .

Art. 23. Statutory Obligation to Effect a Public Rendering of Accounts

(1) The executive committee of the party must draw up a report to render public account of the origin of funds accruing to its party.

. . .

(2) The account of receipts is subdivided to provide separate information on the following items:

1. members' subscription fees (contributions);
2. fees paid by members of the Parliamentary Party and similar regular contributions;
3. Receipts from:
   (a) assets;
   (b) organised events, the sale of pamphlets, publications and other party activities related to pecuniary gain.
4. donations;
5. credit;
6. reimbursement sums pursuant to the fourth section [election expenses];
7. other income . . .

. . .

Art. 25. The Naming of Donors

Donations to a party or to one or several of its regional associations whose total value per calendar year exceeds DM 20,000 must be quoted in the annual report with a statement of the donor's name and address and the total sum of his donation. . . .

[The law goes on to deal with the types of receipts required and the auditing of accounts. There is also a section on the implementation of the ban on unconstitutional parties.]

Document 3

THE ELECTORAL LAW OF THE FEDERAL REPUBLIC OF GERMANY (BUNDESWAHLGESETZ), 7 MAY 1956
Source: Documents on Politics and Society in the Federal Republic of Germany, Inter Nationes, Bonn, 1980, citing BGBl., I, 1975, 2325
Transl.: Official

Electoral System

§ 1: *Composition of the German Bundestag and Suffrage Principles*
    (1) Subject to variations resulting from this law, the German Bundestag shall consist of 518 members.[9] They shall be elected in a universal direct, free, equal and secret ballot by the Germans entitled to vote, in accordance with the principles of proportional representation combined with the personal election of candidates.
    (2) Of the members, 259 shall be elected from constituency nominations in the constituencies and the rest from Land nominations (Land Lists) . . .

. . .

§ 4: *Votes*
Each voter shall have two votes, a first vote to be cast for a Member of Parliament representing a constituency and a second vote be cast for a Land list.

§ 5: *Polling in the Constituencies*
In each constituency one member shall be returned to Parliament. The candidate obtaining the majority of the votes cast shall be deemed elected. . . .

§ 6: *Election by Land List*
    (1) For the distribution of the seats to be occupied on the basis of Land lists, the second votes cast for each Land list shall be added up.[10] In cases where a successful candidate in a constituency is one who has been nominated in accordance

with § 20, subsection (3), or by a party not entitled to submit a Land list in the Land in question, the second votes of those voters whose first votes were cast for him shall be disregarded. There shall be deducted from the total number of Members of Parliament (§ 1, subsection (1)) the number of successful constituency members referred to in the second sentence above or nominated by parties which, in accordance with subsection (4) of the present section, are not to be taken into consideration. The remaining seats shall be distributed among the Land lists in proportion to the totals of their second votes to be taken into account according to the first and second sentence, using the d'Hondt maximum number system. In case of equal maximum numbers the assignment of the last seat shall be decided by the Federal Returning Officer drawing lots.

(2) From the number of members thus arrived at for each Land list, the number of seats won by the party in question in the constituencies of the respective Land shall be deducted. The remaining seats shall be filled from the Land list concerned in the order laid down therein. Candidates who have been elected in a constituency shall be disregarded in the Land list. . . .

(3) Any party shall retain all the seats it has gained in the constituencies even if they exceed the number arrived at in accordance with subsection (1). In this event the total number of the seats (§ 1, subsection (1)) shall be increased by the differences in the numbers; renewed calculation as under subsection (1) of this section shall not take place.

(4) In distributing the seats among the Land lists, only such parties shall be taken into consideration as have obtained at least 5 per cent of the valid second votes cast in the electoral area or have won a seat in at least three constituencies.

. . .

Franchise and Eligibility

§ 12: *Franchise*
(1) All Germans within the meaning of Art. 116 Para. (1) of the Basic Law shall be entitled to vote, provided that on the day of election they:

1. have reached the age of 18 years;
2. have had a domicile or have otherwise been permanently resident for at least three months within the area of application of this Law; and
3. are not disqualified from voting under § 13. . . .

[Art. 13 refers to those incapacitated by mental illness or disqualified by judicial decision.]

. . .

§ 15: *Eligibility to Stand for Parliament*
(1) There shall be eligible to stand for parliament only such persons as, on election day:

1. have been Germans within the meaning of Art. 116 para. (1) of the Basic
   Law for at least one year;
   and
2. have reached the age of 18 years. ...

[Art. 13 also applies to deny eligibility for election to those incapacitated by mental illness or disqualified by the courts.]

Preparations for the Election

§16: *Election Day*
The Federal President shall decide the day on which the general election is to take place (election day). The election day must fall on a Sunday or on a statutory public holiday. ...

...

§ 18: *Right to Nominate Candidates for Election*
(1) Nominations of candidates may be submitted by parties and, in accordance with § 20, by persons entitled to vote. ...

...

§ 20: *Content and Form of Constituency Nominations*
(1) A constituency nomination may only contain the name of one candidate. Each candidate may only be named in one constituency and there only in one nomination. A person may only be nominated if he or she has given his or her consent in writing; such consent shall be irrevocable.
(2) Constituency nominations by parties must bear the personal and handwritten signatures of the executive committee of the Land party organisation ...
(3) Other constituency nominations must bear the personal and handwritten signatures of at least 200 persons entitled to vote from the constituency concerned. ...

§ 21: *Selection of Party Candidates*
(1) A person may only be named as candidate of a party in a constituency if he or she has been selected for this purpose in an assembly of party members for the selection of a constituency candidate or in a special or general assembly of party representatives. ...

...

(3) The candidates and the representatives for the assemblies of representatives shall be selected by secret ballot. Elections may take place at the earliest thirty-two months, in the case of the representatives' assembly at the earliest twenty-

three months, after the beginning of the legislative term of the German Bundestag; this shall not apply if the period of legislature ends prematurely. . . .

. . .

§ 27: *Land Lists*

(1) Land lists may only be submitted by political parties. They must bear the personal and handwritten signatures of the executive committee of the Land party organisation or, where Land organisations do not exist, those of the executive committees of the next lower regional organisations . . . existing within the territory of the Land; moreover, in the case of the political parties mentioned in § 18, subsection (2)[11], they must be so signed by one per 1,000 of the persons entitled to vote in the Land at the last elections to the Bundestag, but by not more than 2,000 persons entitled to vote. . . .

(2) Land lists must show the name of the party submitting them as well as any shortened form of its name if such form is used by it.

(3) The names of the candidates must be listed in recognizable sequence. . . .

(4) A candidate may only be nominated in one Land, and there only in one Land list. Only such persons as have given their consent in writing may be named in a Land list; such consent shall be irrevocable.

§ 30: *Ballot Papers*

. . .

(2) The ballot paper shall contain:

1. for the constituency elections, the names of the candidates of the accepted constituency nominations; additionally, in the case of constituency nominations by parties, it shall show the names of these parties . . .;
2. for elections by Land lists, the names of the parties . . . as well as the names of the first five candidates on the Land lists accepted.

(3) The order of the Land lists of parties which were represented in the last Bundestag shall be determined by the number of second votes which each obtained in the last Bundestag election in the Land concerned. . . .

. . .

Special Regulations for By-elections and Repeat Elections

§ 43: *By-elections*

(1) A by-election shall take place:

1. if an election has not been held in a constituency or a polling district;
2. if a constituency candidate dies after the acceptance of his or her nomination, but before the election. . . .

§ 48: *Appointment of Successors from the Lists, and Replacement Elections*

(1) If an elected candidate dies or refuses to accept election, or if a member dies or subsequently withdraws from the Bundestag for any other reason, the vacant seat shall be filled by an appointment from the Land list of that party for which the departed member stood at the election. In the selection of the successor those candidates on the list who have—subsequently to the drawing up of the Land list—resigned from the party concerned shall not be taken into consideration. If the list is exhausted, the seat shall remain vacant. . . .

Document 4

STATUTES OF THE CDU, 1 JANUARY 1981
Source: Statut der CDU, Bonn, n.d.

Function, Name, Headquarters

§ 1: *Function*
The aim of the Christian Democratic Union of Germany (CDU) is the democratic structuring of public life in the service of the German people and the German fatherland, in accordance with a Christian sense of responsibility and the Christian moral code, and on the basis of personal liberty.

§ 2: *Name*
The name of the party is the Christian Democratic Union of Germany (CDU)

. . .

Membership

§ 4: *Conditions of membership*
Any German can become a member of the Christian Democratic Union of Germany if he is willing to further its objectives, if he is at least sixteen years old and has not been deprived of his electoral rights by judicial decision . . .

. . .

§ 11: *Expulsion from the party*
(1) A member can only be expelled from the party if he has wilfully violated the party's constitution or gravely flouted its principles or regulations, thereby causing it serious harm.

(2) Motions calling for the expulsion of a member are put by the locally responsible constituency or regional executive or by the party's federal executive and

are decided on by the Party Tribunal responsible according to the regulations governing Party Tribunals.

. . .

(5) Decisions taken by the Party Tribunals in expulsion proceedings must be explained in writing.

. . .

§ 12: *Damaging Behaviour*
Behaviour that is damaging to the party is displayed by anyone who

1. belongs to another political party at the same time.
2. makes statements contrary to the official policy of the CDU at meetings of political opponents, in their radio and television broadcasts or their party newspapers.
3. is elected to a representative body as a candidate of the CDU, but withdraws from or refuses to join the CDU caucus.
4. publishes or leaks to political opponents information on confidential party matters.
5. misappropriates funds belonging to or at the disposal of the party. . . .

Organizational Structure

§ 15: *Levels of Organization*
(1) The CDU is organized at the following levels:

1. the federal party
2. the regional associations
3. the constituency associations
4. the local associations or urban district branches . . .

. . .

§ 16: *Regional Associations*
(1) The Christian Democratic Union of Germany is divided into the following regional associations: Baden-Württemberg, Berlin, Brunswick, Bremen, Hamburg, Hanover, Hesse, Oldenburg, the Rhineland, the Rhineland-Palatinate, the Saarland, Schleswig Holstein and Westphalia-Lippe.
(2) A regional association is the organisation of the CDU in a Land or a province.

. . .

§ 28: *Composition of the Federal Party Conference*
(1) The Federal Party Conference is composed of 750 delegates from the regional associations, who are elected by the constituency, district or regional

party conferences, the honorary chairmen and 30 delegates of the CDU in exile
... Of the regional associations' 750 seats, 150 are allotted in proportion to the
number of 'second' votes cast for each of the CDU's State lists at the last election
to the German Bundestag, and 600 in proportion to the number of members
belonging to each regional association.

...

(5) The Federal Party Conference meets at least once every two years and is
convened by the Federal Executive. It must be convened on the motion of the
Federal Committee or at least one-third of the regional associations. ...

...

§ 29: *Powers of the Federal Party Conference*
Functions of the Federal Party Conference:

(1) It lays down the principles of the Christian Democratic Union and its party
programme; these are the basis of the work of the CDU caucuses and CDU-led
governments in Federal and State Parliaments.

(2) It elects in separate ballots the following members to the Federal Executive:

1. the Party Chairman
2. the General Secretary on the recommendation of the chairman
3. seven vice-chairmen
4. the Party Treasurer
5. twenty other members.

...

Document 5

ORGANISATION STATUTE OF THE SOCIAL DEMOCRATIC PARTY OF
GERMANY, DECEMBER 1971 (WITH AMENDMENTS UP TO NOVEMBER
1975)

Source: Organisationsstatut der Sozialdemokratischen Partei Deutschlands, Bonn,
n.d.

Name, Headquarters, Area of Activity

§ 1:

(1) The name of the party is the Social Democratic Party of Germany (SPD).

(2) The area of its activity as defined by the law applying to political parties is
the area within which the Basic Law of the Federal Republic of Germany is
operative.

...

Structure and Organization

§ 8:

(1) The SPD comprises local branches, sub-districts and district associations. Political opinion within the party is formed in these organizations.

(2) The basis of the organization is the district, the boundaries of which are determined by the party executive on the grounds of political and economic expediency. The boundaries of the sub-districts are determined on the same lines by the district executives, those of the local branches by the sub-district executives.

(3) In Länder containing more than one district, regional associations can be formed according to political expendiency as further organisational bodies, provided that all the districts in the Land approve. The status of the districts as the basis of the organisation is not affected by the formation of a regional association.

. . .

Commissions of Arbitration

§ 34:

(1) Commissions of Arbitration are formed at sub-district, district and Party Executive Committee levels. . . .

(2) Commissions of Arbitration are responsible for making decisions regarding:

1. disciplinary proceedings within the party;
2. disputes concerning the application and interpretation of the Statutes of Organization, the Constitutions, the basic precepts . . . and the operational guidelines of the study-groups;
3. procedures for contesting elections or declaring elections null and void . . .

. . .

(5) The members of the commissions of arbitration are elected at Party Conferences by secret ballot for a period of two years. . . .

. . .

(7) The procedures of the commissions of arbitration are governed by a set of rules to be laid down by the Party Conference as an integral part of these statutes.

Disciplinary Proceedings

§ 35:

(1) Disciplinary proceedings are to be taken against a member who damages the interests of the party by persistently flouting decisions of the Party Conference or party organization, or who commits a dishonourable deed or a gross violation of the precepts of the party.

(2) The following sanctions can be imposed as a result of disciplinary proceedings:

1. the censure of a member,
2. the loss for a period of up to three years of the right to hold a specific office or all offices . . . ,
3. the temporary suspension of a specific right or all rights arising from membership for a period of up to three years,
4. expulsion from the party.

(3) A decision to expel a member can only be taken when he or she has wilfully violated the Statutes or gravely contravened the precepts or rules of the party, thereby causing the party serious harm.

(4) A motion calling for disciplinary proceedings to be taken can be submitted by any of the party's structural organizations (§ 8) to the commission of arbitration of the sub-district of which the individual concerned is a member. . . .

Ballot of Party Members

§ 36:
In the event of the Party Conference voting to disband the party or to amalgamate it with another party or parties, a ballot of members shall take place. The resolution of the Party Conference is either confirmed or invalidated by the result of the ballot; it may not be put into effect until it has been confirmed by the ballot.

. . .

Amendments to the Statutes

§ 40:
(1) The Party Statutes can only be amended by a Party Conference with a two-thirds majority.

(2) Motions calling for amendments to the Statutes can only be debated if they have been tabled within the time-limits prescribed by § 18. Failure to comply with the time-limits can be overcome if the Party Conference votes by a three-quarters majority to debate the motion.

. . .

Document 6

THE STATUTES/BY-LAWS OF THE NATIONAL POLITICAL PARTY (THE GREENS)
Source: Translation of the *Satzungen* issued in Karlsruhe, 13 January 1980

The Greens are the fundamental alternative to the conventional parties. They aim for a society which in its development is orientated to the environmental conditions established by nature as well as to the individual and social character of mankind.

...

§ 1: *Name and Location*

(1) The party bears the name The Greens (Die Grünen). The abbreviation is Greens.

(2) The Greens are a political party in the sense of the Basic Law.

...

§ 7: *Executive Bodies (Federal)*

(3) As far as possible all party committees, the governing body, commissions and especially the election lists should be formed equally of women and men.

§ 8: *The Federal Party Conference*

(1) The Federal Conference takes place at least once in the calendar year. Each local group is to be represented by a delegate with voting rights. Where there are more than thirty members every additional thirty members are represented by an extra delegate. The Federal Governing Body appoints a credentials committee to approve delegates. If the number of delegates exceeds 750 then the Federal Conference will designate a new delegate quota ...

...

§ 10: *Structure*

(1) In order to develop a decentralized party organisation and grass-roots democracy the By-Laws confer the greatest possible autonomy on the city, regional and Länder associations. The corresponding members' assemblies are the authoritative bodies.

(2) The regional and Länder associations have autonomy for programme, by-laws, finances and personnel. The programme and by-laws may not contradict the programmatic principles and the aims of the party.

...

Document 7

REGULATIONS GOVERNING FINANCE AND CONTRIBUTIONS TO THE CHRISTIAN DEMOCRATIC UNION (CDU)

Source: Finanz und Beitragsordnung (FBU). See Doc. 4

Passed by the 23rd Federal Party Conference in Mannheim on 23.6.1975 and amended by resolution of the Federal Party Conference on 5.11.1981.

(1) Every member of the party must pay a regular subscription.

(2) The amount to be paid per month is determined by the member's self-assessment of his income.

(3) The following table, agreed by the Federal Party Conference, applies to a member's self-assessment:

net income [per month]	monthly subscription
under 1,500 DM	5—8 DM
1,500—3,000 DM	8—30 DM
3,000—6,000 DM	30—100 DM

Members whose net monthly income is over 6000 DM pay correspondingly higher subscriptions:

(4) In the case of housewives, schoolchildren, students, conscripts of the German Federal Armed Forces (*Bundeswehr*), conscientious objectors doing community service, young people undergoing training, the unemployed, pensioners and members with low income, the constituency associations can make special arrangements regarding the payment of subscriptions. . . .

Document 8

SPD SUBSCRIPTIONS

Source: Organisationsstatut der Sozialdemokratischen Partei Deutschlands (1971 and 1975), Bonn, n.d.

Membership Subscriptions (SPD)

§ 13:

(1) Membership subscriptions are based on net monthly earnings according to the following table:

net monthly earnings		monthly subscription
under	600 DM	4 DM
over	600 DM	5 DM
" "	700 DM	6 DM
" "	800 DM	8 DM
" "	1000 DM	10 DM
" "	1200 DM	12 DM
" "	1400 DM	15 DM
" "	1600 DM	20 DM
" "	1800 DM	25 DM
" "	2000 DM	35 DM
" "	2500 DM	45 DM
" "	3000 DM	60 DM

over	4000 DM	80 DM
" "	5000 DM	120 DM
" "	6000 DM	150 DM
" "	8000 DM	200 DM
" "	10000 DM	250 DM

(2) The monthly subscription for members with no income is DM 2.

(3) Members of the SPD who receive fees or similar gratuities as a result of discharging public offices or holding mandates as members of supervisory administrative or advisory boards, must pay 30% of their gross remuneration to the party at the appropriate organisational level....

(4) It is the Party Conference which, as a matter of principle, fixes the level of subscriptions....

. . .

PARTY PROGRAMMES: THE FUNDAMENTAL PRINCIPLES

Document 9

THE GODESBERG PROGRAMME OF THE GERMAN SOCIAL DEMOCRATIC PARTY, NOVEMBER 1959

Source: Basic Programme of the Social Democratic Party of Germany, Bonn, n.d.

Fundamental Values of Socialism

Socialists aim to establish a society in which every individual can develop his personality and as a responsible member of the community, take part in the political, economic and cultural life of mankind. . . .

Democratic Socialism, . . . in Europe is rooted in Christian ethics, humanism and classical philosophy . . .

The Social Democratic Party is the party of freedom of thought . . . .

We are fighting for democracy. Democracy must become the universal form of state organisation and way of life. . . .

We resist every dictatorship, every form of totalitarian or authoritarian rule. . . .

The Order of the State

The Social Democratic Party of Germany lives and works in the whole of Germany. It stands by the Basic Law of the German Federal Republic. In accordance with the Basic Law it strives for German unity in freedom.

The division of Germany is a threat to peace. To end this division is a vital interest of the German people. . . .

National Defence
The Social Democratic Party affirms the need to defend the free democratic society. It is in favour of national defence. . . .

The Federal Republic of Germany must neither produce nor use atomic or other means of mass destruction. . . .

The armed forces must only be used for national defence. . . .

The Economy

The goal of Social Democratic economic policy is the constant growth of prosperity and a just share for all in the national product. . . .

Economic policy must secure full employment whilst maintaining a stable currency, increase productivity and raise general prosperity. . . .

More than a third of the national income passes through the hands of the government. The question is therefore not whether measures of economic planning and control serve a purpose, but rather who should apply these measures and for whose benefit. . . .

Free choice of consumer goods and services, free choice of working place, freedom for employers to exercise their initiative as well as free competition are essential conditions of a Social Democratic economic policy. The autonomy of trade unions and employers' associations in collective bargaining is an important feature of a free society. Totalitarian control of the economy destroys freedom. The Social Democratic Party therefore favours a free market wherever free competition really exists. Where a market is dominated by individuals or groups, however, all manner of steps must be taken to protect freedom in the economic sphere. As much competition as possible—as much planning as necessary.

Ownership and Power
A significant feature of the modern economy is the constantly increasing tendency toward concentration. . . .

Wherever large-scale enterprises predominate, free competition is eliminated. Those who have less power have fewer opportunities for development, and remain more or less fettered. The consumer occupies the most vulnerable position of all in the economy. . . .

The key task of an economic policy concerned with freedom is therefore to contain the power of big business. State and society must not be allowed to become the prey of powerful sectional groups.

Private ownership of the means of production can claim protection by society as long as it does not hinder the establishment of social justice. . . .

Effective public control must prevent the abuse of economic power. The most important means to this end are investment control and control over the forces dominating the market.

Public ownership is a legitimate form of public control which no modern state can do without. It serves to protect freedom against domination by large economic concerns. . . .

Wage and salary earners whose contribution to production is decisive have so far been deprived of an effective say in economic life. Democracy, however, demands that workers should be given a voice and that co-determination be extended to all branches of the economy. From being a servant the worker must become a citizen of the economy. . . .

Social Responsibility

. . .

Every citizen has the right to a minimum state pension in case of old age or inability to earn a living, or at the death of the family's provider. . . .

The Social Democratic Party . . . demands comprehensive health protection. . . .

All labour and social legislation should be ordered and compiled in a surveyable code on labour legislation and a code on social legislation.

Everyone has a right to a decent place in which to live. It is the home of the family. It must therefore continue to receive social protection and must not be the mere object of private gain. . . .

Woman—Family—Youth
Equality of rights for women should be realised in the legal, economic and social spheres.

. . .

Cultural Life

. . .

Religion and Church

. . .

Socialism is no substitute for religion. The Social Democratic Party respects churches and religious societies. It affirms their public and legal status, their special mission and their autonomy. . . .

Education
Education must give an opportunity to all freely to develop their abilities and capacities. It must strengthen the will to resist the conformist tendencies of our time. Knowledge and the acquisition of traditional cultural values, and a thorough understanding of the formative forces in society, are essential to the development of independent thinking and free judgment. . . .

School systems and curricula must give full scope to the development of talent and ability at all stages. Every gifted pupil should have access to advanced education and training. . . .

The International Community

The greatest and most urgent task is to preserve peace and protect freedom.

Democratic Socialism has always stood for international co-operation and solidarity. . . .

Normal diplomatic and trade relations with all nations are indispensable in spite of differences in system of government and social structure. . . .

[The programme continues with support for International Courts and the U.N.]

Document 10

THE 'FREIBURG THESES' OF THE FREE DEMOCRATIC PARTY, OCTOBER 1971

Source: *Freiburger Thesen der F.D.P. zur Gesellschaftspolitik*, Bonn, n.d.

Introduction

Liberalism is . . . both heir to and champion of the tradition of human liberty and dignity which informed the democratic revolutions in America and France at the end of the eighteenth century.

The liberal tradition grew out of these middle-class revolutions and was later assimilated by reform movements within the state . . .

. . .

In our country a free democratic liberal party has the . . . responsibility of guarding and upholding this tradition of classical liberalism in the face of state measures and social developments which threaten liberty and right.

Today we stand at the beginning of the second phase of a reform movement which stems from the middle-class revolution . . .

This new phase of democratisation and liberalisation . . . springs from a changed understanding of liberty. It opens up the new political dimension of a liberalism which is no longer just democratic, but also social.

. . .

For this social liberalism rights and liberties should not be mere formal pledges given by the state to its citizens, but real opportunities presented to them in their day-to-day life.

. . .

In our party this new spirit of democratisation in society has above all forged ahead in the field of educational policy, in the struggle for equal educational and vocational opportunities, in short for the citizens' right to education. The following theses on liberal social policy outline ways of putting these ideas into political practice. . . .

. . .

Thesis 1: Liberalism stands for human dignity through self-determination. . . .
Thesis 2: Liberalism stands for progress through reason. . . .
Thesis 3: Liberalism calls for the democratisation of society. . . .
Thesis 4: Liberalism calls for the reform of capitalism. . . .

Supported by competition and the individual's will to work, capitalism has led to great economic successes, but also to social injustice. The liberal reform of capitalism aims at halting the imbalance of opportunity and the massing of economic power, which result from the accumulation of money and property and from the concentration of ownership of the means of production in the hands of a few. . . .

Property

Thesis 1: Liberty needs ownership of property. Ownership of property creates liberty. It is a means to the end of preserving and increasing human liberty, not an end in itself. . . .

. . .

Thesis 4: The right of the individual to exploit his property and to use it privately and professionally, must . . . end at the point where this imposes improper and unreasonable restrictions on the freedom of others or interferes with public welfare.

Landed Property

. . .

Thesis 1: The main aims of land policy must be to provide all population groups with sufficient living space and to guarantee humane town-planning. . . .
Thesis 2: The local authorities must be enabled to pursue appropriate land-supply policies. . . .

The Formation of Private Wealth
Worker Participation in Industrial Assets

Preliminary Note:
Today the increment of productive capital arising from profits is concentrated in

the hands of a small number of holders of capital. This is politically dangerous, socially unjust and incompatible with liberal demands for equality of opportunity and for the best possible conditions for the development of individual personality. Liberal policy on the formation of wealth, therefore, aims at a more even distribution of wealth. This is not to be brought about by a once-and-for-all adjustment of the status quo, but rather by the permanent participation of a broader cross-section of the community, particularly in the increment of productive capital . . .

Thesis 1: Above a stipulated figure of capital appreciation, private and public companies will be obliged to grant to the public the right to participate in the companies' capital gains.

. . .

Estate Levy

Preliminary Note:
Death duties, as they have hitherto been in force, perpetuate an outmoded system that has an adverse effect on our economic and social order and its free development.

. . .

These shortcomings and disadvantages are to be overcome by replacing the present death duties by a levy on a dead person's estate and by reorganizing gift taxes correspondingly. Once divested of its tax character, the levy on large fortunes is to be incorporated into the system of participation in industrial assets. By focusing more closely on very great fortunes, proper account is being taken of the fact that very great fortunes cannot normally be acquired without the vital contribution rendered by third parties and society. . . .

[The programme goes on to detail the various conditions of the levy system.]

Co-determination on the Shop Floor[12]

As an employee, the mature and enlightened citizen still wants to be an active individual and not feel himself to be the passive victim of decisions and processes he doesn't understand . . .

[The Free Democrats were concerned that worker participation should not undermine business efficiency, and that managerial staff should play an important role in decision-making.]

As a matter of principle the senior salaried staff have the same social rights as all other employees in the firm. Appropriate account must be taken of their special status as belonging both to the management and to the workforce. . . .

The protection of minorities in a firm is to be intensified. In its composition the workers' council should reflect the social strata of the whole firm and the ratio of men to women. . . .

Co-determination at the Board Level

Preliminary Note

Liberal social policy cannot be satisfied with a form of co-determination that only allows employees to participate in the running of the workshop and in the determining of working conditions on the shop floor.

. . .

. . . the hereafter outlined liberal model for co-determination at the board level on the part of employees in their own company adopts a new approach, both regarding the commensurate participation of the three factors of production—capital, management and labour—and their relative numerical strengths and joint operational procedures. The essence of this approach is co-determination at the board level, organised internally and based on parity.

Thesis 1: Co-determination is to be introduced into the controlling bodies of large-scale industrial enterprises run as joint-stock companies. Such co-determination assumes joint responsibility on the part of the factors capital, management and labour.

. . .

Thesis 4: To ensure the overriding interests of the company, it is vital that on the one hand the share-holders ('capital' factor) should not be absolved from their responsibility; on the other hand, the company employees ('management' and 'labour' factors) must be able to assert their interests without being outvoted.

. . .

Thesis 5: In accordance with the above-mentioned principles, . . . the 'capital', 'labour' and 'management' factors are to participate in the supervision of large-scale industrial enterprises in the ratio 6:4:2. . . .

Thesis 6: The 'management' factor on company boards of supervision is composed of senior salaried staff of the company. Elections are by the majority decision of the senior salaried staff.

. . .

Environmental Policy . . .

Environmental policy is a response to one of the challenges of industrial society. Population increase, urbanisation, urban sprawl, uninhibited technical advances and growing prosperity lead to the overutilisation and destruction of the natural elements—the soil, raw materials, the atmosphere and water. Noise levels, particularly in conurbations, are becoming unbearable; chemicals in the environment are threatening to poison our food. The environmental crisis is world-wide.

. . .

Thesis 1: The protection of the environment has priority over the pursuit of profit and over personal gain. Harming the environment is a criminal offence.

. . .

Document 11

THE FUNDAMENTAL PROGRAMME OF THE CHRISTIAN SOCIAL UNION, 1976

Source: Hans Seidel Stiftung, Institute for Political Co-operation, *Programmes of Tenets of the Parties in Europe. Schriftenreihe* 1.1., Munich, 1979. (Transl. of *Grundsatzprogramm der Christlich Sozialen Union*; CDU–Landesleitung Munich)

Image and Mission . . .

The Christian Social Union sees the foundation of its political work in a concept of man that is governed by Christian values . . .

The Christian Social Union is a conservative party, because it feels committed to an enduring order of values. It accepts progress based on the existing order. It is a liberal party, because it stands up for the citizen's basic rights and freedom. It is a social party, because it works for all men, particularly for the weaker among them. It stands for an equitable social order.

Less State—More Freedom

The Christian Social Union believes in the principles of constitutional administration, parliamentary controls and a permanent [professional] civil service. It does not fall into the socialistic error of thinking that an extended range of State services and a wider State influence in all areas are in themselves to be regarded as progress and that this is the only way to construct a social State . . . .

The Christian Social Union urges that the volume of State responsibilities be restricted. Though little or no scope for a reduction exists in the area of . . . [day-to-day] administration, there are ample opportunities for denationalizing public services in the area of State services and business enterprises. . . .

Freedom through Federalism

The Christian Social Union stands by the principle of federalism. Only a federal structure for Germany can guarantee the necessary counterbalance to centralism. Federalism divides power in the country, safeguards diversity in democratic opinions and keeps the State's actions within the public's field of view. . . .

Education, Science, Culture—Bases of Personal Development and the Future of our Nation

...

Education policies occupy a central position in the arena of individual expectations, economic development, social change and ideological conflicts. Education today is no longer a luxury reserved for the few, but decisive for everyone. ...

Vocational training and general education are equal-ranking tasks and independent areas. To the Christian Social Union's way of thinking, personal education grows out of both practical work and theoretical study. The choice of the right path should be based on personal inclination and abilities, not on out-dated considerations of prestige. Theoretical, practical and artistic elements should be combined in both vocational and general education. An educational system with a vocational and social accent is also the foundation for a humanization of the working world. ...

The State bears the overall responsibility for the school and education system. This obligates it to protect the educational institutions from anti-constitutional activities, as well as to encourage private initiative in the field of education and guarantee freedom, for the teaching staff within the scope of their mission. ...

Social Market Economy—a System to Which There is No Alternative

...

The economic order known as the Social Market Economy is an economic guarantee of the rights of all citizens to freedom. It is therefore an essential condition of a social and State order based on the principle of freedom. The Social Market Economy has proved that it is best able to safeguard these rights. It is based on private ownership, free competition, control of the use of means of production by the market, by freedom of contract and of association, by free negotiation of wages, fair opportunities and optimum social safeguards. ...

In the eyes of the Christian Social Union, reasonable real growth, full employment and stable prices are essential to social security and efficiency. Overtaxing of the economy through rivalry between social groups for the biggest share of the cake or though public spending policies must be resisted. ...

The Christian Social Union supports a consistent policy on competition which will ensure that a healthy level of competition can be maintained and encouraged between small, medium and large enterprises and combat the misuse of market power. ...

The maintenance and strengthening of small and medium business and the middle classes is seen by the Christian Social Union as an important contribution to an overall economic balance, social stability, economic efficiency and adaptability. ...

The Christian Social Union sees agricultural policy as an essential part of economic and social policy. The goal of its policy is to maintain an agricultural structure operated by small farmers and preserve the status of the small farmers as part of a free and independent middle class. ...

[Social Policy]

The Christian Social Union's social policy, based on the principles of solidarity and fair opportunities, is modelled on the ideal of a responsible citizen, is help for self-help and accepts the principle of social justice. . . .

The Christian Social Union is for the expansion of the system of industrial democracy on a functionally appropriate partnership basis where this is in full conformity with the Basic Law. The function of industrial democracy is to reinforce workers' opportunities for sharing in management decisions. But the object of industrial democracy must not be to strengthen the power of organizations foreign to the company. . . . [i.e. the individual firm. This refers to trade unions.]

The Christian Social Union defends the practice of free wage bargaining and believes in trade union plurality as an essential part of a free economic order. It is also for retention of the proven principle of self-administration for business and industry. . . .

The equality of man and woman before the law must be translated into equality in fact. . . .

The Christian Social Union rejects both the traditional idea of the role of man and woman and any ideological egalitarianism. . . .

The Christian Social Union sees the 'C' in its name as imposing special obligations towards the weak, the helpless, the destitute and the socially underprivileged. It therefore does all it can to enable these groups to achieve personal development by participating in the life of society. . . .

Development of the Human Environment

. . .

The Christian Social Union sees it as a major task to maintain a reasonable balance between economic and ecological needs. For this reason, qualitative growth must be put before quantitative. Growth should also give rural areas fresh impetus and not be concentrated only on a few large metropolitan areas. The limits of growth must always be drawn where the environment, nature and the countryside are threatened, not to say destroyed.

Freedom for Germany and Europe

. . .

The Christian Social Union sees the task and goal of German policies as being to obtain freedom, self-determination and unity for the whole of the German people and to help to secure a just peace in Europe and the world that will give all peoples of whatever race, ethnic group or creed full human and community rights and a chance of freedom and economic development. In German foreign policy, the Christian Social Union calls for a greater readiness to assume international responsibilities and an expansion of Germany's own scope for action. . . .

The unilateral policy of 'détente' has not fulfilled expectations. The Soviet Union has used it to consolidate its sphere of power and is constantly increasing its influence in the world. In so doing, it threatens the security of Free Europe. Only a consistent maintenance of the balance of power on all levels can prevent a strengthening and expansion of Soviet power, above all in Europe. . . .

Independence and security for the free portion of Europe are still dependent on the strength and capabilities of the Atlantic Pact. The Christian Social Union therefore supports the continued existence and development of NATO, in the sense of a true partnership in duties and rights. . . .

The Christian Social Union was and is for cooperation with Eastern Europe. But this must be of benefit to the people and their inviolable rights. Treaties must respect the principle of give and take. Mere compliance with the demands of Communist governments cannot lead to reconciliation with the peoples that are oppressed by these governments. . . .

The Christian Social Union's political goal is to unify the German people under one state through free self-determination. Ties with Berlin as one of the states in the Federal Republic of Germany must be strengthened and developed.

Document 12

THE FEDERAL PROGRAMME OF THE GREENS
Source: Die Grünen. Das Bundesprogramm, Bonn, 1980

We are the Alternative to the conventional parties. We have evolved out of a union of 'green', 'motley' and 'alternative' lists and parties. We feel ourselves to be linked to all those who are working in the new democratic movement—the associations committed to conserving life, nature and the environment, the citizens' actions groups, the workers' movements, Christian action groups and the movements engaged in working for Peace, Civil Rights, Women and the Third World. We see ourselves as part of the 'green' movement of the whole world.

The parties established in Bonn behave as though the infinite growth of industrial output were possible on this finite planet of Earth. In this way they are leading us, on their own admission, towards the inescapable decision of choosing between an atomic state and an atomic war, between a Harrisburg and a Hiroshima. The ecological crisis in the world is getting worse from day to day. Raw materials are becoming scarce, there is scandal after scandal over toxic waste, whole species of animals are being wiped out, varieties of plants are dying out, rivers and oceans are turning into sewers, mankind is threatening to waste away both intellectually and spiritually amidst an advanced industrial and consumer society, and we are heaping up a dreadful heritage for future generations.

The destruction of the foundations of life and work and the gradual eroding of democratic rights have reached such a stage that alternative forms of economy, politics and society are becoming a necessity. These are the circumstances which have called forth a spontaneous democratic movement of citizens.

. . .

We feel it necessary to supplement our usual extra-parliamentary activities by work in the municipal and Länder parliaments as well as in the Bundestag. In this way we want to create a public voice and recognition for our alternative ideas. . . .

Ecological

Based on the laws of nature and in particular on the knowledge that unlimited growth is impossible in a limited system, we define an ecological policy as understanding ourselves and our environment as part of nature. Human life too is bound up in the cycles of the ecological pattern: we intervene with our actions and this rebounds on us. We must not be allowed to destroy the stability of the ecological balance. . . .

Social

A future social policy must have as its goal the building up of a stable social system. 'Social' has above all an economic component. . . .

It is a result of competitive economy as well as of economic power, in state and private capitalistic monopolies, that the exploitative compulsion to expand comes, bringing with it the threat of the total pollution and destruction of the foundations of human life. . . .

It is only by the self-determination of those concerned that the ecological, economic and social crisis can be tackled. . . .

Grass-roots Democracy

A policy based on grass-roots democracy means the reinforcing of a decentralized, direct democracy. We are assuming precedence must be given to the decisions of the grass-roots. . . .

Our inner organisational life and our relationship to the people who support us and vote for us is the complete opposite of that which exists in the parties now established in Bonn. These are incapable and unwilling to take up new points of departure and ideas, or to meet the interests of the democratic movement. We are therefore determined to create a party organisation of a new kind whose fundamental structures are constituted on a basis of grass-roots democracy and decentralisation. . . .

Non-violence

Our goal is a non-violent society in which the oppression of man by man and violence perpetrated by man against man is abolished. Our chief principle is that human goals cannot be attained by inhuman means.

Non-violence applies to all freely and without exception, and this means just as much within social groups and society as a whole as between national groups and nations.

The principle of non-violence does not impinge upon the fundamental right to self-defence and includes civil resistance in its many forms. . . .

Document 13

THE PROGRAMME OF THE NATIONAL DEMOCRATIC PARTY OF GERMANY (NPD)

Source: Das Programm der NPD. Düsseldorfer Programm, Neufassung, 1973
. . .

Principles of National Democratic Politics

(1) The NPD supports the national ideal.
We, the National Democrats, stand for the preservation of the German people. We stand for a united Germany in a united Europe, for the indivisible unity of our people and for an alliance of the anti-communist peoples of our continent.

We, the National Democrats, are the guardians of the coming generation. Today's re-educated generation will face the coming one empty-handed because it denied the German people their rights to self-determination and other in-alienable rights. Thus the coming generation will demand its heritage and the rights of its people even more passionately.

. . . The national ideal will develop that explosive force against foreign domination and imperial forces, with which we too will recover German unification and freedom.

(2) The NPD believes in the democratic ideal. We, the National Democrats, are for a democracy in which the will of the people has free expression.

In a democratic state, power should come neither from the presumptuous demands of the so-called mass media, nor from the pressure groups of a so-called pluralistic society, but rather from the people alone, who can speak for themselves and know that they must carry personal and social responsibility. Genuine democracy supports a stronger state, which protects the whole. . . .

Document 14

THE PROGRAMME OF THE GERMAN COMMUNIST PARTY (DKP)
Source: Programm der Deutschen Kommunistischen Partei, Düsseldorf, 1979

... The German Communist Party is the revolutionary party of the working class in the Federal Republic of Germany.

It is the fundamental aim of the DKP to meet the needs and to further the interests of the vast majority of our people—the working class, the farmers, the intelligentsia and other working people—against the power and drive for profit of large-scale capitalism. This is what it is fighting for. It always acts according to the principle: Everything for working people, for their right to social security, democracy, freedom and peace. Everything for social progress.

The DKP has emerged from more than a century of struggle on the part of the German working class movement against capitalist exploitation and repression, against militarism and war. It has inherited the mantle of revolutionary German Social Democracy and of the Communist Party of Germany ...

The Main Driving Force of the World Revolution

The Soviet Union is the main driving force in the community of socialist states and in the movement for revolution in the world as a whole. The workers and farmers of Russia, led by the party of Lenin, created the first ever socialist state. They defended this at great cost against all internal and external enemies. The people of the Soviet Union played the decisive role in the defeat of Hitlerite fascism. It deserves the chief credit for maintaining world peace and for altering international power relationships for the benefit of the forces of peace, democracy and socialism. ...

The German Communist Party is a consistent opponent of imperialism. It strives to enable the working people of our country to make a worthy contribution to the liberation of the peoples of the world from imperialist exploitation and repression by struggling against the imperialism of the Federal Republic and by developing international solidarity. At the same time, this furthers the national interests of the Federal Republic. ...

Document 15

PROGRAMME OF THE WEST GERMAN COMMUNIST LEAGUE (KBW)
Source: Programm und Statut des Kommunistischen Bundes Westdeutschland (June 1973, revised October 1976), Frankfurt/M, 1978

The KBW (West German Communist League) Programme

The originally academic prediction of a world-wide revolution of the proletariat has become a reality. The proletariat has won power first in one, and then in several countries and has initiated the construction of socialism. The proletariat's fight for a social revolution is closely associated with the fight of the oppressed peoples against imperialism. . . .

The West German communists see themselves as a division of the world army of the proletariat. They share the same aim as communists all over the world: to found a classless society which overcomes both exploitation within individual nations and hostile antagonism between them. The aim is determined by the characteristics of capitalist society and the course of its development. . . .

The overthrow of the bourgeois state apparatus and the foundation of a proletariat dictatorship (i.e. gaining and maintaining sufficient political power to allow the proletariat to crush the exploiters' opposition in order to complete the social revolution on a basis of comprehensive and direct democracy), is an essential prerequisite of this social revolution. As long as the bourgeoisie uses armed force to protect its capitalist possessions, the proletariat itself will have to combat political power with armed force. . . .

The greatest hindrance to the unification of the proletariat in the fight for its liberation is that of cleavage due to reformism and revisionism. . . . In any revolutionary crisis the reformists and revisionists tend to side with the bourgeoisie. . . . These people consist mainly of bourgeois and neo-bourgeois elements in the proletarian power structure and its administrative bodies, who have links with remnants of the old bourgeoisie. Only a merciless ideological and political struggle by communists against these elements and against every form of preferential treatment of the bourgeoisie and bureaucratic corruption . . . can prevent political power being snatched from the proletariat. . . .

The German nation is divided. The FGR and West Berlin are in the Western imperialist camp. The GDR is under the immediate influence of Russian social imperialism. . . .

Notes

1. For the English translation, see *The Law on Political Parties* (Inter Nationes, Bonn, 1978), 5–6
2. See also Ch. 5
3. See Table 7
4. See Table 10
5. Figures provided by the SPD *Parteivorstand*, August 1982. For the Christian Democrats, see Christian Fenner, 'Das Parteiensystem seit 1969', in D. Staritz, ed., *Das Parteiensystem der Bunderrepublik*, 2nd edn, Opladen, 1980, 211
6. See Table 8. The process of registration for voting is rendered easier in Germany by the fact that all residents are obliged to register their place of domicile with the authorities
7. See also Ch. 10
8. Cf. Ch. 2, Doc. 8

9. Art. 53 stipulates that, until the law can be fully applied to Berlin, the number of members shall be reduced to 496, of whom 248 shall be directly elected in constituencies

10. This means that the votes in all Länder are added together to arrive at a total for the whole Federal Republic. This does *not* include West Berlin. Para. 53 of the Electoral Law stipulates that Berlin sends twenty-two members to the Bundestag. These are delegated by the parties in the West Berlin parliament (Abgeordnetenhaus) in proportion to their representation there

11. This refers to parties not represented in the Bundestag or Landtag with at least five members

12. See Ch. 10, Doc. 5

9 Public Opinion:
Interest Groups and the Media

Detlev Karsten

In general, interest groups are mediators between the economic and the socio-cultural spheres on the one hand and the political system on the other.* The existence and the official recognition of interest groups is characteristic of a pluralistic society; the underlying assumption is that the commonweal can only be defined as a sum total of many diverging group interests. The legal basis for the foundation and for the activities of interest groups and of the press is to be found in Arts. 5 and 9 of the Basic Law which guarantee the freedom to express opinions and the freedom to form associations.

As in other democratic states, German interest groups pursue their aims by formulating and communicating the viewpoints of their members, although it is not uncommon that the officials develop interests of their own which are not necessarily identical with the interests of the members. In addition to influencing public opinion, interest groups work by feeding information into the political system, by exerting pressure on individual decisionmakers, by direct participation in political processes, e.g. by bringing 'their' representatives into political parties and into administrative positions and parliaments on the local, Länder or federal levels. Occasionally interest groups give support—financial or other—to political parties or individual politicians. Internally, most interest groups—in particular economically motivated groups—perform important functions for their members. They are a source of information and advice especially on matters of economic policy, but also on all kinds of business questions.

Some interest groups entertain close relationships with political parties. Thus, both the CDU/DSU and the FDP enjoy the support of the

---

* Notes for this chapter begin on p. 260

business community; the CDU/CSU reflect to some extent views of the churches; and the interests of the workers and the labour unions are traditionally represented by the SPD.

The overall importance of particular interest groups depends on the interest they represent, on their membership, on their economic strength, on their access to politicians and the media and on the role given to them in the economic and social system. Their influence also depends on whether they act on the local, Länder or federal levels.

In the economic field, the most conspicuous interest groups are the various associations of business firms and the trade unions. The trade unions and the employers' associations are especially important because they are the partners in the collective bargaining over wages and other conditions of employment—a field of action which is legally protected against government interference. The employers' associations and the trade unions are represented in most institutions responsible for social policy.

The associations in which firms are organised are described in Doc. 1. An interesting feature is the fact that the firms are really represented by three categories of associations:

The Chambers of Industry and Commerce (Industrie- und Handelskammern), which on account of their comprehensive and compulsory membership and due to their public law status cannot pursue particular interests of individual industrial branches.

The employers' associations (Arbeitgeberverbände) whose main field is collective bargaining and social policy.

The industrial business associations which represent the economic policy interests of their members and which are in fact the real pressure groups. This is particularly true for the powerful Federation of German Industries (Bundesverband der Deutschen Industrie—BDI). An example of the rather outspoken demands which such industrial business associations put to politicians is Doc. 2.

The existence of the last two groups has the effect that the first can remain fairly moderate in their demands and keep a reasonable working relationship with the trade unions, while at the same time industrial business associations and the Federation of German Industries engage in very strong lobbying by expressing interests and opinions which in content and form disqualify them in the eyes of the trade unions as partners in negotiations.

A special feature of the German system is the unitary trade union;

unions are unitary in a double sense: each union represents *all* the workers in a particular branch of industry, and the unions are, at least in theory, neutral vis-à-vis political parties and religious denominations. The first feature contributes to a reduction of conflict within firms and in the number of industrial disputes: each employer or employers' association has only one partner in collective bargaining. The unitary trade union is an accomplishment of the post-war period. This organizational principle and the ideological neutrality were chosen against the background of negative experiences with professionally organized unions which were also ideologically divided in the Weimar Republic. As an example of a statement of the unions, Doc. 3 gives the trade union view on the issue of lockout. Another important field where the interests and opinions of the employers' federation and the trade unions differ is co-determination at the board level.[1]

The dominant trade union organisation is the Federation of German Trade Unions (Deutscher Gewerkschaftsbund – DGB). The power of the DGB is in a way derived from the power of the individual industrial unions. The Metal Workers' Union (Industriegewerkschaft Metall) occupies a key position in terms of both membership and wealth. About 5.5 million, or 48 per cent (all figures for 1981) of all organized workers are in unions which belong to the Federation of German Trade Unions which is described in Doc. 4. There is also a competing union: the Federation of Christian Trade Unions; its membership is about 290,000, or 2.5 per cent of the total number of workers. In addition there are two organizations which are similar to trade unions: the German Union of Salaried Employees (Deutsche Angestelltengewerkschaft) whose membership was about 500,000 in 1981 and the German Civil Service Federation (Deutscher Beamtenbund) whose membership was about 820,000 in 1981. Altogether, about 42 per cent of the labour force are organized in all these unions.

An interest group which—in spite of comparatively small membership—is politically quite influential is the German Farmers' Association (Deutscher Bauernverband). As an example, Doc. 5 gives its views on the preservation of the family farm.

In addition to these very powerful groups, there are virtually thousands of other organisations covering practically all social activities and interests. These range from automobile associations to sports clubs, from house owners to the associations of refugees, from gardening to literature clubs. Consumer associations, although supported by public funds, have not gained a major significance.

But in addition to these forms of established representation of interests, a new phenomenon—citizens' action groups (Bürger-initiativen)—has developed during the last fifteen years. Most such citizens' action groups were originally formed to prevent something: the construction of a nuclear power station, the building of a highway through a resort area, the demolition of an old quarter of the town, etc.; very often these citizens' action groups have only local significance. By now, there are thousands of such citizens' action groups. Because of their goals and in particular because of their often uncompromising methods of pursuing these goals—some citizens' action groups do not shy away from violence—these citizens' action groups have developed into a major problem for the administrations and for the politicians. Today, citizens' action groups do not restrict themselves to obstruction, but they try to formulate alternatives of an environmentally healthy, socially just, peaceful, decentralized social and political system with strong citizen participation. Since citizens' action groups have also organized themselves into larger structures, e.g. in the form of associations of citizens' action groups, and as they entertain close relationships with the new Green Party[2] they are considered a threat to the established party structure. Doc. 6 gives the views of the Federal Association of Citizens' Action Groups for Environmental Protection (Bundesverband Bürger-initiativen Umweltschutz) on strategic issues.

Both the two dominant churches in Germany, the (Protestant) Evangelical Church in Germany (Evangelische Kirche in Deutschland)[3] and the Catholic Church (Katholische Kirche) have on occasion appeared as powerful pressure groups. About 90 per cent of the population belongs to these Christian Churches, divided almost equally between Catholic and Protestant. The legal position of these two churches in the Federal Republic of Germany is interesting because there is neither a State church nor are the churches merely private associations: the churches have a special status as corporate bodies under public law. There is a church tax which is collected by state revenue offices or local authorities; the churches pay the administrative cost of this service. The churches have a claim to financial allocations from the state which, for example, pays in whole or in part the cost of certain church facilities (e.g. hospitals, old people's homes, etc.). To resign from a church, a member must make a declaration to a state authority. Altogether, the links between the churches and the state are fairly close, a fact which has been criticised for a long time by the Liberal Party, the FDP, with its traditional insistence on a clear separation of state and church (Doc. 7).

The churches themselves are important factors in the forming of public opinion. During election campaigns representatives of the

Catholic Church in particular have occasionally tried to influence the electorate. Sometimes, on issues of lasting importance, the churches publish their views in memoranda which then typically receive considerable public attention. Two examples are reproduced here: Doc. 8 is an excerpt from a memorandum of the lay organisation of the Catholic Church on family policy, and Doc. 9 is an excerpt from the 1981 peace memorandum of the Protestant Church.[4]

In the Federal Republic of Germany, broadcasting falls under the jurisdiction of the Länder. The right to broadcast rests exclusively with self-administered corporations under public law. These corporations are not profit-orientated and most of their revenue derives from license fees rather than from advertising proceeds. On television, the total broadcasting time for commercials is limited to twenty minutes per day; there are no commercials on Sundays and public holidays and after 8 p.m. on any normal day. There are nine independent Länder corporations and two federal broadcasting corporations. These independent corporations cooperate in the Coordinating Association of Broadcasting Corporations governed under Public Law in the Federal Republic of Germany (Arbeitsgemeinschaft der öffentlich-rechtlichen Rundfunkanstalten der Bundersrepublik Deutschland – ARD). In addition, there is a Second German Television (Zweites Deutsches Fernsehen – ZDF) which was founded by an inter-state treaty of all Länder.[5]

In their programmes the broadcasting corporations are obliged to observe political neutrality. Doc. 10 is an example of how this obligation is spelled out. To ensure compliance with these and other regulations, broadcasting corporations are controlled by supervisory bodies called broadcasting or television boards. These boards have considerable influence on the activities of the corporation both by providing guidelines for the programmes and by their control over personnel and budget policy. Doc. 11 shows how in the composition of a television board an attempt is made to arrive at a balanced representation of all interest groups.

In contrast, the printed media are left to private publishers. Here a major problem is the continuing process of concentration of publishing companies. This essentially economically motivated process has resulted in a decline of the total number of publications. Simultaneously the control over the remaining publications is becoming concentrated in fewer hands. This is considered a potential threat to the independent formation of opinion. Attempts legally to guarantee the editorial staff of the various publications independence of the political interest of the owner of the publishing company (commonly referred to as the internal freedom of the press) are important. But the decisive measure to prevent the formation of opinion monopolies seems to be the maintenance of competition between publishing houses, an objective which in 1976 also led to an amendment to Art. 23 of the Act against Restraints of Competition[6] which specified provisions for merger-control of publishing companies. Doc. 12 describes the state of the press.

Document 1

The Federation of German Industries describes the organisation of business interests.

THE ORGANISATION OF BUSINESS INTERESTS

Source: *Bundesverband der Deutschen Industrie (Federation of German Industries),* BDI, Cologne, 1981, 5–11
Transl.: Official

Industry in German business organizations

German business enterprises are organized in associations which safeguard their interests according to their functions. The organizational structure ranges from regional associations to their federation at national level, from sectoral and trade associations to their supra-sectoral and supra-trade representation. These associations represent the complex structure of the modern private enterprise system; they have united to form head organizations.

Industrial business associations primarily represent the economic policy interests of their member enterprises.

This includes general economic, monetary, competition and business policy objectives as well as questions of infrastructure and research policy, financial policy and law or problems of foreign economic policy and European integration.

The head organization of the industrial business associations is the *Federation of German Industries* (Bundesverhand der Deutschen Industrie e.V.).

Employers' associations represent the social and wage policy interests of the entire business sector, i.e. not only those of industry. They are the trade unions' negotiating partners in wage negotiations.

The head organization of the employers' associations is the *Confederation of German Employers' Associations* (Bundesvereinigung der Deutschen Arbeitgeberverbände e.V.).

The Chambers of Industry and Commerce are regional business organizations which as public-law entities and by act of law represent the overall interests of trade and industry established in their respective districts. Contrary to the voluntary membership of the industrial business and employers' associations all enterprises are obliged by law to become members of the Chamber in their particular region.

The head organization of these Chambers is the *Association of German Chambers of Industry and Commerce* (Deutscher Industrie- und Handeistag e.V.).

These organizations have formed a coordinating body, the *Joint Committee of German Trade and Industry* (Gemeinschaftsausschuß der Deutschen Gewerblichen Wirtschaft), together with the head organizations of other business branches—Bundesverband Deutscher Banken (banking business), Bundesverband der Deutschen Volks-und Raiffeisenbanken (agricultural credit cooperatives), Bundesverband des Deutschen Groß- und Außenhandels (wholesale and foreign trade), Centralvereinigung Deutscher Handelsvertreter- und Handelsmakler-Verbände (commercial agents and brokers), Deutscher Hotel- und Gaststättenverband (hotel and catering industry), Deutscher Sparkassen- und Giroverband (savings banks), Gesamtverband der Versicherungswirtschaft (insurance business), Hauptgemeinschaft des Deutschen Einzelhandels (retail trade), Verband Deutscher Reeder (shipping business), Zentralarbeitsgemeinschaft des Straßenverkehrsgewerbes (road transport industry), Zentralverband der Deutschen Seehafenbetriebe (seaport operators), Zentralverband des Deutschen Handwerks (crafts) and the Deutscher Bauernverband (farmers' association). This joint committee is a forum for the discussion and formulation of mutual interest of the aforementioned organizations; it is not a central representative body of the entire German business sector.

Economic and social policy organizations in the Federal Republic have set up the *Institute of German Private Enterprise* (Institut der Deutschen Wirtschaft) in order to conduct scientific studies on economic and social policy developments and to elucidate the mutual objectives of private enterprise, particularly vis-à-vis the general public.

The Federation of German Industries (BDI)

The BDI is the head organization of the industrial business associations in the Federal Republic of Germany. It is thus an 'association of associations'. Its membership consists of thirty-seven parent industrial trade associations organized at national level according to branches of activity. They represent approximately 80,000 private industrial enterprises of varying sizes.

The BDI is therefore the spokesman of the entire German industry. It is obliged by its functions to maintain party-political neutrality.

Functions

The BDI represents the economic policy interests of German Industry in a constant dialogue with the Federal Parliament, the Government and the Opposition, the political parties, trade unions and other social groups, the bodies of the European Communities as well as numerous other national and international institutions.

The BDI supports the work of its member associations by supplying a wide range of information on all areas of economic policy. It coordinates their views and recommendations, organizes the formation of opinions and introduces the results into the economic policy formation process of national and international organizations.

The BDI gives expert advice in the form of suggestions, submissions and interventions and thereby assists in preparing economic policy decisions at national and international level.

The BDI's main spheres of activity are:

General questions relating to the economy, competition and business enterprises:
   general economic policy,
   agricultural policy,
   consumer goods industry and consumer policy,
   cyclical, credit and monetary policy,
   business and administration and statistics,
   competition,
   structural policy.

Infrastructure and research research and vocational training policy:
   energy and nuclear power industry,
   transport policy,
   public tenders,
   defence industry.

Financial policy and law:
   taxation and financial policy,
   law,
   environment,
   insurance.

Foreign economic policy and integration:
   foreign trade and European integration,
   development policy,
   economic relations with the state-trading countries,
   intra-German trade,
   tariff policy and sales promotion.

Central services:
  finance,
  personnel,
  administration.

Small and medium-sized business.

Press and information service.

Document 2

The industrial business associations are quite outspoken in their political demands. The following excerpts are from the address of Ernst-Günter Plutte, the president of the Association of Textile Industries, to the 1982 annual meeting of his organisation. On such occasions, typically highranking politicians both from the Federal Government as well as from the Commission of the European Communities are present.

THE VIEWS OF THE ASSOCIATION OF TEXTILE INDUSTRIES ON FOREIGN TRADE
Source: Press release of Gesamttextil, 26 January 1982

. . .

18. Those wishing to sell textiles on the widest basis within the markets of the Community must be prepared to permit imports as well.
19. We can afford to be generous when it comes to the under-developed countries. But when it comes to the threshold countries and the socialist countries, it should be evident that they have to open their markets after we have already opened ours.
20. In mentioning this 'principle of reciprocity' I have touched on the first point in the programme of an aggressive textile trade and integration policy which has been put forward by the Association of Textile Industries.
21. The principle of reciprocity—and this is the second point—must also be upheld in dealings with other industrial countries. There I am thinking of the USA, Japan and South Africa. Why should the European Community carry on accepting higher tariffs than those she levies herself, or indeed any invisible barriers to trade?
22. The third point is that the duration of the World Textile Agreement III must be used to break down the distortions of competition in the international textile trade.
23. It is not that the producers of the lowest priced textiles are unbeatable because they have the broadest natural advantage in competition. Much

more important in generating this flood of exports is the extent to which exports are subsidized and controlled by the governments of the producing countries. This has already been proved in many ways and no one will deny it.

. . .

25. Points four and five are concerned with the Common Market which in fact is not so common after all. And therefore—fourthly!—we are demanding that existing trade restrictions should be abolished within the European Community and the erection of new barriers should be prevented.

26. A concrete suggestion: There must be no more room in the Common Market for regulations concerning labelling which favour the sale of certain national products or for chicanery at the borders. The French can be accused of the former and the Italians of the latter.

. . .

28. The fifth point of the programme is aimed at the monstrous business of subsidies. The Association of Textile Industries gives this the highest priority. How can the European Community expect fairness in competition from her trading partners when she herself overlooks the breaking of the rules of the game?

29. I will mention in passing that the Association of the Textile Industry is quite prepared to allow demands for the abolition of subsidies on an international level, which I am calling for here, to be measured against its attitudes towards subsidies in its own country. As a matter of principle the textile industry of the Federal Republic rejects subsidies given to special sections of industry. The same is valid for support which comes from public sources in individual cases. In taking this position, we are pre-supposing that any interventions which would result in distortions of competition would in other countries also be prevented by those who are responsible for economic policy.

30. This demand is directed on the one hand at the Federal Government and on the other hand at the European Commission.

. . .

38. State subsidies are unfair since they cheat the entrepreneur who has solved the problems himself of the success of his efforts and of the profit everyone, who does his business well, is entitled to.

39. State subsidies do not even make good economic sense since they prevent the best possible allocation of production to those firms in the European Community in which production is best organized.

40. State subsidies are not a solution to any problem in an oversupplied market. They simply push the problem onto someone else.

. . .

42. In other words: to give subsidies to special sections of industry means to export problems.

43. Subsidies are also enemies of the small and medium-size firm. As a rule it is not the small or medium-sized business which manages to direct the warm rain of subsidy onto its fields. Small businesses fade away even though they can carry great weight in their own locality.

44. If it is inevitable that the cup of hemlock of managerial adjustment goes round in the textile trade then it should be up to the market to decide who drinks it. It should not be dependent on how much support national governments are prepared to offer!

45. It is not enough for the European Commission to lay down conditions on government subsidies to special sections of industry. It must prohibit them!

. . .

Document 3

On certain controversial issues, the German Trade Union Federation publishes its opinion.

THE TRADE UNIONS' VIEW ON LOCKOUT

Source: DGB, The German Trade Union Federation, Cologne, 1981, 33
Transl.: Official

Industrial disputes

If negotiation and mediation fail, the only option left to the labour side to obtain a new collective agreement is to take industrial action. Strike, the joint, organised refusal to work, the ultimate and sharpest trade union weapon, aims to put pressure on the employers to assert worker interests.

Workers' right to strike is guaranteed under Art. 9, Para. 3 of the West German constitution, the Basic Law. In contrast to the lock-out, it thus is constitutionally protected.

A strike requires the approval of the executive of the trade union concerned. As a rule, members vote beforehand in a strike ballot. Only if 75 per cent of the membership vote to down tools does the union leadership call a strike. Only legitimation by so large a majority creates the basis for successful industrial action.

During the action strikers receive no pay from the employer. Trade union members of at least three months' standing receive strike support benefit from their union. Non-unionised workers who strike or are locked out receive no strike support, nor do they get, say, benefits from the Unemployment Insurance.

West Germany is the only European country where the lock-out plays a major part in industrial disputes. One can say that it is the European country with the fewest strikes and the most lock-outs. Arguing a questionable equality of fighting strength, the Federal Labour Court has put the lock-out weapon in employers' hands. And the entrepreneurs make excessive use of it with the aim of weakening the trade unions financially. Just one example: in the Metal Workers' Union 1978 industrial action in the North Württemberg/North Baden contractual region it paid out DM 48 million support to strikers, but more than DM 80 million to members not called out by the union, but locked out by the employers. By means of the lock-out the employers try to break the will of the workers by withdrawing the basis of their livelihood. That violates the fundamentals of human dignity in that workers are used as mere instruments to raise entrepreneurial profits by the threat to their livelihood. The fatuous argument that the lock-out was needed to assure 'fighting parity' is easily refuted. If it were so, there would also have to be perfect parity between employers and workers if the right to strike were taken away! On the contrary, the equality of sorts between employers and workers which only the right to strike established is destroyed by the lock-out. Only those who would deny the socially weaker position of wage-dependent workers and would subject them to the pay dictate of the employers can argue in favour of the lock-out.

'The Federal Republic of Germany is a democratic and social federal state,' says Art. 20, Para. 1 of the Basic Law. As long as hundreds of thousands of workers can be locked out as if it were a matter of course one can seriously doubt this constitutional declaration.

Document 4

In this document, the German Trade Union Federation describes its purposes and its organisational structure. This text does not mention that the German Trade Union Federation also operates an important economic research institute (Wirtschaftswissenschaftliches Institut der Gewerkschaften).

THE STRUCTURE OF THE GERMAN TRADE UNION FEDERATION
Source: DGB, The German Trade Union Federation, Cologne, 1981, 14–15
Transl.: Official

The DGB Constitution

Purpose and tasks of the Federation

The task of the German Trade Union Federation, umbrella organization of seventeen trade unions, is to unify them into an effective unit and to represent their common interests in the fields of general trade union and societal policy, economic and cultural policies.

The Federation and its member unions are democratically structured and—as an essential element of the principle of the unitary union—independent of government, political parties, religious communities, administrations and employers. This party-political independence cannot, however, mean political abstinence. Worker interests have to be represented not only vis-à-vis employers, but also vis-à-vis parliaments, administrations and other institutions in society since these, too, take major decisions affecting the living and working conditions of the dependently employed. In addition to the general set of objectives of working for securing and expanding the social state based on the rule of law and achieving the democratization of the economy, the state and society, this includes the exercising of the right to resist any attempts to overthrow the constitutional order (Art. 20, para. 4 of the Basic Law).

In addition to the political tasks, the Federation also have a number of organizational ones such as unionist schooling, operation of legal aid services, public relations and coordination of trade union activities. The task and objectives laid down in the Constitution are augmented by a Basic Programme and an Action Programme which provide the further guidelines for trade union activities.

Membership and dues

The following seventeen trade unions are members of the Federation:
Building and Construction Workers' Union
Mine and Energy Workers' Union
Chemical, Paper and Ceramic Workers' Union
Printing and Paper Workers' Union
German Railway Workers' Union
Education and Sciences Union
Horticultural, Agricultural and Forestry Workers' Union
Commerce, Bank and Insurance Workers' Union
Wood and Plastic Workers' Union
Art Workers' Union
Leather Workers' Union
Metal Workers' Union
Food, Stimulants and Restaurant Workers' Union
Public Service, Transport and Communications Workers' Union
Police Union
German Postal Workers' Union
Textile and Garment Workers' Union

These unions, which have a combined membership of 7.7 million members, are structured according to the industry-union principle, that is 'one industry, one union', grouping wage earners, salaried staff and, where applicable, civil servants of one sector in one union. In contrast to vocational (or craft) trade unions this strengthens worker unity and underlines the common interests. The individual unions are independent in their bargaining and finance policies.

Prerequisite to a trade union's membership of the DGB is its acceptance of and adherence to the Federation's Constitution.

To finance the umbrella organisation the member unions have to pay it 12 per cent of their membership revenues. For support measures and to finance special trade union activities there is a solidarity fund into which DM 0.30 per individual member is paid per quarter.

Structure and organs of the DGB

The German Trade Union Federation covers the territory of the Federal Republic of Germany, including West Berlin, and parallel to the administrative structure of the West German state is divided into three levels: Federal (Bund), State (Landesbezirke) and County (Kreise) districts.

. . .

Document 5

As in most industrial countries, the agricultural sector is shrinking in the Federal Republic of Germany. Particularly endangered by modernisation is the family farm. In the following document, the German Farmers' Association gives its views on the place of the family farm within the common agricultural policy of the European Community.

THE GERMAN FARMERS' ASSOCIATION'S VIEWS ON THE FUTURE OF AGRICULTURE

Source: Deutscher Bauernverband, *Der Deutsche Bauernverband zur Fortentwicklung der EG-Agrarpolitik, Schriftenreihe des Deutschen Bauernverbands*, Heft 3, 1980, 51–2

The principles of the German Farmers' Association on agricultural, economic and social policy:

It is the chief aim of the German Farmers' Association to ensure the continuation of an agricultural system where the family farm plays an important rôle and thus upholds its undeniable economic and ecological advantages. Its aim is also to make sure that those working in agriculture benefit from the general development of incomes. The German Farmers' Association is ready to share the burden of constructive solutions in the further development of a common agricultural policy in as far as they can be carried out uniformly within the European Community and as long as they safeguard the already existing social status of farmers and improve it in line with the rest of the economy. This is justified by, and in keeping with, the policy of equal treatment for all sections of the population. But at the same time the German Farmers' Association can only agree to suggestions which put the fewest limits on the free entrepreneurial decisions of farmers themselves and ensure that their income remains productivity-orientated. It is indispensable that the socio-political achievements brought about by the agricultural community such as the care for, and upkeep of, the landscape should be appropriately rewarded. It is the task of the state's economic and agricultural policies to set up parity of income as laid down in the Agricultural Law of 1955 and in the Treaty of Rome in 1957.

The family farm system is not self-serving; in the long run it serves the interests of the community as a whole:

In comparison with big industrial farms of either the East or the West it has always shown a high capacity to adapt and to produce.

It forms the economic basis of rurual areas in many parts of Western Europe. The upholding of a minimum level of population in many areas of the Community would not be possible without the family farm system.

The family farm system maintains many flexible decision-making units in farming and in this way guarantees the best possible provision for the population even in times of crisis.

The family farm system provides for a wide distribution of property which is socio-politically desirable and guarantees independence and self-determination at the place of work. In this way it contributes especially to the preservation of democracy in western Europe as well as to the maintenance of social stability in the European Community.

The family farm system as a family business permits a combination with other forms of employment. One of its hallmarks is its ability to co-exist with full and part-time forms of employment.

A family farm means carrying out the business within the working capacity of the family. In this system there is no place for either farm factories which are not dependent on a particular area or agroindustrial methods of cultivation.

The family farm system guarantees the production of food which unquestionably fulfils health standards and guarantees that rural areas will continue to serve as ecological compensators for urban areas.

It must therefore remain the most important common agricultural policy of the European community to maintain and develop the family farm system. Every policy including market, price, foreign trade, social, structural and fiscal policies goes to make up the whole. Decisive statements can only be made after all measures have been considered in relation to each other.

Document 6

Citizens' action groups are very heterogeneous in many ways. They encounter difficulties in defining their purposes and actions in a way which is acceptable to all members. It is not surprising, therefore, that most documents are provisional and preliminary; very often they are published as drafts. This is also true of the document from which excerpts are reproduced here.

CITIZENS' ACTION GROUPS AS SEEN BY THEMSELVES

Source: Orientierungspapier des Bundesverbandes Bürgerinitiativen Umweltschutz e.B. (BBU) — draft of September 1977, reproduced in: Volker Hauff, ed., *Bürgerinitiativen in der Gesellschaft*, Villingen/Schwenningen, 1980, 343–8

Why do citizens' action groups for environmental protection exist?

In the field of environmental protection, citizens' action groups are spontaneously formed where, above all, citizens feel that social developments or state planning measures are encroaching upon their elementary rights. The experience of being helpless in the face of superior economic and political interests induces them to get together with like-minded people to protect their rights. The strength and success of citizens' action groups are still determined by the degree of the citizens' concern about erroneous developments in this society.

Many of us are prepared to offer resistance if a rubbish dump, a motorway or a nuclear power station is being planned right in our front garden, but we return to everyday life whether or not the resistance succeeded. The main thing is to realize that not only our immediate environment but our entire environment is threatened. Only then will the thousand grass roots of single initiatives gradually form a thick green carpet which fundamentally transforms our society and every single one of us.

. . .

What do we want?

We do not merely want to remedy abuses and prevent erroneous developments. On the contrary, we have set ourselves the goal of creating a more just, a freer and a more humane society.

The existing order of society is characterized by the struggle for power, wealth, esteem and knowledge as well as by the fear of powerlessness, poverty, contempt and ignorance. Our society continues to be characterized by the centralization of power, capital, knowledge, etc. We, on the other hand, want to reverse the process of increasing centralization in all areas of society. We want simplification, de-centralization and de-concentration. We want a society in which there is not only the alternative between devouring and being devoured, between winning or perishing; a society in which the antitheses between power and powerlessness, between wealth and poverty are reduced; a society, finally, in which human beings can be human with one another and with nature.

. . .

What is our course?

We think we know that an inseparable connection exists between means and aims. This means that peace cannot be attained by war, justice cannot be attained by injustice, and freedom from violence cannot be attained by force. Consequently, we do not only need the outline of an alternative social order; we also need alternative methods of settling and solving conflicts. These methods are constructive work and non-violent action.

Constructive work means the actual building of the new social order, the realization of alternative ways of living in the economy, society, politics and culture in the environment of every individual and of small groups.

Non-violent action means overcoming existing power relations by non-cooperation (strike, boycott, etc.), citizens' disobedience (breaking unjust laws) and non-violent confrontations (blocking construction sites, road blockades, sit-ins, work-ins, etc.).

The secret of our success

The work of citizens' action groups has so far been successful because it was possible to agree on a number of common principles (minimum consent) which are:

nonpartisanship,
non-violence,
democratic and decentralized organizational structure.

Nonpartisanship does not mean at all that party members are not allowed to work in citizens' action groups. It merely means that they forego party propaganda whilst working in a group (e.g. distributing pamphlets or brochures marked with the party's name). They are free, however, to present their objective arguments.

Non-violence does not mean passivity or burying one's head in the sand; nor does it mean restricting oneself entirely to legal methods of action. Non-violent, direct actions such as occupying a construction site or blocking an approach road by sitting strikers are absolutely reconcilable with the principle of non-violence. But they should be only applied as a last resort after all the legal possibilities have been exhausted.

Democratic organizational structure means that speakers or delegates are *elected* and majority decisions are *approved* as long as they do not offend the individual's conscience.

Due to their loose organizational structure, citizens' action groups run the particular danger of their majority decisions being ignored. In order to avoid irreconcilable differences or even splits, crucial votes should whenever possible be avoided. Where important decisions are concerned, the members of the citizens' action groups should keep talking with one another until the large majority agrees.

Decentralized organizational structure means that every member of a citizens' action group as well as every citizens' action group should be as independent as possible. The strength of citizens' action groups lies in their diversity, activity, spontaneity, imaginativeness and creativity. They live from the interest of *all* members. Regional and national associations should only tackle tasks which cannot be managed by local groups.

In our organization we try to avoid the mistakes which have removed the traditional parties and organizations so far from the real needs of the population. The politicians will have to get used to the idea that a popular movement such as the citizens' action groups cannot be filed away in cosily familiar categories. We resist being taken over by established parties, and we also resist the groups that want to misuse us for their own party's goals.

According to these principles, the BBU (Bundesverband Bürgerinitiativen Umweltschutz: Federal Association of Citizens' Action Groups for Environmental Protection) does not see itself as a representative 'leading organization' of ecologists either. Due to the decentralized organization, its competence is restricted. Its chief tasks lie in the coordination and establishment of a continuous process of information between the groups. However, the Association can also act independently as a 'citizens' action group on a national level' and express its own opinion.

Citizens' action groups and the Basic Law

Citizens' action groups do not want to take over political power. On the contrary, they want to keep power in control, in the long run even reduce power. Even now there are the first signs of parliaments, supported and challenged by citizens' resistance, actually starting to exercise again their control function over the executive.

The active participation of citizens in political life can only be welcomed in a country which states in its constitution: 'All state authority emanates from the people'. But whoever desires a politically active and interested citizen must allow him the right to participate and add his vote in his working and living environment.

We therefore demand a right of participation and codetermination for the citizen who is directly affected by planning decisions. We demand the right of participation and codetermination for the citizen on all political levels. We demand the expansion or else the introduction of plebiscitarian elements in the Länder constitutions and in the Basic Law.

Document 7

The liberal tradition calls for a clearcut separation of Church and State. In 1974 the Free Democratic Party tried to revive the discussion of this issue by publishing its Church Paper, entitled *Free Church in a Free State*

(*Freie Kirche im Freien Staat*). There is, however, little chance of a fundamental change in the situation. The thirteen theses of this paper are reproduced here.

FREE CHURCH IN A FREE STATE

Source: Günter Verheugen,* ed., *Das Programm der Liberalen,* 2nd. ed., Baden-Baden, 1980, 198ff.

1. Churches and ideological communities should make decisions about their own affairs independently of State influences. This requires the State to give up its remaining channels of influence, in particular, with regard to having a share in the regional structuring of the churches, the requirement of the episcopal oath of allegiance to the constitution and its influence on the filling of ecclesiastic offices.

2. The status of 'corporation under public law' is not applicable to religious or ideological groups like the churches because these bodies do not derive their duties from the State. On the other hand, the law regulating associations cannot do justice to the significance of the churches and other large communal bodies. A new law concerning such bodies has therefore to be developed which takes account of their full meaning and public workings. This law should also apply to the churches. Matters concerning religion and ideologies would be taken into consideration within this law.

3. Churches and ideological communities should regulate their membership within the framework of the freedom of religion according to their own laws. In order to leave the church or an ideological community, a declaration of intent addressed to this organization would be required.

   Everybody above the age of fifteen should have the right to choose his/her religion, as is true already in most Länder.

4. No one should be obliged to reveal his religious beliefs. This constitutional principle should be respected everywhere and especially in the law of personal status and in public office.

5. The existing church tax should be replaced by the churches' own contributory system. Appropriate discussions with the churches should be taken up concerning the modalities of transition and to set adequate time limits.

6. The constitutional principle of ideological/religious neutrality of the State should be applicable to the Länder constitutions and law, and rules and customs in public life. The religious convictions of individual groups may not be made binding for everyone.

   Sacred forms and symbols should not be used in the area of public institutions such as courts and state schools. The oath should have a neutral form

---

* Until 1982 secretary general of the Free Democratic Party

and those taking it must be allowed to add any formula which accords with their ideology.

7. Already existing state contracts with the churches (church treaties and concordats) are on account of their special character not a suitable means of regulating relations between Church and State. Such treaties should not therefore be renewed. Existing treaties and concordats, in as far as they are still valid, should be terminated by mutual agreement. The subject matter thereof should, as far as this is required, be settled by new laws or separate agreements.

8. Any payments from the State to the churches which are based on a law, a contract or special legal title should be abolished (as provided for by Art. 140 of the Basic Law and Art. 138, para. 1 of the Weimar Constitution).

Any special privileges concerning tax and payment which the churches or other religious communities enjoy with regard to other public institutions should be terminated.

9. Education, the care of the sick and social welfare should lie within the public domain. The right of independent institutions to be active in these areas should be upheld—although they should not have any privileges. To enable them to render these services independent institutions should receive appropriate state subsidies. Adequate provisions from public funds must be guaranteed to fulfil the need for such institutions which are ideologically neutral and accessible to everyone. Private institutions which receive subsidies from public funds must be accessible to the general public; people of other persuasions must not be subjected to any disadvantages or coercion.

10. The community school which is religiously and ideologically neutral should be the norm for a state school in the entire Federal Republic. Religious instruction is a regular subject according to the existing Constitution. As an alternative, instruction about religion is offered. There should be a free choice between these two subjects. The right to set up and maintain private schools should remain intact.

11. Pastoral care in state institutions such as the Army, the Border Guards and prisons should again become the sole responsibility of the churches. The opportunity of having unrestricted religious care by pastoral workers selected and paid by the churches should be guaranteed. The same right should apply to all religious and ideological communities.

12. Students about to enter the ministry and theology students should have the same rights and duties as other citizens even with regard to military service and conscientious objection.

13. Church representation within public bodies (e.g. broadcasting councils, school committees, youth and social committees, hearings, etc.) should be reexamined having regard to the function of a particular association in a particular area. This principle should also apply to other social groups.

Document 8

The Catholic Church has always attached particular importance to the family as a foundation element of society. Therefore, it has persistently demanded a governmental policy to protect the traditional family. The following excerpts are from a 1979 declaration of the General Assembly of the Central Committee of German Catholics (Zentralkomitee der Deutschen Katholiken), the lay organization of the Catholic Church.

THE CATHOLIC CONCEPT OF FAMILY POLICY

Source: 'Ehe und Familie im Spannungsfeld von personaler Partnerschaft und Institution. Eine Erklärung des Zentralkomitees der Deutschen Katholiken für die Gesellschaftspolitische Diskussion über diese Fragen. Beschlossen von der Vollversammlung des Zentralkomitees der Deutschen Katholiken.' Bonn/Bad Godesberg, 11–12 May 1979

The family finds itself in close mutual interaction with other social groups and processes. The family should be able to expect unlimited support from the forces governing society, not only for the sake of the rôle it plays in personal human development but also because of the service it renders to society.

The mass media—television, the radio, magazines and the daily press—should paint a realistic picture of the family and its importance in our lives as a whole. Ideological images which are hostile to the family and diminish its work unfairly must be replaced by a more constructively critical representation.

For many families working life imposes unnecessary difficulties. Employers in both the public and private sectors should adapt to the needs of the family and offer part-time jobs or flexible working hours.

In their socio-political dealings concerning the family, political parties should rid themselves of tendencies that are one-sidedly individualistic or collectivist and make as a basis for their social and family policies the more complete vision of marriage and the family. Effective cooperation on political matters concerning the family can only be hampered by thinking which is derived from liberal and Marxist principles.

The statement in the Basic Law on marriage and the family is based on a consensus reached after hard-won experience concerning the dignity of human beings, their freedom and their solidarity. We expect organs of the State, in their practical policies, to implement fully those constitutional provisions which present the personal values of marriage and the family as particularly worthy of being protected.

This constitutional undertaking must continue to be fulfilled in several ways: 1) by a relief from financial burdens; 2) through a social infrastructure which has regard for family interests; 3) special forms of aid for families with particular problems. These matters must be a federal concern as well as the responsibility of the Länder and of the local authorities.

In our opinion the following have precedence at the moment: 1) the lawful safeguarding of the family both as an institution and in its original task of bringing up children; 2) the furthering of the willingness to have children; 3) an extension of support for families with three or more children; 4) a regular index-linked child allowance; 5) the extension of maternity leave; 6) the introduction of a regular allowance for mothers bringing up children. Apart from this, considerable efforts must be made to rebuild a relationship of trust between the home and school.

Through a consistent and continuing development of a systematic family policy an important contribution will be made indirectly to a more balanced structure and development of the population. Of principal importance in this are the means to enable a married woman to decide without difficulty to have children. This would count in those cases too where the woman would like—at least temporarily—to be socially or professionally active.

Just as concrete measures are important so also are the language and spirit in which family problems are dealt with in public discussion. Anyone who in this ignores all human relationships casts doubt on himself in a way that he will hardly be able to overcome. Instead of this a positive readiness is called for, a readiness which is not afraid to make the necessary effort to develop further that which has already proved its worth. Each and every individual is called upon to do this.

Document 9

In 1981 the Evangelical Church published its Peace Memorandum: 'The Preservation, Promotion and Renewal of Peace'. This paper emphasizes the need for disarmament and détente in a way which then went beyond the official position of the majority of politicians and in this way encouraged and reinforced the 'peace movement'.

The following excerpt is from the last part of the fifty-eight-page memorandum.

THE PEACE MEMORANDUM OF THE EVANGELICAL CHURCH
Source: 'The Preservation, Promotion and Renewal of Peace, a Memorandum of the Evangelical Church in Germany.' EKD-Bulletin, special issue, 1981
Transl.: Official
. . .

3. Strengthening the Desire for Closer Contacts
. . .

a) International Peace Order (Friedensordnung)

The church's task is first and foremost to witness that peace for the world is only found in Jesus Christ. Political witness and the church's political service for peace cannot ignore the fact that any peace order can only be relative and can always be made obsolete.

The prevention of war is an initial step towards peace. But the absence of war does not make for peace. Peace cannot be conceived of as a political state at all; rather it is a process of gradually broadening the base of those social conditions which make up the quality of peace: the refraining from violent solutions to international conflicts, the abolition of hardship and distress, the guaranteeing of freedom and self-determination for all nations, the elimination of racial or social oppression and discrimination, respect for human rights and the protection of natural environmental conditions for life. Such a peace can only be founded on a close interweaving of different interests and a systematic development of solutions which are of such general benefit that they outweigh the unavoidable disadvantages. Such an order would be the transfer of basic concepts of social welfare and the rule of law to the international level, i.e. the attempt to settle inevitable conflicts on the basis of internationally agreed rules. An international peace order must realise the individual and social human rights, include a common approach to security and prevent the imposition of interests by recourse to force; it has to respect the autonomy of nations and promote regional and international cooperation.

A political road to such an order is scarely within view at the moment, and the projected worldwide peace order, enabling justice and freedom for all, is obviously not feasible at present. It is all the more urgent that the desire for closer contacts be strengthened, that they be neither under-estimated or repudiated, nor themselves mistaken for the further-reaching goals. It is not a question of conserving the present world situation in which peace is so vulnerable. The point is to take steps—however modest—in the direction of an international peace order.

However, the most urgent task is to prevent a war between the two major alliances. Even if opinions differ on whether it can really be prevented, political action must assume that it can, in order to be meaningful. The fact that arms build-up and up-grade continue has altered the nature of the balance and created risks of its own: the possibility of a change of function, to that of triggering off a war instead of guarding against it, is coming into focus more clearly. Since the beginning of the sixties there have thus been efforts towards arms limitation, which must be the first step on the road to disarmament. Most of the expectations in this respect have hitherto been disappointed, however.

The success of such efforts largely depends on the two main power blocs expecting to benefit more from them than from continued arms production. But we are in a situation of heightened confrontation between the superpowers. We Europeans, particularly we Germans, are at present the ones who have the least to gain from a policy of confrontation. It would again restrict the greater room to manoeuvre in the relationship between the two Germanies and reduce the scope for independent political action aimed at a tighter meshing of mutual interests.

Eastern and Western Europe have their own interests, which are not identical with those of the leading powers on either side. On the other hand, Europe is involved in worldwide conflicts of interests from which it cannot extricate itself and which, in a crisis, would rebound on it at the risk of wiping out the achievements of détente. So Europe is bound to be interested in the development of a long-term détente programme involving the superpowers. Even though Europe, specifically the two Germanies, can only play a modest role between the two superpowers, it can contribute to a fresh international perspective. It should not be isolationist, but continually throw its weight into the balance for the sake of peace. Its goal could be to maintain its freedom to seek political strategies aimed at transferring favourable European experience with détente to other world trouble-spots, and encouraging steps in the necessary direction of an international peace order.

In this situation, it is not up to the church to make statements about how such planning could be put into practice. It can however, raise questions for politicians expressing the concerns of many people in the Federal Republic of Germany and their urgent hopes for a new political perspective.

The three major areas for questions are: comprehensive cooperation, typically defensive defence planning and effective disarmament.

b) Towards Comprehensive Cooperation

The present debate highlights control and limitation of arms. These are reasonable and appropriate aims if they are rooted in a broader perspective.

What are the present political chances of a comprehensive cooperative plan being drawn up, involving both the blocs and going beyond arms control and limitation?

Balance cannot be defined solely and satisfactorily in military terms. Moreover, the only promising plans are those taking account of the interests of both power blocs and from which they can both expect to benefit. For these reasons, such an approach would need to include industry, science and technology. The primacy of military confrontation must be replaced by that of political cooperation. This is the only way to reduce the arms production incentive for industry and technological research, and to shift it to other areas of industrial production. Technological and economic constraints are not independent factors: just as they can cut themselves off from politics, and then influence it, different types of policies can also influence the arms industry and give new goals to technology and production.

If military confrontation is to yield to political cooperation, the West must do its best to avoid capitalising on the weak points of the East in such a way as might possibly cause a military reaction. This must certainly not rule out the inclusion of human rights protection in political cooperation.

Such a plan for comprehensive cooperation calls for political imagination which, in turn, needs the latitude of an open political discussion, free of hard lines and insinuation.

c) Towards a Typically Defensive Concept of Armament

What are the chances of stressing the exclusively defensive character of NATO defence, and gradually replacing the weaponry which can also be deployed for purposes of attack? The danger of war can be enhanced by notional threat, and so a defence policy provisionally guaranteeing minimum nuclear deterrence, but emphasising typically defensive weapons, would lessen the danger. This requires the establishing of criteria on what is essential for deterrence and what is superfluous.

There must be a serious discussion in our country and in NATO of this and other alternative defence policies. Here, too, new ways can only be found in a climate of honest public debate.

d) Towards Effective Disarmament

What are the current political prospects for effective arms reduction in the framework of talks on the disturbingly modest objective of cooperative arms control?

In view of the risks entailed by the quantity and quality of existing arsenals, concerned people can only be expected to raise the patience for long-drawn-out arms limitation talks, which have hitherto been only relatively successful, to the extent that they can discern serious intentions and prospects of lessening these risks through effective disarmament.

It is the church's duty to question politicians about ways of breaking the arms production chain, where both sides consider or claim they are reinstating the lost balance. The fact that the striving for parity always means build-up, never reduction, places an intolerable strain on the very concept of balance. Mutual deterrence is provisionally granting scope for political safeguards and if this is not used to break the chain, the time will come when the scandal and risk of the arms race outweighs the effectiveness of the deterrence system.

If calculated unilateral steps can help disarmament talks along, they deserve serious consideration too; we should not be discouraged by the fact that unilateral steps on both sides have not had the effect expected in the past.

Talks on cooperative arms control, arms limitation and disarmament will only be really successful if they aim for agreements also covering foreseeable possibilities of technical advance and systems modernisation.

One way in which the church could strengthen the feeling for rapprochement might be for the Council of the EKD to take the initiative of encouraging the writing of regular expert opinions; on the basis of up-to-date analyses these would make recommendations for possible next steps towards disarmament and political peace orders. In this connection, the Council of the EKD should encourage the continuous flow of reliable news for the general public about basic political developments, dangers to peace, détente and disarmament.

. . .

Document 10

The following quotation is a typical example of how any form of radicalism is banned from a broadcasting corporation.

LAW ESTABLISHING THE 'WESTDEUTSCHER RUNDFUNK KÖLN', 25 MAY 1954

Source: Broadcasting Laws, Documents on Politics and Society in the Federal Republic of Germany, Inter Nationes, Bonn/Bad Godesberg, 1979, 26
Transl.: Official

. . .

Art. 4

Westdeutscher Rundfunk Köln shall maintain its broadcasts within the framework of constitutional good order. It shall take ideological, scientific and artistic factors into account. The moral and religious convictions of the population shall be respected. The ethnic structure of the transmission region shall be given due token. Broadcast of news must be general, independent and objective.

Westdeutscher Rundfunk shall promote international understanding, propagate peace and social justice, defend democratic freedoms and be committed to the truth only. It may not one-sidedly serve the interests of a political party or grouping, an interest-group, faith or ideology. . . .

Document 11

The composition of the television board of the Second German Television reflects the attempt to secure a representation of all relevant social groups. There is, however, the difficulty that many representatives of particular social groups are also members of political parties. Therefore, one may speak of an overrepresentation of party-interests in these bodies.

REPRESENTATION OF INTEREST GROUPS ON THE TELEVISION BOARD OF THE 'SECOND GERMAN TELEVISION'.

Source: Broadcasting Laws, Documents on Politics and Society in the Federal Republic of Germany, Inter Nationes, Bonn/Bad Godesberg, 1979, 60
Transl.: Official

. . .

Art. 14. Composition of the Television Board

(1) The Television Board shall comprise sixty-six members, namely:

a) one representative of each of the Länder entering into this Treaty, to be delegated by the respective Land Government;

b) three representatives of the Federation, to be delegated by the Federal Government;

c) twelve representatives of the political parties in accordance with their strength of representation in the Bundestag, to be delegated by the respective Party Executives;

d) two representatives delegated by the Protestant Church in Germany;

e) two representatives delegated by the Roman Catholic Church in Germany;

f) one representative delegated by the Central Council of Jews in Germany;

g) three representatives of the trades union;

h) two representatives of the Federation of German Employers' Associations;

i) one representative of the Central Committee of German Agriculture;

k) one representative of the Central Association of German Manual Trades;

l) two representatives of the Federation of German Newspaper Publishers;

m) two representatives of the German Journalists' Association (Reg.);

n) four representatives of private charity associations, i.e. one each of the Inner Mission and Relief Scheme of the Protestant Church in Germany; the German Caritas Association (Reg.) (Roman Catholic charity); the German Red Cross and the Central Committee of German Workers' Charity (Reg.);

o) four representatives of the main communal associations, i.e. one each of the Permanent Conference of Municipalities, the Municipalities' Federation, the Permanent Conference of District Councils and the Permanent Conference of Community Councils;

p) one representative of the German Sports' Confederation;

q) one representative of the Federation of Expellees;

r) ten representatives from the fields of education and training, science and the arts, as well as one representative each of

the free professions,

family work,

women's work,

youth work,

. . .

Document 12

In 1978 the Federal Government reported to the Bundestag on the state of the press. Among many other aspects this report deals with the issue of how the freedom of the press is endangered by the process of economic concentration of publishing companies.

THE STATE OF THE PRESS (MEDIENBERICHT)

Source: Report of the Federal Government on the State of Press and Broadcasting in the Federal Republic of Germany (1978), Deutscher Bundestag, 8th legislative period, Drucksache 8/2264, 67–8

II. Freedom of the Press

. . .

The Federal Government reiterated in the Government Declaration of 16 December 1976 that the private-law character of the press should continue to be upheld in the same way as the public-law character of broadcasting. These are two mutually complementary principles on which the system of the media in the Federal Republic is based. Both organisational solutions must be seen in terms of the aim based in the Constitution that every individual be guaranteed the highest level of freedoms and of possibilities in the media. The individual must have a central place in this from which he should be able to inform himself comprehensively and fully, and to form his own opinion freely and to express it, thereby enabling him to have independently responsible participation in the development of a democratic community.

1. Variety in the Press

Whereas the pluralistic internal structure of broadcasting which is regulated by law is supposed to assure the public of a large number of radio and television programmes, exhibiting in themselves a great diversity, and also of a variety of broadcasting organisations, the diversity of information and opinion in the Press is seen as resulting from entrepreneurial competition and market forces.

Indeed the Federal Constitutional Court based its 1961 ruling on the premise that '. . . within the German press a relatively large number of publications exist, which are independent and compete with each other according to their inclination, political leanings and in their basic ideological standpoint'. Implicit in this supposition is that the public has a sufficient number of choices. For this reason the maintenance of variety in what the press offers is principally dependent on maintaining those choices.

1.1 General Variety in the Press

The press in the Federal Republic of Germany corresponds essentially to the image of a wealth of choice represented by a multiplicity of different press publications. This is the case as long as this assessment is based on a broad concept of the press which corresponds and is basic to Art. 5 of the Basic Law. This means that all publications which appear periodically and any which do not, and also, apart from daily newspapers, the wide range of magazines of all kinds and so-called local and regional periodicals with an informative content—regardless of their thematic restriction—are taken into consideration.

. . .

1.2 Limited variety in the regional/local news press and Sunday newspapers
If, however, one considers just the actual daily press as that part of the press
which is important to the formation of opinion, then the present situation does
not come up to the ideal of a desirable competitiveness in the newspaper market
in the two significant areas of the regional/local daily press and the Sunday
newspapers.

There is a wider choice of well-defined independent organs of opinion in the
national dailies and weekly periodicals. There, a pluralistic overview both in
news and commentary is supplied by a number of independent organs with differing political tendencies and standpoints. These include five national
newspapers, three more daily newspapers with a national journalistic reputation,
an economic and financial paper which appears when the Stock Exchange is in
operation and twelve political weeklies. The national Sunday newspaper market
is an exception in that only two publications from the same publisher appear.

. . .

When surveying the landscape of German newspapers one cannot afford to
overlook that a growing number of supplementary press publications—even if
this varies from region to region—have been able to establish themselves, and
these are trying to balance out the gaps in information, mainly concerning local
and communal events, which are no longer covered by the dailies and to fill
demands for information which have recently arisen. the press of the church,
associations and political parties, the so-called 'free newspapers' which serve as
sources of information on citizens' action groups, newpapers for different town
districts and two magazines, local weeklies and advertising newspapers, publications for school children and for young people and community newspapers—all
these contain a multi-layered spectrum of information and opinion which often
transcends social and class groupings. The intention of these papers is to supplement information from the dailies and deepen understanding in certain areas of
expertise.

1.3 Principles for the conservation of the variety in the press.
The future maintenance of variety in the press, according to the Federal Government, should be specifically based on the idea of the best possible supply of
organs of information which are economically and journalistically viable and
which, independent of and in competition with each other, provide altogether a
greater variety of information and opinion and increase the individual's level of
freedom. A concentration into a few market-dominating enterprises, on the other
hand, would narrow down the scope of a press which is multistructured in content. Due to the continual concentration of business interests this cannot be
prevented in the long run even by measures taken within individual enterprises
to ensure a diversity of the publications. At most it can be deferred temporarily in
favourable economic conditions. The reasons for this are the same as the ones
which apply to the behaviour of enterprises which have a dominant position in
the market.

The maintenance of diversity in the Press in the form of an external plurality is therefore absolutely essential. All measures taken within individual publishing houses to ensure diversity within individual publications are therefore no substitute, but rather a concern completely independent thereof.

. . .

Notes

1. Co-determination is documented in Ch. 10, Docs. 5–9
2. See also Ch. 8
3. The Evangelical Church in Germany comprises: the United Protestant Lutheran Church of Germany, the Protestant Church of the Union and the Reformed Alliance
4. See also Ch. 12., Doc. 8
5. See also Ch. 6., Doc. 2b
6. See Ch. 10., Doc. 1

10 Economic and Social Policy

Detlev Karsten

The economic system of the Federal Republic of Germany can be characterized as basically market-orientated, with strong government intervention mainly for social reasons.* A conscious decision in favour of a market system was taken in 1948 when the planned economy with its fixed prices—the heritage of the war and of the extreme poverty of the post-war period—was abandoned. The underlying theoretical concept of the economic system was—and to some extent is—the neo-liberal idea of a 'social market economy'. The basic philosophy of this concept is that economic processes should be regulated by market forces rather than by state control. The market forces, however, can only operate to the best advantage if they are harnessed by a legal framework, the most important element of which is a law to protect competition. As the market forces attribute income only to those who also contribute to production, a social policy has to supplement the system. In Germany, the essence of social policy is seen on the one hand in a strategy which secures growth, prosperity and full employment in a situation of stable prices (the latter being considered an instrumental goal both for the functioning of the economy and also a precondition for an effective social policy). This policy is, on the other hand, supplemented by specific welfare measures in support of those who are unable to work, but which also aim at a reduction of economic inequality by helping the economically weaker persons. This mixture of economic and social policy, which also incorporates a legal strengthening of the position of the weaker party in economic conflicts (e.g. the tenant *vis-à-vis* the landlord, the worker *vis-à-vis* the employer), is considered to be conducive to social stability.[1]

The decision in favour of a market-orientated economic system is now

---

* Notes for this chapter begin on p. 283

largely accepted as non-controversial between the major political parties.[2] This helps to explain the continuity of economic policy regardless of which political parties form the government.

The Basic Law contains few provisions regarding the structure of the economic system. But it does guarantee rights which are necessary for an entrepreneurial system. The most important are:[3]

Art. 2. Rights of Liberty

(1) Everyone shall have the right to the free development of his personality in so far as he does not violate the rights of others or offend against the constitutional order or the moral code.
(2) Everyone shall have the right to life and to inviolability of his person. The liberty of the individual shall be inviolable. These rights may only be encroached upon pursuant to a law.

Art. 9. Freedom of Association

(1) All Germans shall have the right to form associations and societies.
(2) Associations, the purposes or activities of which conflict with criminal laws or which are directed against the constitutional order or the concept of international understanding, are prohibited.
(3) The right to form associations to safeguard and improve working and economic conditions is guaranteed to everyone and to all trades, occupations and professions. Agreements which restrict or seek to impair this right shall be null and void; measures directed to this end shall be illegal. . . .

Art. 12. Right to Choose Trade, Occupation or Profession

(1) All Germans shall have the right freely to choose their trade, occupation or profession, their place of work and their place of training. The practice of trades, occupations, and professions may be regulated by or pursuant to a law.
(2) No specific occupation may be imposed on any person except within the framework of a traditional compulsory public service that applies generally and equally to all.
(3) Forced labour may be imposed only on persons deprived of their liberty by court sentence.

Art. 14. Property, Right of Inheritance, Expropriation

(1) Property and the right of inheritance are guaranteed. Their content and limits shall be determined by the laws.
(2) Property imposes duties. Its use should also serve the public weal.
(3) Expropriation shall be permitted only in the public weal. It may be effected only by or pursuant to a law which shall provide for the nature and extent of the compensation. Such compensation shall be determined by establishing an

equitable balance between the public interest and the interests of those affected. In case of dispute regarding the amount of compensation, recourse may be had to the ordinary courts.

Art. 15. Socialization

Land, natural resources and means of production may for the purpose of socialization be transferred to public ownership or other forms of publicly controlled economy by a law which shall provide for the nature and extent of compensation. In respect of such compensation the third and fourth sentences of paragraph (3) of Art. 14 shall apply *mutatis mutandis.*

Art. 2 implicitly includes the freedom of economic activity. The independence of the trade unions and employers' associations to determine working conditions through collective bargaining is an element of Art. 9, relating to the freedom of association. Art. 15 which allows socialization of the means of production has not gained a major importance. In Art. 20 (1) and Art. 28 (1) the Basic Law refers to the Federal Republic of Germany as a 'social state', a claim which is interpreted not only as an admonition addressed to the legislature but is also directly relevant for the interpretation of all legal provisions and administrative activities.

It is symptomatic of the general political climate and of the awareness of these issues in the Federal Republic of Germany that a discussion arose as to whether the Basic Law had taken a conscious decision in favour of a specific concept of an economic system, the 'social market economy'. The defenders of this idea tried to raise the 'social market economy' to a constitutional principle. This view was refuted in 1954 when the Federal Constitutional Court ruled that the Basic Law was neutral in regard to the economic system. But, in general, the issue of the economic system—mainly in the form of challenging the conformity or compatibility, with the existing system, of a particular economic or social policy measure—remains an important element of political debate.

The law which is fundamental to the market system is the 'Act against Restraints of Competition' of 1957 with important later amendments (Doc. 1).

The recession of the mid-1960s made it apparent that a coordinated economic policy to combat cyclical fluctuations required an effective cooperation of the fiscal authorities of the Federation, the Länder and the municipalities. An attempt to secure this cooperation is the 'Act to Promote Economic Stability and Growth' (Stabilitätsgesetz) of 1967 which largely reflects the then dominant Keynesian view that fiscal policy is the most effective instrument to secure the economic stability (Doc. 2). This law was controversial because it introduced a touch of macroeconomic planning into the existing market system and because it brought an element of centralization into a generally decentralized federal system.[4] The latter was one of the reasons why the Basic Law was amended at the same time to define the financial autonomy of the Federation and the Länder more clearly:

Art. 109. Separate budgets for Federation and Länder

(1) The Federation and the Länder shall be autonomous and independent of each other in their fiscal administration.

(2) The Federation and the Länder shall take due account in their fiscal administration of the requirements of overall economic equilibrium.

(3) By means of federal legislation requiring the consent of the Bundesrat, principles applicable to both the Federation and the Länder may be established governing budgetary law, responsiveness of the fiscal administration to economic trends, and financial planning to cover several years ahead.

(4) With a view to averting disturbances of the overall economic equilibrium, federal legislation requiring the consent of the Bundesrat may be enacted providing for:

1. maximum amounts, terms and timing of loans to be raised by public administrative entities, whether territorial (Gebietskörperschaften) or functional (Zweckverbände), and

2. an obligation on the part of the Federation and the Länder to maintain interest-free deposits in the German Federal Bank (reserves for counterbalancing economic trends).

Authorizations to enact pertinent ordinances having the force of law may be issued only to the Federal Government. Such ordinances shall require the consent of the Bundesrat. They shall be repealed in so far as the Bundestag may demand; details shall be regulated by federal legislation.

A particular feature of the German economic system is that the responsibility for monetary policy lies almost exclusively with the central bank, the 'Deutsche Bundesbank'. As Germany has experienced two massive inflations in the course of this century, Germans are particularly sensitive about inflation. In consequence, the Bundesbank has been made an autonomous body which does not have to follow instructions from the Federal Government although it is obliged to support the Government's policy (Doc. 3). This autonomy of the Bundesbank restricts the Government's control of monetary policy and has occasionally brought into the open conflicts between the Government, whose first priority is the reduction of unemployment even at the cost of a somewhat higher inflation, and the Bundesbank, whose first priority is the fighting of inflation.

In Germany, the first compulsory social insurance schemes were introduced in 1883. Since then, and especially since the Second World

War, the drift has been towards a welfare state. The main reason for this development was the general acceptance of a need for a social policy to support and protect the economically disadvantaged. The present extent of social welfare policy, however, was only reached because of general prosperity, and financial constraints which became apparent in the 1980s may result in far-reaching reforms. The long-lasting prosperity had allowed the financing of social benefits out of public funds, and it had also made possible the burdening of business firms with claims resulting from such legal provisions. Since 1980, an attempt has been made to systematize at least some of the legislative measures in a 'Social Code' (Doc. 4). But this picture remains incomplete without reference to other legal provisions as, for example, the general protection of tenants against expulsion, the protection of juvenile workers, of female workers, the guarantee of holidays, the subsidies for the educational system and many other measures of redistribution in favour of the economically weak.

A particular feature of German economic life is the highly developed German system of co-determination (workers' participation) in industry. Co-determination was practiced informally in the Coal, Iron and Steel Industry as early as 1947, and was codified for this sector in 1951 in the 'Act on the Co-determination of Workers in the Supervisory and Management Boards of Enterprises in the Mining Industry and the Iron and Steel Producing Industry'. Co-determination can be seen as an instrument which improves the economic position of the workers by giving them more rights and more responsibilities in the running of the firm. There is, however, the difficulty that it has a tendency to become co-determination in the interests of the trade unions rather than of the actual workers (which do not necessarily coincide). Since workers' participation is such a specific feature of the German economic system it is dealt with rather more extensively here. Doc. 5 is an excerpt from the — essentially non-controversial — Works Constitution Act (Betriebsverfassungsgesetz) regulating workers' rights at the shop-floor level. Doc. 6 is an excerpt from the Co-determination Act of 1976 which spells out workers' rights of co-determination at the board level. This act was challenged in the Federal Constitutional Court by some firms and employers' federations, and Doc. 7 shows their main arguments. Doc. 8 gives a general idea of the trade unions' position regarding co-determination. Doc. 9 summarizes the relevant decision of the Federal Constitutional Court. The specific issue of co-determination in the Coal, Iron and Steel Industry has been omitted here.

An important current and future challenge for the economic and social system of the Federal Republic of Germany is the presence of a large number of foreign workers. At its height in 1976, foreign workers constituted 10 per cent of the labour force, and today 7 per cent of the inhabitants of Germany are foreigners who are also heavily concentrated regionally. Workers from EEC countries who have a right to work in any member state constitute only a fraction of this foreign labour force. The real problem is represented by workers from non-EEC countries, particularly Turks, who originally were brought to Germany for temporary relief of labour market shortages; they later brought their families,the majority of whom are likely to stay and will thus have to be integrated into German society.[5] There is also a considerable number of political refugees from other continents. The integration of all these people is a difficult process, especially in times of severe unemployment. The whole issue is politically controversial (Doc. 10).

Document 1

The 'Act against Restraints of Competition' of 1957 was passed only after sharp political controversies, especially between the 'purist' defenders of the social market economy concept and the representatives of business and industry who claimed that this law was unnecessarily restrictive and would impair the competitiveness of Germany in the international markets. The main elements are: (1) a general prohibition of cartels and similar arrangements with specified exceptions to this rule, (2) control of abuse by firms which hold a market-dominating position, (3) control and prevention of mergers by larger firms. Articles to protect competition are also contained in the EEC Treaty.

The excerpts reproduced here include later amendments.

ACT AGAINST RESTRAINTS OF COMPETITION (GESETZ GEGEN WETTBE-WERBSBESCHRÄNKUNGEN)
Source: Gesetz gegen Wettbewerbsbeschränkungen, BGBl., I, 1980, 1761ff.
Transl.: OECD

Section 1

(1) Agreements made for a common purpose by enterprises or associations of enterprises and decisions of associations of enterprises shall be of no effect, insofar as they are likely to influence, by restraining competition, production or market conditions with respect to trade in goods or commercial services. This shall apply only insofar as this Act does not provide otherwise.

. . .

Section 15

Agreements between enterprises with respect to goods or commercial services relating to markets located within the area of application of this Act shall be null and void, insofar as they restrict a party to them in its freedom to determine prices or terms of business in contracts which it concludes with third parties in regard to the goods supplied, other goods, or commercial services.

. . .

Section 22

(1) An enterprise is market dominating within the meaning of this Act insofar as, in its capacity as a supplier or buyer of a certain type of goods or commercial services:

1. it has no competitor or is not exposed to any substantial competition, or
2. it has a paramount market position in relation to its competitors; for this purpose, in addition to its share of the market, its financial strength, its access to the supply or sales markets for goods or services, its links with other enterprises and the legal or actual barriers to the market entry of other enterprises shall in particular be taken into account.

(2) Two or more enterprises shall also be deemed market dominating insofar as, in regard to a certain type of goods or commercial services, no substantial competition exists between them, for factual reasons, either in general, or in specific markets, and they jointly meet the requirements of subsection (1).

(3) It shall be presumed that:

1. an enterprise is market dominating within the meaning of subsection (1), if it has a market share of at least one-third for a certain type of goods or commercial services; this presumption shall not apply when the enterprise recorded a turnover of less than DM 250 million in the last completed business year;
2. the conditions specified in subsection (2) are met if, in regard to a certain type of goods or commercial services,
   a) three or less enterprises have a combined market share of 50% or over, or
   b) five or less enterprises have a combined market share of two-thirds or over
   this presumption shall not apply, insofar as enterprises are concerned which recorded turnovers of less than DM 100 million in the last completed business year.

As regards the calculation of the market share and turnover, Section 23 (1), sentences 2 to 10 shall apply, as appropriate.

(4) In regard to market dominating enterprises, the cartel authority shall have the powers set out in subsection (5), insofar as these enterprises abuse their dominating position in the market for these or any other goods or commercial services.

An abuse within the meaning of sentence 1 is present, in particular, if a market dominating enterprise as a supplier or buyer of a certain type of goods or commercial services:

1. impairs the competitive possibilities of other enterprises in a manner relevant to competition on the market in the absence of facts justifying such behaviour;
2. demands considerations or other business terms which deviate from those which would result in all probability if effective competition existed; in this context in particular the practices of enterprises on comparable markets characterised by effective competition have to be taken into account;

. . .

(5) If the conditions laid down in subsection (4) are satisfied the cartel authority may prohibit abusive practices by market dominating enterprises and declare agreements to be of no effect; . . . Prior to such action, the cartel authority shall request the parties involved to discontinue the abuse to which objection was raised.

. . .

Section 23

(1) The merging of enterprises shall immediately be notified to the Federal Cartel Office, if:

1. within the total area of application of this Act or in a substantial part thereof a market share of at least 20% is obtained or increased by the merger or if a participating enterprise has a share of at least 20% in another market, or
2. the participating enterprises together at some date during the completed business year preceding the merger had at least 10,000 employees or recorded a turnover of at least DM 500 million in this period.

. . .

Section 24

(1) If it is likely that a market dominating position will be created or strengthened as a result of a merger, the cartel authority shall have the powers specified in the following provisions, unless the participating enterprises prove that the merger will also lead to improvements in the conditions of competition and that these improvements will outweigh the disadvantages of market domination.

(2) If the conditions of subsection (1) are present, the Federal Cartel Office shall prohibit the merger.

. . .

Document 2

In its section 1, the 'Act to Promote Economic Stability and Growth'

(Stabilitatsgesetz) of 1967 specifies goals of economic policy. The remaining sections stipulate how the actions of all fiscal authorities are to be coordinated to reach these goals. The following document is a description of this Act by the Deutsche Bundesbank.

THE ACT TO PROMOTE STABILITY AND GROWTH (STABILITATGESETZ)

Source: Deutsche Bundesbank, *Instruments of Monetary Policy in the Federal Republic of Germany*, Frankfurt, n.d., 6–8

The Act is based on the recognition that in present and future conditions the efficiency of the system of the free market economy can be safeguarded only if it is supplemented by overall control of the major aggregates of the economy. The Act sets up the necessary institutional machinery. It supplements and improves the traditional instruments of short-term economic and monetary policy and hence widens the Federal Government's and the Bundesbank's freedom of action in the economic policy field. The Act is at the same time designed to create the conditions necessary for achieving balanced economic development which, avoiding undue cyclical fluctuations, help to secure adequate economic growth in the longer term too.

Section 1 of the Act defines the general economic policy objectives. All economic and financial policy measures taken by the Federal Government and the Länder must be designed to 'contribute, in the framework of the free market economy, at the same time to price stability, to a high level of employment and to external equilibrium, along with steady and adequate economic growth'. Compliance with these objectives is required not only of the Federal Government and the Länder, but also of the Federal Railways, the Federal Post Office, the ERP Special Fund and the public boards and corporations directly controlled by the Federal Government. The local authorities and local authority associations must also take account of these basic objectives of economic policy in their budget policy.

To safeguard pursuit of these objectives, the Act provides for principles and measures which have sometimes a direct but sometimes only an indirect relevance for monetary policy; examples of the latter type include in particular the provision under the Act for the preparation of a 'subsidy report' at intervals of two years, and for the forward planning of the revenue and expenditure of the Federal Government and the Länder for a period of five years.

The measures laid down in the Act relate to the following four main fields:

(i) *Information*

A definition of the basic aims of economic policy is given in the Act itself.

The annual economic report of the Federal Government, submitted in January, sets out and explains the economic and financial aims envisaged for the current year and the proposed economic and financial policy. The report also contains a statement of the Federal Government's views on the annual opinion on the general economic trends rendered by the Council of Experts.

The report on subsidies, submitted every two years, similarly throws more light on economic and financial policy.

To enable the Government's economic policy and the autonomous decisions of the parties to collective wage agreements to be coordinated, the Federal Government, if a basic objective of economic policy is endangered, makes available target figures for 'concerted action' by the central, regional and local authorities, trade unions and employers' associations. In practice, these target figures are discussed in advance with the parties concerned. The Deutsche Bundesbank also takes part in these discussions.

(ii) *Financial planning*
The Act introduces forward planning, for a period of several years, of the revenue and the expenditure of the Federal Government and the Länder.

(iii) *Co-ordination among the public authorities*
To improve co-ordination of the measures taken by the Federal Government, the Länder and the local authorities in matters of economic and financial policy, the Act introduces elements of co-operative federalism into financial policy, in particular by establishing a Council on Economic Trends, and, more recently, a Financial Planning Council. The Bundesbank may take part in the discussions of either body.

(iv) *Creation of new instruments of short-term economic policy*
These include the provisions for influencing private demand by tax measures and for influencing the public authorities' investment policy, measures to widen the Bundesbank's room for manoeuvre in liquidity policy, provision for anti-cyclical reserves of the Federal Government and the Länder, rules for the borrowing and debt redemption operations of the public authorities, and provisions for the management of the public authorities' demand for credit.

Document 3

The 1957 'Deutsche Bundesbank Act' specifies the responsibilities of the Bundesbank and its relationship with the Federal Government. In particular, it spells out the autonomy of the central bank.

ACT TO ESTABLISH THE CENTRAL BANK (BUNDESBANKGESETZ), 1957
Source: Gesetz über die Deutsche Bundesbank, BGBl., I, 1957, 745

. . .

§ 3 *Duty*
To safeguard the currency, the Deutsche Bundesbank controls the supply of

money and credits. It does this by exercising the powers in the field of monetary policy assigned to it by this law. It also provides facilities for internal payment transactions as well as those with foreign countries.

. . .

§12 *Relationship of the Bank to the Federal Government*
Subject to the discharge of its duty, the Deutsche Bundesbank is obliged to support the general economic policy of the Federal Government. In the exercise of the powers assigned to it by this law it is independent of instructions from the Federal Government.

§13 *Cooperation*
(1) The Deutsche Bundesbank shall advise the Federal Government in matters of monetary policy which are of substantial importance and furnish the Federal Government with information at its request.
(2) The members of the Federal Government have the right to participate in the discussions of the Central Bank Council. The Central Bank Council (Zentralbankrat) is the policy-making body of the Bundesbank. They have no right to vote, but may propose motions. If they so request, a decision shall be deferred for up to two weeks.
(3) The Federal Government should invite the President of the Deutsche Bundesbank to take part in its discussions on important matters affecting monetary policy.

Document 4

In 1970 a commission was established to codify and systematize social legislation. The first result was the general part of the Social Code which became law in 1976. This Act gives a general impression of the ambitious aims of social policy in the Federal Republic of Germany, although it covers only part of social policy legislation.

SOCIAL CODE (SOZIALGESETZBUCH)

Source: The Federal Minister of Labour and Social Affairs, *Insurance Code/Social Code (extracts)*, Bonn, 1981; BGBl., I, 1975, 3015
Transl.: ILO

Book I. General Part

Division I. Purposes of the Social Code and social rights

1. *Purposes of the Social Code.* (1) The law declared in the Social Code is intended to provide for social benefits, including social and educational assistance, with the object of making a reality of social justice and social security. Its aim is to contribute to—

ensuring an existence worthy of human beings;

providing equal opportunities for the free development of the personality, especially for young persons;

protecting and encouraging the family;

enabling persons to derive a livelihood through freely chosen activity; and

averting or compensating for special burdens in life, inter alia, by helping persons to help themselves.

(2) The law declared in the Social Code is also intended to contribute to ensuring that the social services and institutions required to achieve the purposes specified in subsection (1) are available at the proper time and on the proper scale.

2. *Social rights.* (1) The social rights referred to hereinafter serve to achieve the purposes specified in section 1. Claims in connection with such rights may be advanced or derived only in so far as specific provision for the relevant conditions and constituent elements has been made in the special Parts of this Code.

(2) The social rights provided for hereinafter shall be respected in the interpretation of the provisions of this Code and in the exercise of discretionary powers; every effort shall be made in the process to ensure that such rights are implemented to the broadest possible extent.

3. *Training incentives and employment promotion.* (1) Any person taking part in training corresponding to his inclinations, aptitudes and capacities shall have a right to individual incentives toward such training if the necessary means for the purpose are not otherwise available to him.

(2) Any person taking part, or wishing to take part, in employment shall have a right to—

1. guidance in choosing his form of training and occupation;
2. individual support for his subsequent training (further training and retraining);
3. assistance in obtaining and retaining a suitable job; and
4. financial security in the event of unemployment or the insolvency of his employer.

4. *Social insurance.* (1) Every person shall have a right of access to social insurance, as provided in this Code.

(2) Any person who is covered by social insurance shall have a right, as part of the statutory sickness, accident and pension insurance schemes, including the farmers' old-age assistance scheme, to—

1. the necessary measures to protect, maintain, improve and restore his health and strength; and
2. financial security in the event of sickness, maternity, reduced earning capacity and old age.

An insured person's survivors shall also have a right to financial security.

5. *Social compensation in the event of injuries to health.* Any person sustaining injury to his health shall, if the national community, acting in accordance with the principles laid down in the legislation relating to war victims, assumes responsibility for the consequences of the injury so as to compensate him for any special sacrifice or for other reasons, have a right to—

1. the necessary measures to maintain, improve and restore his health and strength; and
2. appropriate financial relief.

The survivors of a person suffering any such injury shall also have a right to appropriate financial relief.

6. *Deduction of family expenditure.* Any person who provides, or is required to provide, for the maintenance of children shall have a right to a reduction of the resulting financial burdens.

7. *Subsidies for appropriate housing.* Any person who has to incur expenditure in connection with appropriate housing that he cannot reasonably be expected to incur shall have a right to a subsidy towards his rent or comparable expenditure.

8. *Assistance to youth.* Every young person shall have a right to an upbringing for the better development of his personality. This right shall be guaranteed by the youth assistance scheme, through benefits for the general encouragement of youth and family upbringing and, in so far as it is not implemented by the parents, through educational assistance.

9. *Social assistance.* Any person who is not in a position to provide himself with the necessities of life through his own efforts or to help himself in special circumstances and who does not receive sufficient help from any other quarter shall have a right to personal and financial assistance which is in keeping with his special needs, enables him to help himself and take part in the life of the community and ensures that he can lead a life that is worthy of a human being.

10. *Resettlement of handicapped persons.* Any person who is, or is in danger of becoming, physically, mentally or spiritually handicapped shall have a right to such assistance as he needs to—

1. avert, eliminate or improve his handicap, prevent its aggravation or alleviate its consequences;
2. ensure that he obtains a place in the community, and more particularly in employment, corresponding to his inclinations and abilities.

Document 5

The trade unions' demand for co-determination has a long tradition in the Federal Republic of Germany. In 1953, a first Works Constitution Act (Betriebsverfassungsgesetz) regulating co-determination at the shop floor level was passed; in 1972 it was replaced by a new Works Constitution Act. In contrast to co-determination at the board level, co-determination at the shop-floor level is largely non-controversial.

WORKS CONSTITUTION ACT 1972: CO-DETERMINATION AT THE SHOP FLOOR LEVEL

Source: The Federal Minister of Labour and Social Affairs, *Co-determination in the Federal Republic of Germany,* Bonn, 1980, 103; 149–151; BGBl., I, 1972, 13 *Transl.:* ILO

Part I. General provisions

1. Establishment of Works Councils

Works councils shall be elected in all establishments (Betriebe) that normally have five or more permanent employees with voting rights, including three who are eligible.

. . .

87. Right of Co-determination

(1) The works council shall have a right of co-determination in the following matters in so far as they are not prescribed by legislation or collective agreement:

1. matters relating to the order by operation of the establishment and the conduct of employees in the establishment;
2. the commencement and termination of the daily working hours including breaks and the distribution of working hours among the days of the week;
3. any temporary reduction or extension of the hours normally worked in the establishment;
4. the time and place for and the form of payment of remuneration;
5. the establishment of general principles for leave arrangements and the preparation of the leave schedule as well as fixing the time at which the leave is to be taken by individual employees, if no agreement is reached between the employer and the employees concerned;
6. the introduction and use of technical devices designed to monitor the behaviour or performance of the employees;
7. arrangements for the prevention of employment accidents and occupational diseases and for the protection of health on the basis of legislation or safety regulations;
8. the form, structuring and administration of social services where scope is limited to the establishment, company or combine;
9. the assignment of and notice to vacate accommodation that is rented to employees in view of their employment relationship as well as the general fixing of the conditions for the use of such accommodation;

10. questions related to remuneration arrangements in the establishment, including in particular the establishment of principles of remuneration and the introduction and application of new remuneration methods or modification of existing methods;
11. the fixing of job and bonus rates and comparable performance-related remuneration including cash coefficients (i.e. prices per time unit);
12. principles for suggestion schemes in the establishment.

(2) If no agreement can be reached on a matter covered by the preceding subsection, the conciliation committee shall make a decision. The award of the conciliation committee shall take the place of an agreement between the employer and the works council.

Document 6

Co-determination at the board level was practiced successfully for more than twenty-five years in the coal, iron and steel industry. In spite of this positive experience, the Co-determination Act of 1976 which brought co-determination at the board level to all larger companies was passed only after heated public debate.

ACT RESPECTING WORKERS' CO-DETERMINATION (GESETZ ÜBER DIE MITBESTIMMUNG DER ARBEITNEHMER): CO-DETERMINATION AT BOARD LEVEL

Source: The Federal Minister of Labour and Social Affairs, *Co-determination in the Federal Republic of Germany*, Bonn, 1980, 46, 50–1; 65–6; BGBl., 1976, 1153 *Transl.:* ILO

1. Undertakings Covered

(1) Subject to the provisions of this Act, workers shall have a right of co-determination in undertakings which:

1. are run in the legal form of a joint-stock company, a company with limited partners holding share capital, a limited liability company, an incorporated cost-book company under mining law or a co-operative; and
2. normally employ over 2,000 workers.
. . .

7. Membership of Supervisory Boards

(1) The supervisory board of an undertaking:

1. normally employing not more than 10,000 workers shall consist of six shareholders' members and six workers' members;

2. normally employing more than 10,000 but not more than 20,000 workers shall consist of eight shareholders' members and eight workers' members;
3. normally employing more than 20,000 workers shall consist of ten shareholders' members and ten workers' members.

. . .

(2) The workers' members of a supervisory board must include:

1. four workers of the undertaking and two trade union representatives, where the board has six workers' members;
2. six workers of the undertaking and two trade union representatives, where the board has eight workers' members;
3. seven workers of the undertaking and three trade union repesentatives, where the board has ten workers' members.

. . .

27. Chairmanship of Supervisory Boards

(1) The supervisory board shall elect a chairman and vice-chairman from among its own number by a majority of two-thirds of the total number of members of which it is required to be composed.

(2) Where the requisite majority under subsection (1) is not attained during the election of the chairman or vice-chairman of the supervisory board, a second vote shall be taken. In this vote the shareholders' members of the supervisory board shall elect the chairman and the workers' members shall elect the vice-chairman, in each case by a majority of the votes cast.

. . .

29. Voting

(1) The decisions of the supervisory board shall be taken by a majority of the votes cast, . . .

(2) Where voting in the supervisory board results in a tie and a further vote on the same subject also results in a tie, the chairman of the board shall have a casting vote. . . . The vice-chairman shall not have a casting vote.

Document 7

The Co-determination Act of 1976 was strongly criticized by the business world. Their main objection was that co-determination might result in more cumbersome decision-making, and thus adversely affect efficiency. Some firms and employers' associations challenged the legality of the Act in the Federal Constitutional Court. The main arguments of this appeal are summarized here.

THE EMPLOYERS' CRITICISMS OF CO-DETERMINATION AT BOARD LEVEL

Source: The Federal Minister of Labour and Social Affairs, *Co-determination in the Federal Republic of Germany*, Bonn, 1980, 23–4
Transl.: Official

The Constitutional Appeals by the Employers
Constitutional Appeal against the Main Provisions

Even after the German Bundestag passed the new Co-determination Act with an overwhelming majority (including the votes of the Opposition), this did not bring about an end to the constitutional assaults. On 29 June 1977, nine firms and twenty-nine employers' associations lodged an appeal with the Federal Constitutional Court on constitutional grounds against the main provisions of the Co-determination Act.

The employers motivated their constitutional appeals as follows:

- The Co-determination Act contains a provision on the right of employees to an equal say in the supervisory board and this will lead sooner or later to an equal number of employees' and shareholders' representatives in management.
- The provisions of the Co-determination Act and those of the new Works Constitution Act of 1972 mean that the employees' rights will prevail and thus lead to 'supra-parity'.
- Hence, the Co-determination Act infringes the property guarantee contained in Art. 14 of the Basic Law. Shareholders' property is fundamentally affected both in the substance of members' rights as well as in that of their pecuniary rights.
- The Co-determination Act contains elements of an enforced amalgamation between shareholders and employees and thus infringes the free right to form associations and societies pursuant to Art. 9, para. 1 of the Basic Law.
- Furthermore, the Act infringes entrepreneurial freedom as part of the right freely to choose one's trade, occupation or profession (Art. 12 of the Basic Law).
- Finally, the Co-determination Act offends against the right to form associations (Art. 9, para. 3 of the Basic Law). The employers argued that co-determination in undertakings makes the employers' associations dependent on the opposing side and thus renders the collective wage bargaining system unworkable.
- All things considered, the Co-determination Act results in a reshaping of the structure of the economy and of labour, which would only have been admissible by a law enacted to amend the Constitution.

Document 8

The 1978 Congress of the German Federation of Trade Unions emphasized the unions' views on co-determination by accepting the following Motion 17.

THE TRADE UNION VIEW OF CO-DETERMINATION

Source: 11th Full Federal Congress of the German Federation of Trade Unions (Deutscher Gewerkschaftsbund—DGB), Hamburg, 1978

. . .

Motion No. 17 (adopted)

Concerning co-determination in firms and the economy
The Federal Congress is to adopt the following resolution:

The 11th Full Federal Congress of the DGB renews its demand for co-determination on the part of workers in plants, firms and the economy as a whole as a decisive step towards the democratic restructuring of the economy and society. Co-determination in firms is an essential part of the overall demand for democratizing the economy. The demand for co-determination means not only scope for strong, independent and combative trade unions and acceptance of the principle of free collective bargaining over working and economic conditions, but also supervision of control over the means of production wherever economic power is exercised, i.e. co-determination on the shop-floor through shop stewards, works and staff councils; the right of works' and staff councils to full co-determination in all aspects of management and administration; parity co-determination on the supervisory boards of large firms and concerns; co-determination in the economy as a whole.

The economic crisis has clearly shown that jobs and trainee opportunities and other employee interests are endangered when economic and social development is subordinated to the profit motives of firms. Parity co-determination on the basis of the model practised in the Coal, Iron and Steel Industry is necessary for guarding the rights of employees, supervising investment, protecting employees in cases of rationalization, increasing job safety, improving working conditions, exploiting to the full the rights of works councils and for widening the scope of shop stewards.

The following are essential elements in this:

—Parity on supervisory boards. Employees must be represented in equal numbers and with the same voting rights as shareholders.
—Co-determination through uniform employee representation on supervisory boards. The employee side must not be split by granting special rights to higher-grade salaried staff.

—Participation of employee representatives from outside the firm on an equal footing.

—Election and removal of employee representatives by the works councils.

—One Labour Director to be a member of the Board with equal rights. He may not be elected to, or removed from, the supervisory board against the wishes of a majority of the employee representatives.

The 1976 Co-determination Act provides on the other hand only for an extension of employee participation on the supervisory boards of certain larger firms. This is a result in particular of:

—Sham-parity on supervisory boards. A genuine equality is prevented by the special representation given to higher-grade salaried staff and by the chairman's double voting rights.

—The splitting of the employee side as a result of the granting of special rights to higher-grade salaried staff.

—The voting procedure which is complicated and also undermines the solidarity of the employee representatives.

—The Labour Director not being safe-guarded according to the model practised in the Coal, Iron and Steel Industry.

The solidarity of all employees, the board's supervisory functions and the uniformity of representation are endangered. The trade unions are called upon to reject these threats to the representation of their interests and at the same time to exploit realistically the opportunities for an improved employee representation provided by the 1976 Co-determination Act.

For this purpose the following are particularly vital:

—Cooperation of all representatives (trade unions, shop-stewards, works and staff councils, employee representatives on supervisory boards).

—Use of additional means of information and argument for improving the work of trade unions and works councils.

—Elaboration and enforcement of demands relating to plants, firms and particular trades.

The trade unions must elucidate their ideas for the minimum rights of employee representation. Among these are:

—Minimum demands for responsibilities on supervisory boards.

—Effective participation in the election of members of the management board.

—Proposals for information appropriate to co-determination and for the involvement of employee-representatives at the planning stage.

—Preparations for the election, functions and competency of the labour director.

—The division of responsibilities between the employee representatives on the supervisory board.

At the same time it is necessary to link all actions aiming at the full use of the rights of the works council with the potential the trade unions have as a partner in free collective bargaining. This would help to develop and enforce demands of trade union policy on the shop floor. Demands relating to plants and firms must be closely linked to the overall trade union programmes and aims. The demands should draw attention to the firm as a place where social conflicts are argued out and to the diverging interests of labour and capital. They should also involve members and officials in the enforcement of these demands. Spheres of influence might be: jobs and apprenticeships, the social and personal aspects of coming to terms with rationalization measures, income guarantees, working conditions, training and further training, information.

Further requirements for making trade union representation effective are:

—The strengthening of the trade unions on the shop-floor, especially through increasing union membership; strengthening of the position of shop stewards; trade union support for works and staff councils.
—Extending the range of action of wage policy, especially with regard to work place lay-out.
—Pointing to the limitations of the 1976 Co-determination Act and co-determination in firms; no taking of responsibility for the decisions reached by bodies not sufficiently under the influence of the trade unions.
—Setting up economic and social councils at regional, state and federal level as bodies of overal economic co-determination (as demanded by the DGB since 1971).

All trade unionists are called upon to defend the co-determination model of the Coal, Iron and Steel Industry and to fight for its extension to all large-scale firms and for a reduction in the unilateral control of the entrepreneurs in firms and the economy as a whole.

Document 9

In 1979, the Federal Constitutional Court rejected the complaint of the employers. The main reasons for this decision were given in an accompanying statement by the Public Relations Office of the Federal Constitutional Court.

THE FEDERAL CONSTITUTIONAL COURT'S JUDGMENT ON THE CO-DETERMINATION ACT

Source: The Federal Minister of Labour and Social Affairs, *Co-determination in the Federal Republic of Germany*, Bonn, 1980, 38–41. The judgment itself is to be found in *Entscheidungen des Bundesverfassungsgerichts*, Vol. 50, 290ff.
Transl.: Official

Statement by the Public Relations Office of the Federal Constitutional Court

The First Panel of the Federal Constitutional Court today pronounced its judgment in the two proceedings linked together for a joint hearing and decision on the Co-determination Act of 4 May 1976.

. . .

(a) To begin with, the decision clarifies the extent of workers' influence in undertakings pursuant to the Act, which is taken as the basis for further examination by the Court. Neither from the legal standpoint nor in any other way connected with the Act is their influence equal to that of the other side or indeed more than equal. Under the statutory provisions, one cannot proceed on the assumption of parity co-determination because of the second vote accorded to the chairman of the supervisory board, who is normally elected by the shareholders, and because of the non-homogeneous composition of the employees' side comprising workers, salaried employees and senior executives. That also holds true if one includes the partially equal rights of co-determination for the works council. The basic assumption of the complainants that this non-equal representation in reality conceals a fundamentally equal or even more-than-equal representation, which the legislators actually envisaged or wished to facilitate, does not lead to any other judgment, either. There is nothing to indicate that the material substance of the case, which is fundamentally authoritative for an examination of its constitutionality, and the actual impact of the contested normative provisions are divergent in any way.

(b) There is no certainty about what effect this slightly sub-parity co-determination will produce in future. Particular importance attaches to cooperation in individual firms—a cooperation which the law itself can only facilitate and encourage by providing the machinery. If both sides are willing to engage in loyal cooperation, co-determination for employees will produce a different effect than a situation in which the atmosphere of undertakings is dominated by mutual distrust or even enmity. Another factor which may prove significant is whether there is a willingness outside the undertakings to welcome co-determination in its present form in the interest of these individual enterprises as well as of the economy as a whole. Unlike the complainants, the legislators proceeded on the assumption that the effects envisaged by the Act would actually occur and that they would not involve any disadvantageous consequences for the viability of the individual undertakings and for the economy as a whole. The Federal Constitutional Court could only proceed from another assumption if the prognosis made by the legislators about the future effects of the law did not accord with the requirements of the Constitution. This was not the case, as the legislators had based their opinion on an objective and justifiable assessment of the available material.

. . .

Document 10

The presence of a large number of foreigners in Germany—most of them either originally migrant workers, who with their families seem to be remaining in Germany, or political refugees—has resulted in political problems of all kinds. In May 1982 the Federal Government answered an interpellation (Große Anfrage) regarding the policy towards foreigners of the SPD and FDP.

FOREIGN WORKERS AS A CHALLENGE TO POLICY

Source: Der Bundesminister des Innern, *Ausländerpolitik*, Bonn, 1982, 73–7

I. The Federal Government's policy concerning foreigners is directed towards the following:

—To limit effectively the further migration of foreigners into the Federal Republic of Germany

—To strengthen the migrants' readiness to return to their country of origin

—To improve the economic and social integration of foreigners who have been resident in the Federal Republic of Germany for many years and to clarify their right of abode.

II. Only a consistent and effective policy of limiting entry from countries which are not members of the European Community will ensure the indispensable consent of the German people to the integration of foreigners. This is essential for the maintenance of social peace and stability.

Therefore the halt on recruitment of foreigners will be fully upheld. This also excludes the admittance of foreign seasonal workers. Changes of names and dates of birth for the purpose of entry into the country are not binding on internal officials.

The periods of time that family members of foreign workers and those seeking asylum have to wait before entering the labour market remain unchanged.

The entry of family members of foreign workers has to be controlled in a socially reasonable way. On this issue, the Federal Government passed regulations for immediate action on December 2, 1981. The Länder have adopted these regulations with only minor modifications.

Asylum proceedings, while protecting the basic right of asylum, must be so developed that those cases can be decided upon quickly in which application has been made clearly from motives which have nothing to do with the interests of those who are politically persecuted. The Federal Government expects both Bundestag and Bundesrat to complete the discussions on the law governing asylum proceedings without delay.

The law of 15 December 1981 to combat illegal employment has laid down the preconditions for putting an end to the illegal entry of and employment of foreigners. The Federal Government calls upon the Länder who are responsible for carrying out the law to combat illegal unemployment to take full advantage of the legal possibilities.

In the negotiations between the European Community and Turkey on the subject of the final regulation of the free movement of labour, the Federal Government wishes—within the framework of the existing association of Turkey with the European Community—to arrive at a ruling which would exclude any further entry of workers from Turkey.

III. The Federal Government has committed itself to a policy of integration as far as foreigners are concerned who live here permanently. The crucial task is the integration of second and third generation foreigners. It is only through close cooperation between all social groups that a better co-existence between Germans and foreigners can be achieved. For that reason the Federal Government is opposed to any activities which arouse hostility to foreigners.

. . .

Notes

1. The small number of industrial stoppages is an indicator of relatively peaceful labour relations; see Table 15
2. See Ch. 8
3. See also Ch. 5
4. See Ch. 6
5. Foreigners acquire the right of permanent residence in the Federal Republic of Germany after five to eight years, and may be granted German nationality after about ten years. Special regulations apply to workers from EEC countries

11 Foreign Policy

Robert Spencer

In many respects the foreign policy of the Federal Republic of Germany is unique. More dependent than most other states on the international system which gave birth to it, the Republic in its earlier years had to endure a long period of apprenticeship.[*1] It had no foreign ministry until 1951, no foreign minister separate from the chancellor until 1955, the year in which sovereignty was regained in most essentials. Even after that date, however, the Federal Republic remained, as Willy Brandt described it in the 1964 election campaign, 'an economic giant, but a political dwarf'.[2] Just why this pattern should have prevailed after 1949 is explained in part by the Republic's origins. The government established in 1949 was endowed with only a limited and revocable degree of sovereignty, and only gradually were the reins of the occupying powers relaxed (Docs. 1 and 2). From the very start, the goal of political recovery by the Federal Republic meant, as it could only mean, the right to have a foreign policy and to bring about conditions in which it could be exercised.[3]

Other factors also circumscribed Bonn's foreign policy from the start. In the first place, the Federal Republic comprised not all but only a part of the territory of the former German Reich. The importance of this consideration is suggested by the fact that the central goal of foreign policy was laid down in the preamble to the Basic Law: 'The entire German people are called upon to achieve in free self-determination the unity and freedom of Germany.' The Basic Law also committed the Federal Republic to 'serve the peace of the world as an equal partner in a united Europe'. Not only, that is, was the Republic committed to the causes of unification and of peace but, as was the case in a number of other coun-

---

* Notes for this chapter begin on p. 313

tries such as Italy, the goal of European unity was enshrined in its constitution. The regaining of sovereignty was also coupled with the constitutional authority to 'transfer sovereign powers to inter-governmental institutions' and to enter 'a system of mutual collective security' (Art. 24).

In line with these provisions the Bonn government's early steps towards regaining sovereignty were paralleled by an active policy of 'Westpolitik', i.e. participation in the progress towards European integration. In 1950 it overcame its hesitations over the dispute with France over the Saar and entered the newly established Council of Europe in the hope of securing 'appreciable alleviations' in the occupation regime.[4] In the same year it also eagerly embraced the proposal of French Foreign Minister Robert Schuman to pool the resources of heavy industry in Germany, France, Italy and the Benelux countries to form the European Coal and Steel Community on the basis of full equality for the Federal Republic (Doc. 3). After a decade in which the SPD viewed European integration with misgivings, enthusiasm for 'Europe' has spanned the political spectrum from right to left, and the quest for political unity in Western Europe has been a principal theme throughout the Republic's history (Docs. 4 and 5).

In the realm of security policy, with the failure in 1954 of the French proposal for an integrated European army which would have enabled the Germans to make a contribution to the defence of the West without the political risks attendant on the revival of a national German army, the Federal Republic joined in steps which led, a year later on 9 May 1955, to its admission to the North Atlantic Treaty Organization (NATO) as the Alliance's fifteenth member (Doc. 6). Since 1955 the West German partnership in the Atlantic Alliance has been the cornerstone of the country's security policy and the basis of the relationship with the former occupying powers, who until the conclusion of a peace treaty retained special responsibility 'relating to Berlin and to Germany as a whole,'[5] and especially with the United States which provides the vital nuclear shield. A bilateral relationship which was of great importance both within the European community and, more broadly, in the Western Alliance was the Franco–German reconciliation. This, as Adenauer recorded later on, was a special attraction of the Schuman Plan.[6] It was sealed by the Franco–German Treaty of 1963 (Doc. 7), a development of historic proportions.

From the start, the Federal Republic's relations with eastern Europe were governed by the inescapable fact that the Soviet Union and its system of satellites stood in the way of German reunification (Doc. 8).

Moreover, it was perceived in Bonn that any threat to the Federal Republic's security could only come from Moscow. While seeking integration with the West and preparing to contribute to Western defence, the Republic's first chancellor, Konrad Adenauer, did not neglect the need to tackle the problems involved in normalizing relations with the East. His historic visit to Moscow in September 1955, four months after Bonn had joined the North Atlantic Treaty Organization, opened the way to the establishment of diplomatic relations between Bonn and Moscow (Doc. 9); it also recalls the comment by Gustav Stresemann in 1927 on his Locarno policies: 'I never thought more about the East than during the time I was looking for an understanding in the West.'[7] Bonn's hopes to use the link with Moscow to solve the problem of reunification were stillborn, however. In an effort to buttress its position *vis-à-vis* what was referred to as the 'so-called German Democratic Republic', it enunciated the 'Hallstein Doctrine', which promised diplomatic retaliation against third-party states which granted diplomatic recognition to East Berlin (Doc. 10).

West German–Soviet relations deteriorated sharply as the crises over Berlin in 1958 and 1961 demonstrated.[8] But in the early 1960s Foreign Minister Gerhard Schroeder, who after Adenauer's retirement in 1963 was able to exercise greater freedom of action, made significant efforts towards reconciliation with the East, and in its last days the government of Ludwig Erhard, who had succeeded Adenauer as chancellor, launched a broad assault on the problem with the Peace Note (Friedensnote) of March 1966 (Doc. 11). This initiative, too, was stillborn, however. The 'Great Coalition' government of Kurt-Georg Kiesinger, in which the SPD leader Willy Brandt was Foreign Minister, enunciated policies looking to reconciliation with the East which took account of the criticism which the rigidities of the policies hitherto prevailing had encountered; but little progress was recorded. In the end, it was the new Eastern Policy (Ostpolitik) initiated by Chancellor Willy Brandt, following the success of the Social Democratic Party in the elections of September 1969 and the formation of the Socialist–Liberal coalition, which broke the log jam.[9] This opened the way to the abandoning of the outdated and unrealistic concepts of the Hallstein Doctrine and the Alleinvertretungsanspruch (the right of Bonn to speak for all Germans). It led to the conclusion of treaties with Moscow and with Poland in 1970 (Docs. 12 and 13) and, two years later, of the treaty governing relations between Bonn and East Berlin, 'the two states within the German nation' according to the view enunciated by Chancellor Brandt in 1969.[10] Complicated legal questions rather than unwillingness on the part of Bonn to recognize the invalidity of the Munich agreement of 1938 delayed the reconciliation with Czechoslovakia until December 1973 (Doc. 14).

Although the Federal Republic had long been represented at the United Nations by an observer, membership in the organization had to await this settlement in the East. It was thus not until 1973, as a by-product of the Eastern treaties, that the governments of the four occupying powers could support the admission of both the Federal Republic of Germany and the German Democratic Republic to the UN and so enable Bonn to play its full role in the world body (Doc. 15). Well before this, however, the Federal Republic had assumed its share of the obligations of other western industrialized nations in providing assistance to less developed countries (Doc. 16).

While it took until the 1970s for a line to be drawn under the legacy of the Second World War in the East, the process of meeting moral obligations elsewhere had begun two decades earlier. This involved restitution payments to countries such as Norway which had been occupied and despoiled by the Nazis (Doc. 17). The principal thrust in this direction, however, was the much earlier attempt to provide compensation for the special victims of the National Socialist system, the Jews. As early as 1951 Chancellor Adenauer, supported by a broad coalition in the Bundestag which included his own party and the Social Democrats, then in opposition, initiated and executed a policy of substantial restitution payments to Israel which by 1975 had amounted to DM 3.5 billion[11] (Doc. 18).

While restitution policies enjoyed a broad measure of support in the West German political spectrum, other aspects of Bonn's policy have at times provoked sharp controversy. The Adenauer policy of European integration and of adherence to the Atlantic Alliance was at first opposed by the Social Democrats, mainly because they feared this would make difficult, if not impossible, German reunification. However, since about 1960 the Social Democrats have embraced, and indeed enthusiastically endorsed, these aspects of Adenauer's foreign policy. In the late 1960s and the early 1970s, the Christian Democratic opposition violently attacked the Ostpolitik of the Brandt–Scheel government, arguing that Bonn was 'giving' too much through acceptance of the territorial status quo and the 'recognition' of the GDR and not 'receiving' sufficient in return from Moscow and its Warsaw Pact allies. By the end of the 1970s, the Christian Democratic opposition had largely accepted the government's position, and the main features of the Federal Republic's foreign and defence policies enjoyed bipartisan support. The issue of theatre nuclear modernization, however, provoked an outspoken response from the peace movement, made nuclear weapons and foreign policy a subject of controversy in the 1983 election campaign, and confronted the government of Chancellor Helmut Kohl with a vocal source of domestic opposition.[12]

Document 1

A little over a year after giving their approval of the Basic Law for the new Federal Republic of Germany, the Western occupying powers, while retaining their occupation role, projected further steps towards the recovery of sovereignty by the West German state.

DECLARATION BY THE FOREIGN MINISTERS OF GREAT BRITAIN, THE UNITED STATES AND FRANCE, LONDON, 13 MAY 1950

Source: London Conferences. Tripartite Talks between the Foreign Ministers of the United States, United Kingdom and France, May 11–13 1950, London, 1950, Cmd. 7977, 5–6

Following the London Agreements of June, 1948, and the Washington Agreements of April, 1949, the United States, France and the United Kingdom replaced the military authority and the direct administration of the occupied territories in force since 1945 by a civilian regime simply of supervision. ...

Furthermore, by the Agreement of 13th April, 1949, the Allies decided to ease the burden of reparations on Germany. Some months later under the Petersberg Protocol an agreement was reached for a final settlement in regard to the delivery of plant by way of reparations.

In the domain of foreign relations the Petersberg Protocol made provisions for the appointment of German consular and commercial representatives abroad. During the last few months steps have been taken by the Western Powers to secure the accession of the Federal Republic to a number of international organizations, including the Organization for European Economic Co-operation. Finally, she has been invited to join the Council of Europe. ...

...

2. The Allies are resolved to pursue their aim laid down in the Washington Agreement of April 1949 and reaffirmed at the Petersberg that Germany shall re-enter progressively the community of free peoples of Europe. When that situation has been fully reached she will be liberated from controls to which she is still subject and accorded her sovereignty to the maximum extent compatible with the basis of the Occupation régime. This régime is imposed on the Germans and on the Allies by the consequences of the division of Germany and of the international position; until this situation is modified it must be retained in accordance with the common interests of Germany and of Europe.

The Western Powers desire to see the pace of progress towards this end as rapid as possible. . . . The Ministers accordingly agreed to set up a study group in London to undertake the necessary preparatory work to enable the Occupation Statute to be reviewed at the appointed time and to make recommendations for eliminating the major practical inconveniences arising in the countries concerned from the state of war, on the understanding that in the present situation of Europe supreme authority must remain in the hands of the Allied Powers.

. . .

4. While retaining the framework outlined above, the Allies intend to give Germany the possibility of developing freely, while at the same time safeguarding the possibility of peaceful reunification of Germany, which remains the ultimate object of their policy. . . .

Document 2

The Federal Republic's participation in the evolving European institutions—at this stage the Council of Europe and the Coal and Steel Community—involved further steps towards limiting the restrictions of the occupation regime and a consequent regaining of sovereignty.

STATEMENT ON WEST GERMAN SOVEREIGNTY BY THE THREE WESTERN FOREIGN MINISTERS AND THE FEDERAL CHANCELLOR, PARIS, 22 NOVEMBER 1951

Source: United States Department of State Bulletin, Vol. XXV, 649, 3 December 1951, 891–2

The Foreign Ministers of France, the United Kingdom, and the United States met today with Dr. Adenauer.

This meeting, the first occasion on which the Chancellor and Foreign Minister of the German Federal Republic had jointly conferred with the foreign ministers of the three Western Powers, marked in itself a notable advance in the progressive association of the German Federal Republic with the West on the basis of equal partnership.

. . .

. . . The general agreement will be a decisive step toward the realization of the common aim of the three Western Powers and the Federal Government to integrate the Federal Republic on a basis of equality in a European community itself included in a developing Atlantic community.

With the coming into force of the general agreement and the related convention, the Occupation Statute with its powers of intervention in the domestic affairs of the Federal Republic will be revoked, and the Allied High Commission and the Offices of the Land Commissioners will be abolished. The three powers will retain only such special rights as cannot now be renounced because of the special international situation of Germany, and which it is in the common interest of the four states to retain. These rights relate to the stationing and the security of the forces in Germany, to Berlin and to questions concerning Germany as a whole. . . .

The Federal Republic will undertake to conduct its policy in accordance with the principles set forth in the Charter of the United Nations and with the aims defined in the Statute of the Council of Europe.

The four ministers are agreed that an essential aim of the common policy of their Governments is a peace settlement for the whole of Germany freely negotiated between Germany and her former enemies, which should lay the foundation for a lasting peace. They further agreed that the final settlement of the boundaries of Germany await such settlement. . . .

. . .

Document 3

As this document underlines, West German interest in European integration was inspired by more than short-term economic aspirations and looked-to political union on a supranational basis.

KONRAD ADENAUER IN THE BUNDESTAG ON THE EUROPEAN COAL AND STEEL COMMUNITY, 12 JULY 1952

Source: Die Auswärtige Politik der Bundesrepublik Deutschland, Cologne, 1972, 176–9

. . .

It is certainly immediately obvious that such an agreement between six European countries which have different interests and different opinions can only be arrived at after very long conferences and in the course of mutual arrangements, a mutual approximation of interests, and by conviction. It is in the nature of such a contract that none of the participants can carry his own opinion one hundred per cent. Indeed, a participant ought not to start with the idea that only his opinions should be carried through one hundred per cent. As with every agreement, this agreement by six members is a compromise. None of the participants in the negotiations would or could claim that the outcome of the negotiations was a hundred per cent correct or satisfied him a hundred per cent. One should not focus too narrowly on the details of such a set of agreements, but rather consider the basic idea, the purpose of the agreement as a whole, and then see whether the provisions of the whole agreement are constructive and suited to attain this purpose—if one is in favour of the purpose. . . .

I request you not to overlook the dynamic nature of the whole set of agreements. It deals with—I can only stress this again—a construction of a dynamic nature which is designed to take effect over and above the direct sphere of the part of the economy which is organized here. The idea was that when these six European countries had learnt to cooperate in such an extremely important economic field, then the incentive ensuing from this mutual work would suffice in order to achieve cooperation in further economic fields. . . .

It is my opinion and belief that the parliaments of the six European countries which will have to deal with this European Coal and Steel Community realize exactly what it is all about and that in particular they realize that the political goal, the political meaning of the European Coal and Steel Community, is infinitely larger than its economic purpose. . . .

Something further has resulted during the negotiations. I believe that for the first time in history, certainly in the history of the last centuries, countries want to renounce part of their sovereignty, voluntarily and without compulsion, in order to transfer the sovereignty to a supranational structure. . . . I am firmly convinced that after this a beginning has finally been made, when here six European countries transfer part of their sovereignty, and I stress again: voluntarily and without compulsion

(Shout from the KPD (German Communist Party): Who's that laughing?)

to a superordinate institution, then people can follow this process in other fields, too, and in this way nationalism, the inveterate evil of Europe, will be dealt a death blow. . . .

Document 4

The disappointing results of the establishment of diplomatic relations with Moscow and the gloomy outlook for the reunification of Germany in view of the hardening of the lines of division following the entry of the Federal Republic into NATO, suggested to Adenauer the critical importance of moving forward along the road towards European economic and political integration.

MEMORANDUM OF CHANCELLOR ADENAUER TO THE FEDERAL MINISTERS, 19 JANUARY 1956

Source: Die Auswärtige Politik der Bundesrepublik Deutschland, Cologne, 1972, 317–8

The present situation in foreign affairs confronts us with extraordinary dangers. Decisive measures are required to avoid these dangers and to initiate favourable developments. Above all, a clear, positive German attitude to European integration is necessary. . . .

The resulting guideline for our policy is that we must carry out the Messina Resolution in a decisive and honest manner. The political character of this decision must be taken into consideration more strongly than before. It is a decision intended not only to lead to a technical cooperation based on specialized considerations, but to a community which ensures coordination of political purpose and action and is also in the interests of reunification. The OEEC framework does not suffice for this. All technical considerations must enter into the service of these political aims.

In particular the following must apply for the realization of the Messina programme:

(1) Integration of the six members at first is to be furthered by *all* possible methods, i.e. in the field of general (horizontal) integration as well as suitable partial (vertical) integration.
(2) Right from the beginning and as far as possible, the establishing of suitable common institutions is to be aimed at in order to achieve a firm tie between the six members based on the main political goals.
(3) The fairly successful talks on establishing a common European market—i.e. a market which is similar to an inland market—must be vigorously brought to an end. At the same time, European institutions with decision-making rights must be established in order to secure the functioning of the market and simultaneously advance political development.
(4) Based on the idea of the Common Market, a genuine integration of the six with regard to traffic must be strived for. This applies especially to air-traffic; a fundamental refusal or delay in plans for the integrated production, supply and management in this field is politically irresponsible.
(5) The same applies to energy, especially to nuclear energy. It is an absolute political necessity to remove every doubt that we continue to stand by our Messina statements according to which a European Atomic Community with decision-making rights, common institutions and common financial and other operational means should be established. As they have officially stated, the Americans consider a European Atomic Community, which in contrast to the OEEC has its own rights and responsibilities, to be a decisive factor in the political development. They are prepared vigorously to support such an atomic community. . . .

I request that the above be regarded as guidelines of federal government policy and be followed as such.

Document 5

Especially striking—in view of earlier SPD scepticism and indeed outright opposition to European integration—were SPD Chancellor Brandt's early attempts to 'get Europe moving'. This speech was delivered within a few weeks of his enunciation in his first government declaration of his new Ostpolitik.

SPEECH OF CHANCELLOR WILLY BRANDT AT THE EUROPEAN COMMUNITY'S SUMMIT CONFERENCE, THE HAGUE, 1 DECEMBER 1969

Source: Die Auswärtige Politik der Bundesrepublik Deutschland, Cologne, 1972, 716–17

. . .

If things were going well in Europe, we would not have met here today. If our community had been ready to speak out with a united voice, then our main theme would have been foreign policy: the question of a European order of peace, negotiations with the states of Eastern Europe and our interests in view of the conflict in the Middle East.

Therefore, I say in complete frankness: the German parliament and public opinion expect me not to return from this conference without a concrete agreement concerning the question of the broadening of the Community.

We have been occupied with this question for years. The treaty itself has made this one of the basic questions of our Community, and nowhere is it written that we may turn towards this topic only after the period of transition. The German position has been known for years. In my opinion, we may no longer push this topic aside.

Firstly, experience has shown that postponing the expansion of the Community threatens to cripple it.

Secondly, it serves our mutual interests if the Community expands at a time in which we are making efforts to get West and East closer together.

Thirdly, the Community must outgrow the Six if it wants to maintain an economic and technological equivalence with the giants and fulfill its world-wide political responsibility.

I do not hesitate to add a fourth argument: he who fears that the economic weight of the Federal Republic of Germany could prove detrimental to the balance within the Community, should, for this reason, favour expansion.

In any case, I say that without England and the other nations, which are willing to join, Europe cannot be what it should be and what it can be. . . .

The people of Europe wait and urge that state officials must add to the logic of history the will for success. Europe needs our success.

If I again call attention to the younger generation I do so in order to inform you of the wishes of the German government to establish a European 'Jugendwerk' [Youth Exchange Programme]. We feel encouraged through our excellent experiences with the German–French 'Jugendwerk'.

World-wide, politically speaking, our maturing and expanding Community should pursue a dual goal. Through the pooling of its resources, Europe should achieve the means of attaining equal status with the superpowers in economy, science and technology and thereby maintain its identity. At the same time

Europe should enable itself, with all its strength, to take part in the great task which presents itself to the industrialized countries with an ever-growing urgency, i.e. in a policy of aid for the developing countries.

We cannot render our ideals—peace and humanity—any better service.
. . .

Document 6

The Federal Republic's entry into the North Atlantic Treaty Organization within a decade of the defeat of the Third Reich was a dramatic shift from foe to ally and took place within carefully circumscribed limits.

FINAL ACT OF THE NINE-POWER CONFERENCE, LONDON, 28 SEPTEMBER – 3 OCTOBER 1954

Source: Nine-power Conference. Final Act of the Nine-Power Conference held in London, Sept. 28 to Oct. 3, 1954, London, 1954, Cmd. 9289, 10–11

DECLARATION BY THE GOVERNMENTS OF FRANCE, THE UNITED KINGDOM AND UNITED STATES OF AMERICA

The following declarations were recorded at the Conference by the German Federal Chancellor and by the Foreign Ministers of France, United Kingdom and United States of America:

Declaration by Federal Republic of Germany

The Federal Republic of Germany has agreed to conduct its policy in accordance with the principles of the Charter of the United Nations and accepts the obligations set forth in Article 2 of the Charter.

Upon her accession to the North Atlantic Treaty and the Brussels Treaty, the Federal Republic of Germany declares that she will refrain from any action inconsistent with the strictly defensive character of the two treaties. In particular the Federal Republic of Germany undertakes never to have recourse to force to achieve the reunification of Germany or the modification of the present boundaries of the Federal Republic of Germany, and to resolve by peaceful means any disputes which may arise between the Federal Republic and other States.

Declaration by the Governments of the United States of America, United Kingdom and France

The Governments of the United States of America, the United Kingdom of Great Britain and Northern Ireland and the French Republic. . . .

Take note that the Federal Republic of Germany has by a Declaration dated the Third of October, Nineteen hundred and Fifty Four accepted the obligations set forth in Article 2 of the Charter of the United Nations and has undertaken never to have recourse to force to achieve the reunification of Germany or the modification of the present boundaries of the Federal Republic of Germany, and to resolve by peaceful means any disputes which may arise between the Federal Republic and other States:

DECLARE THAT:

1. They consider the Government of the Federal Republic as the only German Government freely and legitimately constituted and therefore entitled to speak for Germany as the representative of the German people in international affairs.

2. In their relations with the Federal Republic they will follow the principles set out in Article 2 of the United Nations Charter.

3. A peace settlement for the whole of Germany, freely negotiated between Germany and her former enemies, which should lay the foundation of a lasting peace, remains an essential aim of their policy. The final determination of the boundaries of Germany must await such a settlement.

4. The achievement through peaceful means of a fully free and unified Germany remains a fundamental goal of their policy.

5. The security and welfare of Berlin and the maintenance of the position of the Three Powers there are regarded by the Three Powers as essential elements of the peace of the free world in the present international situation. Accordingly they will maintain armed forces within the territory of Berlin as long as their responsibilities require it. They therefore reaffirm that they will treat any attack against Berlin from any quarter as an attack upon their forces and themselves.

Document 7

The Franco-German reconciliation—perhaps the most far-reaching and certainly one of the unpredictable developments of the postwar era—culminated in a formal treaty. It was concluded in the last months of Adenauer's tenure as chancellor and had perhaps a symbolic rather than a practical importance.

JOINT DECLARATION BY CHANCELLOR ADENAUER AND PRESIDENT DE GAULLE, 22 JANUARY 1963

Source: Die Auswärtige Politik der Bundesrepublik Deutschland, Cologne, 1972, 490

The Federal Chancellor of the Federal Republic of Germany, Dr. Konrad Adenauer, and the President of the French Republic, General de Gaulle, have

—at the close of the conference from 21–22 January 1963 in Paris, with the participants from the German side being the Federal Foreign Minister, the Federal

Minister of Defence and the Federal Minister for Family and Youth Affairs, and from the French side being the Prime Minister, the Foreign Minister, the Minister of the Army and the Education Minister,

—in the conviction that the reconciliation between the German and French people, which has ended a rivalry of centuries, presents an historical occurence which shapes afresh the relationship between the two peoples from the ground up,

—in view of the fact that the youth in particular have become conscious of this solidarity and that they have been allotted a critical role in the strengthening of the German–French friendship,

—in recognising that the strengthening of the cooperation between both countries means an essential step on the path toward a united Europe, which is the goal of both peoples,

have agreed to the organization and the principles of cooperation between the two states, as they have been laid down in the treaty signed to-day.

. . .

Document 8

Paul Loebe, a member of the SPD and a former speaker of the old Weimar Reichstag, was delegated, as the Bundestag's oldest member, to make this declaration on behalf of all the parties represented in it.

DECLARATION ON THE ODER–NEISSE LINE BY PAUL LOEBE, SPD, THE SENIOR MEMBER OF THE BUNDESTAG, 13 JUNE 1950

Source: H. Siegler, *The Reunification and Security of Germany*, Bonn, 1957, 123–4

In the name of all the Fractions and groups in the Bundestag, with the exception of the Communist Fraction, and with the assent of the Federal Government and the Bundesrat, I make the following declaration:

In the Agreement signed on 6th June 1950 by a delegation of the so-called provisional Government of the German Democratic Republic and by the Government of the Polish Republic, the assertion, untenable in international and constitutional law, is made that a so-called peace frontier has been established between the Soviet Occupied Zone of Germany and Poland. Under the Potsdam Agreement, the German territory east of the Oder and Neisse was handed over as part of the Soviet Occupied Zone of Germany to the Polish Republic only for temporary administration purposes. That territory remains part of Germany.

Ladies and Gentlemen, nobody has the right, of his own despotic will, to sell out a country and its people or to pursue a policy of renunciation. The settlement of this question, as of all other questions affecting the German frontiers, both eastern and western, can be effected only by a peace treaty, and such a treaty must be concluded a soon as possible by a democratically elected German Government as a pact of friendship and good neighbourliness with all nations. Ladies and Gentlemen, the willingness demonstrated by the so-called Provisional Government of the German Democratic Republic to cooperate in demarcating the Oder/Neisse line as the allegedly 'unassailable' East German frontier is evidence of the shameful sycophancy of that agency towards a foreign power. In repudiating that action, the Bundestag knows that it is speaking in the name of the Germans in the Soviet Occupied Zone, too.

. . .

Document 9

Within a few months of the Federal Republic's joining NATO, Chancellor Adenauer journeyed to Moscow in the interests of normalizing diplomatic relations with the USSR. Here, on his return, he defends his Ostpolitik.

CHANCELLOR ADENAUER IN THE BUNDESTAG ON THE AGREEMENT WITH THE USSR, 22 SEPTEMBER 1955

Source: Die Auswärtige Politik der Bundesrepublik, Cologne, 1972, 308–13

. . .

In the course of the talks with representatives of the Soviet government, the delegation of the Federal Republic of Germany has very clearly pointed out that a normalization of relations can, under no circumstances, consist of legalizing the anomalous condition of Germany's division. It was also pointed out that the existence of diplomatic relations between two states was not to be put on a par with a friendly pact relationship; our Soviet discussion partners themselves have stated that they also maintain diplomatic relations with states with which they otherwise have considerable political and ideological differences of opinion. . . .

The establishment of diplomatic relations means that the Federal Republic of Germany, whose effective sovereign power includes three-quarters of our nation and 80% of its productive force and behind whose policy—we are convinced—at least 90% of the population of the Soviet Occupied Zone stands as well, is now also recognized by the Soviet Union. . . .

In due form I wish to declare for myself, for the Federal Government, for the whole German nation in the West and in the East: Germany is a part of the West, in conformity with its spiritual and social structure, its historical tradition and the will of its population. . . .

The establishment of diplomatic relations between the Federal Republic and the Soviet Union does not therefore conflict with Western interests. I even believe I can go further: it serves Western interests. As the Federal Republic, in the role of a clearly Western power which is orientated towards Europe, will now also have a representative in Moscow, it will further strengthen the voice of the West there.

The establishment of relations has yet a further meaning. It contributes to the difficult task of easing the international situation and thereby contributes to world peace. ... We have made the reservations under international law necessary to maintain our juridical standpoint of which the Soviet Union has taken notice. In extremely difficult negotiations, we have extracted as much as was possible out of the given situation for the human and political spheres. ...

Document 10

The Federal Republic's concern to keep open the door for reunification prompted it, in a formal statement, to threaten diplomatic counter-measures against states which recognized what at the time was referred to as the 'so-called German Democratic Republic' or the 'Soviet Occupied Zone'. The resulting 'doctrine' came to be known by the name of the then Under Secretary in the Foreign Office, Walter Hallstein.

GOVERNMENT DECLARATION, 28 JUNE 1956: THE HALLSTEIN DOCTRINE

Source: H. Siegler, *The Reunification and Security of Germany*, Bonn, 1957, 141-2

...

... The recognition of the German Democratic Republic would mean international recognition of the partition of Germany in two States. Reunification would then no longer present itself as the elimination of a temporary disturbance in the organism of our all-German State: it would change into the infinitely more difficult task of uniting two separate States. The history of the unification of Germany in the 19th century illustrates what that can mean. Were the Federal Republic to take the lead in recognition, she would herself contribute to a state of affairs in which Europe and the world would lose consciousness of the anomaly of the present situation and become resigned to it. She would relieve the Four Powers of their responsibility for the re-establishment of the national unity of Germany, a responsibility which they—including the Soviet Union—have so far always recognized. Instead, she would accord to Pieck, Grotewohl and Ulbricht the right of vetoing any reunification. Furthermore, the recognition of the 'German Democratic Republic' would mean that the Federal Republic would relinquish its claim to be the spokesman of the entire German people, a claim established in our constitution and which no Federal Government can ignore.

The Federal Government cannot refrain from making it clear once again that it will feel compelled in future to regard the establishing of diplomatic relations with the so-called German Democratic Republic by third States with which the Federal Republic maintains diplomatic relations, as an unfriendly act calculated to intensify and aggravate the partition of Germany. The Federal Government would in such a case have to re-consider its relations to the State in question.

The question has been variously discussed in recent times as to whether or not it is useful and possible to establish relations with Germany's eastern neighbours. The Federal Government has examined this problem in all its detail and has come to the conclusion that, under present circumstances, diplomatic relations cannot be established with those countries. That does not mean that the Federal Government is not interested in the establishment of normal relations with the countries in question.

. . .

Document 11

The attempt to unfreeze the situation in central Europe through the Peace Note of March 1966—in the last months of the Erhard government—suggests the concern over the dead end into which Adenauer's policies had led the Republic. It was largely without effect as it clung too tenaciously to precepts which were no longer in accord with the prevailing situation.

PEACE NOTE (FRIEDENSNOTE) OF THE FEDERAL REPUBLIC OF GERMANY, 25 MARCH 1966

Source: The Bulletin, 29 March 1966
Transl.: Official

I

The German people wish to live in peace and freedom. They consider it their greatest national task to remove the partition of Germany under which they have suffered for many years. The Government of the Federal Republic of Germany has repeatedly stated that the German people would be prepared also to make sacrifices for the sake of their reunification. They are determined to solve this problem by peaceful means only.

The thought of another war, which would destroy whole countries and nations, even continents, is unbearable to them. . . .

For ·many years now governments have been endeavouring to solve the political problems which lie at the root of tension between world Powers, and to ward off the dangers that arise as a result of the arms race, especially the increase in weapons of mass destruction. . . .

As in the past, the Government of the Federal Republic of Germany still holds the view that a world-wide, general and controlled disarmament must be the objective. Nor will this objective be changed by monotonous propaganda which seeks to question and misrepresent the standpoint of the Federal Government on problems of disarmament and security.

Moved by concern about further developments, it therefore has the honour to present . . . a survey of its policy for peace and to put forward some proposals on disarmament, armaments control and European security.

II

The Federal Government considers that given good will and honest intentions on all sides, even the most difficult problems between nations can be resolved in a peaceful and equitable manner. Thus, on this basis it has reached agreement with Germany's neighbours in the West on all problems that were still open after the war.

The German people desire to live on good terms with all, including their east European neighbours. Hence the Federal Government has been trying in various ways to improve relations with the States and peoples of eastern Europe. . . .

Despite the fact that the Federal Government has made particular efforts to cultivate relations with Poland, the country which suffered most of all among the east European nations in the Second World War, it has made but little progress in this direction. Although the Polish Government is obviously interested in more lively trade between Germany and Poland, it has hitherto not given any indication that it is interested in achieving a conciliation between the two nations. Rather does it hamper the cultural contacts we seek, stand for the continued division of Germany and at the same time calls upon the Federal Government to recognize the Oder-Neisse line, though it is generally known that, under the allied agreements of 1945, the settlement of frontier questions has been postponed until the conclusion of a peace treaty with the whole of Germany and that, according to international law, Germany continues to exist within its frontiers of 31 December 1937 until such time as a freely elected all-German Government recognizes other frontiers.

If, when the occasion arises, the Poles and the Germans enter into negotiations on frontier questions in the same spirit that led to the conciliation between Germany and her western neighbours, then Poles and Germans will also find their way to agreement. For in this question neither emotions nor alone the power of the victor, but rather reason, must prevail.

. . .

The policy pursued by the Federal Government is neither revanchist nor restorative. It is looking forward, not backwards, and its aim is an equitable European order on the basis of peaceful agreements, an order in which all nations can live together freely and as good neighbours.

. . .

The Government of the Federal Republic ... has the honour to submit ... the following ideas and suggestions. ...

V

. . .

4. The Federal Republic of Germany and its Western allies have already exchanged declarations renouncing the use of force. As the Governments of the Soviet Union and some other east European countries have repeatedly expressed their anxiety, unfounded as it is, over a possible German attack, the Federal Government proposed that formal declarations be exchanged also with the Governments of the Soviet Union, Poland, Czechoslovakia and any other east European State, in which either side gives an undertaking to the other people not to use force to settle international disputes.

. . .

6. Finally, the Federal Government is prepared to participate and to co-operate in a constructive spirit in a world disarmament conference or in any other disarmament conference promising success.

VI

The Federal Government considers that these suggestions and proposals stand the best chance, at the present stage, of being carried into effect. It realizes, however, that more far-reaching proposals are required if the world is to be given security in every respect and if it is to be guarded against the risk of nuclear war. It is prepared to co-operate also in such more comprehensive plans; it believes, however, that all efforts to achieve control will fail to bring decisive and lasting success unless there is a simultaneous step-by-step removal of the causes of tension in the world. Looking at Europe, that means, above all, solving the German problem in an equitable manner by granting to the entire German nation the right freely to determine its political way of life and its destiny.

Documents 12a–b

Within a year of taking office as chancellor, Willy Brandt and his associates had concluded a treaty with the Soviet Union in which the Federal Republic accepted 'current realities'. But as the accompanying letter shows, the ultimate right to 'unity in free self-determination' was preserved.

a) TREATY BETWEEN THE FEDERAL REPUBLIC OF GERMANY AND THE UNION OF SOVIET SOCIALIST REPUBLICS, 12 AUGUST 1970

Source: Documentation Relating to the Federal Government's Policy of Detente, Bonn, 1978, 17–19

Art. 1

The Federal Republic of Germany and the Union of Soviet Socialist Republics consider it an important objective of their policies to maintain international peace and achieve détente.

They affirm their endeavour to further the normalization of the situation in Europe and the development of peaceful relations among all European States, and in so doing proceed from the actual situation existing in this region.

. . .

Art. 3

In accordance with the foregoing purposes and principles the Federal Republic of Germany and the Union of Soviet Socialist Republics share the realization that peace can only be maintained in Europe if nobody disturbs the present frontiers.

—They undertake to respect without restriction the territorial integrity of all States in Europe within their present frontiers;
—they declare that they have no territorial claims against anybody nor will assert such claims in the future;
—they regard today and shall in future regard the frontiers of all States of Europe as inviolable such as they were on the date of signature of the present Treaty, including the Oder-Neisse line which forms the western frontier of the People's Republic of Poland and the frontier between the Federal Republic of Germany and the German Democratic Republic.

. . .

b) LETTER ON GERMAN UNITY, 12 AUGUST 1970

Source: ibid., 20

On the occasion of the signing of the Treaty, the Federal Government handed over in the Soviet Foreign Ministry the following letter:

Dear Mr. Minister,

In connection with today's signature of the Treaty between the Federal Republic of Germany and the Union of Soviet Socialist Republics the Goverment of the Federal Republic of Germany has the honour to state that this Treaty does not conflict with the political objective of the Federal Republic of Germany to work for a state of peace in Europe in which the German nation will recover its unity in free self-determination.

I assure you, Mr. Minister, of my highest esteem.

Walter Scheel

Documents 13a – c

In view of the long history of German/Polish hostility and of the suffering inflicted on the Poles by the Third Reich (and of the fact that Poland was the chief beneficiary of the partition of Germany) the reconciliation between Bonn and Warsaw was of special importance. A very sensitive issue was the repatriation of many Germans who still lived in these former East German territories (Doc. 13c).

a) TREATY BETWEEN THE FEDERAL REPUBLIC OF GERMANY AND THE PEOPLE'S REPUBLIC OF POLAND, 7 DECEMBER 1970, CONCERNING THE BASIS FOR NORMALIZING THEIR MUTUAL RELATIONS, AND RELATED STATEMENTS

Source: Documentation Relating to the Federal Government's Policy of Detente, Bonn, 1978, 28ff.

THE FEDERAL REPUBLIC OF GERMANY
AND
THE PEOPLE'S REPUBLIC OF POLAND

Considering that more than 25 years have passed since the end of the Second World War of which Poland became the first victim and which inflicted great suffering on the nations of Europe,

Conscious that in both countries a new generation has meanwhile grown up to whom a peaceful future should be secured,

Desiring to establish durable foundations for peaceful coexistence and the development of normal and good relations between them,

Anxious to strengthen peace and security in Europe,

Aware that the inviolability of frontiers and respect for the territorial integrity and sovereignty of all States in Europe within their present frontiers are a basic condition for peace,

Have agreed as follows:

Article I

(1) The Federal Republic of Germany and the People's Republic of Poland state in mutual agreement that the existing boundary line the course of which is laid down in Chapter XI of the Decisions of the Potsdam Conference of 2 August

1945 as running from the Baltic Sea immediately west of Swinemunde, and thence along the Oder River to the confluence of the western Neisse River and along the western Neisse to the Czechoslovak frontier, shall constitute the western State frontier of the People's Republic of Poland.

(2) They reaffirm the inviolability of their existing frontiers now and in the future and undertake to respect each other's territorial integrity without restriction.

(3) They declare that they have no territorial claims whatsoever against each other and that they will not assert such claims in the future.

Article II

(1) The Federal Republic of Germany and the People's Republic of Poland shall in their mutual relations as well as in matters of ensuring European and international security be guided by the purposes and principles embodied in the Charter of the United Nations.

(2) Accordingly they shall, pursuant to Articles 1 and 2 of the Charter of the United Nations, settle all their disputes exclusively by peaceful means and refrain from any threat or use of force in matters affecting European and international security and in their mutual relations.

Article III

(1) The Federal Republic of Germany and the People's Republic of Poland shall take further steps towards full normalization and a comprehensive development of their mutual relations of which the present Treaty shall form the solid foundation.

(2) They agree that a broadening of their co-operation in the sphere of economic, scientific, technological, cultural and other relations is in their mutual interest.

Article IV

The present Treaty shall not affect any bilateral or multilateral international arrangements previously concluded by either Contracting Party or concerning them.

. . .

Done at Warsaw on December 7, 1970 in two originals, each in the German and Polish languages, both texts being equally authentic.

For the	For the
Federal Republic	People's Republic
of Germany	of Poland
Willy Brandt	*Józef Cyrankiewicz*
Walter Scheel	*Stefan Jedrychowski*

b) NOTE FROM THE FEDERAL GOVERNMENT TO THE THREE WESTERN POWERS, 19 NOVEMBER 1970

. . .

The German Federal Foreign Office presents its compliments to Her Britannic Majesty's Embassy and has the honour to communicate to the Embassy the following text of a note of today's date of the Government of the Federal Republic of Germany to the Government of the United Kingdom of Great Britain and Northern Ireland:

. . .

In the course of the negotiations which took place between the Government of the Federal Republic of Germany and the Government of the People's Republic of Poland concerning this Treaty, it was made clear by the Federal Republic that the Treaty between the Federal Republic of Germany and the People's Republic of Poland does not and cannot affect the rights and responsibilities of the French Republic, the United Kingdom of Great Britain and Northern Ireland, the Union of Soviet Socialist Republics, and the United States of America as reflected in the known treaties and agreements. The Federal Government further pointed out that it can only act in the name of the Federal Republic of Germany.[13]

The Government of the French Republic and the Government of the United States of America have received identical notes

. . .

c) INFORMATION FROM THE GOVERNMENT OF THE PEOPLE'S REPUBLIC OF POLAND (UNDATED)

The Government of the People's Republic of Poland has communicated to the Federal Government the following information on measures for a solution of humanitarian problems:

(1) In 1955 the Polish Government recommended the Polish Red Cross to conclude an agreement with the Red Cross of the Federal Republic of Germany on the reunion of families; under that agreement, roughly one-quarter million people left Poland up to 1959. Between 1960 and 1969, an additional 150,000 people have departed from Poland under normal procedures. In carrying out measures to reunite families, the Polish Government has been guided above all by humanitarian motives. However, it could not, and still cannot, agree that its favourable attitude regarding such reunions be exploited for the emigration of Polish nationals for employment purposes.

(2) To this day, there have remained in Poland for various reasons (e.g. close ties with their place of birth) a certain number of persons of indisputable ethnic German origin and persons from mixed families whose predominant feeling over

the past years has been that they belong to that ethnic group. The Polish Government still holds the view that any persons who owing to their indisputable ethnic German origin wish to leave for either of the two German States may do so subject to the laws and regulations applicable in Poland.

Furthermore, consideration will be given to the situation of mixed and separated families as well as to such cases of Polish nationals who, either because of their changed family situation or because they have changed their earlier decision, express the wish to be reunited with near relatives in the Federal Republic of Germany or in the German Democratic Republic.

(3) The appropriate Polish authorities have not received anything like the number of applications from persons wishing to leave the country for the FRG as is maintained in the FRG. According to the inquiries so far made by the Polish authorities, some tens of thousands of people may fall under the criteria possibly entitling them to leave Poland for the FRG or the GDR. The Polish Government will therefore issue appropriate instructions for careful examination of whether the applications submitted are justified, and for their early consideration.

The Polish Government will authorize the Polish Red Cross to receive from the Red Cross of the FRG lists of the persons whose applications are held by the German Red Cross in order that they may be compared with the lists held by the appropriate Polish authorities, and carefully examined.

(4) Co-operation between the Polish Red Cross and the Red Cross of the FRG will be facilitated in any way necessary. The Polish Red Cross will be authorized to receive from the German Red Cross explanatory comments on the lists and will inform the German Red Cross of the outcome of examinations by the Polish authorities of transmitted applications. The Polish Red Cross will further be authorized to consider jointly with the Red Cross of the FRG all practical questions that might arise from this action.

(5) As regards the traffic of persons in connection with visits to relatives, the appropriate Polish authorities will, after the entry into force of the Treaty concerning the basis for normalizing relations between the two States, apply the same principles as are customary with regard to other States of Western Europe.

Documents 14a–b

While there were many former Sudeten Germans living in the Federal Republic after having been expelled by the Czechs, it was less the pressure from expellees than the more complicated legal questions resulting from the Czechoslovak demand that the Munich Treaty of 1938 (to which Britain, France and Italy were also parties) be declared invalid *ab initio* which delayed the settlement with Czechslovakia until 1973.

a) TREATY BETWEEN THE FEDERAL REPUBLIC OF GERMANY AND THE
CZECHOSLOVAK SOCIALIST REPUBLIC, 11 DECEMBER 1973

Source: Documentation Relating to the Federal Government's Policy of Detente,
Bonn, 1978, 68–71
Transl.: Official

. . .

Article II

(1) The present Treaty shall not affect the legal effects on natural or legal persons of the law as applied in the period between 30 September 1938 and 9 May 1945.

This provision shall exclude the effects of measures which both Contracting Parties deem to be void owing to their incompatibility with the fundamental principles of justice.

(2) The present Treaty shall not affect the nationality of living or deceased persons ensuing from the legal system of either of the two Contracting Parties.

(3) The present Treaty, together with its declarations on the Munich Agreement, shall not constitute any legal basis for material claims by the Czechoslovak Socialist Republic and its natural and legal persons.

Article III

(1) The Federal Republic of Germany and the Czechoslovak Socialist Republic shall in their mutual relations as well as in matters of ensuring European and international security be guided by the purposes and principles embodied in the United Nations Charter.

(2) Accordingly they shall, pursuant to Articles 1 and 2 of the United Nations Charter, settle all their disputes exclusively by peaceful means and shall refrain from any threat or use of force in matters affecting European and international security, and in their mutual relations.

Article IV

(1) In conformity with the said purposes and principles, the Federal Republic of Germany and the Czechoslovak Socialist Republic reaffirm the inviolability of their common frontier now and in the future and undertake to respect each other's territorial integrity without restriction.

(2) They declare that they have no territorial claims whatsoever against each other and that they will not assert any such claims in the future.

. . .

b) EXCHANGE OF LETTERS ON THE EXTENSION OF ARTICLES II AND V
OF THE TREATY TO BERLIN (WEST)
Source: Documentation Relating to the Federal Government's Policy of Detente,
Bonn, 1978

Mr. Minister,

On behalf of the Government of the Federal Republic of Germany I have the
honour to confirm the agreement reached in the negotiations that the validity of
Article II of the Treaty signed today on Mutual Relations between the Federal
Republic of Germany and the Czechoslovak Socialist Republic shall, consistent
with the Quadripartite Agreement of 3 September 1971, be extended to Berlin
(West) in accordance with established procedures.

The Federal Republic of Germany and the Czechoslovak Socialist Republic
propose to agree in each individual case on the extension to Berlin (West), consistent with the Quadripartite Agreement of 3 September 1971, of treaties arising
out of the implementation of the provisions of Article V of the present Treaty, in
accordance with established procedures.

I would ask you to confirm your agreement to the above.

Accept, Mr. Minister, the assurances of my highest consideration.

Walter Scheel

Mr. Bohuslav Chnoupek, Eng.,
Minister of Foreign Affairs
of the Czechoslovak Socialist Republic

Mr. Minister,

On behalf of the Government of the Czechoslovak Socialist Republic I have the
honour to confirm receipt of your letter of today's date . . .

The Government of the Czechoslovak Socialist Republic agrees to the above.

Accept, Mr. Minister, the assurances of my highest consideration.

B. Chnoupek

Herr Walter Scheel,
Minister for Foreign Affairs
of the Federal Republic of Germany

Document 15

Not until the two German states had come to an understanding in the
Basic Treaty of 1972 (see Ch. 14, Doc. 4) was it possible for the Federal
Republic, along with the GDR, to seek full membership in the United
Nations.

DECLARATION OF THE GOVERNMENTS OF THE UNITED STATES, FRANCE, THE USSR AND GREAT BRITAIN, 18 JUNE 1973

Source: The Federal Republic of Germany, Member of the United Nations, 3rd ed., Bonn, 1977, 170

The Governments of the United States of America, the French Republic, the Union of Soviet Socialist Republics and the United Kingdom of Great Britain and Northern Ireland, having been represented by their Ambassadors, who held a series of meetings in the building formerly occupied by the Allied Control Council, are in agreement that they will support the applications for membership in the United Nations when submitted by the Federal Republic of Germany and the German Democratic Republic, and affirm in this connection that this membership shall in no way affect the rights and responsibilities of the Four Powers and the corresponding related quadripartite agreements, decisions, and practices.

Document 16

From the 1960s onwards, German government statements (and policy) reflect an increasing preoccupation with the question of developmental assistance. What follows is an excerpt from a statement issued by Chancellor Schmidt's socialist–liberal coalition.

POLICY PAPER ON GERMAN CO-OPERATION WITH DEVELOPING COUNTRIES

Source: Policy Paper on German Cooperation with Developing Countries, Bonn, 1980, 7–11

. . .

Goals, Tasks and Methods of German Development Policy

Goals

(6) The object of German development policy is to promote economic and social development in countries of the Third World. It sets out to help the people there to improve their living conditions by using their own ideas and resources, develop their personalities and share in economic growth. It is a policy designed to secure peace on a long-term basis because development helps to eliminate hardship and constraints, as well as the tension and potential conflicts which originate in the prosperity gap which exists between North and South, among the developing countries themselves as well as inside individual developing countries. Development co-operation is based on the idea of the reconciliation of interests between North and South and on the principle of international solidarity.

(7) After three decades of international development policy, we need to take a more critical and more discriminating look than before at the concept, objective and methods of development. There is no single universally valid course of development. The goals and course chosen depend on a country's political, economic, cultural and social circumstances and values. The countries of the Third World should be guided by their own ideas and principles regarding progress. Therefore, development assistance means, above all, helping people to help themselves. Without economic growth, development is impossible, yet growth alone is no guarantee of development for all. Only where there is freedom from degrading dependence, domination and oppression, and where basic needs have been met, can there be development.

Past experience has shown that while progress is possible, it requires time and patience. It is inconceivable that there could be similar living standards in the North and the South in the foreseeable future. The first need is to ensure the basic requisites of a dignified existence.

(8) The principles and priorities of German development policy set out here are the basis on which the Federal Government conducts its negotiations with developing countries. But because the situation differs from country to country, the instruments and measures of co-operation are adjusted to the particular requirements of each partner, taking into account the country's own priorities.

(9) The development of the Third World requires measures both in the developing and in the industrialized countries, along with the further development and improvement of international economic relations. The Federal Government is collaborating in all these spheres. It co-operates bilaterally with developing countries, concentrating on fields in which external aid is possible and in which it can make effective contributions. It supports multilateral development organizations. In the North–South dialogue, it lends its support for improvements in the world economic system and is in favour of equal opportunities for developing countries. At home, it is facilitating the inevitable structural changes.

Tasks and Methods

The Fight against Absolute Poverty

(10) The greatest challenge to international solidarity is the mass poverty in the developing countries. Combating it is the primary task of German development policy. This means, first and foremost, satisfying basic needs: food, clean drinking water, health, clothing, housing and education. Progress towards satisfying such basic needs tends to increase people's capability for work and thereby their productivity which in turn provides the basis for sustained, independent economic growth. Measures designed to satisfy the basic needs should be of direct benefit to those living in absolute poverty; insofar as possible, they should be invited to participate in the planning and execution of such measures. The Federal Government will increase its support for those countries which direct their own efforts particularly to combating absolute poverty.

The Developing Countries' Independence and Responsibility

(11) The Federal Government is resolutely opposed to any attempt on the part of foreign powers to build up hegemony or establish spheres of influence in the Third World. Development policy sets out to strengthen the autonomy and political independence of the developing countries so that they remain free of onesided dependence and foreign control and can make decisions for themselves. This task is long-range in nature. Thus, development co-operation, being based on long-range considerations, is principally independent of internal political changes in the partner countries.

(12) German development policy supports economic co-operation among the developing countries themselves. Extra support is given to regional projects and joint projects which benefit several developing countries at once. The importance of such projects is reflected by the favourable terms and conditions granted for them.

(13) The promotion and protection of human rights is one of the basic objectives of the Federal Government's policy.

. . .

A notable feature of the Federal Republic's foreign policy has been the assumption of responsibility for the crimes committed during wartime by the Third Reich. Doc. 17 illustrates the pattern in which this obligation was discharged in Europe. The much more far-reaching attempt, very early in the history of the Federal Republic, to provide some form of restitution for Nazi crimes against the Jews is suggested by Doc. 18.

Document 17

TREATY BETWEEN THE FEDERAL REPUBLIC OF GERMANY AND THE KINGDOM OF NORWAY, 7 AUGUST 1959.

Source: Die Auswärtige Politik der Bundesrepublik Deutschland, Bonn, 1972, 410

The Federal Republic of Germany and the Kingdom of Norway have agreed as follows:

Art. I

(1) The Federal Republic of Germany will pay 60 million German marks to the Kingdom of Norway for the benefit of the Norwegian citizens concerned who have been persecuted by the National Socialists because of their race, belief or Weltanschauung, who have thereby endured injury to their freedom or health, as

well as for the benefit of the bereaved of those who died as a result of this persecution.

(2) The distribution of the amount is left to the discretion of the Kingdom of Norway.

Art. II

The Federal Republic of Germany will place at the disposal of the Kingdom of Norway the aforementioned sum in three equal instalments, whereby the first instalment is payable no later than one month after this treaty takes effect, the second no later than 1 May 1960 and the third no later than May 1961. . . .

Document 18

STATEMENT BY CHANCELLOR ADENAUER TO THE BUNDESTAG CONCERNING THE ATTITUDE OF THE FEDERAL REPUBLIC TOWARDS THE JEWS, 27 SEPTEMBER 1951

Source: Die Auswärtige Politik der Bundesrepublik Deutschland, Bonn, 1972, 179−81

. . .

Of late, the world public opinion has repeatedly been concerned with the attitude of the Federal Republic of Germany towards the Jews. Here and there doubts have arisen as to whether our new policy is guided, in regard to this important question, by principles which take into account the terrible crimes of the past epoch and which place the relationship between the Jews and the German people on a new and healthy footing.

The attitude of the Federal Republic of Germany to its Jewish citizens is clearly defined through the Basic Law. . . . These legal norms are the law of the land and oblige every German citizen, and especially every state official, to reject any form of racial discrimination. In the same spirit, the German government has also signed the Human Rights Convention adopted by the Council of Europe and has pledged itself to the realization of the legal concepts laid down in this Convention.

. . . . The German government, and with it the majority of the German people, are conscious of the immeasurable sorrow that was brought upon the Jewish people in Germany and in the occupied territories during the period of National Socialism. There was a predominant majority of German people who abhorred the crimes committed against the Jews and did not take part in them. There were many Germans during the time of National Socialism who, at their own risk, showed their willingness to help their Jewish compatriots for religious reasons, in a conflict of conscience, and out of shame because the German name had been disgraced. The unmentionable crimes committed in the name of the German people demand a moral and material restitution. This includes both the damages inflicted on individual Jewish people and on Jewish property for which the individuals entitled to restitution no longer exist. The first steps have been taken in this area. Much more, however, remains to be done. The German government will see to a quick settlement concerning the restitution legislation and its fair implementation. A part of the identifiable Jewish property has been returned; additional restorations will follow.

As to the extent of the restitution, which in view of the vast destruction of Jewish assets as a result of National Socialism is a very serious problem, limits are imposed by the fact that the Germans are confronted, through a bitter necessity, with the need to care for the countless war victims and the relief of the refugees and expellees. The Federal Government is ready, together with representatives of Jewish interests and the State of Israel, which received so many homeless Jewish refugees, to bring about a solution of the material restitution problems and thereby to prepare the way to a moral adjustment of this infinite sorrow. The German government is deeply convinced that the spirit of true humanity must be revived and made fruitful again.

To serve this spirit is regarded by the German government as the most outstanding obligation of the German people. . . .

Notes

1. Alfred Grosser, *Germany in Our Time: A Political History of the Postwar Years*, New York, 1971, 291
2. Cited in Philip Windsor, 'West Germany in Divided Europe,' in F.S. Northedge, ed., *The Foreign Policies of the Powers*, London, 1968, 237
3. Wolfram F. Hanrieder, *The Stable Crisis. Two Decades of German Foreign Policy*, New York, 1970, 45; Grosser, *Germany in Our Time*, 291
4. Konrad Adenauer, *Memoirs 1945–1953*, transl. Beate Ruhm von Oppen, London, 1965, 259
5. Protocol on the Termination of the Occupation Regime in the Federal Republic of Germany, 23 October 1954, *Selected Documents on Germany and the Question of Berlin, 1944–1961*, London, HMSO, Cmnd. 1552, 209. See also Ch. 12
6. Konrad Adenauer, *Memoirs 1945–1953*, 260
7. Cited in Gerald Freund, *Unholy Alliance: Russo–German Relations from the Treaty of Brest–Litovsk to the Treaty of Berlin*, London, 1957, 245
8. See below, Ch. 13
9. Karl Kaiser, *German Foreign Policy in Transition. Bonn Between East and West*, London, 1969, 90–5. See also Ch. 14
10. See above, Ch. 4
11. Total restitution payments by then amounted to some DM52 billion. See *Die Auswärtige Politik der Bundesrepublik Deutschland*, Cologne, 1972, 954
12. See Chs. 8, 14
13. This reservation has been strongly re-emphasised by a part of the CDU/CSU, after they came into power in 1982

12 Defence policy and the armed forces

Carl-Christoph Schweitzer

The Basic Law stipulates very clearly 1) the exclusively defensive aim of West Germany's foreign and defence policies; 2) the exclusive power of the Federation to set up federal armed forces (Bundeswehr) and to subject them to rigorous political control and 3) the principle both of compulsory military service, if need be, and of the right of 'conscientious objection', the latter being linked to the obligation to serve the country in a 'civilian alternative service' (Ziviler Ersatzdienst).

The constitutionally binding preamble of the Basic Law made it absolutely clear that the foreign and defence policies of the Federal Republic are committed to three basic goals: '. . . to preserve its *national and political unity* and to serve the *peace* of the world as an equal partner in a *United Europe*'.

Art. 26 (1) elaborates on the problem of war and peace in the context of these goals and states that 'acts tending to and undertaken with the intent to disturb the peaceful relations between nations, especially to prepare for aggressive war, shall be unconstitutional. They shall be made a punishable offence'.

Hence even to draw up offensive plans for military action would for the first time in German history constitute a violation of the constitution. Another significant break with the German past was the fact that a General Staff (Generalstab) was not established again when the Federal Republic was finally permitted to set up a new military force in 1955.

The rearming of West Germany was debated for some five years and would possibly not have materialised at all, certainly not so relatively early after 1945/49, had it not been for the outbreak of the Korean War in 1950[1]*. Chancellor Adenauer, when 'offering' German rearmament

---

to the Western Powers in 1950, was obviously motivated by German security interests (Doc. 1). The actual setting up of the new armed forces was, in the end, part of a package which included West Germany's entry into the NATO alliance, her regaining of national sovereignty (with the continuing exception of reservations previously imposed by agreements made at Potsdam in 1945 and Paris in 1954) and the renunciation of any further attempt to produce ABC weapons.[2] In addition the founding fathers themselves had made provision for giving up national sovereignty rights in favour not only of a 'supra-national' European organization but also of 'collective security arrangements' expressly referred to in Art. 24 of the Basic Law. In this connection it is important to point out that from the beginning practically all the German armed forces have been assigned to NATO's supreme command even in peace-time—quite in contrast to other NATO countries, above all to France, which in 1966 withdrew from the integrated military command of NATO altogether. The Federal Republic provides some 50 per cent of the NATO's land forces in Central Europe (excluding France), 50 per cent of the ground-based air-defence, 30 per cent of the combat aircraft, 100 per cent of the naval air forces in the Baltic and nearly 100 per cent of the naval forces in the Baltic. In absolute figures West Germany makes the second biggest financial contribution to NATO, which adds up to a considerable portion of the overall federal budget.[3]

Apart from the articles that were in the Basic Law from the beginning, amendments were enacted in the field of defence after the allied decision of 1955 to rearm the Federal Republic. A first set of these amendments concerned the organizational structure of the armed forces. Art. 87a, enacted in 1956, stating that the 'numerical strength and general organizational structure shall be shown in the annual budget', was intended to ensure that parliament would not only provide the necessary money, but would also exercise a general oversight. Furthermore, Arts. 65a and 115 (as amended) of the Basic Law made certain that the supreme political control over the armed forces could not be called into question again. Here the law-makers were mindful of the Kaiserreich (1871–1918) and the Weimar Republic (1919–1933), not to speak of the Nazi regime.[4] In peace-time the supreme authority over the armed forces lies in the hands of a civilian minister of defence; in wartime it would be in the hands of the chancellor. Chancellor and minister of defence are, of course, politically responsible to Parliament.

The Bundestag has a special instrument of control through its Defence Commissioner (Wehrbeauftragter), a sort of Ombudsman for the armed forces. A continuous legal overview is guaranteed by its Committee on

Defence. Finally, only the Bundestag as a whole, or its emergency sub-parliament (Gemeinsamer Ausschuß)[5] can determine constitutionally that the Federal Republic of Germany is at war, which would then be legally proclaimed by the head of state. Euphemistically, the Basic Law does not envisage a 'state of war', but a 'state of defence'. In possible 'internal upheavals', the powers of the federal government to use troops would be very narrow indeed. Art. 87a (4) states: '... should ... the police forces and the Federal Border Guard [Bundesgrenzschutz] be inadequate, the Federal Government may use the armed forces to support the police and the Federal Border Guard in the protection of civilian property and in combating organized and military armed insurgents ...'.

In accordance with Art. 12a the Bundestag, in 1956, passed the Law of Compulsory Military Service (Wehrpflichtgesetz, Doc. 2a) as well as that for Civilian Alternative Service (Ziviler Ersatzdienst, Doc. 2b). Today a very heated and still 'open' public debate revolves around the problem of how to improve the process of recognition of a conscientious objector. The difficulty lies in defining and proving a point of conscience.[6] An additional factor in this problem is that in the future the Federal Republic seems likely to have a serious shortage of professional soldiers. Additional constitutional provisions have been introduced for the calling-up of men *and* women in times of a national emergency, with women serving in non-military activities. In an age of equality between men and women and, above all, in view of the shortages in the nursing profession, another as yet undecided public debate has turned on the possibility of once more revising the Basic Law in order to make a call-up of women possible even in peace-time. So far the political odds are against such an innovation.

One of the main features of the new (West) German armed forces has been the extreme care devoted to, and emphasis put on, the safeguarding of democratic standards in the day-to-day life of conscripts and professional soldiers. The Germans have given this phenomenon the overall term (as peculiar as it is untranslatable) of Innere Führung (Leadership) (Doc. 3), meaning certain principles of conduct within the armed forces. A very extensive Central Service Regulation (Zentrale Dienstvorschrift) of 1972 was devoted to this problem which has since been the subject of further official pronouncements. The principle of Innere Führung was given legal force by Parliament through the Soldiers' Act (Soldatengesetz, Doc. 4) and the Military Appeal (Complaint) Act (Wehrbeschwerdeordnung) for the armed forces (Doc. 5). Innere Führung is based on the central hypothesis that it is necessary in a democratic society with a viable military establishment to strike a balance between obligations and rights of the individual in the armed forces. Its members have obligations, above all, to defend their country. While on this duty, they have to forego some basic civil rights 'for the time being', such as the right to assemble at any time or to associate themselves with others. They retain, however,—and this is the main point—other important rights, since they remain citizens, or citizens in uniform, as another German concept puts it. This was very clearly embodied in the Central Service Regulation dealt with in Doc. 3. Above all, the members of the armed services can claim to be treated in accordance with their basic constitutional right to the 'inviolability of their human dignity' (Art. 1, Basic Law); they have the right to make complaints against superiors (Doc. 5), and they are part of a community in which other principles are supposed to be cherished, such as comradeship, loyalty, determination of purpose, tradition (Doc. 6) or the claim to a continuing general and professional education within the forces. The latter applies especially to the field of civics studies, which is on the weekly curriculum for all units. All these rights are committed—over and above the normal enforcement of laws—to the special care and supervision of the Defence Commissioner. He receives complaints directly from any member of the armed services, investigates them and issues a yearly report on his findings to the Bundestag (Doc. 7).

Throughout its relatively short history of twenty-five years, the Bundeswehr has been confronted by problems not of its own making, i.e. by problems emerging from the overall domestic and international environment. In the first years of its existence the Bundeswehr had to grapple with the legacies of the Third Reich. In the 1950s most Germans did not, really, want an army again. In those years, especially after the stationing of the first atomic weapons on German soil, the country resounded with slogans such as the famous 'count me out' ('Ohne mich') in regard to the rearming of West Germany. These views were by no means confined to the young. All this explains the decrees and laws mentioned above, to provide a maximum of democratic guarantees for the members of the armed forces—to be used as guide-lines, also, for the formation of a new corps of officers.

Now in the 1980s, new developments are taking place in the national and international situation. A second peace movement has arisen some of whose aims are reflected in the slogan of young demonstrators at the National Conference of the German Protestant Churches (Kirchentag) in Hamburg in 1981: 'What will the governments do when they start their war and we just won't show up?'[7] The West German peace movement has not only been part of a larger Western European peace-movement,[8] but it is actually at the forefront of that effort. Hundreds of thousands have marched for peace in West Germany in 1981 and 1982. There have been in the Federal Republic a great number of calls for peace (Friendensappelle) from all walks of life.[9] The most radical one was the Krefelder Appell of 1981, directed against the famous Nato dual-track decision of 1979 (Doc. 8). The people behind such appeals could by no means be dismissed as communist stooges, as was also made clear by the last Social-Democratic defence minister Hans Apel in a key address in October 1982 (Doc. 9).

The peace debate is still open-ended in West Germany, in Western Europe, in the Western world and, one hopes, in the East as well. There, however, it has so far been very restricted and officially controlled.

Document 1

MEMORANDUM OF CHANCELLOR KONRAD ADENAUER TO THE ALLIED HIGH COMMISSION ON THE SECURITY OF THE FEDERAL REPUBLIC, 29 AUGUST 1950

Source: K. von Schubert (ed.), *Sicherheitspolitik der Bundesrepublik Deutschland, Dokumentation*, Teil I, 79ff.

I.

The development in the Far East has aroused alarm and uncertainty within the German population. Confidence that the western world would be prepared swiftly and effectively to react to aggression against Western Europe is in the process of dwindling to such an extent as to cause fear, and has led to a dangerous lethargy in the German population. . . .

II.

According to confirmed reports, two corps of mobile troops with nine motorized divisions and four tank corps with thirteen divisions, that is to say, a total of twenty-two motorized and tank divisions of Soviet troops are presently located in the East Zone . . . . Their deployment displays the motorized mobile troops on the front line, the heavy tank units behind them, with special artillery and anti-aircraft units in between. This picture must be designated as a marked offensive deployment.

The number of tanks ready for action must be assumed to be 5000 to 6000 . . .

In addition to these extraordinarily strong Soviet Russian forces, the building up of the Volkspolizei [People's Police] has made considerable progress in the last few months. Their development from police force to police army demands attention. In the last few months, around 70,000 men have been taken out of the

General Police of the East Zone and organized into military-like formations and have been militarily trained . . . .

It can be assumed that the Volkspolizei will have some 150,000 men in the near future who, according to the overall plan, should be brought up to around 300,000 men.

All information regarding the setting of the objective, which is being given to these troops by the Soviet and East Zone governments indicates that it would be their task in the near future to free West Germany from its allied tyrants, to eliminate the 'collaborating government' of the Federal Republic, and to unify West Germany with the East Zone in a satellite-like state. Along with the public declarations of the East German politicians Pieck and Ulbricht, one must assume that preparations are being made in the East Zone for an operation which, from many viewpoints, brings to mind the development of the action in Korea . . . .

III.

As a counteracting force to this adversary there are two American and British divisions apiece, and one French unit in West Germany. Apart from the weak forces comprising the customs guards, the Federal Government has no power at its disposal. In the British Zone there is a police force which is organized on a local level . . . .

IV.

The problem of the security of the Federal Republic, to begin with, is a problem of foreign affairs. The defence of the Federation against outside attacks lies primarily in the hands of the occupation troops. The Chancellor has repeatedly requested a strengthening of the occupation troops and, herewith, renews this request in a most urgent form. For the strengthening of the allied occupation troops alone can make visibly known to the people the determination of the Western powers that West Germany will actually be defended under emergency conditions . . . .

The Chancellor has furthermore repeatedly made clear that he is prepared, if an international West European army is to be set up, to provide a contribution in the form of a German contingent. It has since been clearly stated that the Chancellor rejects a remilitarization of Germany through setting up independent national military forces.

V.

The security problems of the Federal Territory present themselves moreover under a domestic perspective . . . .

The Federal government, therefore, proposes to set up immediately, on a federal basis, a police force which must be strong enough to guarantee its internal security

. . .

Because preparations must be immediately begun, it is necessary that the Allied High Commission furnish the Federal government with the directive for the necessary steps to initiate the creation of this police force.

The democratic control of this police force shall be guaranteed through a committee set up by the Bundestag which would be given the power to inspect the build-up and the personnel arrangements of this police force.

International control of this force could be exercised by the Allied Office for Military Security . . . .

Documents 2a–b

From 1956 right through to the present the Federal Ministry of Defence has relied on calling up males above the age of 18—roughly 51,500 every three months to make up between 45 and 50 per cent (i.e. some 220,000 men) of the total strength of the three services. There is now a serious shortage of senior NCOs whose duties are, therefore, often assigned to corporals or junior sergeants.[10]

a) COMPULSORY MILITARY SERVICE ACT (WEHRPFLICHTGESETZ) 21 JULY 1956

Source: BGBl., I, 1956, 651ff.

1. Extent of Compulsory Military Service . . .

§1 *General Compulsory Military Service*

(1) From the age of 18 onwards all men who are German citizens according to the Basic Law are obliged to perform military service, if the following conditions are fulfilled:

1. If they have a permanent residence within the domain of this law or
2. If they have their residence outside the territory of the German Reich as it stood on December 31, 1937 and either
   a) had their last German permanent residence within the domain of this law or
   b) possess a passport or certificate of nationality of the Federal Republic of Germany or have put themselves under its protection in some other way.

(2) Compulsory military service is suspended for Germans who have their permanent residence and means of subsistence outside the Federal Republic of Germany if the facts support the belief that they intend to keep their permanent residence abroad. This applies particularly to German citizens with a dual nationality.

. . .

§ 5 *Basic Military Service*

(1) Conscripts up to the age of twenty-eight perform a basic military service. Those conscripts who are used mainly for special military duties because of their professional qualifications or those who were not conscripted before the age of twenty-eight because of a military service exemption ... have to perform military service up to the age of thirty-two. Basic military service lasts for fifteen months and begins as a rule in the calendar year when the conscript reaches his nineteenth birthday. Applications from the conscript to perform basic military service before the call-up of conscripts of his age should be met but not before the conscript's eighteenth birthday.

...

§ 12 *Temporary Exemption from Military Service*

(1) Those who are temporarily exempt from military service are:

1. those who are temporarily unable to perform military service
2. those who ... are serving a prison sentence or ... are being cared for in a psychiatric hospital or ... are in a social-therapeutic institution or in an institution where withdrawal treatment for addicts is administered.
3. Anyone who is currently placed in the care of a guardian.

(2) Conscripts who are preparing themselves for holy orders ... are exempted on application.

(3) If a conscript has agreed to stand for an election to the Bundestag or to one of the Länder parliaments he will be exempted until that election. If he has taken his seat, he may only be called up for service during parliamentary recesses for the duration of his term of office unless he requests otherwise.

(4) A conscript should be exempted from military service,

1. if being called up for military service would mean for him a special personal, in particular, a domestic, economic or professional hardship. Such would be the case, as a rule, if the calling up of a conscript put at risk either a) his provision for his family or needy relatives or other needy people for whom he must supply a livelihood on either legal or moral grounds or b) if particular distress were to result for his nearest kin.
2. If the conscript is indispensable for the upkeep and maintenance of his own or his family's farm or firm.
3. If the calling up of the conscript would interfere with

   a) a period of training which was already greatly advanced
   b) his secondary education leading to a university degree or a diploma of higher education
   c) primary professional training or the first part thereof

   and in the case of c) when neither a university degree nor a diploma of an institution of higher education has been obtained, nor when the normal length of the training or part of the training exceeds four years.

. . .

§ 25 *Effects of Conscientious Objection*

Anyone who objects to taking part in an armed conflict between states for reasons of conscience and therefore refuses to perform armed service in war must render civilian service outside the armed forces. He can be recruited to unarmed service within the armed forces if he applies for this.

b) CIVILIAN ALTERNATIVE SERVICE ACT (ZIVILDIENSTGESETZ), 3 JANUARY 1960, HERE AS AMENDED 26 JUNE 1981
Source: BGBl., I, 1981, 553ff.

The alternative civilian service (in hospitals, nursing homes for the aged and disabled, in forestry work etc.) lasted one month longer for conscripts recognized as conscientious objectors than the term for those serving in the armed forces. Hitherto special tribunals have had to take the decision to recognize conscientious objectors. It has now been decided to abolish these tribunals and to extend the term for those serving in the 'civilian alternative' to twenty months, as against fifteen months in the armed forces.

1. *Duties of Civilian Alternative Service*

In civilian alternative service, recognized conscientious objectors fulfil duties which serve the public welfare with priority in the social services area.

2. *Organization of Civilian Alternative Service*

(1) This law will be executed by the federal administration, in so far as not otherwise determined herein.

. . .

7. *Fitness*

Fitness for civilian alternative service is determined by the fitness standard applied to the military service. Those qualified for military service can be drafted into civilian alternative service; those momentarily not fit for military service are momentarily not fit for civilian alternative service, and those not fit for military service are not fit for civilian alternative service. In compliance with Art. 8, Para. 2 of the law of compulsory military service, types of employment established on the basis of the physician's examination must be taken into consideration in the assignment of activities for the men who are liable to serve.

8. *Unfit for Civilian Alternative Service*

Not to be called upon for civilian alternative service are:

(1) those not capable of civilian alternative service,
(2) those under guardianship.

. . .

19. *Conscription*

(1) Those liable to serve will be called up for civilian alternative service according to the conscription regulations of the Minister for Labour and Social Affairs [now Minister of Youth, Family and Health Affairs], as long as they are not transferred according to section (2) below to a term of employment according to this law. Those who are discharged from the basic military service after having been recognized as conscientious objectors should be called up immediately for civilian alternative service.

(2) Service in the armed forces already begun can be commuted through an agreement in the form of a written reply from one of the administrative offices set up by the Federal Minister of Defence to a term of employment according to this law, if the soldier is recognized as a conscientious objector.

. . .

24. *Length of Civilian Alternative Service*

(1) Men liable to serve who have not yet completed their twenty-eighth year render civilian alternative service. Those liable to serve who, with their consent, intend to fulfil particular duties in the civilian alternative service remain liable, after completion of their professional training, to render civilian alternative service until the completion of their thirty-second year. Civilian alternative service lasts sixteen months. . . .

Document 3

REGULATION 10/1 OF 1972 (ZDV), ISSUED BY THE MINISTRY OF DEFENCE, ON PRINCIPLES OF LEADERSHIP (INNERE FÜHRUNG) IN THE ARMED FORCES

Source: Ministry of Defence

. . .

Chapter 2: Leadership

I. *Aims*

. . .

202. It is the aim of *Innere Führung* (Leadership) to enforce the performance of

the soldier's duties, and at the same time to guarantee his rights. The principles of Leadership, on which the order of the federal armed forces depends, balance out the tension between the rights and the duties of the soldier . . .

205. The principles and practices of Leadership are adaptable to the intellectual, political, and technical development within society . . .

II. *Principles*

206. (1) *Innere Führung* (Leadership) serves the federal armed forces' state of preparedness within the framework of our legal order. The principles of Leadership are therefore firmly established in the Basic Law, in military laws, decrees, ordinances, and service regulations.

(2) The senior officer should utilize the latitude which these regulations allow, in exercising Leadership . . .

. . .

210. The legally determined duties of the soldier are derived from the requisites of military service.

. . .

212. Senior officers and subordinates alike are responsible for cohesion within the federal armed forces. This presupposes trust, which must be valued and which demands mutual respect.

(1) The representatives of the other ranks (Vertrauensmänner), of the non-commissioned officers and the officers should contribute to, and thereby strengthen, in the areas for which they have been elected, the inner order of the federal armed forces towards responsible cooperation between superiors and subordinates, as well as the maintenance of trust between comrades . . . (the election of the Vertrauensmänner is prescribed by law).

. . .

IV. *Self-Image of the Soldier*

222. The federal armed forces have many relationships with society at large. The federal armed forces, in so far as their tasks permit, take part in the intellectual, political and technical development of society.

223. Today's soldier is not only a soldier. He may also be, for example, a member of a church, a party, a professional organization, association or other organizations. From this, many links have been forged between the federal armed forces and society.

224. Our liberal society is characterized by a plurality of interests, opinions, conceptions of values and aims (Pluralism). Willingness for objectivity, com-

promise, and democratic decisions guarantee that conflicting interests and opinions can be resolved without use of force. This willingness also applies to the federal armed forces if, during the fulfillment of duties, they come into conflict with other groups . . .

. . .

232. Soldiers can be proud of their profession. Like members of other professions, this pride in the soldier's profession depends on his own performance but, above all, on the performance of the group, the unit, or the task force.

. . .

234. The tasks of the federal armed forces in the midst of a modern industrial society demand from each superior

—Education and specialized knowledge,
—Powers of judgement and decision,
—Commitment and ability to differentiate,
—Loyalty and comradeship.

. . .

Document 4

FEDERAL LAW GOVERNING THE LEGAL STATUS OF SOLDIERS (SOLDIERS' ACT, SOLDATENGESETZ), 19 MARCH 1956, AS AMENDED IN 1975

Source: BGBl., I, 1975, 2275ff.

. . .

§ 6 *A Soldier's Rights as a Citizen*

A soldier enjoys the same rights as any other citizen. His rights are limited within the framework of the requirements of military service through the obligations placed on him by law.

§ 7 *The Basic Duty of a Soldier*

A soldier has the duty to serve the Federal Republic of Germany loyally and to defend valiantly the rights and liberties of the German people.

§ 8 *Commitment to the Democratic Basic Order*

A soldier must recognize the free democratic basic order as defined by the Basic Law and show himself committed to its preservation by his whole behaviour.

§ 9 *The Oath and Solemn Pledge*

(1) Professional soldiers and short-service soldiers must take the following oath of office:

'I swear to serve the Federal Republic of Germany loyally and to defend valiantly the rights and liberties of the German people, so help me God.'

The oath can also be taken without the words 'so help me God'. If a Federal law allows members of a religious body to use another term of affirmation instead of the words 'I swear' the member of the religious body may use this form of affirmation.

(2) Soldiers performing military duty because they are required to by compulsory military service pledge themselves to their duties by the following solemn promise 'I promise to serve the Federal Republic of Germany loyally and to defend valiantly the rights and liberties of the German people'.

§ 10 *Duties of a Superior Officer*

(1) A superior officer must set an example by his behaviour and devotion to duty.
(2) He has the duty to supervise and is responsible for the discipline of those under his command.
(3) He must take care of those under his command.
(4) He may only give orders in the exercise of duty and in compliance with international law, the national law and service regulations.
(5) He must bear the responsibility for his orders. He must see that orders are carried out in a way that is appropriate to the circumstances.
(6) Officers and non-commissioned officers must, both on and off duty, preserve that restraint in their language which is necessary to uphold the confidence and trust placed in them as superior officers.

§ 11 *Obedience*

(1) A soldier must obey his superiors. He must carry out their orders to the best of his ability, to the letter, conscientiously and promptly. A soldier is not guilty of disobedience if he refuses to carry out an order which violates human dignity or which has not been given in the line of command. The false supposition that such an order had been given only absolves the soldier from responsibility if the mistake was unavoidable and if he could not, in the circumstances known to him, be expected to oppose the order by lawful means.
(2) An order may not be followed when a punishable offence would thereby be committed. If the soldier carries out the order notwithstanding he can be blamed only if he recognizes or if it is apparent from the circumstances known to him that a punishable offence is thereby being committed.

§ 12 *Comradeship*

The cohesion of the armed forces rests essentially on comradeship. This obliges every soldier to respect the dignity, honour and rights of his comrades and to stand by them in distress and danger. This includes the mutual recognition of, consideration and respect for, different outlooks and ideas.

. . .

§ 15 *Political Activity*

(1) A soldier may not while on active service promote or discredit a particular political view. The right of the soldier to express his own opinion among his comrades remains intact.

(2) Within military quarters and installations and off duty the right of free expression is restricted by the basic rules of comradeship. A soldier must behave in a way that does not seriously disturb the cooperative spirit of the service. Above all a soldier may not actively canvas support for a political group by holding meetings, disseminating literature or working as a representative of a political organisation. Mutual respect must not be put at risk.

(3) A soldier may not wear uniform at a political meeting.

(4) A soldier may not as a superior officer influence his subordinates for or against a political opinion.

§ 16 *Behaviour in Other Countries*

Outside the domain of the Basic Law a soldier is forbidden to involve himself in the affairs of the country where he is residing.

§ 17 *Behaviour On and Off Duty*

(1) A soldier must maintain discipline and respect the rank of a superior officer also off duty.

(2) His behaviour must be fitting to the high standing of the armed forces as well as to the respect and trust which his duties as a soldier command. When off duty and not present in his military quarters or on military installations he must behave in such a way that he does not seriously impair the high standing of the armed forces or the respect and trust which his official position demands.

. . .

Document 5

MILITARY APPEAL (COMPLAINT) ACT (WEHRBESCHWERDEORDNUNG), 23 DECEMBER 1956

Source: BGBl., I, 1956

The Bundestag has passed the following law:

§ 1 *The Right of Complaint*

(1) A soldier may complain, if he considers himself to have been improperly

treated by a superior or a section of the armed forces or if he feels himself to have been hurt by the unsoldierly behaviour of his comrades.

(2) A complaint can also be based upon the fact that no response to a petition of his has been forthcoming after two weeks have elapsed without adequate reasons being given.

(3) A complaint against an official judgement of personal performance cannot be entertained.

(4) Collective complaints are not permitted. The Right of Petition according to Art. 17 of the Basic Law is thus restricted.

. . .

§ 4 *Mediation and Expression of Views*

(1) The complainant may, before registering a complaint, call upon a mediator, if he feels personally offended and a favourable settlement seems possible to him.

(2) The mediator may be called upon at the earliest after one night has elapsed and must be called upon within a week of the complainant's becoming aware of the cause for complaint.

(3) A complainant must choose as a mediator a soldier who enjoys his personal confidence and who has no part in the matter. A soldier who has been called upon as a mediator may only refuse with good reason to carry out the mediation. Direct superiors of the complainant or the one about whom the complaint is being made . . . and the 'man of confidence' (Vertrauensmann) may not take on the rôle of mediator.

(4) The mediator should personally familiarise himself with the subject matter of the complaint and make an effort to ensure a settlement.

(5) If a complainant asks the person he has complained about to have a discussion either before the mediation or instead of it then the latter must give him the opportunity to put forward his point of view.

. . .

§ 7 *Failure to Meet the Deadline*

If the complainant is prevented from adhering to a deadline either by military duty, act of God or other unavoidable occurrence, the deadline will not expire until three days after the ending of the obstruction.

. . .

§ 10 *Preparation of the Decision Regarding the Complaint*

(1) The superior who takes the final decision in the matter has to clarify the issue by way of oral or written proceedings. He may commission an officer to clarify the issue. A short concluding report must be made on all oral proceedings, in writing. . . .

. . .

§ 12 *Notification of the Final Decision*

(1) The decision must be made in writing. The reasons for the decision must be given. . . .

(2) In so far as the substance of the complaint concerns an action which is subject to prosecution under the legal code involved, the matter must be handed over immediately to the relevant office of the public prosecutor. . . .

. . .

§ 13 *Contents of the Decision*

(1) In so far as the complaint proves to be justified, the decision must be complied with. . . . In this connection orders or measures which are proved to have been out of order or irrelevant [unzulässig oder unsachgemäß] must be revoked or changed. If the relevant order has been already executed, or become irrelevant, it must be made clear [in the decision] that the order should not have been given. Measures called for but not taken must be executed, as far as this is still possible.

. . .

Document 6

This directive is the second of its kind, the first having been issued in 1965 by the then CDU-governed Cabinet. In its introduction to the new directive of 1982 the then Social Democratically-led Ministry of Defence said, interestingly enough, that 'for instance' para. 17 of the old directive was 'historically not tenable'; this paragraph had asserted that it was 'a part of the good tradition of the German military, that ever since the time of the Prussian reforms [during and after the Napoleonic Wars] the German army has participated in political thinking and been ready to take on political responsibilities'.

NEW DIRECTIVE ON THE PROBLEM OF TRADITIONS IN THE ARMED FORCES (NEUE TRADITIONSRICHTLINIEN DER BUNDESWEHR), ISSUED BY THE MINISTRY OF DEFENCE 20 SEPTEMBER 1982

Source: Ministry of Defence press release, 20 September 1982

I. *Basic Principles*

1. Tradition is the passing on of values and norms. They are formed through a value-orientated analysis of the past. Tradition binds generations, safeguards an identity, and builds a bridge between the past and the future. Tradition is an essential foundation of man's culture. It presupposes an understanding of the historical, political and social context.

2. The yardsticks for an understanding and preservation of traditions in the German Federal armed forces are the Basic Law and the delegated assignments and duties of the army. The Basic Law is the response to history. It allows much latitude yet entails definite limits.

   The portrayal of common, united values and a democratic awareness of the armed forces is the foundation of the preservation of their tradition.

5. Political-historical education contributes decisively to the development of a common understanding of tradition in conformity with the Basic Law and an up-to-date preservation of that tradition. This demands an approach that incorporates the whole of German history and omits nothing.

6. The history of the German armed forces has not been without abrupt changes of a serious nature. The armed forces were both instruments and victims of political abuse during the period of National Socialism. An unjust regime, such as the Third Reich, cannot found a tradition.

   . . .

15. In the preservation of tradition in the German Federal armed forces, such records of conduct and experiences from history should be preserved which, as ethical and constitutional, free and democratic traditions, can serve as examples and are worthy of remembrance today.

16. In the preservation of tradition in the German Federal armed forces, events should be remembered such as those in which soldiers, beyond their military performance, took part in progressive political activities which contributed to the emergence of a mature citizenry and led the way to a free, republican and democratic Germany.

17. In maintaining the tradition of the German Federal armed forces special emphasis should be placed on the following political stances and modes of behaviour:

    1) Critical acceptance of German history, love of the homeland and mother-country, orientation not only towards success and the successful, but also towards the suffering of the persecuted and the humiliated.

    2) Political participation and common responsibility, awareness of democratic values, judgment without prejudice, tolerance, readiness and ability to discuss the ethical aspects of military service, the will for peace.

    3) Conscientious obedience and loyal fulfilment of duties in everyday life, comradeship, determination and will to fight when defence is required.

    . . .

20. The German Federal armed forces preserve their own established traditions, which should be further developed. Those included above all are:

    1) The mission to preserve peace in freedom as the foundation of a soldier's commitment.

2) Abstention from creating ideologically-motivated images of an enemy or from cultivating feelings of hatred.

3) Participation in the Atlantic Alliance and comradely cooperation with Allied troops on the basis of common values.

4) The model of 'Citizen in Uniform' and the principles of Innere Führung.

5) The active contribution to the shaping of democracy through the role of the soldier as a citizen.

6) An open-minded attitude to social change and the readiness for contact with the civilian citizen.

7) Assistance to the civilian population in emergency and catastrophe at home and abroad.

These are unchangeable characteristics of the German Federal armed forces.

Document 7

These annual reports, regularly debated in Parliament, often touch on points of principle relating to the overall situation of the armed forces within state and society to-day. Their main purpose is, however, to list, evaluate and act upon complaints lodged by the members of the forces. In 1980 (dealt with in 1981, see Deutscher Bundestag, 9th leg. per., Drucksache 9/1406) for instance, 400 complaints were brought forward. Of those sixty-nine concerned problems of conscientious objectors, sixty-eight questions of human dignity, sixty-six the principle of equality, fifty-three general principles of the Basic Law, forty-nine violations of the inviolability of the individual, forty-five problems of freedom of expression and so on. The incident listed below may be seen as typical of the work of the Defence Commissioner. One of the most serious incidents investigated by the Commissioner (and brought to court) occurred in 1962 in Nagold during a river-crossing as part of a military exercise which led to loss of life.

REPORT OF THE DEFENCE COMMISSIONER TO THE BUNDESTAG FOR THE YEAR 1963, ISSUED 1965

Source: Deutscher Bundestag, 4th legislative period, Drucksache 4/2305, 13

4. *Maltreatment of a Subordinate*

A company 1st sergeant kicked a soldier who was lying on his bed and sleeping during barracks' detail, in order to wake him. The company 1st sergeant was sentenced to detention.

. . .

Private 1st class A., member of a signal company, filed a complaint with the Defence Commissioner regarding the following incident:

After reveille, he and a few other soldiers from his unit were ordered to stay in quarters until 8 a.m. There they lay down fully dressed upon the beds and he, the complainant, fell asleep. At around 7.40 a.m. the company 1st sergeant woke him with a 'kick in the loins'. He requested verification of his grievances.

The regimental commander, whom the Defence Commissioner had requested to investigate the matter, established that the statements of private 1st class A.did not prove true on all counts. According to his findings, the incident occurred in the following manner:

Following the end of reveille, private 1st class A. and some other soldiers who were not taking part in the company's general detail, were sent to the quarters for barracks' detail.

As the company 1st sergeant went through the mens' quarters during this detail, he established that the private 1st class, and soldiers B. and C., were lying on their beds sleeping. Upon his loud shout, B. and C. got up, while A. remained lying. In order to motivate him to get up, the company 1st sergeant kicked him in the hip region.

The assertion of private 1st class A. that he received a kick 'in the loins' was not confirmed by the medical officer who had examined him; signs of use of violence were not established. And furthermore, because witnesses agreed that they had not had the impression that the company 1st sergeant had intended to abuse private 1st class A., the incident was not reported to the public prosecutor's office. The company 1st sergeant was sentenced to three days detention. In light of the company 1st sergeant's irreproachable conduct up to the time of the incident, the sentence was suspended in favour of a five months probation period.

The Defence Commissioner considered the settlement of the matter appropriate. . . .

Document 8

This appeal, one of many at the time in the Federal Republic, but the most widely publicized, was issued jointly by individuals and groups from the churches, the trade unions, the ecological movements, youth organizations (in particular from the socialist and liberal parties), some members of the Bundestag (of the Social Democratic Party only), teachers, doctors, university professors, novelists, former officers of the Bundeswehr and, last but not least, sections of the Communist Party of Germany (DKP). Already by the end of 1981 some one million signatures were claimed.

APPEAL OF KREFELD (KREFELDER APPELL) AGAINST NATO'S DUAL-TRACK DECISION OF 1979, ISSUED IN NOVEMBER 1980

Source: Unsere Zeit, 8 November 1980

NATO resolution a fateful mistake
European nations should not be exposed to unbearable risks

More and more obviously the NATO rearmament resolution of 12 December 1979 is proving to be a fateful mistake. The hope for agreements between the USA and the Soviet Union over a restriction of Euro-strategic arms systems before a new generation of American middle-range nuclear weapons is stationed in Western Europe will apparently not be fulfilled.

A year after Brussels, not even the commencement of such talks is in sight. On the contrary: the newly elected president of the USA frankly declares that he does not even want to accept the Salt II treaty on the restriction of Soviet and American strategic nuclear weapons and therefore does not want to pass it on to the Senate for ratification.

However, the American refusal to ratify the treaty would unavoidably push the chance of talks on restricting Euro-strategic nuclear arms into the distant future. A suicidal arms race would not be stopped at the last moment; its increasing acceleration together with increasingly specific speculations about the possibility of limiting a nuclear war necessarily exposes the European nations, above all, to unbearable risks.

The participants in the Krefeld Talks of 15 and 16 November 1980 therefore jointly appeal to the Federal government:

To withdraw their consent to stationing Pershing II rockets and cruise missiles in Central Europe; to take an attitude within the alliance which no longer leaves room to suspect our country of wanting to be the forerunner of a new nuclear arms race which would endanger the Europeans above all.

Worry about recent developments is growing among the general public. The possibilities of an alternative security policy are being discussed with more and more determination. Such deliberations are of great importance for the democratic process of opinion-forming and can contribute to preventing our nation from suddenly being confronted with a *fait accompli*.

The whole population is therefore asked to support this appeal in order to enforce by unceasing and increasing pressure of public opinion a security policy:

which does not permit Central Europe to be equipped as a nuclear arms platform for the USA; disarmament is considered more important than deterrent; the development of the armed forces is to be orientated to achieve these goals.

Krefeld, 16 November 1980

Document 9

SPEECH BY THE LONG-SERVING SOCIAL DEMOCRATIC MINISTER OF DEFENCE, HANS APEL, DELIVERED ON 27 OCTOBER 1982 TO THE COMMANDING OFFICERS OF ALL THREE SERVICES AT THEIR REGULAR (25th) MEETING IN INGOLSTADT

Source: Ministry of Defence press release, 27 October 1982

. . .

20. The Bonn peace demonstration and its non-violent course made it clear to everyone that it expresses the motives and anxieties of parts of our population. Before and after the event this somehow seemed to some people to be a centrally-steered, remote-controlled Communist campaign. In actual fact it was nothing of the sort, but was rather the result of innumerable individual initiatives in our country's towns and villages. Certainly, part of the organization lay in the hands of Communist groups which are trained in organizing such meetings. According to my information there were 23,000 Communists amongst the 250,000 to 300,000 demonstrators. That is a lot, if you remember that there are only 40,000 Communist Party members in the Federal Republic of Germany. But they were lost amongst the masses of people who made up this demonstration: ecologists, neutralists, pacifists, supporters of unilateral disarmament, entire school classes, unionists, feminists and above all Protestant and Catholic youth groups. The two Protestant Church organizers, the Aktion Sühnezeichen and the Aktionsgemeinschaft Dienst für den Frieden, were themselves surprised by the number of demonstrators who travelled to Bonn and the high participation rate of Christians.

Nevertheless, we should not let ourselves be impressed by the number of participants at demonstrations. This becomes clear, if you compare the percentage of demonstrators to the electorate. Not only the size of a demonstration counts, but rather the goals it seeks to advance.

21. It is the fight against so-called rearmament which unites all groups. Apart from this, the peace movement has hardly one common platform. So far, no consensus of the various groups on a constructive alternative to the existing security policy is in sight.

22. Certain anti-American tones are not representative of our population's opinion. Today 56 per cent are in favour of closer cooperation with the United States; in May 1973 it was only 36 per cent. Especially in difficult political times, the Germans know that they cannot have security without American protection. Likewise it is certain that the majority of the public supports NATO's dual-track decision. This summer, two surveys showed that 58 per cent of the population agree with the dual-track decision as a means of making the Soviet Union negotiate. About 30 per cent are against any form of rearmament. Only 10 per cent are correctly informed about the contents of the dual-track decision, i.e. to

station all planned American medium-range systems, if concrete arms limitation measures have not been agreed by the end of 1983. About 30 per cent think the decision only concerns rearmament. This is also a result of poor information.

23. References to and evidence for the fact that deterrence has functioned for thirty-six years do not suffice in a debate with young people. This deterrence system is certainly not a guarantee of eternal peace; it has its own built-in dynamics which stem from technical progress and the necessity of maintaining a balance of power. This is, however, the prerequisite, if deterrence is to remain plausible. In the long run, this deterrence system is only bearable, if it is supplemented by arms control and if thereby the balance of power is kept on the lowest level possible. We must say and explain this to our public which has become more critical on questions of security policy. And we must tell them that we cannot have unilateral arms limitation and arms control. The Soviet Union has to put a stop to its rearmament spiral. Unilateral Western concessions made in advance increase the danger of martial conflicts. Our country can only secure its future in a Western alliance and on that basis pursue its détente policy with a chance of success.

24. The main accusation levelled by critics of our security policy amounts to the statement that defence is no longer possible today. It is true that defence, in the sense of effective protection of our country and its inhabitants in a nuclear war, is out of the question. But that is not the issue. The issue is deterrence. We must have armed forces as a protection against war and military threat so that we are not faced with foreign demands or ideological situations we do not want. It is a matter of preventing war. . . .

25.

. . .

Questions concerning our security policy are posed more critically and probably more intelligently today. 'Critical peace research' which did not exist originally [as a discipline] has effectively prepared the ground for the present peace movement. We, too, should seek to talk with serious peace researchers. Discussions with critics of this security policy have become more difficult. . . . Each generation has to think over the basic questions of peace anew, and the political and ethical legitimation of our security policy and armed forces as a part of this policy has to be transmitted to each generation. This inner credibility can only be created by open debate.

The armed forces cannot avoid taking an active part in this debate. Explaining the rationale of security policy is certainly a task for politicians as well as for the whole of society, especially for parents and schools. When questions of the legitimacy of their mission are involved, however, the federal armed forces also must become responsive to the intellectual challenge. In the eyes of young people in particular, the task of the federal armed forces cannot be separated from our democracy and the duty of every one of us to support it daily.

26. I ask you to take every opportunity to discuss and publish information on the basic questions of our security policy. You should be guided therein by three principles:

Firstly: The soldier's contribution to securing peace in freedom is his actual and most important task. However, this contribution is only credible if the armed forces possess combat effectiveness. At this point, the critics of deterrence have to be told that it is necessary to be *able* to fight in order not to have to fight.

Secondly: We all long for and want peace. However, that does not suffice for a credible security policy. Allow me to put it differently: a highly admirable, individually ethical pacifism or neutralism is not a security policy which the Federal Republic of Germany can afford.

Thirdly: I emphatically reject those who see a cause for tension and dangers of war in the armed forces and claim that they alone know the right way to keep peace. On several public occasions I have stressed the fact that the Federal Government and the armed forces let no one surpass them in their desire and determination to preserve peace in freedom.

Notes

1. The relevant volume of the series *Foreign Relations of the United States* for the year 1950 shows that not only the Joint Chiefs of Staff were already considering a West German rearmament before the outbreak of the Korean War, but also the British government. Here, no doubt, the prime motive was to reduce the financial liabilities in regard to the British Army of the Rhine. The impression which the then US High Commissioner in Bonn, John McCloy, cabled home to his government was that Adenauer pressed for rearmament both for security reasons and for pressuring the Western allies into hastening the process of the Federal Republic regaining sovereignty.

2. See also Ch. 11 on foreign policy. The whole issue came to the fore again in 1982 as new reports spread about the stationing of chemical weapons of the US army on German soil. Very strong protests, especially from the trade unions in the Palatinate, followed. The Federal Constitutional Court was appealed to.

3. See in general: White Paper 1979, *The Security of the Federal Republic of Germany and the developments of the Federal armed forces*, published in English by the Ministry of Defence in Bonn 1979. See also Figures below, 418ff.

4. In the Weimar Republic the German army had become what was then called a 'state within the state'—one of the reasons for the collapse of the Republic in the early 1930s.

5. See Ch. 2 for the Law on the Defence Commissioner, the Bundestag Committee on Defence and the 'emergency parliament'.

6. The Social Democratic government and its majority in the Bundestag had wanted to make it possible for potential conscientious objectors to claim their status 'by postcard', as it were, i.e. doing away with special boards. The new Christian–Democratic government of Chancellor Kohl introduced a new bill in parliament because the Federal Constitutional Court had stepped in.

7. See Ch. 9, Doc. 9.

8. In the German Democratic Republic the Protestant Church hosted some very courageous efforts especially by the younger generation to call for disarmament in East and West under the slogan: 'Swords into plough shares'. Otherwise 'calls for peace' in all Communist countries have, ever since the 1950s, been officially sponsored as part of an overall Moscow diplomatic strategy and, therefore, been restricted to demands for disarmament by NATO.

9. Other calls for peace, more in line with the policies of the then government and of NATO were issued above all by the trade unions.

10. See White Paper, 1979, above (n.3), 229ff., 261ff. and Figures, 417ff.

13 Berlin

Robert Spencer

Berlin, from 1445 the seat of the Prussian rulers and from 1871 to 1945 the capital of the German Reich, has occupied a unique position in Germany and in Europe since the end of the Second World War. The old core of the city on the banks of the Spree and the districts to the east, now the capital of the German Democratic Republic, today house the communist state's principal institutions. The larger part of Berlin to the west, comprising 54.4 per cent of the 883 square kilometre area included in Greater Berlin in 1922, with a population in 1980 of 1,998,000, still ranks as West Germany's largest city and includes extensive farmlands, lakes, and wooded areas, but is a city without a hinterland. Organized as a city-state, the status of present day West Berlin rests on the wartime agreements among the Allied powers[1]* and the important restatement of its position contained in the agreements of 1971 (Docs. 1a–d).

West Berlin's government is based on the constitution drawn up by the West Berliners and approved by the three Western powers in 1950 (Doc. 2). It provides for a 16-member Senate (Senat) or executive nominated by the Governing Mayor. These nominations have to be confirmed by a popularly elected House of Representatives which first has to vote the Mayor into office. The Senate exercises both state and municipal functions. The Social Democratic Party, revived in June 1945, has dominated West Berlin's politics, outvoting the CDU in every election until 1975 and producing distinguished Governing Mayors such as Ernst Reuter (1945–53) and Willy Brandt (1957–66). In the elections of 10 May 1981, however, the CDU scored a victory, winning 48 per cent of the vote. Richard von Weizsäcker, who had unsuccessfully tried to topple the SPD two years earlier, was elected Governing Mayor

---

* Notes for this Chapter begin on p. 371

and formed a minority government supported by the majority of the FDP deputies. Political change in Berlin (or in Bonn), however, has not weakened determination to preserve the position of West Berlin and its vital links with the Federal Republic (Docs. 3, 4, 5, and 6).

In 1983, as since 1945, Berlin remains a barometer of East–West relations, and concern for its future is a reflection of the city's postwar history which was punctuated by a series of crises. The most dramatic of these was the blockade, by the Soviet Union, of the land and water access routes passing through the surrounding Soviet occupied zone in 1948/49.[2] For an eleven-month period (24 June 1948 to 29 May 1949), the only link between the Western sectors and the West was the airlift, which, by bringing in food and fuel in quantities up to 12,940 tons daily, enabled the city to survive. This operation, unparalleled in the history of aviation, depended on the earlier Four-Power agreements on the establishment of air corridors and the Berlin Air Safety Centre (Doc. 7). The successful defence of Berlin was also due to the determination of the city's population to resist communist pressure, and the blockade marked a decisive stage in forging the partnership of West Berliners with what henceforth became known as the 'Protecting Powers'.

When the blockade was lifted, East and West Berlin both had separate governments, administration and utilities. In subsequent years the lines of division hardened still further, with the formation of the German Democratic Republic and the integration of the Federal Republic into the Western Alliance. The blockade had dealt a severe blow to West Berlin's economic recovery. In 1950 one in three West Berliners was unemployed. Aided by the government of the Federal Republic (Doc. 8), however, West Berlin recovered from the blow and for a decade was the centre of world attention as a unique 'democratic island in a red sea', with an open frontier to the communist East. It served, as an English journalist remarked at the time, as a token of the Four-Power pledge to reunite Germany, as a refuge for the tens of thousands who after 1949 fled East Germany, and as a shop window of the West in the heart of a hostile, but still accessible East.[3]

For the communist East, West Berlin was, as Soviet Party Secretary Nikita Khrushchev put it, 'a bone which stuck in my throat', an anachronism which prevented the consolidation of the German Democratic Republic and the source of a serious drain on its population. In 1958 he set out to solve this problem in his own way (Doc. 9a). Although firm Western resistance led to abortive Four-Power talks, the stalemate was prolonged (Docs. 9b and c). In June 1961, Khrushchev tried to challenge the West again, this time the new U.S. President John F. Kennedy.

After a summit meeting in Vienna, Kennedy insisted on the basic right of the Western powers to be in Berlin and on the 'commitment to sustain—and to defend, if need be', West Berlin and its inhabitants.[4] Less than three weeks later, the government of the GDR made a desperate attempt to stop the human flood through the escape hatch of Berlin, resulting from a form of Torschlusspanik which had seized many of its citizens. Despite SED Party Secretary Walter Ulbricht's statement at a press conference on 15 June that 'nobody intends to build a wall',[5] the German Democratic Republic, with the full backing of its Warsaw Pact allies, proceeded to do just that. On the night of 12–13 August 1961, in a move which the SED leadership said was designed to put an end to 'the hostile activities of the revanchist military forces of Western Germany and West Berlin', the border between the Western and the Soviet sectors was sealed (Docs. 10a–c). From that date East Germans have remained imprisoned by what Governing Mayor von Weizsäcker described on the twentieth anniversary of the construction of the Wall as 'a petrified rejection of humanity'. Despite the 45-kilometre-long, increasingly formidable barriers cutting through the centre of a great city, just under 39,000 East Germans have managed to escape to West Berlin since 1961; 71 persons lost their lives in doing so.[6]

In 1961 West Berlin suffered a severe political, economic and psychological blow. Yet Soviet aims—the creation of a subordinate 'free city'—were frustrated. As the 1960s wore on and West Berliners endured what Willy Brandt referred to as 'the ordeal of co-existence'[7] (Doc. 10c), attempts were made by the West Berlin authorities to lessen the impact of division. In 1963, without compromising the policy of non-recognition of the GDR, the West Berlin Senate succeeded in negotiating an agreement whereby West Berliners could visit relatives in East Berlin (Docs.11a and b). Later in the decade the governments of the Western Alliance insisted on the conclusion of a satisfactory arrangement over Berlin as a precondition for moving towards a preparation of the conference on European security for which the Soviet Union had been calling ever since the XXIII Congress of the CPSU in March 1966 (Doc. 12). Negotiations between the four powers began in the old Control Council building in West Berlin on 26 March 1970 and led, a year and a half later, to the initialling of an agreement on 3 September 1971. With the conclusion of subsequent agreements on traffic and other matters between the Federal Republic and the German Democratic Republic and the ratification by Bonn of the Moscow and Warsaw treaties, the Four-Power agreements came into effect on 3 June 1972.

In the decade since the conclusion of the agreements over Berlin, the tensions over Berlin have largely disappeared and, as former Chancellor Helmut Schmidt put it, 'the existence of Berlin is secured'.[8] Nevertheless, there have been many thousands of complaints over their implementation, arrests along the access routes, and reminders of the continuing element of precariousness in the situation through the reinforcing of the physical barriers by what Governing Mayor von Weizsäcker described as a 'financial wall' in the shape of major increases in the minimum currency exchange requirements. But since 1972 trade and traffic to and from West Berlin has increased, the passage across the German Democratic Republic has been immeasurably eased, telephone communications between West Berlin and East Berlin and the German Democratic Republic have approached 'normalcy', and several millions of West Berliners and West Germans visit the East annually.[9] Apart from pensioners, however, Berliners and East Germans are still precluded from visiting the West. The withdrawal of their city from the point of acute tension between East and West has enabled West Berliners to concentrate on economic problems consequent on their isolated location and to tackle social problems such as those resulting from an unfavourable age structure (23 per cent of West Berlin's population is over 65) and the very large foreign community (over 10 per cent of West Berlin's population, mostly migrant workers from the Mediterranean). Bold new housing developments have been constructed and attempts have been made to develop West Berlin into a conference centre and to add new dimensions to the city's already rich cultural and intellectual life.

Documents 1a–d

The 1971 agreements on Berlin constitute a landmark in the city's postwar history. The protracted East–West negotiations were conducted at three levels: between the Western Powers on the one hand and the Soviet Union on the other; and, following the essential Four-Power agreement of 3 September, between the Federal Republic and the German Democratic Republic and between the Berlin Senate and the German Democratic Republic to reach supplementary agreements. In essence both sides clung to their respective legal views on the status of the divided city and on this basis agreed on general provisions for transit to West Berlin from the Federal Republic and for traffic between the two halves of the former capital.

a) THE FOUR-POWER AGREEMENT ON BERLIN, 3 SEPTEMBER 1971, WITH APPENDICES

Source: Press and Information Office of the Federal Republic, *Documentation relating to the Federal Government's Policy of Détente*, Bonn, 1978, 87–106

The Governments of the United States of America, the French Republic, the Union of Soviet Socialist Republics, and the United Kingdom of Great Britain and Northern Ireland, represented by their Ambassadors, who held a series of meetings in the building formerly occupied by the Allied Control Council in the American Sector of Berlin,

Acting on the basis of their quadripartite rights and responsibilities, and of the corresponding wartime and postwar agreements and decisions of the Four Powers, which are not affected,

Taking into account the existing situation in the relevant area,

Guided by the desire to contribute to practical improvements of the situation,

Without prejudice to their legal positions,

Have agreed on the following:

PART I

General Provisions

1. The four Governments will strive to promote the elimination of tension and the prevention of complications in the relevant area.
2. The four Governments, taking into account their obligations under the Charter of the United Nations, agree that there shall be no use or threat of force in the area and that disputes shall be settled solely by peaceful means.
3. The four Governments will mutually respect their individual and joint rights and responsibilities, which remain unchanged.
4. The four Governments agree that, irrespective of the differences in legal views, the situation which has developed in the area, and as it is defined in this Agreement as well as in the other agreements referred to in this Agreement, shall not be changed unilaterally.

PART II

Provisions Relating to the Western Sectors of Berlin

A. The Government of the Union of Soviet Socialist Republics declares that transit traffic by road, rail and waterways through the territory of the German Democratic Republic of civilian persons and goods between the Western Sectors of Berlin and the Federal Republic of Germany will be unimpeded; that such traffic will be facilitated so as to take place in the most simple and expeditious manner; and that it will receive preferential treatment.

Detailed arrangements concerning this civilian traffic, as set forth in Annex I, will be agreed by the competent German authorities.

B. The Governments of the French Republic, the United Kingdom and the United States of America declare that the ties between the Western Sectors of Berlin and the Federal Republic of Germany will be maintained and developed, taking into account that these Sectors continue not to be a constituent part of the Federal Republic of Germany and not to be governed by it.

Detailed arrangements concerning the relationship between the Western Sectors of Berlin and the Federal Republic of Germany are set forth in Annex II.

C. The Government of the Union of Soviet Socialist Republics declares that communications between the Western Sectors of Berlin and areas bordering on these Sectors and those areas of the German Democratic Republic which do not border on these Sectors will be improved. Permanent residents of the Western Sectors of Berlin will be able to travel to and visit such areas for compassionate, family, religious, cultural or commercial reasons, or as tourists, under conditions comparable to those applying to other persons entering these areas.

. . .

ANNEX I

Communication from the Government of the Union of Soviet Socialist Republics to the Governments of the French Republic, the United Kingdom and the United States of America.

The Government of the Union of Soviet Socialist Republics, with reference to Part II A of the Quadripartite Agreement of this date and after consultation and agreement with the Government of the German Democratic Republic, has the honour to inform the Governments of the French Republic, the United Kingdom and the United States of America that:

1. Transit traffic by road, rail and waterways through the territory of the German Democratic Republic of civilian persons and goods between the Western Sectors of Berlin and the Federal Republic of Germany will be facilitated and unimpeded. It will receive the most simple, expeditious and preferential treatment provided by international practice.

2. Accordingly,

   (a) Conveyances sealed before departure may be used for the transport of civilian goods by road, rail and waterways between the Western Sectors of Berlin and the Federal Republic of Germany. Inspection procedures will be limited to the inspection of seals and accompanying documents.

   . . .

   (c) Through trains and buses may be used for travel between the Western Sectors of Berlin and the Federal Republic of Germany. Inspection procedures will not include any formalities other than identification of persons.

(d) Persons identified as through travellers using individual vehicles between the Western Sectors of Berlin and the Federal Republic of Germany on routes designated for through traffic will be able to proceed to their destinations without paying individual tolls and fees for the use of the transit routes. Procedures applied for such travellers shall not involve delay.

The travellers, their vehicles and personal baggage will not be subject to search, detention or exclusion from use of the designated routes, except in special cases, such as may be agreed by the competent German authorities, where there is sufficient reason to suspect that misuse of the transit routes is intended for purposes not related to direct travel to and from the Western Sectors of Berlin and contrary to generally applicable regulations concerning public order.

(e) Appropriate compensation for fees and tolls and for other costs related to traffic on the communication routes between the Western Sectors of Berlin and the Federal Republic of Germany, including the maintenance of adequate routes, facilities and installations used for such traffic, may be made in the form of an annual lump sum paid to the German Democratic Republic by the Federal Republic of Germany.

3. Arrangements implementing and supplementing the provisions of Paragraphs 1 and 2 above will be agreed by the competent German authorities.

ANNEX II

Communication from the Governments of the French Republic, the United Kingdom and the United States of America to the Government of the Union of Soviet Socialist Republics.

The Governments of the French Republic, the United Kingdom and the United States of America, with reference to Part II B of the Quadripartite Agreement of this date and after consultation with the Government of the Federal Republic of Germany, have the honour to inform the Government of the Union of Soviet Socialist Republics that:

1. They declare, in the exercise of their rights and responsibilities, that the ties between the Western Sectors of Berlin and the Federal Republic of Germany will be maintained and developed, taking into account that these Sectors continue not to be a constituent part of the Federal Republic of Germany and not to be governed by it. The provisions of the Basic Law of the Federal Republic of Germany and of the Constitution operative in the Western Sectors of Berlin which contradict the above have been suspended and continue not to be in effect.

2. The Federal President, the Federal Government, the Bundesversammlung, the Bundesrat and the Bundestag, including their Committees and Frak-

tionen, as well as other state bodies of the Federal Republic of Germany will not perform in the Western Sectors of Berlin constitutional or official acts which contradict the provisions of Paragraph 1.

3. The Government of the Federal Republic of Germany will be represented in the Western Sectors of Berlin to the authorities of the three Governments and to the Senat by a permanent liaison agency.

ANNEX III

Communication from the Government of the Union of Soviet Socialist Republics to the Governments of the French Republic, the United Kingdom and the United States of America

. . .

1. Communications between the Western Sectors of Berlin and areas bordering on these Sectors and those areas of the German Democratic Republic which do not border on these Sectors will be improved.
2. Permanent residents of the Western Sectors of Berlin will be able to travel to and visit such areas for compassionate, family, religious, cultural or commercial reasons, or as tourists, under conditions comparable to those applying to other persons entering these areas. In order to facilitate visits and travel, as described above, by permanent residents of the Western Sectors of Berlin, additional crossing points will be opened.
3. The problems of the small enclaves, including Steinstücken, and of other small areas may be solved by exchange of territory.
4. Telephonic, telegraphic, transport and other external communications of the Western Sectors of Berlin will be expanded.
5. Arrangements implementing and supplementing the provisions of Paragraphs 1 to 4 above will be agreed by the competent German authorities.

ANNEX IV

A. Communication from the Governments of the French Republic, the United Kingdom and the United States of America to the Government of the Union of Soviet Socialist Republics.

The Governments of the French Republic, the United Kingdom and the United States of America, with reference to Part II D of the Quadripartite Agreement of this data and after consultation with the Government of the Federal Republic of Germany, have the honour to inform the Government of the Union of Soviet Socialist Republics that:

1. The Governments of the French Republic, the United Kingdom and the United States of America maintain their rights and responsibilities relating to the representation abroad of the interests of the Western Sectors of Berlin and

their permanent residents, including those rights and responsibilities concerning matters of security and status, both in international organizations and in relations with other countries.

2. Without prejudice to the above and provided that matters of security and status are not affected, they have agreed that:

(a) The Federal Republic of Germany may perform consular services for permanent residents of the Western Sectors of Berlin.

(b) In accordance with established procedures, international agreements and arrangements entered into by the Federal Republic of Germany may be extended to the Western Sectors of Berlin provided that the extension of such agreements and arrangements is specified in each case.

(c) The Federal Republic of Germany may represent the interests of the Western Sectors of Berlin in international organizations and international conferences.

(d) Permanent residents of the Western Sectors of Berlin may participate jointly with participants from the Federal Republic of Germany in international exchanges and exhibitions. Meetings of international organizations and international conferences as well as exhibitions with international participation may be held in the Western Sectors of Berlin. Invitations will be issued by the Senat or jointly by the Federal Republic of Germany and the Senat.

3. The three Governments authorize the establishment of a Consulate General of the USSR in the Western Sectors of Berlin accredited to the appropriate authorities of the three Governments in accordance with the usual procedures applied in those Sectors, for the purpose of performing consular services, subject to provisions set forth in a separate document of this date.

. . .

The Four-Power agreement paved the way for negotiations between the German authorities in West and East to reach more detailed, supplementary agreements within, however, the framework of previous agreements with the Western powers.

b) LETTER OF CHANCELLOR WILLY BRANDT TO THE AMBASSADORS OF THE UNITED STATES, THE UNITED KINGDOM, AND FRANCE.

Source: Press and Information Office of the Federal Republic, *Documentation relating to the Federal Government's Policy of Détente*, Bonn, 1978, 107–8

. . .

I have the honour to confirm receipt of the letter of the Ambassadors of France, the United Kingdom and the United States of America of September 3 together with which the text of the Quadripartite Agreement signed on September 3, 1971, in Berlin was communicated to the Government of the Federal Republic of Germany.

I also have the honour to confirm receipt of the letter of the three Ambassadors of the same date containing clarifications and interpretations which reflect what their Governments understand by the declarations contained in Annex II to the Quadripartite Agreement with regard to the relationship between the Federal Republic of Germany and the Western Sectors of Berlin.

The Government of the Federal Republic of Germany intends taking steps immediately in order to arrive at agreements on concrete arrangements relating to civilian traffic as envisaged in Part IIA of the Quadripartite Agreement.

The Government of the Federal Republic of Germany has taken note of the contents of Your Excellency's letter which were communicated to it in exercising the rights and responsibilities which were retained in pursuance of Article 2 of the Convention on Relations between the Federal Republic of Germany and the Three Powers of May 26, 1952, as amended on October 23, 1954, and which will continue to be respected by the Government of the Federal Republic of Germany.

The Government of the Federal Republic of Germany shares the view and the determination that the ties between the Federal Republic of Germany and Berlin shall be maintained and developed.

In the negotiations between Bonn and East Berlin agreement was reached, for the first time in Berlin's postwar history, on the procedures by which transit traffic between the isolated Western sectors of the city and the territory of the Federal Republic should flow 'unimpeded' and even 'receive preferential treatment' on the access routes.

c) AGREEMENT BETWEEN THE GOVERNMENT OF THE FEDERAL REPUBLIC OF GERMANY AND THE GOVERNMENT OF THE GERMAN DEMOCRATIC REPUBLIC ON TRANSIT TRAFFIC OF CIVILIAN PERSONS AND GOODS BETWEEN THE FEDERAL REPUBLIC OF GERMANY AND BERLIN (WEST), 17 DECEMBER 1971

Source: Press and Information Office of the Federal Republic, *Documentation relating to the Federal Government's Policy of Détente*, Bonn, 1978, 115–31

The Government of the Federal Republic of Germany and the Government of the German Democratic Republic,
Desiring to render a contribution to détente in Europe, and
In accordance with the arrangements of the Agreement of 3 September 1971 between the Governments of the French Republic, the Union of Soviet Socialist Republics, the United Kingdom of Great Britain and Northern Ireland, and the United States of America,
Have agreed to conclude the following Agreement:

Article 1

The subject of this Agreement is the transit traffic by road, rail and waterways through the territory of the German Democratic Republic of civilian persons and goods between the Federal Republic of Germany and the Western Sectors of Berlin—Berlin (West)—hereinafter referred to as transit traffic.

Article 2

1. Transit traffic shall be facilitated and unimpeded. It will receive the most simple, expeditious and preferential treatment provided by international practice.

...

Article 21

This Agreement shall enter into force simultaneously with the Agreement of 3 September 1971 between the French Republic, the Union of Soviet Socialist Republics, the United Kingdom of Great Britain and Northern Ireland, and the United States of America, and shall remain in force together with it.

...

In negotiations between the West Berlin Senate and the government of the German Democratic Republic agreement was reached which permitted West Berliners to visit, for the first time since the expiry of the earlier pass agreement in 1965, East Berlin and the areas of the GDR bordering on West Berlin.

d) ARRANGEMENT BETWEEN THE SENATE AND THE GOVERNMENT OF THE GERMAN DEMOCRATIC REPUBLIC CONCERNING THE FACILITA-TION AND IMPROVEMENT OF TRAVEL AND VISITOR TRAFFIC, 20 DECEMBER 1971

Source: Press and Information Office of the Federal Government, *Documentation relating to the Federal Government's Policy on Détente*, Bonn, 1978, 132–3

In accordance with the arrangements of the Agreement of 3 September 1971 between the Governments of the French Republic, the Union of Soviet Socialist Republics, the United Kingdom of Great Britain and Northern Ireland and the United States of America, and desiring to render a contribution to détente, the *Senat* and the Government of the German Democratic Republic have agreed to facilitate and improve the travel and visitor traffic of permanent residents of the Western Sectors of Berlin/Berlin (West) as follows:

Article 1

(1) Permanent residents of Berlin (West) shall be granted entry one or more times into areas bordering on Berlin (West) and those areas of the German Democratic Republic which do not border on Berlin (West) for visits totalling thirty days a year.

(2) Entry under paragraph (1) above shall be approved for compassionate, family, religious and cultural reasons, and for touring.

Article 2

(1) For entry, permanent residents of Berlin (West) shall require their valid identity card and an entry permit, and for exit, an exit permit of the German Democratic Republic. The required permits are to be applied for with the competent authorities in accordance with the regulations of the German Democratic Republic.

(2) Accompanying children must be entered in the identity card of a parent or guardian or be in possession of their own identity card or a certified photographic likeness. In exceptional cases (for family reasons, vacations), entry may also be permitted for children up to the age of sixteen who are not accompanied by adults.

(3) Permanent residents of Berlin (West) not in possession of an identity card shall require for entry an identity document formally issued in Berlin (West). An appropriate document may also be issued, on application and on payment of a fee, by the competent authorities of the German Democratic Republic, once the identity of the traveller has been established.

Article 3

(1) Entry by permanent residents of Berlin (West) shall take place via the boundary crossing points designated for this purpose.

(2) Permanent residents of Berlin (West) shall be issued with entry permits at the boundary crossing points on the basis of entitlement certificates or telegrams endorsed by the competent authorities of the German Democratic Republic.

Article 4

(1) Permanent residents of Berlin (West) may be granted entry for urgent family and compassionate reasons even though their total visiting time referred to in Article 1 of the present Arrangement has already been exhausted. The permits required for entry may be issued at the boundary crossing points on the basis of officially endorsed telegrams.

. . .

Documents 2a–b

In approving the 1950 Berlin Constitution (which could of course only be applicable to the Western Sectors) the Western occupying powers were concerned to reserve their special rights by denying to Berlin the legal status of a constitutional federal state (Bundesland) within the Federal Republic.

a) STATEMENT ISSUED BY WEST BERLIN COMMANDANTS, 29 AUGUST 1950

Source: Documents on Berlin, 1943–1963, Munich, 1963, 121–2

. . .

1. The Allied Kommandatura has studied the draft Berlin Constitution which was submitted to the Allied Kommandatura on April 22, 1948, and the supplement and amendment which were passed by the Berlin City Assembly on August 4, 1950, and submitted for approval on the same date.

2. In approving this Constitution and the proposed changes thereto, the Allied Kommandatura makes the following reservations:

(a) The powers vested in the city government by the Constitution are subject to the provisions of the Statement of Principles which was promulgated on May 14, 1949, or any modifications thereof.

(b) Article 1, Paragraphs 2 and 3 are suspended.

(c) Article 87 is interpreted as meaning that during the transitional period Berlin shall possess none of the attributes of a twelfth Land. The provisions of this Article concerning the Basic Law will only apply to the extent necessary to prevent a conflict between this law and the Berlin Constitution.

Furthermore, the provisions of any Federal law shall apply to Berlin only after they have been voted upon by the House of Representatives and passed as a Berlin law.

b) CONSTITUTION OF BERLIN, 1 SEPTEMBER, 1950

Source: Documents on Berlin, 1943–1963, Munich, 1963, 122–3

Pursuant to Article 35 of the Temporary Constitution of Greater Berlin the City Assembly (Stadtverordnetenversammlung) has drafted the following Constitution and passed it on August 4, 1950, with the approval of the City Executive (Magistrat). It is hereby promulgated:

Preamble

In the resolve to protect the freedoms and rights of all individuals, to regulate the community and the economy on a democratic basis, to serve the spirit of social progress and peace, and in the desire to remain the capital of a new united Germany, Berlin has adopted this Constitution:

Chapter I
Fundamental Provisions

Article 1

(1) Berlin is a German Land and at the same time a City.
(2) Berlin is a Land of the Federal Republic of Germany.
(3) The Basic Law and the laws of the Federal Republic of Germany are binding on Berlin.

Article 2

(1) All public power derives from the whole of the German citizens having their domicile in Berlin.
(2) Under this Constitution the citizens manifest their will, directly, by election of the Popular Representative Body and by referendum, indirectly through the Popular Representative Body.

Article 3

(1) Legislative power is exclusively vested in the Popular Representative Body and, by means of referendum, in the people. Executive power is in the hands of the Government and the Administration subordinate to it, judicial power in the hand of independent Courts.
(2) The tasks of Berlin as a municipality, an association of municipalities (Gemeindeverband) and a Land, are dealt with by the Popular Representative Body, the Government and the Administration.

Article 4

(1) Berlin comprises the area of the former Territorial Corporation of Greater Berlin, the boundaries being those of the date when this Constitution comes into force. Any territorial change requires the consent of the Popular Representative Body.
(2) Berlin is divided into twenty Boroughs (Bezirke). Borough boundaries may be changed and the number of the Boroughs reduced or increased by law only.

Article 5

The heraldic bear will appear in the flag, the coat-of-arms and the seal of Berlin, the colours of the flag being white and red.

. . .

Article 87

(1) Article 1, paragraphs (2) and (3) of this Constitution shall come into force as soon as the application of the Basic Law for the Federal Republic of Germany is no longer subject to any restriction in Berlin.

(2) In the transition period the City Council can establish by law that any specific law of the Federal Republic of Germany is applicable to Berlin also without change.

(3) Insofar as the application in Berlin of the Basic Law for the Federal Republic of Germany is not subject to any restriction (paragraph 1) in the transition period, Basic Law provisions are effective in Berlin also. They override the provisions of the Constitution. In specific cases the City Council can, with a two-thirds majority of the members present, decide to the contrary. . . .

(4) As far as possible, the constitutionally-established official agencies of Berlin should, in the transition period, observe the Basic Law provisions governing the relations of the Federation and the Länder as a pattern of legislation and administration.

. . .

Document 3

Elected Governing Mayor in 1981, the respected CDU leader Richard von Weizsäcker confronted new social problems as well as more familiar ones stemming from West Berlin's isolation.

STATEMENT ON GOVERNMENT POLICY BY GOVERNING MAYOR RICHARD VON WEIZSÄCKER, 2 JULY 1981

Source: Presse- und Informationsamt, VI, No. 27, Berlin, 1981

I. *The Political Change*

For the first time since the war, the Berliners have brought about a political change in an election. For the first time in the history of Berlin, a Senate made up entirely of the Berlin CDU appears before the House of Representatives. The Senate is grateful to everyone who made this possible. It is aware of its responsibility to all citizens.

. . .

IX. *Foreigners*

The number of foreign fellow citizens has risen to approximately 233,000, of which about 114,000 are Turkish. The figures continue to rise rapidly. Responsible cooperation on the part of all involved is imperative in order to prevent increasing grounds for conflict. It is necessary for our foreign fellow citizens to make decisions affecting their whole lives. It is necessary for us to throw genuine life-lines to the foreigners who are willing to integrate. But this can only succeed if the number does not increase.

In the view of the Senate, our foreign fellow citizens must in the long run choose between two possibilities:

—either they return to their native country; the Senate will offer material incentives and support,
—or they remain in Berlin; this includes the decision to become naturalized Germans in the long run.

A third way is no permanent solution, i.e. to stay here but not and never to want to become a Berliner. This would lead to a constant and mutual isolation of these sections of the population. Several cities within one city, that is bound to go wrong. Berlin has to put up with the Wall. Our city cannot on top of this put up with fences which we erect ourselves or which we permit [to exist].

Every conceivable help is to be given to those prepared to accept integration. The Senate will favour integration programmes which allow room for the cultural independence of the foreigners.

We Berliners must be prepared to cooperate with the foreigners. Prejudices and hostilities between sections of the population must not grow in the free part of the city. It is necessary to develop the awareness that Germans and foreigners can respect and enrich one another. . . .

X. *Rule of Law*

. . .

The Senate will take its stand in every discussion which serves the purpose of remedying social abuses. It will also protect the right of all citizens openly to stand up for their convictions and to demonstrate. In order to secure these fundamental freedoms the Senate will protect the rule of law with determination. It will oppose every deed of violence.

The foremost task for the Senate is to restore safety in the streets. It will relieve the police from administrative occupations, check the regulations for duty hours and ensure that outside duty is intensified. It will meet the need for security of senior citizens in particular by reinforcing the foot patrols in their areas. . . .

. . .

XIV. *Berlin Policy and German Policy*

1. Many of the major tasks in our city also exist in other big cities. In so far as they appear earlier and more acutely in Berlin than elsewhere, we shall take the opportunity to find solutions which may serve as examples for others.

However, there is no real comparison between Berlin and other metropolises. The exposed situation of our city produces particular problems. It prevents solutions which are available elsewhere. Divided in the middle, with no surrounding countryside, separated by hundreds of kilometres from one part of Germany and by a wall and barbed wire from the other, under the sovereignty of the protecting powers, with no individual contribution towards defence; all this compared with any other city involves drastically different living habits, population structure, age structure and above all changes in the motives for people to come or go.

In dealing with bottlenecks in the city, we cannot escape to the surroundings as others do. Some powerful neighbours therefore speculate upon a slow, internal wasting away of our strength. It is thus even more important for us to avoid wrong developments and internal shortcomings on our own. For this is also a prerequisite of our external security.

In no other metropolis is there this inseparable Berlin connection between internal vitality and external existence.

We Berliners seek neither crises or herioc roles. In the long run, we can gain the inner strength which we need under the difficult conditions of our situation from the prospect of the future. This prospect is and remains peacefully to overcome the division of Europe, Germany and Berlin. . . .

2. We stand up for these aims in the freedom which our protecting powers guarantee us. The Senate thanks the United States of America, Great Britain and France for their unbreakable commitment. The Berliners are and remain reliable friends of the protecting powers and all their civilian and uniformed members.

. . .

Document 4

SPEECH BY FEDERAL PRESIDENT KARL CARSTENS ON SIGNING THE GOLDEN BOOK, 13 JULY 1979

Source: Karl Carstens, *Reden und Interviews*, Presse-und Informationsamt, I, Bonn, 1981, 31–3

It is with the greatest of pleasure that I follow the example set by my predecessors to pay the first visit outside of Bonn after taking office to Berlin. I am grateful to you for your friendly welcome.

Every German has Berlin at heart in a special way. In the last 100 years the history of Berlin has mirrored the fate of our people. This city is a symbol of German unity and German separation. And it is an indication of the freedom and the desire to uphold this freedom and the basic values of our democratic state system.

. . .

This modern metropolis does not only make a large contribution to the economic strength of the Federal Republic of Germany and the European Community; it does not only shelter great memories for the whole of Germany, but it is also the seat of important cultural institutions such as the National Gallery, the State Library, the Philharmonic Orchestra, the German Opera, the Foundation for Prussian Cultural Treasures (Stiftung Preußischer Kulturbesitz) and many others, whose effectiveness influences our whole country. Everyone who comes here feels the pulsating intellectual life. I am confident that Berlin can make full use of its intellectual position between East and West as a city of human, political and scientific meetings, as a city of congresses and exhibitions. The whole of Europe will benefit therefrom.

The fact that we can make a confident prognosis for this city today is thanks to the love of freedom and the sober political sense of the Berlin population, to the prudence and caution of Berlin's politicians and last but not least to the determination and care of the three powers under whose protection this part of the city rests. This is an act of friendship which the three powers perform for Germany. We are gratefully aware of this.

. . .

Document 5

SPEECH BY US PRESIDENT RONALD REAGAN IN BERLIN, 11 JUNE 1982

Source: United States Department of State Bulletin, Vol. 82, No. 2064, June 1982, 37–8

It was one of Germany's greatest sons, Goethe, who said that 'There is strong shadow where there is much light'. In our times, Berlin, more than any other place in the world, is such a meeting place of light and shadow, tyranny and freedom. To be here is truly to stand on freedom's edge and in the shadow of a wall that has come to symbolize all that is darkest in the world today, to sense how shining and priceless—and how much in need of constant vigilance and protection our legacy of liberty is.

This day marks a happy return for us. We paid our first visit to this great city more than 3 years ago, as private citizens. As with every other citizen of Berlin or visitor to Berlin, I came away with a vivid impression of a city that is more than a place on the map—a city that is a testament to what is both most inspiring and most troubling about the time we live in.

Thomas Mann once wrote that 'A man lives not only his personal life, as an individual, but also, consciously or unconsciously, the life of his epoch . . .'. Nowhere is this more true than in Berlin where each moment of everyday life is spent against the backdrop of contending global systems and ideas. To be a Berliner is to live the great historic struggle of this age, the latest chapter in man's timeless quest for freedom.

As Americans, we understand this. Our commitment to Berlin is a lasting one. Thousands of our citizens have served here since the first small contingent of

American troops arrived on July 4, 1945, the anniversary of our independence as a nation. Americans have served here not as conquerors but as guardians of the freedom of West Berlin and its brave, proud people.

... My visit here today is proof that this American commitment has been worthwhile. Our freedom is indivisible.

The American commitment to Berlin is much deeper than our military presence here. In the 37 years since World War II, a succession of American presidents has made it clear that our role in Berlin is emblematic of our larger search for peace throughout Europe and the world. Ten years ago this month, that search brought into force the Quadripartite Agreement on Berlin. A decade later, West Berliners live more securely, can travel more freely, and, most significantly, have more contact with friends and relatives in East Berlin and East Germany than was possible 10 years ago. These achievements reflect the realistic approach of allied negotiators who recognized that practical progress can be made even while basic differences remain between East and West.

... The United States remains committed to the Berlin agreement. We will continue to expect strict observance and full implementation in all aspects of this accord, including those which apply to the eastern sector of Berlin. ...

And let there be no doubt: The United States will continue to honor its commitment to Berlin. Our forces will remain here as long as necessary to preserve the peace and protect the freedom of the people of Berlin. For us the American presence in Berlin, as long as it is needed, is not a burden. It is a sacred trust. ...

Document 6

SPEECH BY FEDERAL CHANCELLOR HELMUT KOHL AT SCHLOSS CHAR-
LOTTENBURG, BERLIN, 18 OCTOBER 1982

Source: Presse- und Informationsamt der Bundesregierung, *Bulletin*, No. 97, 26
October 1982, 897–9

... To come directly to the point: I do find it perfectly natural that the first trip of a newly elected Federal Chancellor takes him to Berlin. I find it natural because I am one of those people who not only says today, but has always said and felt that for many reasons we must take the part of Berlin and give this city a great deal; yet we have also received a lot and continue to do so. ...

It is not the fault of the Berliners that they have fully to suffer the effects of German history, that they have to bear the division of their city and the division of their mother-country with all the results and consequences. None of us, in any single city, in any single village of the Federal Republic of Germany has the right to say: it has nothing to do with me. For it is in Berlin that the fate of the Germans will be decided in peace and freedom.

During the next few weeks, when we talk with heads of business and leading representatives about the economy, we shall also have to consider the foolish argument that some people offer: after all, is Berlin actually safe? My answer can be but brief: if Berlin is not safe, then my home town Ludwigshafen is not safe any longer, either. We are all in the same boat. . . .

I think it should also be stressed more strongly what a European city Berlin has always been, a European capital. Just now, in this Schloss, we looked at the designs for the manufacture of china in former times. From Petersburg to London, from Lyon and Dijon to Paris and Antwerp, everything from this large European society of times gone by was naturally represented.

Today, Berlin does of course still have its natural rank and position as a European capital and a European city. And all that together provides a chance for me to take the measure of Berlin in daily politics, to learn in Berlin that we will be judged by the perspectives that have been historically anchored in this city, by the history of our own people and, in retrospect, by later generations of our children or grandchildren, and that we quite simply have to stand examination by History's yardstick in these critical times. . . .

Document 7

While no precise agreements dealing with civilian land and water transit traffic through the Soviet-occupied Zone were concluded at the start of the Allied occupation of Berlin, the agreement reached on air traffic survived the blockade and subsequent crises.

FLIGHT RULES BY ALLIED CONTROL AUTHORITY AIR DIRECTORATE FOR AIRCRAFT FLYING IN AIR CORRIDORS AND IN BERLIN CONTROL ZONE, 22 OCTOBER 1946

Source: Documents on Berlin, 1943–1963, Munich, 1963, 39–41

Section I

General

1. a. *Object.* To ensure the maximum safety in flight of all aircraft flying in the corridors and in the Berlin Control Zone under all conditions.

. . .

2. *Air Corridors in Germany.* The following air corridors have been established.

> Frankfurt–Berlin
> Bückeburg–Berlin
> Hamburg–Berlin

Each of the above corridors is 20 English miles (32 kilometers) wide, i.e. 10 miles (16 kilometers) each side of the centre line. It is probable that from time to time additional corridors may be established, and these rules apply equally to any such corridors.

3. *Berlin Control Zone (B.C.Z.)*

a. The Berlin Control Zone is defined as the air space between ground level and 10,000 feet (3000 meters) within a radius of 20 miles (32 kilometers) from the Allied Control Authority Building in which is established the Berlin Air Safety Center (B.A.S.C.)

b. The Berlin Control Zone is a zone of free flight for all aircraft entering the zone to land on the Berlin airfields or taking off to depart therefrom.

. . .

4. *Berlin Air Safety Center (B.A.S.C.)* The Berlin Air Safety Center has been established in the Allied Control Authority Building with the object of ensuring safety of flight for all aircraft in the Berlin area. The safety Center regulates all flying in the Berlin Control Zone and also in the corridors extending from Berlin to the boundaries of adjacent control zones.

. . .

Document 8

The following law, the third of its kind, laid down the validity of federal law in Berlin and specified that grants would be made annually to the Land Berlin from the federal budget.

BERLIN AND THE FEDERAL REPUBLIC: THIRD TRANSFER LAW, 4 JAN-UARY 1952

Source: BGBl., I, 9 January 1952

. . .

§ 11 *Continued Validity of Existing Laws*

Laws in force before the first constituent meeting of the Bundestag which had become Federal law in the other territories within the purview of the Basic Law and which continue to be valid in the Land Berlin will be Federal law in the Land Berlin when this law is put into force in the Land Berlin according to § 19 (1) . . .

. . .

§ 13 *Other Federal Laws*

Other Federal laws which are promulgated for territories within the purview of the Basic Law simultaneously with this law or after it has come into force and the validity of which is explicitly stated for the territory of the Land Berlin, shall be put into force in the Land Berlin within one month of its promulgation in the

Federal Law Gazette or the Federal Gazette in accordance with article 87, § 2 of the Constitution of Berlin . . .

. . .

§ 15 *General Regulations Concerning Legal Alignment*

(1) Insofar as no other stipulations arise from this law and its supplements, the Land Berlin will adopt the Federal law with the same text with which it is in force in the other territories within the purview of the Basic Law. Deviations are permissible only insofar as they are determined by:

1. reference to previously differing regulations of the Land Berlin,
2. the special laws of the Land Berlin permitted by this law,
3. differing titles of authorities in the Land Berlin.

(2) The Federal government is authorized to extend the purview of the Federal law which is not yet in force in the area of the Land Berlin by authority of a special regulation, by an administrative order to the area of the Land Berlin, insofar as it is put into force in the Land Berlin according to Article 87, § 2 of its Constitution.

§ 16 *Federal Grant to the Budget of the Land Berlin*

(1) The Land Berlin receives a grant to cover the deficit in the Land budget with effect from April 1, 1951. The amount of the Federal grant is determined by law on establishing the Federal budget. The Federal grant is to be transferred to the Land Berlin in monthly instalments.

(2) The Federal grant is to be assessed so that the Land Berlin can fulfill the tasks arising from its special position. . . .

. . .

§ 19 *Legal Take-Over in Berlin*[10]

(1) This law shall come into force as soon as the Land Berlin decides to apply it according to Article 87, § 2.

(2) The application of this law by the Land Berlin is a prerequisite of the financial contributions to the Land Berlin to which the Federation is committed by the terms of this law.

. . .

Documents 9a–c

What follows is a drastically shortened version of the Soviet Note which marked the opening of the second Berlin crisis and inaugurated a pro-

longed war of notes and a series of conferences which failed to resolve
East–West differences over Berlin.

a) NOTE FROM THE GOVERNMENT OF THE USSR TO THE GOVERNMENT
OF THE UNITED STATES, 27 NOVEMBER 1958

Source: Documents on Berlin, 1945–1963, Munich, 1963, 181–95

The problem of Berlin, which is situated in the center of the German Democratic
Republic but the western part of which is cut off from the GDR as a result of
foreign occupation, deeply affects not only the national interests of the German
people but also the interests of all nations desirous of establishing lasting peace in
Europe. . . . A situation of constant friction and tension has prevailed for many
years in this city. . . . Berlin . . . has now become a dangerous center of contradiction between the Great Powers, allies in the last war. . . .

The policy of the U.S.A., Britain, and France with respect to West Germany
had led to the violation of those provisions of the Potsdam Agreement designed to
ensure the unity of Germany as a peace-loving and democratic state. . . . The
Government of the FRG, encouraged by the Western Powers, is systematically
fanning the 'cold war,' and . . . is nurturing plans for abolishing the GDR and
strengthening at the latter's expense its own militaristic state. . . .

There is another program for uniting Germany, . . . advocated by the German
Democratic Republic, . . . for uniting Germany as a peace-loving and democratic
state, . . . that is, through agreement and contacts between the two German states
and through the establishment of a German confederation. . . . The Soviet
Union, as well as other states interested in strengthening the peace in Europe,
supports the proposals of the German Democratic Republic for the peaceful
unification of Germany. . . . Consequently, the policy pursued by the United
States, Great Britain and France, directed as it is toward the militarization of
West Germany and toward involving it in the military bloc of the Western
Powers, has also prevented the enforcement of those provisions of the Potsdam
Agreement that pertain to Germany's unity.

Actually, of all the Allied agreements on Germany, only one is being carried
out today. It is the agreement on the so-called quadripartite status of Berlin. On
the basis of that status, the Three Western Powers are ruling the roost in West
Berlin, turning it into a kind of state within a state and using it as a center from
which to pursue subversive activity against the GDR, the Soviet Union, and the
other parties to the Warsaw Treaty. The United States, Great Britain, and
France are freely communicating with West Berlin through lines of communication passing through the territory and the airspace of the German Democratic
Republic, which they do not even want to recognize.

The governments of the Three Powers are seeking to keep in force the long-
since obsolete part of the wartime agreements that governed the occupation of
Germany and entitled them in the past to stay in Berlin. At the same time, as

stated above, the Western Powers have grossly violated the Four-Power agreements, including the Potsdam Agreement, . . . The Four-Power status of Berlin came into being because Berlin, as the capital of Germany, was designated as the seat of the Control Council established for Germany's administration during the initial period of occupation. This status has been scrupulously observed by the Soviet Union. . . . The U.S.A., Great Britain, and France . . . have chosen to abuse in a flagrant manner their occupation rights in Berlin and have exploited the Four-Power status of the city for their own purposes to the detriment of the Soviet Union, the German Democratic Republic, and the other Socialist countries. . . .

It is obvious that the Soviet Union, just as the other parties to the Warsaw Treaty, cannot tolerate such a situation any longer. For the occupation regime in West Berlin to continue would be tantamount to recognizing something like a privileged position of the NATO countries, for which there is, of course, no reason whatsoever. . . .

In this connection, the Government of the U.S.S.R. hereby notifies the United States Government that the Soviet Union regards as null and void the 'Protocol of the Agreement between the Governments of the Union of Soviet Socialist Republics, the United States of America, and the United Kingdom on the zones of occupation in Germany and on the administration of Greater Berlin,' of September 12, 1944, and the related supplementary agreements. . . . The Soviet Government will enter into negotiations with the Government of the GDR at an appropriate time with a view to transferring to the German Democratic Republic the functions temporarily performed by the Soviet authorities by virtue of the above-mentioned Allied agreements and under the agreement between the U.S.S.R. and the GDR of September 20, 1955. . . .

Should the Government of the United States be unwilling to contribute in such a way to the implementation of the political principles of the Allied agreements on Germany, it will have no reason, either legal or moral, for insisting on the preservation of the Four-Power status of Berlin. . . .

An independent solution to the Berlin problem must be found in the very near future. . . . It is necessary to prevent West Berlin from being used any longer as a springboard for intensive espionage, sabotage, and other subversive activities against Socialist countries, the GDR, and the U.S.S.R. or, to quote the leaders of the United States Government, to prevent its being used for 'indirect aggression' against the countries of the Socialist camp. . . .

Of course, the most correct and natural way to solve the problem would be for the western part of Berlin, now actually detached from the GDR, to be reunited with its eastern part and for Berlin to become a unified city within the state in whose territory it is situated.

However, the Soviet Government . . . would consider it possible to solve the West Berlin question at the present time by the conversion of West Berlin into an independent political unit—a free city, [which] could have its own government and run its own economic, administrative, and other affairs.

The Four Powers which shared in the administration of Berlin after the war could, as well as both of the German states, undertake to respect the status of West Berlin as a free city. . . .

For its part, the Soviet Government would have no objection to the United Nations also sharing, in one way or other, in observing the free-city status of West Berlin. . . . The Soviet Government is prepared to enter into negotiations with the Government of the United States of America and with those of the other states concerned on granting West Berlin the status of a demilitarized free city. In case this proposal is not acceptable to the Government of the U.S.A. then there will no longer remain any topic for negotiations between the former occupying powers on the Berlin question. . . . The Soviet Government proposes to make no changes in the present procedure for military traffic of the U.S.A., Great Britain, and France from West Berlin to the FRG for half a year. . . . If the above-mentioned period is not utilized to reach an adequate agreement, the Soviet Union will then carry out the planned measures through an agreement with the GDR. It is envisaged that the German Democratic Republic, like any other independent state, must fully deal with questions concerning its space, i.e., exercise its sovereignty on land, on water, and in the air. At the same time, there will terminate all contacts still maintained between representatives of the armed forces and other officials of the Soviet Union in Germany and corresponding representatives of the armed forces and other officials of the U.S.A., Great Britain, and France on questions pertaining to Berlin. . . .

Caught off balance by the Krushchev ultimatum, the Western powers firmly reasserted their rights in Berlin, but wavered between toughness and conciliation as they sought a negotiated solution.

b) COMMUNIQUÉ OF THE FOREIGN MINISTERS OF THE UNITED STATES, THE UNITED KINGDOM, FRANCE, AND THE FEDERAL REPUBLIC OF GERMANY, PARIS, 14 DECEMBER 1958

Source: Documents on Berlin, 1943–1963, Munich, 1963, 136–7

The Foreign Ministers of France the Federal Republic of Germany, the United Kingdom and the United States [who] met on December 14, 1958, in Paris to discuss developments in the Berlin situation . . . had the benefit of an oral statement on the situation in Berlin by Herr Brandt, Governing Mayor of that city.

The Foreign Ministers of France, the United Kingdom and the United States once more reaffirmed the determination of their governments to maintain their position and their rights with respect to Berlin including the right of free access.

They found unacceptable a unilateral repudiation by the Soviet Government of its obligations to the Governments of France, the United Kingdom and the United States in relation to their presence in Berlin and the freedom of access to that city or the substitution of the German authorities of the Soviet Zone for the Soviet Government insofar as those rights are concerned.

. . .

The Western Powers' stand was backed by the NATO Council, whose declaration was subsequently repeatedly cited to underline the Alliance's commitment to Berlin.

c) COMMUNIQUÉ ISSUED FOLLOWING MINISTERIAL MEETING OF THE NORTH ATLANTIC COUNCIL, PARIS, WITH APPENDED DECLARATION ON BERLIN, 16–18 DECEMBER 1958

Source: NATO Final Communiqués, 1949–1974, Brussels, n.d., 121–4

. . .

2. In a comprehensive survey of the international situation, the Council gave first place to the question of Berlin. The Member countries made clear their resolution not to yield to threats. Their unanimous view on Berlin was expressed in the Council's Declaration of 16th December. The Council will continue to follow this question with close attention and will shortly discuss the replies to be sent to the Soviet notes of 27th November.

. . .

DECLARATION ON BERLIN

The North Atlantic Council examined the question of Berlin.

2. The Council declares that no State has the right to withdraw unilaterally from its international engagements. It considers that the denunciation by the Soviet Union of the inter-allied agreements on Berlin can in no way deprive the other parties of their rights or relieve the Soviet Union of its obligations. Such methods destroy the mutual confidence between nations which is one of the foundations of peace.

3. The Council fully associates itself with the views expressed on the subject by the governments of the United States, the United Kingdom, France and the Federal Republic of Germany in their statement of 14th December.

4. The demands expressed by the Soviet Government have created a serious situation which must be faced with determination.

5. The Council recalls the responsibilities which each member state has assumed in regard to the security and welfare of Berlin, and the maintenance of the position of the Three Powers in that city. The member states of NATO could not approve a solution of the Berlin question which jeopardised the right of the three

Western Powers to remain in Berlin as long as their responsibilities require it, and did not assure freedom of communication between that city and the free world. The Soviet Union would be responsible for any action which had the effect of hampering this free communication or endangering this freedom. The two million inhabitants of West Berlin have just reaffirmed in a free vote their overwhelming approval and support for that position.

6. The Council considers that the Berlin question can only be settled in the framework of an agreement with the USSR on Germany as a whole. It recalls that the Western Powers have repeatedly declared themselves ready to examine this problem, as well as those of European security and disarmament. They are still ready to discuss all these problems.

. . .

Documents 10a–c

The three documents which follow are intended to illustrate the decision of the German Democratic Republic, backed by the Warsaw Pact powers, to erect barriers along the sector boundary, the anxiety in West Berlin resulting from the uncertain response of the Western powers to the East German move and the Berlin government's policy in a period in which it had perforce to 'live with the Wall'.

a) DECREE OF THE MINISTER OF THE INTERIOR OF THE GERMAN DEMOCRATIC REPUBIC, EAST BERLIN, 12 AUGUST 1961

Source: Documents on Berlin, 1943–1963, Munich, 1963, 273–4

By virtue of the resolution [sic] of the Government of the German Democratic Republic of August 12, 1961, the Minister of the Interior issues the following direction [sic], to come into effect immediately:

1. In road traffic between West Berlin and Democratic Berlin, the following crossing-points remain open to motor-cars and other vehicles and to pedestrians:

Kopenhagener Strasse	Heinrich-Heine-Strasse
Wollankstrasse	Oberbaum Brücke
Bornholmer Strasse	Puschkinallee
Brunnenstrasse	Elsenstrasse
Chausseestrasse	Sonnenallee
Brandenburger Tor	Rudower Strasse
Friedrichstrasse	

2. For the visit of a person to West Berlin, citizens of the German Democratic Republic, including citizens of the capital of the German Democratic Republic (Democratic Berlin) require a permit from either the competent People's Police

circuit office (Kreisamt) or the competent People's Police inspectorate (Inspektion). . . .

3. Peaceable citizens of West Berlin may cross at these points into Democratic Berlin on the presentation of their West Berlin identity card (Personalausweis).

4. For the visit to the capital of the German Democratic Republic (Democratic Berlin), inhabitants of Western Germany receive, as hitherto, permits covering a one-day's stay at the four allocating centres Wollankstrasse, Brandenburger Tor, Elsenstrasse and the Friedrichstrasse railway-station on presentation of their identification documents (identity card or passport).

5. For foreign nationals the existing regulations continue to be valid. For members of the Diplomatic Corps and of the Western Occupation Forces the system in force at present continues.

6. Citizens of the German Democratic Republic who do not work in Berlin are asked to refrain from travelling to Berlin until further notice.

b) LETTER FROM GOVERNING MAYOR WILLY BRANDT TO PRESIDENT JOHN F. KENNEDY, 16 AUGUST 1961

Source: Bundesministerium für innerdeutsche Beziehungen, *Dokumente zur Deutschlandpolitik*, IV. Reihe, Vol. 7, Frankfurt, 1976, 48ff.

. . . The actions of the Ulbricht regime, supported by the Soviet Union and the rest of the East bloc, have almost fully destroyed what remained of the Four-Power status. While the commandants of the Allied Powers have previously protested against the parades of the so-called People's Army, the military occupation of the Eastern Sector by the People's Army leaves little more open to them than tardy and rather indecisive action. The illegal sovereignty of the government of East Berlin has been recognized through acceptance of the restriction of crossing points and of entry into the Eastern Sector. I consider this a serious turning-point in the postwar history of this city, such as has not been experienced since the Blockade.

This development has not altered the will to resistance of the population of West Berlin, but it has succeeded in casting doubt upon the capability and determination of the Three Powers to react. In this connection it is very significant that the West has always appealed immediately to the existing Four-Power status. I am well aware that the guarantees of the freedom of the population, of the presence of the troops and of free access apply, only to West Berlin. Nevertheless, the issue is that this is a serious turning-point in the life of the German people as well as an expulsion [of the Western allies] from areas of collective responsibility (Berlin and Germany as a whole) which will affect collective Western prestige. The political and psychological danger can be seen in two areas:

1. Inaction and purely defensive action could unleash a crisis of confidence in the Western powers.

2. Inaction and purely defensive action could lead to excessive confidence on

the part of the East Berlin regime, whose newspapers today boasted of the success of the demonstration of military strength.

The Soviet Union has used the People's Army to achieve half of its proposals for a 'free city'. Act Two is only a question of time. After Act Two we would find a Berlin which resembles a ghetto. Having lost not only its function as the refuge of freedom and the symbol of hope for reunification, it will also be cut off from the free section of Germany. Then, instead of a refugee movement into Berlin, we might see the beginning of a flight out of Berlin.

I consider it appropriate in this situation that the Western powers demand, as a matter of course, the reestablishment of Four-Power responsibility, but at the same time proclaim a Three-Power status in West Berlin. The Three Powers should repeat the guarantee of their presence in West Berlin until German reunification and if necessary have that underpinned by a plebiscite of the population of West Berlin and the Federal Republic. The present situation also calls for a clear statement that the German question is in no way resolved in the eyes of the Western Powers, but rather that they will insist on a peace settlement which reflects the self-determination of the German people and the security of all concerned. Apart from this, I believe that the West, on its own initiative, should bring the Berlin question before the United Nations, at least on the basis of a blatant Soviet violation of the Declaration of Human Rights. It seems to me to be better to force the Soviet Union into the role of an accused committed for trial rather than to let the same issue be discussed on the basis of petitions from other states.

I do not expect any substantial material change in the present situation to result from such measures and recall the reasons formerly given for rejecting discussions with the Soviet Union with some bitterness. The rationale then was that one should not negotiate under pressure. Now that we are faced with complete extortion, I am beginning to hear the argument being made that negotiations are unavoidable. In such a situation, when the chances of initiating a deal are already so limited, it is even more important at least to show political initiative.

Following the acceptance of Soviet action which is illegal and has been labelled illegal and in view of the many tragedies now taking place in East Berlin and in the Soviet zone, we will continue to live under the ultimate threat. A certain visible strengthening of the American garrison would be most welcome. . . .

c) POLICY DECLARATION OF THE BERLIN GOVERNMENT, READ BEFORE THE BERLIN PARLIAMENT BY GOVERNING MAYOR WILLY BRANDT, 18 MARCH 1963

Source: Documents on Berlin, 1943–1963, Munich, 1963, 354–7

. . .

The Senate will continue to pursue unchanged the present principles of Berlin policy approved by the House of Representatives which have repeatedly met with the express approval of the Federal Government and the Bundestag.

. . .

The starting-point of this policy is the realisation that there is no isolated Berlin problem. From the very beginning it has formed a part—even if an integral one—of the German problem, and it will remain inextricably tied up with the German problem: . . .

The status of this city and the situation in it are not the cause, but only one of the effects, of the antagonisms and tensions between East and West. This status is not in the least a hindrance to the efforts being made to bring about a relaxation of international tensions. On the contrary, from the Soviet Union's policy vis-à-vis Berlin it is possible to infer how far it is really interested in a relaxation of tension internationally, above all in Europe.

The Senate sticks firmly to the opinion that there is no reason to change the status of Berlin prior to a peace settlement for Germany. There is, however, no way leading to a peace settlement for Germany as a whole which by-passes the right of the German people to self-determination. As long as the Soviet Union debars the German people from exercising the right to self-determination there is no genuine solution to the German problem.

Until that point is reached the Western Powers must keep up firmly their legal claim to the whole of Berlin. Their original rights in Berlin are valid until a peace settlement for Germany has been reached. The Soviet Union cannot dispose of these rights unilaterally.

All the same, the fundamental distinction between the superiority of the legal claims and the political reality in this city must not be overlooked.

Berlin's four-Power status has been undermined to the extreme limits by the unilateral and unlawful measures taken by the Soviet Union.

The erection of the Wall represents the most grievous attack on the Four-Power status. To all intents and purposes it signifies the de facto annexation of the Eastern Sector by the Zonal authorities that the Soviet Union desires and encourages.

At present the Western Powers are in a position to exercise their full rights and responsibilities only in and in respect of West Berlin, and unfortunately, not in respect of Berlin as a whole.

The guarantees holding good for West Berlin give expression to this special responsibility of the Three Powers for West Berlin. This special responsibility is the strongest support of our security and of our life in freedom. Its most visible expression lies in the presence of the Western troops. This responsibility must be upheld to the full.

That cannot and must not prevent the Federal Government from sharing to the full, politically and in practice, the responsibility for West Berlin. Its unreserved commitment does not weaken but strengthens the West's position in Berlin.

There cannot be, and must not be, a Four-Power status restricted solely to West Berlin. The Soviet Union must not retain and exercise rights in West Berlin beyond those granted to the Western Powers in the Eastern Sector of the city.

The Western Powers have entered into the strongest commitment in regard to West Berlin it is possible to conceive. In stipulation and repeated confirmation of the three basic essentials they have given unmistakable expression to their readiness to face an extreme risk should it be a matter of safeguarding the presence of their troops in the city, the free access to Berlin, and the freedom and vitality of the population.

. . .

The Senate of Berlin is prepared to cooperate in an interim which leaves the foundation of the city's existence untouched and which helps to ease the life of its citizens.

It is the view of the Senate that, in any possible interim solution, the following conditions must be fulfilled:

(1) The United States, Britain and France must keep their troops stationed in Berlin and bear full responsibility for the security of Berlin until the Wall comes down and the German problem is settled.

(2) With the approval of the Three Powers, with the knowledge of the Soviet Union, and through the will of the population concerned, West Berlin in the last fifteen years has become interwoven economically, financially, juridically and politically with the remainder of the Federal Republic. These ties which have developed are vital. They should be strengthened so far as this is possible in international law and consonant with security.

(3) Never must the right of the population concerned to settle their own affairs themselves and to be free to determine their own future be left out of account.
. . .

(4) The particularly brutal consequences of the Wall must be rendered less severe. In regard to East Berlin, in any event the West Berliners must be placed on an equal footing with all other people. In the interests of humanity and reason and to re-tie the bonds between families and friends in the two parts of the city that have been so arbitrarily torn asunder no one will be able to strike this item off the agenda.

(5) Just as today by air, free access to Berlin on the surface must be realised and guaranteed. An international access authority, its actions based on the principle of free traffic, could signify a material improvement on the present situation.

(6) As we have confidently represented to the allied Protective Powers, obsolete claims of Soviet Zone officials are to be replaced by arrangements doing justice to Berlin's needs. This applies particularly to the former German railway system and thus for the city railway too. . . .

The Senate reaffirms its readiness to help in the settlement, on a reasonable basis, of technical problems within the whole of Berlin. For this purpose, above all the services of existing institutions, capable of being enlarged, are already available between the two German currency areas.

Documents 11a–b

The Pass agreement of 1963, which permitted West Berliners for the first time since 1961 to travel to East Berlin, is an interesting example of the result of negotiations between parties which did not recognize each other in a diplomatic sense.

a) PROTOCOL OF AGREEMENT ON PASSES, 17 DECEMBER 1963

Source: Presse-und Informationsamt, *Zur Passierscheinfrage*, I, Berlin 1964, 36

After an exchange of views introduced by a letter from the Deputy Chairman of the Council of Ministers of the German Democratic Republic, Mr. Alexander Abusch, dated 5 December 1963 and addressed to the Governing Mayor of Berlin, Mr. Willy Brandt, State Secretary Erich Wendt and Senate Councillor Horst Korber met from 12 to 17 December 1963 for seven talks on the issuing of passes for West Berlin residents to visit their relatives in East Berlin, the capital of the GDR, from 18 December 1963 to 5 January 1964.

Notwithstanding the different political and legal standpoints, both sides were guided by the idea that it should be possible to realize this humanitarian objective. During the talks which took place alternatively in Berlin (West) and Berlin (East), capital of the GDR, the agreement hereby attached was reached.

. . .

b) PUBLIC NOTICE OF PASS AGREEMENT (PASSIERSCHEINABKOMMEN) BY THE BERLIN SENATE, 17 DECEMBER 1963

Source: Ibid., 41–2

. . .

I

During discussions with the authorities in the other part of Berlin, the Berlin Senate settled the technical requirements to enable you to visit your relatives in East Berlin from 19 December 1963 to 5 January 1964.

A visit by parents, children, grandparents, grandchildren, brothers and sisters, aunts and uncles, nieces and nephews as well as the marriage partners of this group of individuals and a visit between husbands and wives are all considered to be visits to relatives.

II

1. A requirement for visiting relatives is the possession of a pass which is issued on application.

2. A permit office has been installed in every administrative district. They are signposted by notices with the following text:

'Day-Passes
Applications—Issue'

. . .

III

1. Application forms as well as forms for currency and for goods—the latter to be shown at the crossing-point—are distributed at the permit offices.

2. These forms are to be filled out by the applicants. The form is to be handed in where it was issued. Applications can be immediately rejected, if it is obvious that no relationship according to I [above] exists.

Children under sixteen do not require an application of their own. Instead, their particulars are to be entered on the applications of the accompanying adults, as long as they are included on the identity cards of these adults.

3. When applying for or collecting passes, valid Berlin identity cards are to be submitted.[11] The registration offices at the police stations are open until 8 p.m. on weekdays.

4. Applications are handled and decided upon in Berlin (East).

5. Basically, passes will be handed over on the weekday following the day the application was handed in.

. . .

IV

1. Each pass is only valid from 7 a.m. to midnight on the calendar date marked on the pass.

. . .

Document 12

In the East–West negotiations which marked the high point of détente at the end of the 1960s and the beginning of the 1970s Berlin was a key element, as the following document, dating from the early days of Willy Brandt's chancellorship, demonstrates.

DECLARATION OF THE NORTH ATLANTIC COUNCIL, 5 DECEMBER 1969

Source: NATO Final Communiqués, 1949–1974, Brussels, n.d., 229–31

1. Meeting at Brussels on 4th and 5th December 1969, the Ministers of the North Atlantic Alliance reaffirmed the commitment of their nations to pursue effective policies directed towards a greater relaxation of tensions in their continuing search for a just and durable peace.

. . .

Germany and Berlin

8. The Ministers welcome the efforts of the governments of the United States, Great Britain and France, in the framework of their special responsibility for Berlin and Germany as a whole, to gain the co-operation of the Soviet Union in improving the situation with respect to Berlin and free access to the city. The elimination of difficulties created in the past with respect to Berlin, especially with regard to access, would increase the prospects for serious discussions on the other concrete issues which continue to divide East and West. Furthermore, Berlin could play a constructive role in the expansion of East–West economic relations if the city's trade with the East could be facilitated.

9. A just and lasting peace settlement for Germany must be based on the free decision of the German people and on the interests of European security. The Ministers are convinced that, pending such a settlement, the proposals of the Federal Republic for a modus vivendi between the two parts of Germany and for a bilateral exchange of declarations on the non-use of force or the threat of force would, if they receive a positive response, substantially facilitate co-operation between East and West on other problems. They consider that these efforts by the Federal Republic represent constructive steps toward relaxation of tension in Europe and express the hope that the governments will therefore take them into account informing their own attitude toward the German question.

10. The Ministers would regard concrete progress in both these fields as an important contribution to peace in Europe. They are bound to attach great weight to the responses to these proposals in evaluating the prospects for negotiations looking toward improved relations and co-operation in Europe.

. . .

Notes

1. See Ch. 1, Doc. 1
2. See above, Ch. 1, Doc. 2
3. Sebastian Haffner, *Encounter*, Vol. XVII, No. 4, October 1961, 62–3. See also Ch. 14
4. United States *Department of State Bulletin*, Vol. XLV. No. 1155, 14 August 1961, 267

5. *Dokumente zur Berlin–Frage 1944–1962*, Munich, 1962, 419

6. See also Ch. 14

7. Willy Brandt, *The Ordeal of Coexistence* (The Gustav Pollak Lectures, Harvard University, 1962), Cambridge, Mass., 1963

8. Bundesministerium für innerdeutsche Beziehung, *Zehn Jahre Deutschland politik*, Bonn, 1980, 431

9. See Ch. 14 and Table 12

10. Such a 'Berlin–Klausel' was thereafter part of any federal laws passed by Parliament in Bonn

11. Ever since 1945, inhabitants of West Berlin have special Berlin identity-cards, i.e. different from those in use in the other parts of the Federal Republic

14 The Federal Republic and the German Democratic Republic

Carl-Christoph Schweitzer

As an analyst of postwar German history once remarked, the division of the former German Reich in 1945 and after resulted not so much from any specific agreement by the wartime allies to bring about such a state of affairs, but from their fundamental disagreements about the future order in Germany, in Europe and in the world at large. The main powers concerned—the USA and the USSR—wanted a reunification of Germany only on their own terms, if at all,[1]* i.e. on the condition that such a united Germany would be part of their respective economic, political, military and ideological spheres of influence. Most of the positions adopted in the many diplomatic exchanges that occurred during the first decade after 1945, urging a reunited Germany at some future date, were almost certainly a mixture of rhetoric, lip-service and tactical manoeuvering.[2]

Neither of the German states which finally came into existence by the end of 1949 was, or is, a free agent in deciding on the future of Germany.[3] Things have, however, turned out differently for the two Germanies: East Germany (the GDR, German Democratic Republic) is to this day a rigidly organized communist state without free elections, guaranteed human and civil rights in practice, or even the fundamental freedom for its citizens to leave their own country.[4] Above all, it is contained within a satellite system under the tight control of Moscow. The Federal Republic of Germany, on the other hand, has a Western democratic constitution with all due rights and liberties for the individual, including free elections. It is part of the NATO alliance—theoretically of equals, although, of course, here too a superpower, the USA, plays a dominant role.

It is against this international background that one has to consider the

---

development and present-day position of the two Germanies in European and world affairs. For the purposes of this relatively short chapter in a documentary collection based on the Federal Republic of Germany the emphasis will be on an evaluation of the positions adopted by Bonn and East Berlin on the all-German question, since under international law this German question is still 'open'. (The term 'all-German' [gesamtdeutsch] will be used to describe policies which stress the continuing existence of links between the two states.)

From this angle it seems useful to take as a starting point the pronouncements made and definitions used in the respective constitutional documents of the two German states on the all-German problem and on the concept of a *German nation*, which is, as it were, in abeyance. The constitutional postion of the Federal Republic of Germany has remained absolutely unchanged and consistent on these questions.

Basically the all-German policies of all Bonn governments have been guided—and will continue to be guided constitutionally in the future—by the goal expressed in the preamble of the Basic Law:

> The entire German people are called upon to achieve, in free self-determination, the unity and freedom of Germany.

The logical consequence of this stand was, and is, that the Federal Republic of Germany sticks rigorously to its constitutionally guaranteed 'one German citizenship'. It considers all German inhabitants of the German Democratic Republic as Germans of the same sort as the citizens of the Federal Republic of Germany, if they wish to claim this continuing citizenship and demand, for instance, protection and help from West German diplomatic missions in third countries. The Basic Law is very explicit about this in its Articles 16 and 116:

> No one may be deprived of his German citizenship . . . Unless otherwise provided by law a German within the meaning of this Basic Law is a person who possesses German citizenship or who has been admitted . . . to the territory of the German Reich within the frontiers of 31 December 1937 as a refugee or expellee of German stock (Volkszugehörigkeit) or as the spouse or descendant of such a person. . . .

In contrast the German Democratic Republic has changed its policy and, therefore, also its legal code (both its constitution and various laws) in this whole regard several times since 1949. One could demonstrate that these changes correspond, each time, to a changed international environment, above all to the changing 'German policy' of the Soviet Union, her relations with the other superpower and the relations between the NATO and Warsaw Pact alliances. In the first years after 1945

Moscow and East Berlin may still have entertained hopes for a united Germany on communist lines. The East German constitution of 1949, therefore, used at several points an 'all-German' language (Doc. 1a). As the Cold War developed more and more and especially as the two Germanies each became part of a military, political, economic and ideological alliance 'antagonistic' to the other side, the East felt constrained finally in 1961 to put an end to all real or feigned attempts to arrive at some kind of all-German solution, be that in the form of a confederacy or federation or something else.[5] The Wall built in that year along the whole border between the two Germanies and right through the former capital of Berlin stopped any further opportunities for the East Germans to 'vote with their feet' by going West, which millions had done up to that time.[6] For many years after that—actually to this very day—the Federal Republic could only get people out of the German Democratic Republic by paying, for example and strictly behind the scenes, between 40,000 DM for a factory worker and 120,000 DM for a medical practitioner.

The logical consequence of the new policy of the GDR after 1961 was a double one: the amendment of the constitution in 1968 to emphasize a separate Socialist state of the German nation (Doc. 1b) *and* the enactment of a separate GDR citizenship law (Staatsbürgerschaftsgesetz, Doc. 2). Both documents were an expression of a rigorous policy of 'fencing off' (Abgrenzung) and of an increasing desire on the part of the East German regime to get itself nationally and internationally acknowledged as a separate entity under international law.[7]

The year 1969 marked a turning point in the internal political environment of the Federal Republic in line with a changed international environment. For the first time ever a Social Democratic chancellor took over in Bonn — and this above all with the avowed intention of achieving a détente, a change through rapprochement (Wandel durch Annäherung) within the context of Germany, in Central Europe and between the East–West camps generally.[8] The following three years saw the breakthrough towards a new Ostpolitik, i.e. Bonn's treaties with Moscow, Warsaw, Prague, the Four-Power Treaty on Berlin and last but not least, the treaty with the German Democratic Republic.[9] As regards the latter the groundwork had been laid by the new Chancellor Willy Brandt in his meetings with the Prime-Minister of the German Democratic Republic, Willy Stoph, in West German Kassel and in East German Erfurt in 1970. The new West German policy guide-lines for intra-German relations (innerdeutsche Beziehungen)[10] were enunciated by Brandt in his so-called Kassel Points (Doc. 3).

The treaty between Bonn and East Berlin of 1972 (Grundlagen-vertrag) with its various sub-agreements and protocol annexes (Docs. 4a–f) not only made it possible for the German Democratic Republic to be finally recognized under international law by the rest of the international community — including the Western allies of the Federal Republic of Germany[11] — but put the relations between the two German states on a new footing of mutual recognition of each other's sovereignty. However, the West German government of Willy Brandt — as that of Helmut Schmidt — made it clear that for constitutional and other reasons the Federal Republic could not and would not, in connection with these agreements, herself recognise the GDR under international law, that for Bonn the question of the future of an 'all-Germany' was open and that, therefore, an all-German citizenship continued to exist (Docs. 4a–f). Bonn has not, for that reason, established full diplomatic relations with East Berlin. Even if a West German government or political party wanted to bridge this continuing, decisive area of disagreement between Bonn and East Berlin, it could not do so, unless the constitution itself could be changed — with a two-thirds majority of both Houses. This legal position was reiterated authoritatively by the Federal Constitutional Court (Bundesverfassungsgericht) in an important judgement handed down in 1972 (Doc. 5).

The consequences of Bonn's new Ostpolitik, especially of the new relationship between the two Germanies, cannot, in the context of this documentation, be analyzed in detail. Suffice it to say that, above all, the possibilities of individual contacts between Germans in the West and their many friends and relatives in the East of the former single Germany have increased enormously,[12] even if only in a one-way-traffic from West to East! There can be little doubt that the overall success of the policy of détente in Germany in this so-called 'human field' was one of the main reasons for the second amendment of the GDR constitution in 1974 (Doc. 1c). This time, references to an all-German nation, in being or in abeyance, were completely eliminated. The East German regime probably felt that the all-German 'germ' was getting too dangerous by virtue of these increased contacts and had to be eradicated semantically as well as politically. In this connection one must not forget that the viewing of Western TV — which can now no longer be stopped by the authorities — has a tremendous impact in the German Democratic Republic.

Considerable headway in intra-German relations has been made, for example, in the fields of public health and of road construction between Berlin and the Federal Republic of Germany. Since this is, if anything, even more in the interest of the German Democratic Republic (with

Bonn providing most of the money), not too much can or should be made of such improvements when assessing the extent of normalization between the two states. By contrast, progress has been slight in regard to the delimitation of the exact border-line between the two states on the river Elbe; the code of practice permitting officially recognized activities by journalists has time and again been breached; there has been—to mention just one other important point—no progress at all in regard to the signing of a formal cultural agreement, mainly due to differences over the status of West Berlin in this connection. So, all in all, one would have to say that in many fields singled out for more cooperation in the 1972 agreements the actual progress so far achieved in ten years has been disappointingly small or not in evidence at all.[13]

The guiding principle of the GDR's policy has apparently remained the same ever since Erich Honecker, the General Secretary of East Germany's Communist Party, the SED, moved the threshold for the intra-German process of normalisation higher up with a speech made in the East German city of Gera in 1980 (Doc. 6). Since Honecker must know that the Federal Republic of Germany cannot comply with his demands for settling the all-German question legally in the direction of the GDR's wishes (in the field of citizenship, diplomatic recognition etc.), it seems clear that the Eastern side is mainly interested in a leverage to exact other advantages from the West. Furthermore, the East German government created new and even stiffer barriers against meetings of West Germans with their friends and relatives in the East by increasing the amount of currency which visitors from the West are forced to exchange when entering the GDR (Doc. 7).

The talks between Schmidt and Honecker in December 1981 in East Germany did not help to defuse intra-German grievances, except that they underscored once more a very important point of mutual consensus. It was made officially clear on the lines of Brandt's point 7 at Kassel (Doc. 3) that both German governments, in spite of their unbridgeable ideological differences, remain determined to 'prevent another war ever taking German soil as its starting point again', to quote from the communiqué issued after the meeting.[14]

There remains one other noticeable joint German policy approach worth mentioning: the fact that even the East German government does not want to give up the concept of a 'special relationship' between the two German states in the economic sphere, i.e. regarding trade relations. Through keeping up this special relationship the GDR can make sure that it will continue to profit indirectly from the EEC treaties, since the Federal Republic of Germany made certain, when signing those treaties in 1957, that its trade with the East German side would be considered as domestic trade, not subject to external tariffs and controls imposed by the EEC on trade with countries outside the Community (Doc. 8).

Altogether then, the question of future relations between the Western democratic Federal Republic of Germany with its two-thirds numerical preponderance, and the Eastern communist German Democratic Republic seems to remain, nationally and internationally, an open one.

Documents 1a–c

THE GERMAN NATION—AS SET OUT IN THE CONSTITUTION OF THE GERMAN DEMOCRATIC REPUBLIC

a) ART. 1 OF THE CONSTITUTION OF 1949

Source: S. Mampel, *Die Verfassung der Sowjetisch besetzten Zone*, Frankfurt, 1965, 37

Germany is an indivisible democratic republic, composed of German states [Länder].

The republic determines all matters which are essential for the existence and development of the German people as a whole; all other matters are to be determined independently by the states. The decisions of the republic are in principle to be carried out by the states.

There is only one German citizenship.

b) AMENDMENT TO THE CONSTITUTION, 1968

Source: Friedrich-Ebert-Stiftung (ed.), *Honecker's Verfassung*, Bonn, 1981, 49f.

Because of our responsibility to point the way to the entire German nation to a future of peace and socialism ... the people of the GDR ... have given themselves this socialist constitution:

Art. 1

The German Democratic Republic is a socialist state of the German nation. It is the political organization of the working people in the city and the country, who together bring socialism into reality under the leadership of the working class and its Marxist–Leninist Party.

c) AMENDMENT TO THE CONSTITUTION, 1974

Source: Ibid.

In continuation of the revolutionary traditions of the German working class, ...

the people of the German Democratic Republic have given themselves this socialist constitution:

Art. 1

The German Democratic Republic is a socialist state of the worker and the farmer. It is the political organization of the working people in the city and the country under the leadership of the working class and its Marxist–Lenninist Party.
. . .

Documents 2a–b

a) THE LAW ON CITIZENSHIP (GESETZ ÜBER DIE STAATSBÜRGER-SCHAFT DER DEUTSCHEN DEMOKRATISCHEN REPUBLIK, STAATSBÜRGERSCHAFTSGESETZ), 20 FEBRUARY 1967

Source: Gesetzblatt der DDR, I, No. 2, 23 February 1967

The citizenship of the German Democratic Republic came into existence, in accordance with international law, upon establishment of the German Democratic Republic. It is an expression of the German Democratic Republic's sovereignty and contributes to the further strengthening of all socialist countries.

The citizenship of the German Democratic Republic is membership of its residents in the first peace-loving, democratic and socialist German state, in which the working class exercises political power in alliance with the farmers' cooperative class, the socialist intelligentsia and other labouring people.

§ 1

A citizen of the German Democratic Republic is one who:

a) was a German national at the time of the establishment of the GDR, had his place of official or permanent residence in the German Democratic Republic and has not lost his German Democratic Republic citizenship since then;
b) was a German national at the time of the establishment of the GDR, had his official or permanent residence outside the German Democratic Republic, has obtained no other citizenship thereafter and, corresponding to his declaration of intent is enrolled, through registration at one of the authorised German Democratic Republic's agencies, as a citizen of the German Democratic Republic;
c) obtained the citizenship of the German Democratic Republic, according to valid regulations, and has not lost it since.

§ 2

(1) The citizenship of the German Democratic Republic guarantees that the citizens of the German Democratic Republic can avail themselves of their constitutional rights; and demands from them the implementation of their constitutional duties [Pflichten].

(2) The German Democratic Republic affords its citizens protection and supports them in the assertion of their rights outside the German Democratic Republic.

§ 3

(1) According to generally accepted international law, citizens of the German Democratic Republic can claim no rights or duties of another citizenship in relation to the German Democratic Republic.

(2) A citizen of the German Democratic Republic who intends to acquire citizenship from another country, requires the assent of the authorised central agencies of the German Democratic Republic. . . .

§ 4

The citizenship of the German Democratic Republic is obtained through:

a) descent;
b) birth within the territory of the German Democratic Republic;
c) naturalization.

. . .

§ 10

(1) With the permission of the responsible agency of the German Democratic Republic, a citizen can on application be released from the status conferred on him by his citizenship of the German Democratic Republic if he has, or desires to take, residence outside the German Democratic Republic, holds or intends to apply for another citizenship, and if no compelling reason exists to prevent his relinquishing his citizenship of the German Democratic Republic.

(2) The release from the citizenship of the German Democratic Republic will be acknowledged in an official document.

. . .

§ 13

Citizens who have official or permanent residence outside the German Democratic Republic can be deprived of their citizenship for serious violation of civil duties.

. . .

_____

Here the point to be noticed is that Germans who flee from the GDR automatically lose their GDR citizenship.

b) ADDITIONAL LAW ON QUESTIONS OF CITIZENSHIP (...ZUR REGELUNG VON FRAGEN DER STAATSBÜRGERSCHAFT), 16 OCTOBER 1972

Source: Gesetzblatt der DDR, I, No. 18, 17 October 1972

§ 1

(1) Citizens of the German Democratic Republic who, in violation of the laws of the Worker and Peasant State [Arbeiter-und Bavernstaat] left the German Democratic Republic before 1 January 1972, and who have not taken up residence in the German Democratic Republic again, lose their citizenship of the German Democratic Republic with the coming into force of this Law.

(2) Descendants of persons referred to in (1) lose their citizenship of the German Democratic Republic with the coming into force of this Law in so far as they have their residence outside the German Democratic Republic without the authorization of governmental agencies of the German Democratic Republic.

§ 2

Persons referred to in § 1(1) will not be liable to criminal prosecution for leaving the German Democratic Republic without authorization.

. . .

Document 3

Chancellor Willy Brandt and the GDR's Chairman of the Council of Ministers, Willi Stoph, met twice in 1970, first in Erfurt and then in Kassel. Brandt's visit to Erfurt in March 1970 was the first ever by a West German chancellor and led to such an enthusiastic reception for him by the East Germans that the authorities in the Eastern part of the country have never again incurred the risk of a West German chancellor meeting with the people of the German Democratic Republic. This fact was very much in evidence some eleven years later, when Chancellor Helmut Schmidt met with Erich Honecker, the leader of the GDR since 1971, in a secluded place near Berlin (December 1981). Schmidt was completely cordoned off during his visit to the town of Guestrow in the GDR. At their second meeting of 1970, in Kassel, Brandt and Stoph exchanged views and notes on the guidelines each side was putting forward to normalize relations between the two states. The excerpts below are part of a total of '20 Points' which Brandt put forward.

KASSEL MEMORANDUM OF WILLY BRANDT

Source: Austwärtiges Amt (ed.), *Die Außenpolitik der Bundesrepublik Deutschland,* Bonn, 1972, 754

. . .

Our conception of the guidelines and treaty elements for the regulation of an equal relationship between the Federal Republic of Germany and the German Democratic Republic is as follows:

1. The Federal Republic of Germany and the German Democratic Republic, which are both constitutionally based on the concept of the unity of the nation, in the interest of peace as well as for the future and coherence of the nation, agree on a treaty, which regulates the relationship between both German states, improves the link between the people and both states and contributes to the elimination of existing discrimination.

   . . .

5. Both sides respect the independence and self-sufficiency of each of the two countries in matters which concern their domestic jurisdiction.
6. Neither of the two German states can act for the other or represent the other.
7. The treaty-making partners declare that a war must never again begin from German soil.

   . . .

10. The treaty must proceed from the consequences of World War II and from the special situation of Germany and the Germans, who live in two states and yet understand themselves to be citizens of *one* nation.

    . . .

Documents 4a–f

a) TREATY ON THE BASIS OF RELATIONS BETWEEN THE FEDERAL REPUBLIC OF GERMANY AND THE GERMAN DEMOCRATIC REPUBLIC

Source: Documentation relating to the Federal Government's policy of détente, Press Information Office, Bonn, 1978, 178ff.

Transl.: Official

The High Contracting Parties,

In consideration of their responsibility for the preservation of peace,

Anxious to contribute to détente and security in Europe,

Conscious that the inviolability of frontiers and respect for the territorial integrity and sovereignty of all States in Europe within their present frontiers are a fundamental condition for peace,

Recognizing that therefore the two German States are to refrain from the threat or use of force in their relations,

Proceeding from the historical facts and without prejudice to the differing views of the Federal Republic of Germany and the German Democratic Republic on questions of principle, including the national question,

Desiring to create the conditions for co-operation between the Federal Republic of Germany and the German Democratic Republic for the benefit of the people in the two German States,

Have agreed as follows:

Article 1

The Federal Republic of Germany and the German Democratic Republic shall develop normal good neighbourly relations with each other on the basis of equal rights.

. . .

Article 3

In accordance with the United Nations Charter, the Federal Republic of Germany and the German Democratic Republic shall settle their disputes exclusively by peaceful means and refrain from the threat or use of force.

They reaffirm the inviolability now and in the future of the border existing between them and undertake fully to respect their territorial integrity.

Article 4

The Federal Republic of Germany and the German Democratic Republic proceed on the assumption that neither of the two States can represent the other internationally or act in its name.

. . .

Article 7

The Federal Republic of Germany and the German Democratic Republic state their readiness to regulate practical and humanitarian questions in the process of the normalization of their relations. They will conclude agreements with a view to developing and promoting cooperation in the fields of economics, science and technology, traffic, judicial relations, posts and telecommunications, health, culture, sport, environmental protection, and in other fields, on the basis of the present Treaty and for their mutual benefit. The details have been agreed in the Supplementary Protocol.

Article 8

The Federal Republic of Germany and the German Democratic Republic will exchange permanent missions. They will be established at the respective seat of government.

Pratical questions relating to the establishment of the missions will be dealt with separately.

Article 9

The Federal Republic of Germany and the German Democratic Republic are agreed that the present Treaty does not affect the bilateral and multilateral international treaties and agreements previously concluded by them or concerning them.[15]

. . .

b) LETTER FROM THE GOVERNMENT OF THE FEDERAL REPUBLIC OF GERMANY TO THE GOVERNMENT OF THE GERMAN DEMOCRATIC REPUBLIC ON GERMAN UNITY, 21 DECEMBER 1972

Source: Ibid., 182

In connexion with the signing today of the Treaty on the Basis of Relations between the Federal Republic of Germany and the German Democratic Republic, the Government of the Federal Republic of Germany has the honour to state that this Treaty does not conflict with the political aim of the Federal Republic of Germany to work for a state of peace in Europe in which the German nation will regain its unity through free self-determination.

c) SUPPLEMENTARY PROTOCOL TO THE TREATY ON THE BASIS OF RELATIONS BETWEEN THE FEDERAL REPUBLIC OF GERMANY AND THE GERMAN DEMOCRATIC REPUBLIC

Source: Ibid., 183–4

I

Re Article 3

The Federal Republic of Germany and the German Democratic Republic have agreed to form a Commission composed of representatives of the Governments of the two States. They will review and, where necessary, renew or supplement the marking of the border existing between the two States and draw up the necessary documentation on the course of the border. In the same way, the Commission will contribute to regulating other problems connected with the course of the border, e.g., water management, energy supply and the prevention of damage.

. . .

II

Re Article 7

(1) Trade between the Federal Republic of Germany and the German Democratic Republic shall be developed on the basis of the existing agreements.

The Federal Republic of Germany and the German Democratic Republic will conclude long-term agreements with a view to promoting a continuous development of economic relations, adapting outmoded arrangements, and improving the structure of trade.

(2) The Federal Republic of Germany and the German Democratic Republic state their intention to develop co-operation in the fields of science and technology for their mutual benefit and to conclude the necessary treaties for this purpose.

. . .

(4) The Federal Republic of Germany and the German Democratic Republic state their readiness to regulate by treaty their judicial relations as simply and expediently as possible in the interests of those seeking justice, especially in the fields of civil and criminal law.

(5) The Federal Republic of Germany and the German Democratic Republic agree to conclude an agreement on posts and telecommunications on the basis of the Constitution of the Universal Postal Union and the International Telecommunication Convention. They will notify such agreement to the Universal Postal Union (UPU) and the International Telecommunication Union (ITU).

The existing agreements and the procedures beneficial to both sides will be taken over in that agreement.

(6) The Federal Republic of Germany and the German Democratic Republic state their interest in co-operation in the field of health. They agree that the relevant treaty shall also regulate the exchange of medicaments and, as far as possible, the treatment of patients in special clinics and sanatoria.

(7) The Federal Republic of Germany and the German Democratic Republic intend to develop cultural co-operation. To this end they will enter into negotiations on the conclusion of intergovernmental agreements. . . .

d) STATEMENTS ON RECORD
Source: Ibid., 187

The Federal Republic of Germany states on record:

'Questions of nationality have not been regulated by the Treaty.'

The German Democratic Republic states on record:

'The German Democratic Republic proceeds from the assumption that the Treaty will facilitate a regulation of questions of nationality.'

e) EXPLANATORY NOTES REGARDING THE EXCHANGE OF LETTERS ON THE REUNITING OF FAMILIES, THE FACILITATION OF TRAVEL AND THE IMPROVEMENT OF NON-COMMERCIAL GOODS TRAFFIC

Source: Ibid., 191–2

With the entry into force of the Treaty on the Basis of Relations the following facilitations will take effect:

1. *Solution of problems connected with the reuniting of families*

—Reuniting of married couples
—Movement of parents requiring the care of their children, especially if only one parent is still alive. The same applies to the movement of grandparents to join their grandchildren.
—In special exceptional cases, permission to marry.

2. *Improvement of border-crossing travel and visitor traffic*

—Extension of the number of urgent family reasons for which GDR citizens may be permitted to travel to the FRG to include silver and golden wedding anniversaries.
—Extension of the category of GDR citizens entitled to apply for travel for urgent family reasons to include half-sisters and half-brothers (same mother).
—Extension of the procedure regarding the issue of transit visas in transit between the FRG and Berlin (West) to include other transit by rail and inland waterway (requirement for written application ceases).
—Possibility of interrupting transit travel (except in Berlin traffic), provided that bookings to that effect have been made with the GDR travel bureau.
—Permission for FRG passengers on freight vessels calling at GDR seaports to go ashore for a one-day stay in the port town concerned (including overnight accommodation if booked through the GDR travel bureau).

. . .

———————

Under Secretary Bahr (of the Federal German Republic) and Under Secretary Kohl (of the GDR) exchanged letters with the following identical content (in Herr Kohl's letter 'Federal Republic of Germany' and 'German Democratic Republic' were exchanged as appropriate).

f) EXCHANGE OF LETTERS CONCERNING WORKING POSSIBILITIES FOR JOURNALISTS, 8 NOVEMBER 1972

Source: Ibid., 206–7

. . .

The Federal Republic of Germany shall within the framework of its applicable legislation accord journalists from the German Democratic Republic and their assistants the right to engage in their professional activities and freely to acquire and report information. It will enable journalists to carry on their activities as travelling correspondents and, on the basis of reciprocity, to take up residence and engage in their professional activities as permanent correspondents, in each case on condition that their professional activities remain within the limits of the law.

. . .

Journalists working as permanent correspondents of the German Democratic Republic in the Federal Republic of Germany will be required:

—to be accredited or established in accordance with the applicable modalities in the Federal Republic of Germany;
—to observe the laws and regulations enacted in the interest of security, crime prevention, protection of public health and of the rights and liberties of others.

. . .

Document 5

The government of Bavaria had applied to the Federal Constitutional Court on 28 May 1973 to declare the treaty between the Federal Republic of Germany and the German Democratic Republic of December 1972 unconstitutional, on the grounds that certain provisions of that treaty constituted a violation of the preamble and other articles of the Basic Law, all of which make it legally binding on any government in Bonn to work for a reunification of Germany. The Court rejected the Bavarian government's complaint, but emphasised the limitations placed on government action by the Basic Law. Below follow extracts from the ruling of the Court.

BASIC PRINCIPLES UNDERLYING THE RULING OF THE FEDERAL CON-STITUTIONAL COURT ON THE VALIDITY OF THE TREATY OF DECEMBER 1972 (LEITSÄTZE, 31 JULY 1973)

Source: Bundesanstalt für Gesamtdeutsche Aufgaben, Bonn, 1974, special issue

1) Article 59, § 2 of the Basic Law lays down that all treaties regulating the political relations of the Federation or relating to issues of federal legislation are subject to parliamentary supervision. Whether the state which is a party to the treaty is deemed by the Basic Law to be a foreign country or not, a law of ratification must be passed by Parliament.

. . .

3) For the Executive to circumvent legal proceedings pending in the Federal Constitutional Court is irreconcilable with the stipulation in the Basic Law establishing the primacy of the Constitutional Court.

Should, by way of exception, a situation arise—as in this case—in which the implementation of a treaty seems, in the opinion of the Executive, to be imperative before proceedings in the Constitutional Court have been concluded, then the constitutional bodies responsible must answer for all consequences so arising.

4) It follows from the precept of reunification that no constitutional body of the Federal Republic of Germany may abandon the restoration of national unity as a political goal and that it is the duty of all constitutional bodies to work towards the attainment of this goal in their policies and to refrain from doing anything that would thwart the aim of reunification. This involves a requirement to keep alive the claim to reunification at home and to insist on it unwaveringly abroad.

5) The Constitution forbids the Federal Republic of Germany to renounce a legal title enshrined in its Basic Law, by means of which it can work towards the realization of reunification and self-determination, or to create a legal title incompatible with the Basic Law, or to be party to the establishment of a legal title which may be cited against it in its pursuit of this goal.

6) The treaty has dual character; in essence it is a treaty under international law; in substance it is specifically a treaty regulating inter-German relations.

7) Art. 23 of the Basic Law forbids the Federal Government to enter into a contractual dependence as a result of which it would no longer be able to effect the incorporation of other parts of Germany on its own, but only with the approval of the other party to the contract.

8) Art. 16 of the Basic Law assumes that the 'German citizenship', to which reference is also made in Art. 116, Para. 1 of the Basic Law, is at the same time the citizenship of the Federal Republic of Germany. It follows according to the spirit of the Basic Law that not only citizens of the Federal Republic of Germany are German citizens.

9) Any German entering the area of authority ... of the Federal Republic of Germany is entitled to the full protection of the courts of the Federal Republic of Germany and to the fundamental rights guaranteed by the Basic Law.

Document 6

SPEECH BY ERICH HONECKER, GENERAL SECRETARY OF THE SED AND CHAIRMAN OF THE COUNCIL OF STATE (STAATSRATSVORSITZENDER), ON 'TOPICAL QUESTIONS OF THE DOMESTIC AND FOREIGN POLICY OF THE GDR', AT GERA, 13 OCTOBER 1980

Source: Neues Deutschland (the official newspaper of the SED in the GDR), 14 October 1980

. . .

The GDR has made many attempts at improvements

The German Democratic Republic strives for good neighbourly relations with the Federal Republic of Germany and, just as in our policy towards other Western states, we pursue here, too, a policy of peaceful coexistence. On this basis we have done much in the past to smooth the path for progress in the relations between the German Democratic Republic and the Federal Republic of Germany. It was possible to negotiate numerous treaties and agreements which function fairly well. The results thereof were important prerequisites for a mutually advantageous cooperation based on equal rights.

Obviously it cannot be overlooked that many problems between the German Democratic Republic and the Federal Republic of Germany continue to exist and that we still have a long way to go before complete normality is attained. The main reasons for this are the Federal Republic of Germany's continued attempts, when dealing with the GDR, to disregard decisive principles of the sovereignty of our state, thereby violating the Basic Treaty [Grundlagenvertrag]. In this relationship, however, it is only possible to take a step forward when the existence of two sovereign states, which are independent of one another and which have different forms of society, is unconditionally accepted. Every effort to revise the European postwar arrangement must put a strain on the normalization of the relations between the two German states; indeed it puts them in doubt.

The Federal Republic of Germany prevents solutions

It is absolutely vital that the principle of non-interference is accepted without limitation by both sides in the bilateral relations as well as in the relationship to third states. The Basic Treaty obliges its members to do this, of course. In particular, disregard of the principle of non-interference which was, after all, also signed by the Federal Republic of Germany in Helsinki, is in no way compatible with more normal relations. More extensive solutions of various kinds which would be of advantage to the people of the Federal Republic of Germany and the German Democratic Republic are still being heavily obstructed by the Federal Republic of Germany. We have often pressed to have the obstructions removed, but have received no cooperation. This is true above all of the recognition of the citizenship of the German Democratic Republic. As the Federal Republic of Germany adheres to ideas which are not in accordance with international law and as they refuse to respect the citizenship of the German Democratic Republic, the jurisdiction of our state is being denied. But it is certainly a fact that there are two sovereign German states, independent of one another. There are, and this is also a fact, citizens of the socialist German Democratic Republic and citizens of the capitalist Federal Republic of Germany.

We consider it necessary for the FRG to accept reality at last, something it will not be able to avoid in the long run, in any case. This would make it easier to settle the most urgent practical questions in tourist travel, in legal aid and in various other fields. The so-called 'Registration Centre' [Zentrale Erfassungsstelle] at Salzgitter should have been dissolved long ago. An end must be put to the issuing of temporary passports for GDR citizens when staying in the Federal Republic, as well as to the issuing of FRG passports for GDR citizens by FRG embassies in third countries.

We also consider it time to exchange ambassadors as is usual in the relations between two sovereign states independent of one another, i.e. to transform the offices of the permanent representatives of the GDR and the FRG into what conforms with international law—into embassies. This would be a visible step towards a normalization of the relations between the two German states.

Of great importance is the situation at the border of the two states, which is also the dividing line between the Warsaw Pact States and NATO. The common Border Commission of the two German states has achieved positive results and important agreements have been arrived at. It would serve the interests of peace and good neighbourly relations, if the border line along the river Elbe could be determined according to international law, an agreement which has so far failed due to the unacceptable positions adopted by the Federal Republic. . . .

Document 7

The GDR authorities first introduced the following in 1964 under the name of 'obligatory minimum exchange'. The regulation of the 25 November 1964 to this effect applied to 'all visitors from West Germany, other non-socialist countries and West Berlin who enter the GDR for a private visit'. The amount of compulsory currency exchange was then fixed at 5 DM per diem per person (for West Berliners, 3 DM). This was changed to 10 DM in 1968 and to 20 DM in 1972 for all categories including West Berliners. Exempted had been women over sixty, men over sixty-five and young people under sixteen. Old people were temporarily included again in November 1973 and again in November 1974, but the amount was then reduced. Interestingly enough only five weeks later, i.e. in December 1974, pensioners were again exempted. This was the position that prevailed until 1980. The new law, quoted below, increased the amount to 25 DM and, what was even more objectionable to the Bonn government, again included pensioners. Children between the ages of six and fourteen had to pay 7.50 DM; exemption was granted only for children under the age of six. As of October 1983 children under the age of fourteen were exempted.

REGULATION CONCERNING THE OBLIGATORY MINIMUM CURRENCY EXCHANGE [ON ENTERING THE GDR] (ANORDNUNG ÜBER DIE DURCHFÜHRUNG EINES VERBINDLICHEN MINDESTUMTAUSCHES VON ZAHLUNGSMITTELN) 10 OCTOBER 1980

Source: Gesetzblatt der DDR, Teil I, No. 29, 9 October 1980

§ 1

This regulation applies to persons residing temporarily in non-socialist countries and in West Berlin, who enter the German Democratic Republic for visits of limited duration.

§ 2

1) For each day of their stay in the German Democratic Republic including its capital city, persons referred to in § 1 must exchange foreign currency equivalent in value to at least

25 marks of the German Democratic Republic

at the rates of exchange currently applying in the German Democratic Republic.
2) The minimum exchange in accordance with 1) must be carried out in a convertible currency.

§ 3

1) Currency exchanged according to § 2, 1) into marks of the German Democratic Republic cannot be reconverted.
2) Unused marks of the German Democratic Republic can be deposited or paid into an account with all bureaux of exchange and all branches of the State Bank of the German Democratic Republic. Such sums can be drawn upon in full in marks of the German Democratic Republic at any time on reentry into the German Democratic Republic.

Document 8

THE WEST GERMAN UNDERSECRETARY OF STATE FOR FOREIGN AFFAIRS (STAATSSEKRETÄR) WALTER HALLSTEIN, SPEAKING IN THE BUNDESTAG ON THE SPECIAL TRADE RELATIONSHIP BETWEEN THE TWO GERMAN STATES, 21 MARCH 1957

Source: Auswärtiges Amt (ed.) *Die Aussenpolitik der Bundesrepublik Deutschland,* Bonn, 1972, 354f.

Hallstein emphasized that the federal government had, when signing the Treaties of Rome (EEC and Euratom), made clear that a reunited Germany would be free to decide on its own accession to the treaties and he went on to say in this connection: '... we have taken special care to safeguard the position of Berlin and the whole process of the 'intra-German trade' [Interzonen-handel]... we are very much interested in not only preserving this instrument of intra-German trade, but in actually developing it further. For this reason the treaty on the Common Market *expressis verbis* contains the provision—I quote—that the execution of the community treaty will entail neither any change in regard to the regulations for the intra-German trade as of now nor any change in the actual conduct of this same trade. It is, therefore, absolutely clear that the present state of affairs by which the intra-German trade is a purely domestic one will remain intact; the demarcation line with the Eastern zone [Zonengrenze, frontier with the German Democratic Republic] will continue not to be a customs frontier. The federal government retains its full freedom of action in regard to this intra-German trade'.

Notes

1. See, for instance, US National Security Document No. 5727, declassified in Washington in 1982, on the policy of the United States towards the German question as of December 1957—interesting in retrospective as well as for its prospective considerations and indicating a high degree of continuity. We read in the hitherto unpublished document: '. . . Germany is of vital importance to the United States: a) Germany's location in the heart of Europe and its considerable material and human resources make it a key area in the struggle between the Communist and free worlds; b) the division of Germany is a chronic source of European instability and East–West friction and a possible source of major armed conflict; c) the future development and orientation of the Federal Republic will significantly affect the development of Europe as a whole . . . West German military association with Western Europe is very important to strengthen NATO capabilities in Europe . . . (major policy guidance): . . . make clear that reunification is essential to any genuine relaxation of tension between the USSR and the West, but that the US will not agree to any reunification involving a) Communist domination of a reunified Germany; b) a federated Germany which perpetuates the existing government of the German Democratic Republic; c) the withdrawal of US and other allied forces from West Germany without an effective military quid pro quo from the Soviets and the satellites . . .' See C.C. Schweitzer, *Weltmacht USA; Kontinuität oder Wandel ihrer Aussenpolitik nach 1945*, Munich, 1983, 68ff.
2. For the exchange of diplomatic notes between West and East on German reunification in the crucial years 1952–1954 see e.g. Beate Ruhm von Oppen, ed., *Documents on Germany under Occupation 1945–1955*, London, 1955, and H. Siegler, *The Reunification and Security of Germany*, Bonn, 1957; see also Ch. 11 above.
3. See B. Ruhm von Oppen, ed., op. cit., for the treaties between the Western powers and the Federal Republic 1952–55 with the Western allied reservations on Germany as a whole and Berlin.
4. See Art. 12 of the International Pact on Civic and Political Rights of 1966, United Nations, 1966
5. The idea of a confederacy was first put on the overall East–West agenda by the GDR in 1956; see statement by Walter Ulbricht, the then Secretary of the East German Communist Party, of 29 December 1956, published in the official newspaper *Neues Deutschland*, 30 December 1956: 'Confederacy between the two German states as a transition stage for reunification'. The motives behind such proposals were manifold, *inter alia* to influence public opinion in West Germany against a further integration of the Federal Republic into the overall Western system (the founding of the EEC then

being imminent), the achievement of international recognition for the GDR under international law etc. For literature, see n. 2 above.

6. See Table 12. From 1949 to 1961, i.e. up to the building of the Wall, 2,686,942 people fled from East to West Germany.

7. The claim to 'solely represent the whole German people' on the grounds of the democratic legitimacy of the system was—and is—part of the Basic Law, especially its preamble. For some fifteen years (from 1955 onwards) it was further entrenched in the Hallstein Doctrine (see Ch. 11, Doc. 10).

8. The new Ostpolitik had already begun under the so-called 'grand coalition' of SPD and CDU/CSU in 1966–69 (see Ch. 11, on foreign policy). With Willy Brandt as Chancellor, the Social Democrats took over such an office again for the first time since 1930.

9. See Ch. 11, on foreign policy and Ch. 13, on Berlin.

10. Chancellor Willy Brandt changed the name of the Federal Ministry in charge of relations with the GDR from: Ministry for All-German Affairs into Ministry for Intra-German relations, the official term ever since.

11. The United States, for instance, recognized the German Democratic Republic under international law in May 1974.

12. The figures for those granted visas to visit the GDR from the Federal Republic rose from approximately 1.1m in 1969, when the government of Willy Brandt took office, to 2.2m in 1973, 1.9m in 1974, 3.1m in 1975 and 1976, 2.9m in 1977 and 3.1m again in 1978 (compounded from official statistics, here quoted from Margit Roth, *Zwei Staaten in Deutschland*, Opladen, 1981). The figures for those over the age of 65 granted permission by the GDR authorities to visit the West show a total of approximately 1m in 1969, 1.2m in 1973 and approximately 1.3m for the years 1974–8. There was also a significant increase in the number of exit permits given to people in East Germany to visit the West on 'urgent family grounds' (such as the marriage or death of a near relative); numbers rose from 11,421 in 1973 to 48,695 in 1978.

13. At the time of going to press it is possible to comment that, after one year of the new CDU/CSU/FDP coalition in Bonn a continuation of the Federal Republic's overall GDR policies has been observed; no further significant progress has as yet been achieved in certain decisive issue areas, despite a DM one billion loan from the West—some dismantling of lethal devices on the Eastern side of the border notwithstanding.

14. At the time of going to press it appears that the present governments in both East and West Germany are still anxious to prevent a renewal of the freeze, even if the overall conflict on disarmament remains, as yet, unsolved.

15. This constitutes further evidence of the continuing Four-Power responsibility for both Berlin and the whole of Germany, referred to above.

Statistical tables

Table 1. **Overall demographic structure of the Federal Republic (end of 1980)**

Age	Population Total In '000s (absolute fig.)	%	Male %	Of these Married %	Foreigners %
Under 15	11,003	17.8	51.2	00	11.4
15–39	22,518	36.5	51.5	47.0	10.2
40–64	18,602	30.2	47.5	81.7	4.9
65 and older	9,535	15.5	35.8	46.4	1.2
Total	61,658	100.0	47.8	49.0	7.4

Source: Statistisches Bundesamt, ed., *Datenreport,* Bundeszentrale für Politische Bildung, Bonn, 15 March 1983, 45

Table 2. **National income/employment**
Gross value added and employment by sector (1981)

	Gross value added		Employment	
	DM million	%	1,000	%
Agriculture, forestry, fishery	34.0	2.2	1,495	5.8
Manufacturing	728.6	46.3	11,358	44.2
Trade and transport	231.2	14.7	4,551	17.7
Services	368.9	23.4	5,106	19.9
Government, non-profit organizations, services to private households	212.0	13.5	3,170	12.3
	1574.7		25680	

62.2% of all people employed were male. 9.2% of the people employed were foreigners; the largest group of which comes from Turkey (581,000 workers)

End use of Gross National Product (1981)

	DM million	%
Private consumption	860.9	55.5
Government consumption	325.8	21.0
Investment	353.0	22.7
Export–import	12.2	0.8
	1551.9	100.0

Source: Bundesministerium für Wirtschaft, ed., *Leistung in Zahlen 1981,* n.d.

Table 3. **Standard of living**
Standard of living statistics distinguish three types of households:
Type 1: 2-person household with low income (living on social security/pension)
Type 2: 4-person household with medium income (worker)
Type 3: 4-person household with higher income (salaried employee/civil servant)

Provision of households with selected durable consumer goods (1981 percentages)

	Type 1	Type 2	Type 3
Private car	18.8	83.8	96.0
Telephone	77.5	89.6	98.8
TV (black and white)	52.5	52.4	61.8
TV (colour)	57.5	78.7	69.8
Typewriter	43.8	69.1	87.1
Washing machine	81.9	99.5	99.1
Vacuum cleaner	98.8	98.7	99.8
Dish-washer	1.3	28.2	65.8

Source: Statistisches Jahrbuch 1982 für die Bundesrepublik Deutschland, 456

The accessibility of infrastructural facilities is reflected in the following statistics (1978)

	Distance living quarter—infrastructural facility in minutes walking				
	up to 5	6–10	11–20	more than 20	unknown
	Per cent of households				
Shopping facilities	46	29	12	7	6
Medical doctor	31	24	18	19	8
Public park	49	20	13	9	9
Public transport	60	25	8	3	4
Kindergarten (households with children only)	30	28	17	13	12
Primary schools (households with children only)	25	28	22	16	9
Public children's playground (households with children only)	29	23	12	10	16

Source: Statistisches Bundesamt, ed., *Datenreport,* Bonn, 1983, 128

Table 4. **Number of Bundestag committees of all categories between 1949 and 1979**

Legislative period	1949–53	1953–57	1957–61	1961–65	1965–69	1969–72	1972–76	1976–79
Number of Standing Committees at the beginning of each legislative period	36	36	26	26	23	17	19	19
Number of Standing Committees during the course of the legislative period	40	38	26	28	23	17	19	-
Total number of meetings of Committees and their Subcommittees	5,111	4,083	2,435	2,863	2,500	1,312	1,973	1,418
Number of Special Committees of Enquiry	9	3	0	2	2	1	1	
Total number of meetings of Special Committees of Enquiry	174	34	0	37	101	26	77	48
Number of Enquete-Commissions[1]	-	-	-	-	-	2	3	2
Number of meetings of Enquete-Commissions	-	-	-	-	-	52	89	20

[1] These Enquete-Commissions correspond to the British Royal Commissions and are intended to give guidance to the government for enacting new legislation. Ch. 7 above (Federalism: Intergovernmental Relations and Finance) refers to the Enquete-Commission on constitutional reform.

Source: Deutscher Bundestag, ed., *30 Jahre Deutscher Bundestag, Dokumentation, Statistkik, Daten,* Bonn, 1979, 220, (translation here slightly adapted, absolute figures only given)

Table 5. **Professions of the members of the Bundestag elected on 6.3.1983 before they entered Parliament[1] (10. Deutscher Bundestag)**

	CDU/CSU	SPD	FDP	GREENS	TOTAL
1. *Members of the government*					
a. Bundeskanzler, Bundes-minister	14	—	3	—	17
b. Parlamentarische Staatssekretäre (including Staatsminister)	22	—	3	—	25
Total	36		6		42 (=8.1%)
[CDU/CSU/FDP had already been members of the caretaker government for the five months previous to the election of March 1983]					
2. *Beamte* (Civil Servants in the narrower sense, see Ch. 7)					
a. So-called 'political' civil servants[2]	1	4	1	—	6
b. Other civil servants in the higher echelons of the administration of Bund, Länder and municipalities	31	21	3	1	56
c. As b, but in the lower echelons	7	7	—	—	14
d. Judges and attorneys	3	6	—	—	9
e. Professional members of the armed forces	2	2	—	1	5
f. Elected mayors	10	15	—	—	25
g. Professors at universities and colleges	5	6	1	2	14
h. Other academic staff at universities and colleges	2	4	1	1	8
i. Teachers at secondary schools	11	12	—	3	26
j. Teachers at elementary schools	5	11	—	2	18
Total	77	88	6	10	181 (=34.8%)
3. *Salaried employees in the civil service and other relevant bodies* (such as the broadcasting system, foundations etc.)					
Total	9	13	1	2	25 (=4.8%)
4. *Salaried employees in the administration of the European community*					
Total	—	1	—	1	2 (=0.4%)

Table 5 cont.	CDU/CSU	SPD	FDP	GREENS	TOTAL
5. *Theologians* (Protestant and Catholic clergy)					
Total	1	2	—	1	4 (=0.8%)
6. *Salaried employees of political parties and other organisations:*					
a. Political parties and caucuses	3	17	2	—	22
b. Trade Unions and other employee organisations	3	21	—	1	25
c. In other institutions including those in the field of cultural and social activities (*charitable*)	6	7	2	3	18
Total	12	45	4	4	65 (=12.5)
7. *Salaried employees in industry:* (Industry, trade, commerce, crafts etc.)					
Total	32	17	5	1	55 (=10.6)
8. *Self-employed*					
a. In industry, trade, commerce, crafts etc.	32	4	5	—	41
b. In agriculture and forestry	16	2	3	—	21
Total	48	6	8	—	62 (=11.9)
9. *Professions*					
a. Lawyers and notaries	19	7	3	1	30
b. Doctors, pharmacists, architects, engineers, journalists, tax-advisors etc.	15	7	2	3	27
Total	34	14	5	4	57 (=11.0)
10. *Housewives:*					
Total	3	4	—	—	7 (=1.3)
11. *Wage earners* [3]					
Total	2	10	—	2	14 (=2.7%)

Table 5 cont.	CDU/CSU	SPD	FDP	GREENS	TOTAL
12. *Others*					
Total	1	2	—	3	6 (= 1.1%)
The caucuses	255	202	35	28	520 (= 100%)

[1] This table was compiled on the basis of data given by the newly-elected members of parliament themselves.

[2] Who lose office after a political change of the government.

[3] In addition, those members of Parliament who were wage-earners at the beginning of their working career may have later practised another profession far more characteristic of the statistical categories of this table. A comparatively large number from group 6 above entered themselves as 'wage-earner' to denote a previous profession.

Source: Deutscher Bundestag, Verwaltung, *Parlamentsrecht*, 25 May 1983 (adapted)

Table 6. **Progress of Bills introduced in the Parliament of the Federal Republic 1.1.1949–31.7.1979**

Legislative periods	1949–53	1953–57	1957–61	1961–65	1965–69	1969–72	1972–76	1976–79
Bills introduced (total)	805	877	613	635	665	577	670	322
By the Government	472	446	401	378	417	362	461	210
By the Bundestag	301	414	207	245	227	171	136	79
By the Bundesrat	32	17	5	121	21	44	73	33

(Bills may be introduced by any of these three bodies. They reach the statute books when passed after a third reading by the Bundestag, after the assent of the Bundesrat (where required) and the final signature by the President. *Editor's note.*)

Bills passed by Parliament

Total, of those originating	545	507	424	427	453	335	516	201
Government	392	368	348	329	368	259	427	161
Bundestag	141	132	74	96	76	58	62	22
Bundesrat	12	7	2	2	9	13	17	10

Bills which failed to become law in the course of proceeding through Parliament

Total	174	212	96	95	80	74	80	33
Government bills	-[1]	26	13	15	16	9	2	1
Bundestag bills	-[1]	180	82	77	57	53	47	22
Bundesrat bills	-[1]	6	1	3	7	12	31	10

Bills which could not be steered through Parliament before the end of a legislative period

Total	86	158	93	113	132	169	71	-[1]
Government bills	-[1]	52	40	34	33	89	30	-[1]
Bundestag bills	-[1]	102	52	72	94	60	21	-[1]
Bundesrat bills	-[1]	4	2	7	5	20	20	-[1]

Appeals to the Mediation Committee of both Houses (Vermittlungsansschuß)[2]

Total	75	65	49	39	39	33	104	44
Appeal by Government	3	3	3	3	4	2	7	3
Appeal by Bundesrat	70	59	46	34	34	31	96	41
Appeal by Bundestag	2	3	0	2	1	0	1	0
Of those, the number of appeals on any given bill, more than once								
Twice	3	1	0	2	1	2	6	3
Three times	0	1	0	0	1	0	1	0
Finally enacted, after appeal	63	56	47	35	29	30	89	40
Not enacted, after appeal	9	6	2	2	7	1	7	1
Absolute veto by Bundesrat[2]	12	9	6	7	10	3	19	1
Finally enacted, after procedures in the Mediation Committee	4	5	4	4	8	2	11	0
Not enacted, after veto	8	4	2	3	2	1	8	1
Suspensive veto by Bundesrat[2]	1	1	3	0	0	1	6	5
Overridden by final vote of Bundestag and thereby								
enacted	0	1	1	0	0	1	5	5
Not enacted	1	0	2	0	0	0	1	0

[1] Figures not available   [2] Ch. 2 explains this in detail
Source: Deutscher Bundestag,ed., 30 Jahre Deutscher Bundestag, Dokumentation, Statistik, Daten, Bonn,1979, 270, 276, (translation here slightly adapted, absolute figures given only)

Table 7. **The d'Hondt system of proportional representation**

This system works on what is called the 'greatest average' principle. The total number of votes cast for each party is divided successively by 1, by 2, by 3 and so on. The resulting quotients are put in order and seats allocated to the highest quotients until all the seats are exhausted. Thus if three parties A, B and C were to win 480, 300 and 180 votes respectively and there are six seats to divide between them the result would be:

| Divided by: | Party | | |
	A	B	C
1	*480*	*300*	*180*
2	*240*	*150*	90
3	*160*	100	60
4	120	75	45
5	96	60	36

The six largest quotients are: 480, 300, 240, 180, 160, 150. So Party A wins three seats, Party B two seats and Party C one seat.

Table 8. **Electoral participation in the elections for the Bundestag, 1957–80**

The percentage of the electorate which voted in the Bundestag elections was as follows:

1957	87.8%
1961	87.7%
1965	86.8%
1969	86.7%
1972	91.1%
1976	90.7%
1980	88.6%

Source: Statistisches Bundesamt, Wiesbaden, *Statistisches Jahrbuch 1982 für die ... Bundesrepublik Deutschland*, Stuttgart/Mainz, 1982, 83

Table 9. **Bundestag election results, 1949–80 ('000s)**

	14.8.1949 31.2 mill. 24.5 mill. 78.5			6.3.1953 33.1 mill. 28.5 mill. 85.8			15.9.1957 35.4 mill. 31.1 mill. 87.8			17.9.1961 37.4 mill. 32.8 mill. 87.7		
Eligible / Turnout / % voting	a	b	c	a	b	c	a	b	c	a	b	c
CDU/CSU	7,359	31.0	139	12,440	45.2	243	15,008	50.2	270	14,298	45.3	242
SPD	6,935	29.2	131	7,945	28.8	151	9,496	31.8	169	11,427	36.2	190
FDP	2,83	11.9	52	2,628	9.5	48	2,307	7.7	41	4,029	12.8	67
KDP/DKP	1,362	5.7	15	0,607	2.2	-	-	-	-	-	-	-
DP[d]	0,94	4.0	17	0,898	3.3	15	1,007	3.4	17	GDP	2.8	-
BHE[d]	-	-	-	1,614	5.9	27	1,374	4.6	-	0,871		-
Centre[d]	0,728	3.1	10	0,217	0.8	2	0,086	0.3	-	-	-	-
Bavaria Party[d]	0,986	4.2	17	0,466	1.7	-	0,168	0.5	-	-	-	-
WAV[d]	0,682	2.9	12	-	-	-	-	-	-	-	-	-
DRP/NPD	0,429	1.8	5	0,296	1.1	-	0,309	1.0	-	0,263	0.8	-
DFU[d]	-	-	-	-	-	-	-	-	-	0,61	1.9	-
Others	1,481	6.2	4	0,433	1.4	-	0,15	0.5	-	0,052	0.2	-

Table 9 cont.

	19.9.1965 38.5 mill. 33.4 mill. 86.8			28.9.1969 38.7 mill. 33.0 mill. 86.7			19.11.1972 41.4 mill. 37.8 mill. 91.2			3.10.1976 42.0 mill. 38.1 mill. 90.7			5.10.1980 43.2 mill. 38.3 mill. 88.7		
	a	b	c	a	b	c	a	b	c	a	b	c	a	b	c
CDU/CSU	15,524	47.6	245	15,195	46.1	242	16,794	44.8	225	18,397	48.6	244	16,900	44.5	226
SPD	12,813	39.3	202	14,066	42.7	224	17,167	45.9	230	16,099	42.6	213	16,262	42.9	218
FDP	3,097	9.5	49	1,903	5.8	30	3,129	8.4	41	2,995	7.9	39	4,030	10.6	53
KPD/DKP	-	-	-	0,197	0.6	-	0,114	0.3	-	0,141	0.4	-	0,080	0.2	-
GDP															
Centre[d]															
Bavaria Party[d]															
WAV[d]															
DRP/NPD	0,664	2.0	-	1,422	4.3	-	0,207	0.6	-	0,122	0.3	-	0,067	0.2	-
DFU[d]	0,434	1.3	-	-	-	-	-	-	-	-	-	-	-	-	-
Others	0,088	0.3	-	0,022	-	-	0,027	0.1	-	0,070	0.2	-	0,599	1.6	-

Notes: [a] Total votes gained (000s)   [c] Number of seats, excl. deputies of West Berlin
[b] Percentage of vote   [d] Disappeared or included in 'Others'
Sources: Tormin, 288; Kaack, 356; Inter Nationes, 25; *Das Parlament*, 11.10.1980.

Table 10. **Seats won in the Bundestag elections of 1972, 1976 and 1980**[1]

	Total 1972	Total 1976	Total 1980	SPD 1972	SPD 1976	SPD 1980	CDU 1972	CDU 1976	CDU 1980	FDP 1972	FDP 1976	FDP 1980	CSU 1972	CSU 1976	CSU 1980
Schleswig-Holstein .... a	22	22	23	11	10	11	9	10	9	2	2	3	-	-	-
b	11	11	11	9	6	11	2	5	-	-	-	-	-	-	-
Hamburg .... a	16	14	13	9	8	7	5	5	4	2	1	2	-	-	-
b	8	8	7	8	8	7	-	-	-	-	-	-	-	-	-
Lower Saxony .... a	62	62	63	30	29	30	27	28	26	5	5	7	-	-	-
b	30	30	31	23	18	23	7	12	8	-	-	-	-	-	-
Bremen .... a	4	5	4	3	3	3	1	2	1	-	-	-	-	-	-
b	3	3	3	3	3	3	-	-	-	-	-	-	-	-	-
North Rhine Westphalia .... a	148	148	147	75	70	70	61	66	60	12	12	17	-	-	-
b	73	73	71	52	45	44	21	28	27	-	-	-	-	-	-
Hesse .... a	47	47	46	23	22	22	19	21	19	5	4	5	-	-	-
b	22	22	22	20	17	19	2	5	3	-	-	-	-	-	-
Rheinland-Pfalz .... a	31	31	32	14	13	14	15	16	15	2	2	3	-	-	-
b	16	16	16	9	6	7	10	10	-	-	-	-	-	-	-
Baden-Württemberg .... a	72	71	72	28	26	27	36	38	36	8	7	9	-	-	-
b	36	36	37	12	4	6	6	24	32	31	-	-	-	-	-
Bavaria .... a	86	88	89	33	29	30	-	-	-	5	6	7	48	53	52
b	44	44	45	13	4	5	-	-	-	-	-	-	31	40	40

Table 10 cont.

	Total			SPD			CDU			FDP			CSU		
	1972	1976	1980	1972	1976	1980	1972	1976	1980	1972	1976	1980	1972	1976	1980
Saar ....a	8	8	8	4	4	4	4	4	4	-	-	-	-	-	-
b	5	5	5	3	3	3	2	2	2	-	-	-	-	-	-
Federal Republic without Berlin ..a	496	496	497¹	230	214	218¹	177	190	174	41	39	53	48	53	52
b	248	248	248	152	114	127	65	94	81	-	-	-	31	40	40
Berlin (West)	22	22	22	12	10	10	9	11	11	1	1	1	-	-	-
Total	518	518	519¹	242	224	228¹	186	201	185	42	40	54	48	53	52

a: Elected directly as well as off lists   b: Elected directly only

¹This includes an extra seat in Schleswig-Holstein because the SPD obtained one more directly elected seat than its list vote would otherwise have entitled it to hold

Source: Statistisches Bundesamt Wiesbaden, ed., *Statistisches Jahrbuch 1982 für die Bundesrepublik Deutschland,* Stuttgart/Mainz, 1983, 85

Table 11a. **German nationals expelled and repatriated from the eastern and south-eastern states of Europe between 1950 and 1969.**

Numbers include those persons who defected to the Federal Republic from the states in question. Figures in brackets give the monthly average of persons entering the Federal Republic

From countries	1950	1951	1952	1953	1954	1955	1956	1957	1958	1959	1960	1961	1962	1963	1964	1965	1966	1967	1968	1969	1950-1969
Poland	31,761 (2,647)	10,791 (899)	194 (16)	147 (12)	664 (55)	860 (72)	15,674 (1,306)	98,290 (8,191)	117,550 (9,796)	16,252 (1,354)	7,739 (643)	9,303 (773)	9,657 (805)	9,522 (794)	13,611 (1,134)	14,644 (1,220)	17,315 (1,443)	10,856 (905)	8,435 (703)	9,536 (795)	402,801
USSR	- (-)	1,721 (143)	63 (5)	- (-)	18 (2)	154 (13)	1,016 (85)	923 (77)	4,122 (344)	5,563 (464)	3,272 (273)	345 (29)	894 (75)	209 (17)	234 (20)	366 (31)	1,245 (104)	1,092 (91)	598 (50)	316 (26)	22,151
CSSR	13,308 (1,109)	3,524 (294)	146 (12)	63 (5)	128 (11)	184 (13)	954 (80)	762 (64)	692 (58)	600 (50)	1,394 (116)	1,207 (101)	1,228 (102)	973 (81)	2,712 (226)	3,210 (268)	5,925 (494)	11,628 (969)	11,854 (988)	15,602 (1,300)	76,094
Hungary	3 (-)	157 (13)	30 (3)	15 (1)	43 (4)	98 (8)	160 (13)	2,193 (183)	1,194 (100)	507 (42)	319 (27)	194 (16)	264 (22)	286 (24)	387 (32)	724 (60)	608 (51)	316 (26)	303 (25)	414 (35)	8,215
Roumania	13 (1)	1,031 (86)	26 (2)	15 (1)	8 (1)	44 (4)	176 (15)	384 (32)	1,383 (115)	374 (31)	2,124 (177)	3,303 (275)	1,675 (140)	1,321 (110)	818 (68)	2,715 (226)	609 (51)	440 (37)	614 (51)	2,675 (223)	19,748
Yugoslavia	179 (15)	3,668 (306)	3,407 (284)	7,972 (664)	9,481 (790)	11,839 (987)	7,314 (610)	5,130 (428)	4,703 (392)	3,819 (318)	3,308 (276)	2,053 (171)	2,003 (167)	2,543 (212)	2,331 (194)	2,195 (183)	2,078 (173)	1,881 (157)	1,391 (116)	1,325 (110)	78,620
others	1,901 (158)	175 (15)	182 (15)	84 (7)	50 (4)	23 (2)	8 (1)	8 (1)	11 (1)	21 (2)	15 (1)	9 (1)	12 (1)	15 (1)	6 (-)	13 (1)	33 (3)	14 (1)	6 (-)	5 (-)	2,591
Total	47,497 (3,958)	24,765 (2,064)	13,369 (1,114)	15,410 (1,284)	15,424 (1,285)	15,788 (1,316)	31,345 (2,612)	113,946 (9,496)	132,228 (11,019)	28,450 (2,371)	19,169 (1,597)	17,161 (1,430)	16,415 (1,368)	15,483 (1,290)	20,842 (1,737)	24,342 (2,029)	28,193 (2,349)	26,475 (2,206)	23,397 (1,950)	30,039 (2,503)	659,738

Source: Der Bundesminster des Innern, VtK 14–933 600/2

Table 11b. **German nationals expelled and repatriated from the eastern and south-eastern states of Europe, 1.1.1970 –31.5.1983.**

As in table 11a, numbers include defectors; figures in brackets give the monthly average of persons entering the Federal Republic

From countries:	1970	1971	1972	1973	1974	1975	1976	1977	1978	1979	1980	1981	1982	1970–82	1950–82	1.1.83–31.5.83
Poland	5,624 (469)	25,241 (2,103)	13,482 (1,124)	8,903 (742)	7,825 (652)	7,040 (587)	29,364 (2,447)	32,857 (2,738)	36,102 (3,009)	36,274 (3,023)	26,637 (1,970)	50,983 (4,249)	30,355 (2,530)	310,687	765,669	8,593 (1,719)
USSR	342 (29)	1,145 (95)	3,420 (285)	4,493 (374)	6,541 (545)	5,985 (499)	9,704 (809)	9,274 (773)	8,455 (705)	7,226 (602)	6,954 (580)	3,773 (314)	2,071 (173)	69,363	91,535	538 (108)
CSSR	4,702 (351)	2,337 (195)	894 (75)	525 (44)	378 (32)	516 (43)	849 (71)	612 (51)	904 (75)	1,058 (88)	1,733 (144)	1,629 (136)	1,776 (148)	17,418	93,512	395 (79)
Hungary	517 (43)	519 (43)	520 (44)	440 (37)	423 (35)	277 (23)	233 (19)	189 (16)	269 (22)	370 (31)	591 (49)	667 (56)	589 (49)	5,604	13,819	189 (38)
Roumania	6,519 (543)	2,848 (237)	4,374 (365)	7,577 (631)	8,484 (707)	5,077 (423)	3,766 (314)	10,989 (916)	12,120 (1,010)	9,663 (805)	15,767 (1,314)	12,031 (1,003)	12,972 (1,081)	112,187	131,935	6,367 (1,273)
Yugoslavia	1,372 (114)	1,159 (97)	884 (74)	783 (65)	646 (54)	419 (35)	313 (26)	237 (20)	202 (17)	190 (16)	287 (24)	234 (20)	213 (18)	6,939	85,559	57 (44)
others	9 (1)	23 (2)	6 (-)	11 (1)	18 (2)	15 (1)	19 (2)	5 (-)	9 (1)	21 (2)	15 (1)	19 (2)	16 (1)	186	2,777	– (–)
Total	18,949 (1,579)	33,637 (2,803)	23,895 (1,991)	23,063 (1,922)	24,507 (2,042)	19,657 (1,638)	44,402 (3,700)	54,251 (4,521)	58,123 (4,844)	54,887 (4,574)	52,071 (4,339)	69,455 (5,788)	48,170 (4,014)	525,067	1,184,806	16,177 (3,236)

Source: Der Bundesminister des Innern, Vtk I 4–933 600/2

Table 12. **Escapees from the German Democratic Republic and East Berlin to the Federal Republic of Germany**

	Total	1.People who left GDR with official permission	2.Refugees who left GDR without permission	3. Numbers of 2. who faced lethal obstacles (after 13.8.1961)	Others[1]
a. 1949 to 12.8.1961 (erection of Wall)	2,686,942	-	-	-	-
b. From 13.8.61					
1961	51,624	-	51,624	8,507	
1962	21,356	4,615	16,741	5,761	
1963	42,632	29,665	12,967	3,692	
1964	41,876	30,012	11,864	3,155	
1965	29,552	17,666	11,886	2,329	
1966	24,131	15,675	8,456	1,736	
1967	19,573	13,188	6,385	1,203	
1968	16,036	11,134	4,902	1,135	
1969	16,975	11,702	5,273	1,193	
1970	17,519	12,472	5,047	901	
1971	17,408	11,565	5,843	832	
1972	17,164	11,627	5,537	1,245	
1973	15,189	8,667	6,522	1,842	
1974	13,252	7,928	5,324	969	
1975	16,285	10,274	6,011	673	
1976	15,168	10,058	5,110	610	
1977	12,078	8,041	4,037	721	
1978	12,117	8,271	3,846	461	
1979	12,515	9,003	3,512	463	
1980	12,763	8,775	2,976	424	1,012
1981	15,433	11,093	2,900	298	1,440
1982	13,208	9,113	2,565	283	1,530
Total b.	453,854	260,544	189,328	38,433	3,982
Total a. + b.	3,140,796				

[1] Statistically registered as from 1.1.1980. Before that listed under 'refugees'
Source: Federal Ministry of the Interior, 1983

Table 13. **Public finance**

The consolidated budget of all three levels of government (Federal Government, Länder, local authorities) amounted to public expenditure of DM 496 billion in 1980, which is 34.2% of the Gross National Product (GNP). The most important items of expenditure were (% of total):

Social security	22%
Education, research and culture	18%
Defence	8%
Transport and communication	6%
Public health, sport and recreation	6%

In the budget of the Federal Government alone, defence accounted for 17.5% of all expenditure.

Important elements of public finance are the para-statal institutions of social security which are financed mainly by contributions, but which also receive sizeable public subsidies. If the budget of these institutions is included in public expenditure, then the total consolidated public budget amounts to DM 711 billion in 1980, which is 48% of the GNP. Spending on social security alone accounted for 28% of the GNP; the most important items were old-age pensions.

Sources: Statistisches Bundesamt, ed., *Statistisches Jahrbuch 1982;* Statistisches Bundesamt, ed., *Datenreport,* Bonn, 1983

Table 14. **External trade**

As an exporter, the Federal Republic of Germany ranks second in the world with about 9% of world exports. Total exports from the Federal Republic amounted to DM 396.9 billion in 1981, which was 25.6% of the Gross Domestic Product. Total imports amounted to DM 369.2 billion in the same year. The Federal Republic has had export surpluses since 1955. The surplus is needed to earn the foreign exchange required for the income transfers of the large number of foreign workers (their total number was 1.9 million in 1981) and for the deficit in tourism. In 1981 DM 39.6 billion in foreign exchange were spent by German tourists, which resulted in a deficit of DM 25.5 billion in this field.

Exports

The six most important categories of exports were

	(1981; % of total exports)
Vehicles	17.9%
Machinery (except electric machinery)	17.4%
Chemicals	13.4%
Iron and iron products	9.5%
Electric goods (including electric machinery)	9.3%
Textiles	5.0%

The six most important countries of destination of these exports were

	(1981; % of total exports)
France	13.1%
Netherlands	8.5%
Italy	7.9%
Belgium/Luxemburg	7.3%
Great Britain	6.6%
USA	6.5%

All Eastern bloc countries together received about 5% of all exports

Imports

The six most important categories of imports were

	(1981; % of total imports)
Crude oil and derived products	23.6%
Chemicals	8.5%
Textiles	8.0%
Vehicles	7.6%
Machinery (without electric machinery)	6.4%
Electronic products (including electric machinery	6.2%

Table 14 cont.

The six most important countries of origin of these imports were

	(1981; % of total imports)
Netherlands	12.0%
France	10.9%
USA	7.7%
Italy	7.5%
Great Britain	7.4%
Belgium/Luxemburg	6.7%

All Eastern bloc countries together accounted for about 6% of all imports.

Soure: Bundesministerium für Wirtschaft, *Leistung in Zahlen 1981;* Statistisches Bundesamt, *Wirtschaft und Statistik 2/83;* Statistisches Bundesamt, ed., *Datenreport*, Bonn, 1983

Table 15. Industrial Stoppages

Working days lost per 1000 employees

	1979	average 1970–75
Federal Republic of Germany	19	36
France	209	211
Italy	1600	1309
Netherlands	77	43
Belgium	197	269
Luxemburg	—	—
United Kingdom	1276	570
Ireland	1905	789
Denmark	83	260

Source: Eurostat, *Review 1970-1979,* 140

Table 16. Working time and holidays

The actual weekly working time was 40 hours in 1980. In addition to the high number of public holidays in the Federal Republic of Germany, workers and salaried employees had paid holidays as follows (figures for 1980)

From 3 to under 4 weeks	5%
From 4 to under 5 weeks	22%
From 5 to under 6 weeks	69%
6 weeks or more	4%

Source: Statistisches Bundesamt, ed., *Datenreport, Zahlen and Fakten über die Bundesrepublik Deutschland,* Bonn, 1983, 137

Table 17. **Elections to the Tenth Federal Parliament, 6.3.1983**[1]

	Number	1983 %
Electorate	44,088,935	
Votes cast	39,279,529	
Turn-out		89.1
Invalid second votes	338,841	0.9
Valid second votes	38,940,687	
of which for		
CDU/CSU	18,998,545	48.8
SPD	14,865,807	38.2
FDP	2,706,942	7.0
Greens	2,167,431	5.6
Others, including Communists, NDP etc.	201,942	0.4
Valid first votes	38,841,230	
of which for		
CDU/CSU	20,259,428	52.1
SDP	15,684,450	40.4
FDP	1,088,857	2.8
Greens	1,607,665	4.1
Communists	97,414	0.3

Distribution of Seats 1983

Party	Constituency seats	Land list	Total excl. Berlin	incl. Berlin
CDU/CSU	180	64	244	255
SPD	68	125	193	202
FDP	-	34	34	35
Greens	-	27	27	28

[1]*Source:* Bulletin, 25 March 1983

Figures

Fig. 1. **Defence expenditure of the Federal Republic of Germany 1970–78** (DM thousand million, growth rate in per cent)

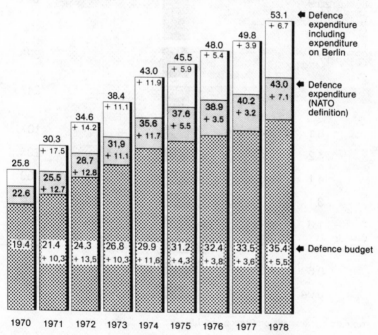

Source: White Paper 1979. The Security of the Federal Republic of Germany and the Development of the Federal Armed Forces, Federal Minister of Defence for the Federal Government, Bonn, 1979, 119, 270

Fig. 2. **Defence expenditure of NATO countries 1978**

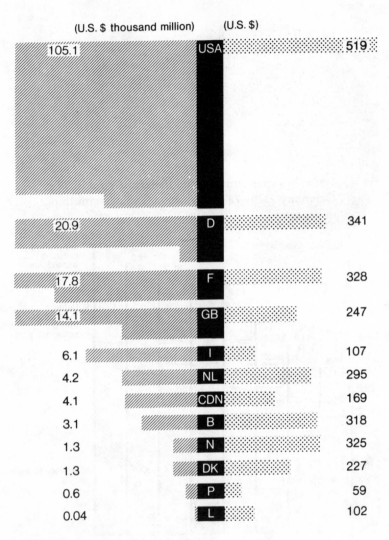

No data are available on Greece and Turkey.

Source: White Paper 1979. The Security of the Federal Republic of Germany and the Development of the Federal Armed Forces, Federal Minister of Defence for the Federal Government, Bonn, 1979, 277

Fig. 3. **Breakdown of defence expenditure 1979** (DM thousand
million and per cent)

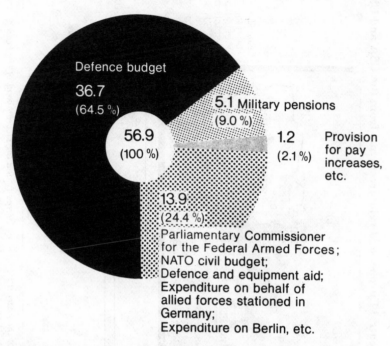

Defence budget
36.7
(64.5 %)

56.9
(100 %)

5.1 Military pensions
(9.0 %)

1.2
(2.1 %)

Provision
for pay
increases,
etc.

13.9
(24.4 %)

Parliamentary Commissioner
for the Federal Armed Forces;
NATO civil budget;
Defence and equipment aid;
Expenditure on behalf of
allied forces stationed in
Germany;
Expenditure on Berlin, etc.

*Source: White Paper 1979. The Security of the Federal Republic of Germany and the
Development of the Federal Armed Forces,* Federal Minister of Defence for the
Federal Government, Bonn, 1979, 271

420

Fig. 4. Land and air forces in Central Europe, and reinforcements from the USA and USSR

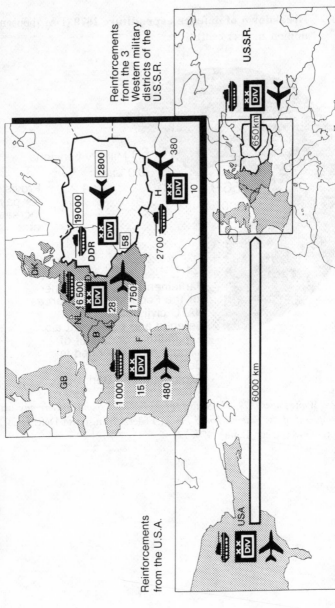

Source: White Paper 1979. The Security of the Federal Republic of Germany and the Development of the Federal Armed Forces, Federal Minister of Defence for the Federal Government, Bonn, 1979, 119

Select Bibliography

BIBLIOGRAPHIES

Hereford-Price, Arnold, *The Federal Republic of Germany. A Selected Bibliography of English Language Publications*, 2nd rev. edn., Washington, 1978
Merritt, Anna J. and Richard L., *Politics, Economics and Society in the Two Germanies 1945–1975*, Champaign-Urbana, 1978

GENERAL WORKS ON THE POLITICAL SYSTEM OF THE FEDERAL REPUBLIC OF GERMANY

Childs, D. and Johnson, J., *West Germany: Politics and Society*, London, 1981
Conradt, David P., *The German Polity*, New York, 1978
Dahrendorf, R., *Society and Democracy in Germany*, London, 1968
Heidenheimer, Arnold J. and Kommers, Donald P., *The Governments of Germany*, 4th edn., New York, 1975
Paterson, William E. and Smith, Gordon, *The West German Model. Perspectives on a Stable State*, London, 1981
Sontheimer, Kurt, *The Government and Politics of West Germany* New, York, 1973

CHAPTER 1. *The Origins of the Federal Republic of Germany, 1944–1949*

Adenauer, Konrad, *Memoirs 1945–53*, London, 1966
Balfour, Michael, *West Germany*, London, 1968
——, 'Four-Power Control in Germany 1945–1946' in Balfour, Michael and Mair, John, *Four-Power Control in Germany and Austria*

1945–1946. Survey of International Affairs, 1939–1946, (ed.) Arnold Toynbee, London, 1956

Chalmers, Douglas A., *The Social Democratic Party of Germany, From Working-class Movement to Modern Political Party*, New Haven, 1964

Edinger, Lewis J., *Kurt Schumacher*, Oxford, 1965

Feis, Herbert, *Between War and Peace. The Potsdam Conference*, Princeton, 1960

Gimbel, John, *The American Occupation of Germany*, Stanford, 1968

Heidenheimer, Arnold J., *Adenauer and the CDU. The Rise of the Leader and the Integration of the Party*, The Hague, 1960

Merkl, Peter H., *The Origin of the West German Republic*, New York, 1963

Pridham, Geoffrey, *Christian Democracy in Western Germany. The CDU/CSU in Government and Opposition, 1945–1976*, London, 1977

Smith, Jean Edward, (ed.), *The Papers of General Lucius D. Clay: Germany 1945–1949*, 2 vols., Bloomington, 1974

Stolper, Gustav, Häuser, Karl and Borchardt, Knut, *The German Economy, 1870 to the Present*, New York, 1967

Wallich, H.C., *Mainsprings of the German Revival*, New Haven, 1955

Wheeler-Bennett, John W. and Nicholls, Anthony, *The Semblance of Peace, The Political Settlement after the Second World War*, London, 1972

Willis, F. Roy, *The French in Germany, 1945–1949*, Stanford, 1962

de Zayas, Alfred, M., *Nemesis at Potsdam, the Anglo-Americans and the Expulsion of the Germans: Background, Execution, Consequences*, London, 1977

CHAPTER 2. *Parliamentary Democracy—The Bundestag*

Braunthal, Gerard, *The West German Legislative Process*, Ithaca, 1972

Burkett, T. and Schnettemeyer, S., *The West German Parliament*, London, 1982

Loewenberg, Gerhard, *Parliament in the West German Political System*, Ithaca, 1966

Schäfer, Friedrich, *Der Bundestag*, Opladen, 1982

Schellknecht, Helmut, and Ziller, Gebhard, 'The Parliamentary Institutions in the Federal Republic of Germany', *Constitutional and Parliamentary Information, 29*, Geneva, 1979, *117*, 15–24

Schweitzer, Carl-Christoph, *Der Abgeordnete im parlamentarischen Regierungssystem der Bundesrepublik, Deutschland*, Opladen, 1979

CHAPTER 3. *Chancellor, Cabinet and President*

Dyson, Kenneth, 'The German Federal Chancellor's Office', *Political Quarterly (July–September)*, 45, 364–71

Johnson, Nevil, *Government in the Federal Republic of Germany*, Oxford, 1973

Junker, E.U., *Die Richtlinienkompetenz des Bundeskanzlers*, Tübingen, 1965

Laufer, Heinz, *Der parlamentarische Staatssekretaer*, Munich, 1969

Mayntz, Renate, and Scharpf, Fritz, *Policy-Making in the German Federal Bureaucracy*, Amsterdam, 1975

Merkl, Peter Hans, *Germany, Yesterday and Tomorrow*, New York, 1965

Prittie, Terrence, *Willy Brandt*, New York, 1974

Rausch, H., *Der Bundespräsident*, Munich, 1979

Ridley, F.F., 'Chancellor Government as a Political System and the German Constitution', *Parliamentary Affairs*, 19, February 1966, 446–61

CHAPTER 4. *The Judiciary*

Geck, Wilhelm K., 'The Reform of Legal Education in the Federal Republic of Germany', *American Journal of Comparative Law*, 25, 1977, 86–119

Heyde, Wolfgang, *The Administration of Justice in the Federal Republic of Germany*, Bonn, 1971

Laufer, Heinz, *Verfassungsgerichtsbarkeit und politische Prozess*, Tübingen, 1968

Leibholz, Gerhard, *Politics and Law*, Leyden, 1965

Kommers, Donald, P., *Judicial Politics in West Germany: A Study of the Federal Constitutional Court*, London, 1976

McWhinney, Edward, *Constitutionalism in Germany and the Federal Constitutional Court*, Leyden, 1962

Pakuscher, Ernst K., 'Administrative Law in Germany—Citizen v. State', *American Journal of Comparative Law*, 16, 1968, 309–31

Rheinstein, Max, 'Approach to German Law', *Indiana Law Journal*, 34, 1959, 546–58

Schmidt, Richard, *Justiz in der Bundesrepublik*, Pfullingen, 1967

Schram, Glenn N., 'The Recruitment of Judges for the West German Federal Courts', *American Journal of Comparative Law*, 21, 1973, 691–711

CHAPTER 5. *Basic Rights and Constitutional Review*

American Council of Germany, *Civil Liberties and the Defense of Democracy Against Extremists and Terrorists: A Report on the West German Situation*, New York, 1980

Benda, Ernst, 'New Tendencies in the Development of Fundamental Rights in the Federal Republic of Germany', *John Marshall Journal of Practice and Procedure, 11,* 1977, 1–15

Kauper, Paul, and Halberstadt, Rudolf, 'Religion and Education in West Germany: A Survey and an American Perspective', *Valparaiso University Law Review, 4,* 1969, 1–42

Klein, Ekkehart, 'The Principle of Equality and its Protection in the Federal Republic of Germany' in Koopmans, *Constitutional Protection of Equality,* Leyden, 1975

Kommers, Donald P., 'The Jurisprudence of Free Speech in the United States and the Federal Republic of Germany', *Southern California Law Review, 53,* 1980, 654–95

Krieger, Leonard, *The German Idea of Freedom,* Boston, 1975

Lautner, Gerd, *Die Freiheitliche Demokratische Ordnung,* Athenaum, 1982

Lee, Orlan, and Robertson, T.A., *'Moral Order' and the Criminal Law: Reform Efforts in the United States and West Germany,* The Hague, 1973

Meyer-Teschendorf, Klaus G., *Staat und Kirche in pluralistischen Gemeinwesen,* Tübingen, 1979

CHAPTERS 6 AND 7. *Federalism: Bund and Länder/Federalism: Intergovernmental Relations and Finance*

Blair, Philip, *Federalism and Judicial Review in West Germany,* Oxford, 1981

Bundesminister für Bildung und Wissenschaft, *Report of the Federal Government on Education 1970; The Federal Government's Concept of Educational Policy,* Bonn, 1970

Cole, R. Taylor, 'Federalism and Universities in West Germany: Recent Trends', *American Journal of Comparative Law, 21,* Winter, 1973, 45–68

——, 'West German Federalism Revisited', *American Journal of Comparative Law, 23,* 1975, 2, 325–36

Hearnden, Arthur, *Education, Culture and Politics in West Germany,* Oxford/Frankfurt, 1976

Hesse, Konrad, *Der unitarische Bundesstaat*, Karlsruhe, 1962

Laufer, Heinz, *Das Föderative System der Bundesrepublik Deutschland*, Munich, 1981

Merkl, Peter Hans, 'The Financial Constitution [Finanzverfassung] of West Germany', *American Journal of Comparative Law, 6*, 1957, 327–40

Pinney, Edward L., *Federalism, Bureaucracy and Party Politics in Western Germany: Role of the Bundesrat*, Chapel Hill, 1963

Reuter, Konrad, *Föderalismus. Grundlagen und Wirkungen in der Bundesrepublik Deutschland*, Heidelberg/Hamburg, 1983

CHAPTER 8. *Political Parties*

Balfour, Michael, *West Germany*, rev. edn., London, 1982

Burkett, Tony, *Parties and Elections in West Germany. The Search for Stability*, London, 1974

Fisher, Stephen L., *The Minor Parties of the Federal Republic of Germany. Toward a Comparative Theory of Minor Parties*, The Hague, 1974

Grosser, Alfred, *Germany in our Time. A Political History of the Post-War Years*, London, 1971

Kaack, Heino, *Geschichte und Struktur des Deutschen Parteiensystems*, Opladen, 1971

Kinz, Rainer, *et al.*, *Programme der politischen Parteien in der Bundesrepublik Deutschland*, Munich, 1979

Kitzinger, Uwe, *German Electoral Politics. A Study of the 1957 Campaign*, Oxford, 1960

Pridham, Geoffrey, *Christian Democracy in Western Germany. The CDU/CSU in Government and Opposition, 1945–1976*, London, 1977

Schellenger, Harold K., *The SPD in the Bonn Republic*, The Hague, 1968

Smith, Gordon, *Democracy in Western Germany. Parties and Politics in the Federal Republic*, London, 1979

CHAPTER 9. *Public Opinion: Interest Groups and the Media*

Claessens, Dieter, *et al.*, *Sozialkunde der Bundesrepublik Deutschland*, new edn., Düsseldorf/Cologne, 1981

Beyme, Klaus, *Interessengruppen in der Demokratie*, 5th edn., Munich, 1980

Guggenberger, Bernd, *Bürgerinitiativen in der Parteiendemokratie*, Stuttgart/Berlin/Cologne/Mainz, 1980

Weber, Jürgen, *Die Interessengruppen im politischen System der Bundesrepublik Deutschland*, Stuttgart/Berlin/Cologne/Mainz, 1977

Braunthal, G., *The Federation of German Industry in Politics*, Ithaca, 1965

CHAPTER 10. *Economic and Social Policy*

Claessens, Dieter, et. al., *Sozialkunde der Bundesrepublik Deutschland*, new edn., Düsseldorf/Cologne, 1981

Hallet, G., *The Social Economy of West Germany*, London, 1973

Helmstädter, Ernst, et. al., *Wirtschaftskunde der Bundesrepublik Deutschland*, Düsseldorf/Cologne, 1975

Lampert, Heinz, *Die Wirtschafts-und Sozialordnung der Bundesrepublik Deutschland*, 5th edn., Munich, 1976

Owen-Smith, E., *The West German Economy*, London, 1982

Wünsche, Horst Friedrich, *Standard Texts on the Social Market Economy*, Stuttgart/New York, 1982

CHAPTER 11. *Foreign Policy*

Deutsch, Karl W., and Edinger, Lewis J., *Germany Rejoins the Powers. Mass Opinion, Interest Groups, and Elites in Contemporary German Foreign Policy*, Stanford, 1959

Griffiths, William E., *The Ostpolitik of the Federal Republic of Germany*, Cambridge, Mass., 1978

Hanrieder, Wolfram F., *The Stable Crisis. Two Decades of German Foreign Policy*, New York, 1970

——, ed., *West German Foreign Policy, 1949–1979*, Boulder, 1979

Kaiser, Karl, *Germany Foreign Policy in Transition. Bonn Between East and West*, London, 1969

——, and Morgan, (eds.), *Britain and Western Germany. Changing Societies and the Future of Foreign Policy*, London, 1971

Merkl, Peter H., *German Foreign Policies, West and East. On the Threshold of a New European Era*, Santa Barbara, 1974

Morgan, Roger, *The United States and West Germany, 1945–1973: A Study in Alliance Politics*, London, 1974

Richardson, James L., *Germany and the Atlantic Alliance. The Interaction of Strategy and Politics*, Cambridge, Mass., 1966

Stent, Angela, *From Embargo to Ostpolitik. The Political Economy of*

West German–Soviet Relations, 1955–1980, Cambridge, 1981

Whetten, Lawrence L., *Germany's Ostpolitik. Relations between the Federal Republic and the Warsaw Pact Countries*, London, 1971

Willis, F. Roy, *France, Germany and the New Europe, 1945–1963*, Stanford, 1965

Windsor, Philip, *Germany and the Management of Détente*, London, 1971

CHAPTER 12. *Defence Policy and the Armed Forces*

Barth, Peter, (ed.), *Die Bundeswehr in Staat und Gesellschaft*, Munich, 1982

Haftendorn, Helga, 'West Germany and the Management of Security Relations: Security Policy under the Conditions of International Inter-dependence', in *The Foreign Policy of West Germany*, London, 1980, 7–31

Leber, Georg, 'Principles Underlying German Defense Policy', *The Atlantic Community, 14, 2*, Lexington, 1976, 218–24

Ministry of Defence, (ed.), White Paper, 1979, *The Security of the Federal Republic of Germany and the Development of the Federal Armed Forces*, Bonn, 1979

von Schubert, Klaus, *Sicherheitspolitik der Bundesrepublik Deutschland. Dokumentation 1945–1977*, 2 vols., Cologne, 1979

Schwarz, Jürgen, (ed.), *Grundlagen und aktuelle Aspekte der deutschen Sicherheitspolitik*, Munich, 1982

CHAPTER 13. *Berlin*

Bowers, Stephen Reed, *The West Berlin Issue in the Era of Superpower Détente: East Germany and the Politics of West Berlin*, Tennessee, 1975

Brandt, Willy, *The Ordeal of Coexistence. The Gustav Pollak Lectures at Harvard University, 1962*, Cambridge, Mass., 1963

Catudal, Honoré M. Jr., *The Diplomacy of the Quadripartite Agreement on Berlin. A New Era in East–West Politics*, Berlin, 1978

Clay, Lucius D., *Decision in Germany*, New York, 1950

Davison, W. Phillips, *The Berlin Blockade*, New York, 1958

Mander, John, *Berlin: Hostage for the West*, London, 1962

Schick, Jack M., *The Berlin Crisis, 1958–1962*, Philadelphia, 1971

Slusser, Robert M., *The Berlin Crisis of 1961. Soviet American Relations and the Struggle for Power in the Kremlin, June–November, 1961*, Baltimore, 1973

Smith, Jean Edward, *The Defense of Berlin*, Baltimore, 1963
Speier, Hans, *Divided Berlin. The Anatomy of Soviet Blackmail*, London, 1961
Windsor, Philip, *City on Leave. A History of Berlin 1945–1962*, London, 1963

CHAPTER 14. *The Federal Republic and the German Democratic Republic*

Bundesminister für innerdeutsche Beziehungen, (ed.), *Bericht der Bundesregierung und Materialien zur Lage der Nation 1972*, Kassel, 1972
Bundesminister für innerdeutsche Beziehungen, (ed.), *Materialien zum Bericht zur Lage der Nation 1974*, Berlin, 1974
Doeker, Günther, and Brückner, Jens A., eds., *The Federal Republic of Germany and the German Democratic Republic in International Relations*, New York, 1979
Romoser, George K., 'The State of the German Nation', in *European Journal of Political Research*, Amsterdam, 1975, 425–35
Roth, Margit, *Zwei Staaten in Deutschland — Die sozialliberale Deutschlandpolitik und ihre Auswirkungen 1969–1978*, Opladen, 1981
Schierbaum, Hansjürgen, *Intra-German Relations. Development, Problems, Facts*, Munich, 1979
Schweitzer, Carl-Christoph, *Die deutsche Nation. Aussagen von Bismarck bis Honecker. Dokumentation*, 2nd edn., Cologne, 1979

Glossary

(This glossary lists technical terms and abbreviations applied in the political system of the Federal Republic of Gemany which are either untranslatable, and therefore used in this volume in German only, or so uncommon for Anglo-Saxon readers that they need to be explained, or used differently in Britain and the United States.)

Anfrage (pl: Anfragen) = written questions addressed to the government in parliament, usually with many supplementary questions.

Aktuelle Stunde = ad-hoc debate in parliament, put on the agenda on the motion of any one party, lasting an hour.

Art. (= Artikel) = synonymous in German legal text with paragraph (§) or section (US), therefore used interchangeably in this volume.

Bund = Federation, also synonymous with the source of federal power.

Bundesgesetzblatt (BGBl) = Statute Book of federal laws enacted by Parliament.

Bundeskabinett = Bundesregierung = Federal government, synonymous with cabinet.

Bundeskanzler = Federal chancellor.

Bundesminister = Federal minister

Bundespräsident = Federal president, head of state.

Bundesrat = Council of Constituent States (Länder, see *infra* Land).

Bundesrepublik Deutschland = Federal Republic of Germany.

Bundestag, Deutscher = Federal Parliament.

Bundestagspräsident = Speaker.

Bundesverfassungsgericht = Federal Constitutional Court.

Bundesversammlung = Federal Convention, to elect the Federal president.

Bundeswehr = federal armed forces, services.

CDU (Christlich-Demokratische Union) = Christian Democratic Union.

CSU (Christlich-Soziale Union) = Christian Social Union, in Bavaria.

Deutsche Demokratische Republik = GDR (German Democratic Republic, East).

DGB (Deutscher Gewerkschaftsbund) = German Federation of Labour (TUC, AFL/CIO).

DKP (Deutsche Kommunistische Partei) = German Communist Party.

Evangelische Kirche in Deutschland = German Council of Protestant Churches.

Fraktion = caucus (US), parliamentary party (GB) in parliament.

Freiheitlich-demokratische Grundordnung = free democratic constitutional or basic order, a term frequently used in connection with activities which are regarded as threats to this order.

FDP (Freie Demokratische Partei) = Free Democratic Party.

Geschäftsordnung = Standing Orders (GB), Rules (US)—of parliament, but also of other bodies.

Gesamtdeutsch = all-German, referring jointly to the Federal Republic and the GDR.

Gesetz = Law, Act or Statute.

Grundgesetz = Basic Law, constitution of the Federal Republic.

Grüne = The Greens (ecology party).

KBW (Kommunistischer Bund Westdeutschlands) = Communist League of West Germany.

KPD (Kommunistische Partei Deutschlands) = Communist Party of Germany originally outlawed in 1956.

Konstruktives Misstrauensvotum = constructive vote of no-confidence (in the Bundestag).

Land (pl: Länder) = federal state (US), e.g. Bavaria.

Legislaturperiod = legislative period (or term)

Ministerpräsident = minister-president = Prime Minister of a Land; in Hamburg, Berlin and Bremen: Bürgermeister (Regierender or First Minister).

Mitbestimmung = co-determination.

NDP (Nationaldemokratische Partei) = National Democratic Party of Germany.

Öffentlicher Dienst = Civil Service (federal, of the Länder and local).

Parlamentarischer Rat = Parliamentary Council = Constituent Assembly to draw up Basic Law.

Parlamentarischer Staatssekretär = Parliamentary Secretary of State, deputizing for the minister in parliament, of which he is a member.

Parteitag = Party Congres or Conference = US Convention.

Rechtsstaat = German tradition of government based on due process of law.

Reich = Old German Empire.

SPD (Sozialdemokratische Partei Deutschlands) = Social Democratic Party of Germany.

SRP (Sozialistische Reichspartei) = former neo-Nazi party, outlawed in 1952.

Soziale Marktwirtschaft = social market economy.

Ständige Konferenz der Kultusminister = Permanent Conference of the Ministers for Cultural Affairs (and education) of the Länder.

Staatssekretär = (Permanent) Under-Secretary (of State) in a ministry (GB), Assistant Secretary of State (US).

Tagesordnung = Agenda, Order Paper in parliament—also pertaining to the order of business of other bodies.

Notes on the Editors

Carl-Christoph Schweitzer
Professor of Political Science at the University of Bonn, he graduated from Oxford and received his PhD at the University of Freiburg. He has written books on contemporary international affairs, European integration and on the problems of parliamentary government: *Amerika's Chinesisches Dilemma*, Opladen, 1969; *Die nationalen Parlamente in der Gemeinschaft, ihr schwindener Einfluß in Bonn und Westminster auf die Europagesetzgebung*, Bonn, 1978; *Bremer Bundeswehrkrawalle–Gefahren für unseren Staat und ihre Verschleierung im Streit der Politischen Parteien im parlamentarischen Untersuchungsverfahren*, Baden-Baden, 1980, and *Weltmacht USA: Kontinuität und Wandel ihrer Außenpolitik nach 1945*, Munich, 1983. For five years he was a member of the German Bundestag, where he served on the Committees for Foreign Relations and Defence.

Detlev Karsten
Professor of Economics and the Didactics of Economics at the University of Bonn, he was previously Professor at Stuttgart University (1970–5) and Visiting Professor of Economics in Ethiopia (1964–70). He is the author of *Wirtschaftsordnung und Erfinderrecht*, 1964, and *The Economics of Handicrafts in Traditional Societies*, Munich, 1973, as well as articles on the economics of development, environmental policy and European integration. He has also written textbooks for schools and teaching material for courses on economics.

Robert Spencer
Professor of History and Director of the Graduate Centre for International Studies Centre in the University of Toronto, Canada. He has written books and articles on recent and contemporary German and European

history, as well as on international relations and Canadian foreign policy. Since 1959 he has been the co-editor of the quarterly journal of the Canadian Institute of International Affairs, *International Journal*. A specialist in nineteenth- and twentieth-century German history, his publications include co-authoring *Modern German History*, 4th ed., London, 1968, and *The Shaping of Postwar Germany*, London, 1960.

R. Taylor Cole

James B. Duke Research Professor Emeritus of Political Science and provost of Duke University from 1960 to 1969. He has served as president of the American Political Science Association and the Southern Political Science Association and as editor of the *American Political Science Review* and the *Journal of Politics*. He is a member of the American Academy of Arts and Sciences.

From 1943 to 1944, he acted as special assistant to the United States minister in Stockholm and, during the early post-war period, as consultant to the United States military government in Germany. He was awarded the Medal of Freedom for his contributions during this period.

He is the author of *Recognition Policy of the United States since 1901* and *The Canadian Bureaucracy*; co-author of *Responsible Bureaucracy, Government in Wartime Europe and Japan, European Political Systems* and *The Nigerian Political Scene*.

He received his AB and MA degrees from the University of Texas and his PhD degree from Harvard University.

Donald P. Kommers

Professor of Government and International Studies at the University of Notre Dame and editor of *The Review of Politics*. He received his PhD from the University of Wisconsin, where he also studied law. He has been a Visiting Scholar at the Harvard Law School, an Alexander von Humboldt Fellow at the University of Cologne, and Director of the Notre Dame Law School's Centre for Civil and Human Rights. He is author of *Judicial Politics in West Germany*, 1976, and co-author of *The Governments of Germany*, 4th ed., 1975; *Human Rights and American Foreign Policy*, 1979, and the forthcoming *Comparative Political Systems*.

Anthony J. Nicholls

Official Fellow and University Lecturer, St. Anthony's College, Oxford, he was educated at Merton College, Oxford. The author of *Weimar and the Rise of Hitler*, co-author (with Sir John Wheeler-Bennett) of *The Semblance of Peace: the Political Settlement after the Second World War* and co-editor (with Erich Matthias) of *German Democracy and the Triumph of Hitler*.

Index